THE GARDENER'S COMPANION

The Gardener's Companion

A BOOK OF LISTS AND LORE

Roberta M. Coughlin

Drawings by Elizabeth L. Drake
and Richard T. Smyth

Woodcuts from herbals in the
University of Connecticut Library Special Collections

HarperPerennial
A Division of HarperCollinsPublishers

TO MDM AND RWC

FIRST EDITION

Designed by Karen Savary

Library of Congress Cataloging-in-Publication Data

Coughlin, Roberta M., 1934–
    The gardener's companion: a book of lists and lore/Roberta
Coughlin; illustrated by Elizabeth Lum Drake and Richard T. Smyth.
—1st ed.
        p. cm.
    Includes bibliographical references.
    ISBN 0-06-271531-3
    ISBN 0-06-273069-X (pbk.)
    1. Gardening—Miscellanea. I. Title.
SB453.C755 1991 89-45643
635.9—dc20

---

91 92 93 94 95 CC/RRD 10 9 8 7 6 5 4 3 2 1
91 92 93 94 95 CC/RRD 10 9 8 7 6 5 4 3 2 1 (pbk.)

Contents

Acknowledgments

I AM INDEBTED TO MANY PEOPLE FOR HELP WITH this book. In addition to those listed elsewhere, I would like to give special thanks to my family, who kept me well supplied with botanical items, as well as to the following people: J. Affolter, S. Agarwal, G. Anderson, A. Campbell, J. Carey, M. Conover, M. Dickson, C. L. Drake and E. T. Drake, G. Dreyer, K. Fisher, R. Flasher, H. Forbes, R. Gilman, L. Jacobs, B. Janes, K. and A. Kawakami, J. Koths, G. Krewer, A. Kennell and J. P. Huie, E. Launius, P. Lytton, E. Marrotte, C. Monroe, M. Rhodes, B. Roberts, E. Sampson, G. Tantaquidgeon, P. Van der Leun, J. Walker, G. Waters and many others not mentioned.

Introduction:
Our Gardens, Ourselves

ULY 4, 1989: THE FIRST JAPANESE BEETLES
emerged today, first seen appropriately enough on Japanese Yew.
Very soon they will find the roses, raspberries and gooseberries, if
they haven't already, and picking beetles will be added to the task of
pulling weeds for the next few weeks. Traps have been abandoned as a
means of bettle control; last year's traps were full of beetles, but so were
the roses, raspberries and gooseberries. Milky spore disease, caused by a
bacillus that attacks beetle larvae, is another option. Researchers are
working on ways to make this insect pathogen even more lethal and to
make other bacteria infectious to bettle larvae. Small wasp-like insects
may also prey on Japanese beetle grubs; other enemies include largely
unappreciated starlings, English sparrows, moles and skunks. It's too bad
we cannot welcome these handsome, glossy, coppery-green beetles but
bad habits and sheer numbers can turn an attractive (and even useful)
species into an enemy. Ask the Dandelion!

Meanwhile, the perennials thrive. Coreopsis and Oenothera are gold
and yellow; orange Calendula has reseeded itself. The blossoms of Nepeta,
Lavender, Campanula and a few lingering Polemonium flowers provide

the garden with lavender/blue. Tiny lilac flowers cover Creeping Thyme, which has formed solid mats over the paving stones. Lady's Mantle has a frothy yellow-green display above its handsome gray-green leaves. Gardens need good foliage plants. They add substance to a planting, rest the eyes and provide interest throughout the growing season. The blue-gray swords of Bearded Iris are also part of my garden. Out of bloom now, Iris foliage is an asset all summer. Astilbe, another fine foliage plant, is blooming with feathery pink plumes. Unexpectedly tall, Dusty Miller commands attention with gray leaves and shocking pink flowers, small but bright. Chalky-white common Yarrow is a standout at dusk; its more refined cousins, with pale gold flowers, are due to bloom any day, as are mahogany and apricot Daylilies, Gooseneck Loosestrife and Purple (but really pink) Coneflower, which will attract its annual army of butterflies. Siberian Iris has produced many fat, green seed pods that will be attractive in winter bouquets, as will the seed pods of Oriental Poppy ripening across the driveway. The dried spires of Astile will likewise grace the autumn garden, remaining erect through the winter if not removed. Presiding over this assortment and standing 6 feet tall (garden books did not warn me*) is Valerian, or Garden, Heliotrope, the strange fragrance of its long-lasting white flowers perfuming the air. A once-famous seda- tive, the rank odor of its crushed leaves is said to attract both cats and mice, a reason, perhaps, why Valerian was also thought to be a favorite of witches.

By now it is embarrassingly evident that my garden is not blessed with coherent composition, with proper attention paid to blooming times and flower color. It was not designed. Parts of it were inherited, and it has provided a home for gift plants from generous friends and relatives over the years. Usually it is even more colorful with an added assortment of annuals; this year I must be content with the zonal Pelargoniums that bloomed indoors all winter and now bloom on the doorstep and the variegated Impatiens that did likewise.

Edibles also thrive—mainly the perennial easy-care kind like Egyp- tian onion, Rhubarb and Jerusalem artichoke, although the usual spring planting of Basil, Tomatoes, Parsley and cress is in place. Other crops (as well as perennials) have been tried and abandoned, victims of disease and/or the local fauna. Plants are not the independent food machines many perceive them to be. Most of our hybrids and cultivars depend

---

*Could I have the "Water Valerian" that Culpepper describes as growing "promiscuously in marshy grounds and moist meadows"?

totally upon us for survival, and our fellow creatures ensure the pollination and seed dispersal of many others. If animals disappeared from the
face of the earth, colorful flowers and luscious fruit would also vanish;
only the green world of grasses and wind-pollinated trees, conifers,
birches and willows would remain.

In return for our efforts, plants produce the sugars and vitamins that
sustain us and manufacture toxins (for their own protection) that have
also been used to enhance human health. Few Americans actually need
the plants they raise to fill these basic needs; supermarkets, drugstores and
farmstands are plentiful. And yet the symbiotic bond between Earth's
flora and fauna is very strong and very old. I cannot imagine myself
without my garden. It is my time machine. When I step into the garden
I leave my century, my millennium; I join hands with ancient ancestors
who also tilled the soil, watched the plants, rejoiced over the first ripe
berry.

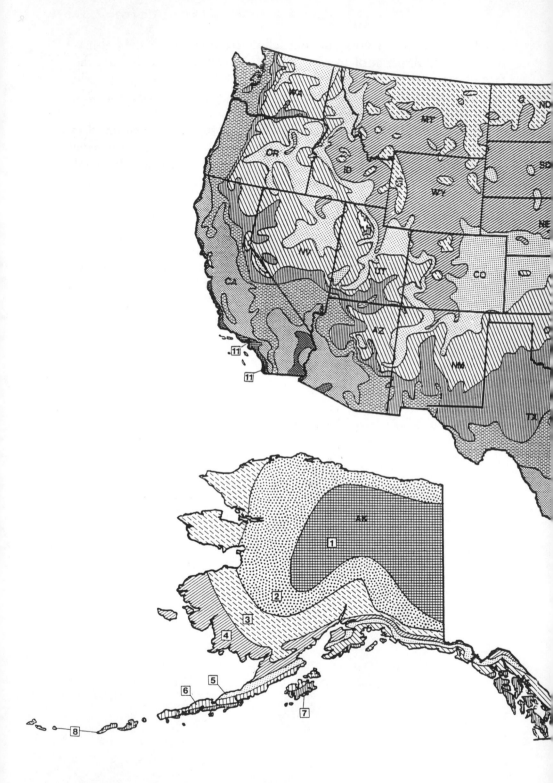

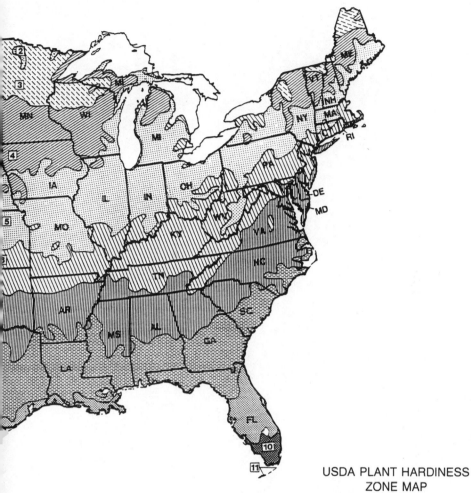

USDA PLANT HARDINESS ZONE MAP

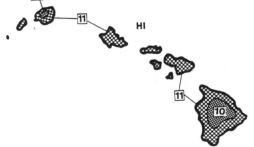

RANGE OF AVERAGE ANNUAL MINIMUM TEMPERATURES FOR EACH ZONE

ZONE 1	BELOW −50°F	
ZONE 2	−50° TO −40°	
ZONE 3	−40° TO −30°	
ZONE 4	−30° TO −20°	
ZONE 5	−20° TO −10°	
ZONE 6	−10° TO 0°	
ZONE 7	0° TO 10°	
ZONE 8	10° TO 20°	
ZONE 9	20° TO 30°	
ZONE 10	30° TO 40°	
ZONE 11	ABOVE 40°	

THE GARDENER'S COMPANION

1

Roses

THE ROSE, A PRIMITIVE FLOWERING PLANT, HAS blossomed on earth for millions of years. Long before there were humans to smell them, the sweet scent of roses wafted through the early Cenozoic air, perhaps giving pleasure to strange, now-extinct mammals whose dusty bones languish in museums of natural history. More than one authority claims that the rose originated in Asia. If this is true, it is strange that it became the best-loved flower not of the East, but of the Western world. In the words of poets, in song, in art, in the language itself we have ample evidence of the West's long love affair with the rose.

Most species of roses are hardy and tough; some can even become weedy and pestiferous—a far cry from their glamorous garden cousins. While there is renewed interest today in species and the highly desirable old rose varieties, most gardeners plant the beautiful but more demanding Hybrid teas, Floribundas and Grandifloras. These roses are the result of intense efforts on the part of rose hybridizers in many countries during the past several hundred years. Many hybrid roses are worth the extra effort, but others are not. Some garden catalogs carry enticing pictures of what are in reality inferior plants, almost sure to disappoint. But the lists that follow should help gardeners select strong, beautiful, disease-resistant and (last but not least) fragrant roses.

NATIONAL RATINGS FOR ROSES

The American Rose Society publishes a small "Handbook for Selecting Roses," which is available from ARS for $1.00. The booklet lists alphabetically all roses currently available in the United States and rates them on a scale of 1 to 10, with 10 being the perfect rose (a distinction as yet unachieved).

9.0–9.9	Outstanding
8.0–8.9	Excellent
7.0–7.9	Good
6.0–6.9	Fair
5.9 and lower	Of questionable value

Rose growers, amateur and professional, from all over the country participate in the surveys to establish ratings; therefore, the ratings in the Handbook are national averages. Gardeners should bear in mind that a rose may actually rate higher in a certain region of the country than its composite rating in the Handbook would indicate and a rating for a particular rose may change over the years. The Handbook also contains other information rose lovers will find valuable. They are published yearly in the late fall. Check with the American Rose Society, P. O. Box 30,000, Shreveport, LA 71130, phone (318) 938–5402.

Two Excellent Species Roses

Species roses are, of course, the oldest roses of all. Botanists still argue over the definition of a species or "wild" rose though most seem willing to agree that species roses have five-petaled (or "single") flowers that can self-pollinate and produce seedlings that resemble the parent plant. Two fine Asian roses that deserve a place in the larger rose garden or shrub border are:

Rosa hugonis (9.1)—Also called the Golden Rose of China or Father Hugo's Rose, R. hugonis can reach six feet in height and width and produces 2-inch yellow flowers (only slightly fragrant) very early in the season. The leaves are fine textured and fernlike and reddish fruit is produced in late summer. This rose likes it warm and sunny and will do well in rather poor soil.

Rosa rugosa alba (8.2)—Native to Japan, it is hardy and very fragrant; it will tolerate some shade and produces white

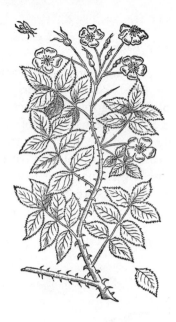

Rosa damascena. A hardy (zone 5) rose introduced into Europe from Asia Minor.

flowers, good yellow fall color and attractive red fruit. The dark, somewhat glossy foliage is deeply veined, giving rise to the common name of Wrinkled Rose; it is also known as Saltspray Rose because it thrives in seaside gardens. It grows 5 to 6 feet tall and benefits from yearly renewal pruning. R. rugosa rubra has mauve flowers and a similar "Excellent" rating. Several Rugosa hybrids (or "shrub roses") have also received high ratings. Blanc Double de Coubert (8.0; 1892), has double white flowers, good fall color and a rich perfume. Frau Dagmar Hartopp (8.9), introduced in 1914, is a smaller shrub without much fragrance but it does have single silver-pink flowers with decorative stamens and large orange-red fruit. Hansa (8.5), introduced in 1905, is another hardy Rugosa with a rich fragrance; it has large, double mauve flowers and recurrent bloom.

Two other roses that the American Rose Society classifies as species and gives high ratings to are Rosa banksiae lutea and Rosa glauca. The former, from China, is a climber with double yellow flowers and hardy to zone 7; the latter is a very hardy European rose with red-tinged, glaucous foliage, small pink to red blossoms and attractive winter fruit. Hortus Third classifies 'Lutea' as a cultivar of R. banksiae; R. glauca is listed there as R. rubrifolia.

An American Native: Virginia's Rose

A beautiful native, R. virginiana grows along roadsides and shorelines, in moist spots and in dry ones, obviously tolerant of salts that could damage other plants. Height is variable; it can grow 5 to 6 feet tall, but often is smaller. Leaves are glossy green and the single, softly scented rose-pink flowers (with a thick ring of golden stamens) are usually produced several to a stem. Foliage turns red in the fall; red fruit and red stems are attractive in winter. Although Virginia Rose is perhaps the finest of our native roses for landscape use, two others deserve mention: lower-growing R. carolina (the Pasture Rose) and R. setigera (the Prairie Rose), which has pink flowers, red fall color and a broad, arching habit that makes it suitable for large-scale plantings.

Rosa virginiana. Very hardy (zone 4) rose native to eastern North America. There is a double-flowered cultivar.

Two Other Highly Rated Shrub Roses

Blanc Double de Coubert, Frau Dagmar Hartopp and Hansa (see "R. rugosa," pages 2–3) are all known as "shrub roses"; the name is confusing because all roses are shrubs. Nevertheless, the term is usually applied to the more recent hybrids of species roses and other old garden roses and to roses that cannot be placed in other categories, such as Hybrid tea and Floribunda. In general, these roses, like species (or "wild") roses and vintage roses, are hardy, tough, and often shade-tolerant and fragrant. They are suitable for shrub borders or for growing alone as specimens. Two of the best are:

Cornelia (9.1)—A hybrid Musk Rose, Cornelia (1925), has fragrant double pink flowers flushed with apricot and glossy green/bronze leaves. Flowers are rather small but abundantly produced in large clusters; bloom is recurrent. Cornelia's only drawback is that it may be susceptible to mildew in certain areas.

Golden Wings (8.7)—A hybrid of the old Scotch Rose R. spinosissima, the delightful Golden Wings was introduced in 1956. Winner of an ARS National Gold Medal Certificate in 1958, this very hardy rose produces large single flowers, pale yellow in color and decorated with a circle of red and gold stamens. Called only "slightly fragrant" by many, I have always found its spicy perfume distinctive and was recently gratified when my niece, who usually does not notice roses that are not many-petaled and red (or pink), found Golden Wings irresistible because the fragrance reminded her of the ribbon candy served at holiday time.

Bonica '82 (also listed under the name Meidomonac) is the only shrub rose to win the All-America Rose Selection (AARS) award. Introduced in 1982 this hardy pink-flowered rose has nearly evergreen R. sempervirens in its lineage. Widely advertised as fragrant, ARS describes it as having "no fragrance," and I agree. It does have dark green, glossy foliage and many-petaled flowers. The shrub is bushy, spreading and low-growing. It has recently been rated 7.8 by the ARS.

DIFFERENT TYPES OF MODERN ROSES

Hybrid Tea—Large flowered rose, averaging 3 to 5 feet in height, which blooms almost continuously from spring until frost. Hybrid teas first appeared on the rose scene about 120 years ago; they are the most common roses found in gardens today. Many varieties need some winter protection in zones 3 through 6.

Floribunda—In 1924 a cross between a Hybrid tea and a Polyantha (low-growing, very hardy rose that blooms continuously, producing large clusters of small flowers) gave us the hardy Floribunda. Floribundas bloom almost continuously and produce clusters of medium-sized flowers on bushes that grow 2 to 3 feet tall. In general this group is a little hardier than Hybrid teas and Grandifloras.

Grandiflora—A cross between a Hybrid tea and a Floribunda produced the first Grandiflora in 1954. The blossoms are a bit larger than Floribunda flowers and stems are longer. Grandifloras are often taller than their parents; most varieties grow 3 to 6 or more feet high and should be planted in back of Floribundas and most Hybrid teas.

Miniature—While sometimes there is disagreement about whether a new rose introduction should be classified Hybrid tea, Floribunda or Grandiflora, classification of miniatures presents fewer problems. These small roses grow from 3 to 18 inches tall; average size is about one foot, with leaves and flowers correspondingly tiny. All types of roses can be found in miniature, including climbers that can reach several feet. Unlike the three categories above, which are grafted, miniatures are grown on their own roots and are easy to propagate.

Top Exhibition Roses

Listed below are the cultivars that won the most points in rose shows across the country in 1988. The lists appeared in the *American Rose,* May 1989, and were compiled by F. O. Dollinger, who has prepared lists of winning roses for many years. Most of the following are fine garden subjects as well as show roses.

HYBRID TEAS

Touch of Class*	Pink blend
Keepsake	Pink blend
Pristine	White/pink edges
Olympiad*	Medium red
Uncle Joe	Dark red
Folklore	Light orange/dark orange
Color Magic*	Pink blend
Double Delight*	Red/white bicolor
Royal Highness*	Light pink
Paradise*	Mauve blend
First Prize*	Rose pink/ivory trim
Marijke Koopman	Medium pink

GRANDIFLORAS

Gold Medal	Deep yellow
Pink Parfait*	Dawn pink/cream blend
Queen Elizabeth*	Clear pink
Sonia	Coral pink/yellow blend
Aquarius*	Light pink/dark pink blend

FLORIBUNDAS

Showbiz*	Medium red
Europeana*	Dark red
First Edition*	Orange blend
Gene Boerner*	Medium pink
Impatient*	Orange red
Playgirl	Medium pink

MINIATURES

Jean Kenneally**	Apricot blend
Minnie Pearl	Pink blend
Snow Bride**	White
Party Girl**	Yellow blend
Rainbow's End**	Yellow blend

*All-America Rose Selection   **Award of Excellence Winner

Gardeners interested in showing roses may want to read the ARS publication "Guidelines for Judging Roses."

Gold Medal Certificate Winners

The American Rose Society established the Gold Medal Certificate award in 1948 to recognize varieties that showed especially good performance over a five-year period. The award was discontinued in 1980. The thirteen winners are:

Carrousel (GR)	**Peace** (HT)
Chrysler Imperial (HT)	**Queen Elizabeth** (GR)
City of York (CLIMBER)	**Spartan** (F)
Fashion (F)	**Toy Clown** (MINIATURE)
Frensham (F)	**Tropicana** (HT)
Golden Wings (SHRUB)	**Vogue** (F)
Montezuma (GR)	

F—Floribunda   GR—Grandiflora   HT—Hybrid Tea

Outstanding Roses

A high rating generally indicates that a rose has performed well in all sections of the country. The following roses are among the few that have an American Rose Society rating of 9.0 (Outstanding) or better.

Beauty Secret* (MINIATURE)	Medium red	9.2
Double Delight* (HT)	Red/white bicolor	9.0
Dortmund (CLIMBER)**	Red/white center	9.2
Europeana (F)	Dark red	9.1
First Prize (HT)**	Medium pink/ivory blend	9.1
Magic Carrousel	White/red edges	9.3
(MINIATURE)		
Mister Lincoln* (HT)	Deep red	9.1
Queen Elizabeth (GR)**	Medium pink	9.1
Rise 'n' Shine (MINIATURE)	Medium yellow	9.0
Starina (MINIATURE)***	Orange red	9.6

* Fragrant.
** Slightly fragrant.
*** The highest rated rose to date.

Highly Rated Old Garden Roses

"Old" roses may be loosely defined as those roses grown in gardens before the advent of the Hybrid teas. The American Rose Society has set 1867 as the dividing line between "old" and "modern" roses. In that year the Guillots of France introduced "La France," the first Hybrid tea, to an eager world. Here at last was a hardy rose that produced large, attractively shaped flowers throughout the season; no wonder these beautiful newcomers replaced many of the older varieties in the rose garden. Fortunately, however, old roses have many champions. Besides being historically important and beautiful, many old roses are hardy, disease-resistant, fragrant and some are shade tolerant. Many (like R. rugosa) have good fall color and attractive fruit. Old roses not grown in beds do not need much pruning; in fact their only drawback is that, except for the Bourbons and Hybrid perpetuals that have genes from China roses, most old roses bloom just once in a season. Among the best (all are eligible for American Rose Society's "Dowager Queen Award") are:

Apothecary's Rose	gallica	Deep pink	9.3
Celsiana	damask	Light pink	9.3
Mme. Hardy	damask	White	9.0
Maiden's Blush	alba	Pale pink	7.9
Petite de Hollande	centifolia	Medium pink	8.5
Reine des Violettes	hybrid perpetual	Lavender	7.3
Rosa Mundi	gallica, striped	Light/dark pink	9.1
Souvenir de la Malmaison	bourbon	Light pink	8.5
Tuscany Superb	gallica	Dark mauve/red	8.4
William Lobb	moss	Mauve blend	8.4

A BRIEF HISTORY OF LISTED ROSES

It is very difficult to unravel the complex history of the rose. It is safe to say that humans have, for a very long time, muddied the waters by cultivating, moving plants (sometimes great distances) and selecting the roses that best pleased. In recent years chromosome studies have helped to shed some light on the confusing subject of rose history. For example, until recently it was believed that the centifolia rose was an ancient species. Recent studies have shown it to be a complex hybrid, perhaps developed by the Dutch in the seventeenth and eighteenth centuries.

Most agree that gallica roses, probably native to the Middle East and southern Europe, were known to the ancient world. R. gallica is the rose celebrated in the rose windows of Europe's great cathedrals. Thirteenth-century Provins (France) was the center of a large industry, where the petals of Apothecary Rose, which become more fragrant as they dry, were sold for medicinal and cosmetic purposes. Rosa Mundi, a sport of Apothecary Rose and perhaps the world's first striped rose, may have been named for Henry II's mistress, Fair Rosamund, who died in 1176. Both these roses tolerate some shade and produce attractive fruit. Tuscany Superb (1848), is a sport of Tuscany, an old variety grown in the Middle Ages. These hardy gallicas are all fragrant; most gallicas are more tolerant of poor soil than other roses.

The damask rose, with its mysterious name and delicious scent, is truly a mystery to rose historians. Tradition says it was brought back from Damascus by returning Crusaders, and although it may be native to Asia Minor there is much evidence that it was known and cultivated in ancient Greece and Italy. Taller than gallica roses, and differing in leaf and flower, the damasks still resemble gallicas so much that some think they may be gallica hybrids, created by anonymous rose breeders long ago. Grown before 1750, fragrant Celsiana has a long midseason bloom and is neat and attractive when not in bloom. Mme. Hardy (1832), suspected of having R. centifolia in its ancestry, is a beautiful white rose with a green center. Both roses tolerate poorer soils; Mme. Hardy tolerates some shade.

The alba rose is believed to be the result of a cross between a gallica or damask and the European dog rose (R. canina). It is thought that this fragrant and hardy rose was known also to the ancient world; it is more certainly documented from the Middle Ages, when it was recommended for hedge planting. The alba rose Maiden's Blush, with its blue-green leaves and strong fragrance, was cultivated in the seventeenth century, or perhaps earlier.

The fragrant moss rose, noted for "mossiness" of buds and stems, is the result of a mutation, probably in the early 1700s, of the centifolia, or "Cabbage" rose. Cabbage roses, also known as "Provence" roses, once were thought to be very ancient but now are believed to be hybrids of rather recent origin. William Lobb (1855) may grow tall enough to require support; it produces big clusters of fragrant flowers and lots of pine-scented moss. Petite de Hollande (1800), a smaller rose with fragrant pink blossoms, is considered by some to be the best centifolia for a small garden. Rose de Meaux (8.3) is even smaller, growing about two feet tall and also producing sweet-smelling medium pink flowers.

China is rich in roses and there is evidence that they were cultivated and hybridized there since ancient times. Some China roses may have reached Italy in the sixteenth century but it wasn't until the eighteenth century that they were introduced to Western roses and the revolution in rose history began. Europe had a rose, the "Autumn Damask," that sometimes bloomed twice a year, but most roses grown at that time bloomed only once. Returning travelers talked of continually blooming Chinese roses, and when these somewhat tender plants were crossed with Europe's roses, the ancestors of our modern, free-flowering roses were born. Chinese Tea roses (together with the Austrian Briar from western Asia) also brought the color yellow to modern roses.

The first *Bourbon* roses (which reigned in rose gardens from 1820 to 1870) resulted from natural hybridization between China roses and damask roses on the Isle de Bourbon (now Réunion) around 1820. These hybrids were hardier than Chinas, with larger flowers and recurrent bloom; some say they bloom especially well in fall.

Souvenir de la Malmaison (1843), named for Empress Josephine's rose garden at Malmaison, is said to be a sparse bloomer that does not open well in wet weather, yet old-rose expert Peter Beales calls this fragrant rose, when at its best, "the most beautiful of all Bourbons."

Hybrid perpetuals, the most popular roses cultivated in Victorian times, were a group created from crosses between Bourbons and Portlands (damask, gallica, and China), as well as Noisettes (China and Rosa moschata, the musk rose) and teas. Hybrid perpetuals, when crossed with teas produced the modern Hybrid tea. Reine des Violettes (1860), with gray-green leaves and fragrant, lavender flowers, is one of the loveliest of the Hybrid perpetuals. Another excellent (8.2) Hybrid perpetual is Mrs. John Laing, introduced in 1887. Although the date makes it too late to qualify as an "old" garden rose, this fragrant pink rose was one of the best and most popular Hybrid perpetuals grown in its day.

Hardiness Notes

Hardiest are the gallicas, damasks, centifolias and mosses. Hybrid perpetuals vary; among the hardiest are Baronne Prevost and Reine des Violettes. Bourbons may need protection in colder areas; Chinas are approximately as hardy as Hybrid teas. Tea roses (and the Noisettes) do best in the South.

Old-Rose Experts

The American Rose Society maintains a list of "old-rose experts" who can assist in the selection of the best "old" roses for your area. There is also a Heritage Rose Group, which publishes a quarterly news booklet; some regions have subgroups that meet several times a year. For more information contact the American Rose Society, PO Box 30,000, Shreveport, LA 71130, Phone (318) 938–5402.

Overrated Roses

One rose grower's delight may be another's dud; individual preferences aside, local climate conditions can make or break a rose's performance. Ray Reddell, a commercial grower in California who grows roses for blossom sale, calls the following All-America Rose Selections poor picks. Bear in mind that one of them could be a star in *your* rose garden. (AARS award won in the year indicated.)*

1968 Miss All-American Beauty (HT)	8.5
1972 Portrait (HT)	7.2
1975 Oregold (HT)	7.4
1975 Rose Parade (F)	7.7
1983 Sun Flare (F)	7.8
1983 Sweet Surrender (HT)	7.1
1984 Impatient (F)	8.0
1984 Intrigue (F)	7.3
1985 Showbiz (F)	8.1
1988 Prima Donna (GR)	7.6

F—Floribunda GR—Grandiflora HT—Hybrid Tea

Mr. Reddell finds mildew a problem on Garden Party, but also objects to Tropicana and Miss All-American Beauty, both fragrant and disease-resistant; the former he calls "so dumpy that it doesn't even look like a rose," the latter has "formless blooms too large for its stubby stems."

Disappointing Roses

Each June, when the new All-America Rose Selection winners are announced, there is a rush to buy and plant the new award winners. These

---

*From an article written by Mr. Reddell in *Horticulture: The Magazine of American Gardening,* February 1988, and *The American Rose,* October 1988.

winners have been grown in test gardens for two years, and many of them are exceptional roses. However, not all of them live up to their promise, and when American Rose Society ratings are established several years later some award winners are rated only "fair"—or worse. Cautious gardeners may want to wait for ARS ratings; hasty purchase of new award winners could result in problem roses. The following roses were all award winners in the year indicated:

1949	**Forty-niner** (HT)	5.8
1950	**Sutter's Gold** (HT)	6.5
1954	**Mojave** (HT)	6.2
1955	**Jiminy Cricket** (F)	6.9
1958	**Gold Cup** (F)	5.4
1969	**Commanche** (GR)	6.8
1972	**Apollo** (HT)	5.0
1973	**Gypsy** (HT)	6.1
1975	**Arizona** (GR)	6.1
1981	**Bing Crosby** (HT)	6.9

F—Floribunda GR—Grandiflora HT—Hybrid Tea

REGIONAL LISTS

Portland Medal Winners

In the cool and misty weather of the Pacific Northwest roses with many petals sometimes fail to open properly and mildew can be a problem. The following roses have won the Portland (Oregon) Gold Medal for good performance in that region.

Bewitched (HT)	Medium pink	7.2
Chrysler Imperial (HT)	Crimson red	8.2
Electron (HT)	Deep pink	8.0
Europeana (F)	Dark red	9.1
Fragrant Cloud (HT)	Orange red	8.1
Handel		
(BIG-FLOWERED CLIMBER)	Cream edged in pink	8.2
Little Darling (F)	Yellow/pink blend	8.8
Paradise (HT)	Lavender edged in red	8.8

Pascali (HT)	White	8.7
Peace (HT)	Yellow edged in pink	8.9
Pink Parfait (GR)	Medium to light pink	8.7
Pristine (HT)	White, shaded pink	8.9
Queen Elizabeth (GR)	Medium pink	9.1
Spartan (F)	Orange red	7.2
Tiffany (HT)	Pink blend	8.3

F—Floribunda GR—Grandiflora HT—Hybrid Tea

Roses for the Middle South*

Century Two	Medium pink	8.5
Double Delight (HT)	White/red	9.0
Fragrant Cloud (HT)	Orange red	8.1
Garden Party (HT)	White	8.8
Gold Medal (GR)	Dark yellow	7.8
Honor (HT)	White	7.6
Olympiad (HT)	Medium red	8.1
Pink Parfait (GR)	Medium to light pink	8.7
Pristine (HT)	White, pink edges	8.9
Royal Highness (HT)	Light pink	8.6
Summer Fashion (F)	Yellow blend	7.6
Sunsprite (F)	Deep yellow	8.9
Swarthmore (HT)	Pink blend	8.5
Tiffany (HT)	Pink blend	8.3
Uncle Joe (HT)	Dark red	7.9

*From the consulting rosarians of the Tenarky (Tenn., Ark., Ky.) district. The American Rose Society maintains a list of consulting rosarians from the eighteen ARS districts. To request a list of the rosarians near you, write the American Rose Society. Consulting rosarians will be glad to help you with questions concerning roses.

F—Floribunda GR—Grandiflora HT—Hybrid Tea

Roses for the North

Consulting rosarians in the North-Central district recommend the following:

Cherish (F)	Medium pink	8.0
Chicago Peace (HT)	Pink blend	8.4
Dainty Bess (HT)	Light pink	8.6
Double Delight (HT)	White/red	9.0
Europeana (F)	Dark red	9.1

Garden Party (HT)	White	8.8
Iceberg (F)	White	8.9
Little Darling (F)	Yellow/pink blend	8.8
Olympiad (HT)	Medium red	8.1
Paradise (HT)	Lavender edged in red	8.8
Peace (HT)	Yellow edged in pink	8.9
Pristine (HT)	White, shaded pink	8.9
Queen Elizabeth (GR)	Medium pink	9.1
Sunsprite (F)	Deep yellow	8.9
Tropicana (HT)	Orange-red	8.6

F—Floribunda GR—Grandiflora HT—Hybrid Tea

Dainty Bess, a vintage Hybrid tea that appeared in 1925, has silvery-pink single petals, showy golden stamens, a sweet clove scent and healthy foliage. The new pink Grandiflora Tournament of Roses came through its first New England winter well. An AARS winner, its rating has not yet been established.

Floribundas generally are somewhat hardier than Hybrid teas. Most roses can withstand occasional drops in temperature to 10 degrees F, but if winter temperatures remain below 10 degrees F for more than several weeks at a time, winter protection should be provided. The most common method is to cover the crown of the plant with 6 to 8 inches of soil (from another part of the garden). Avoid "rose cones." Check with your local Agricultural Extension Service for the best method of protection in your area.

Blast Furnace Rose Gardening

The Rose Society of Tucson, Arizona, has compiled a book of advice for rose gardeners in the hot Southwest: "Blast Furnace Rose Gardening," which may be ordered from the Rose Society of Tucson, 2049 E. 9th Street, Tucson, AZ 85719 (please enclose $5.00 plus $1.50 for postage and handling). Ben Corbin, a consulting rosarian for the Tucson district and a test rose-grower for Jackson and Perkins, suggests the following varieties for that sun-baked area:

Double Delight (HT)	Red/white bicolor	9.0
Brandy (HT)*	Apricot blend	7.3
Royal Highness (HT)*	Light pink	8.6

*Best where winters are mild.
F—Floribunda GR—Grandiflora HT—Hybrid Tea

Honor (HT)	White	7.6
First Prize (HT)	Medium pink/ivory	9.1
Olympiad (HT)	Medium red	8.1
Peace (HT)	Yellow edged in pink	8.9
Chrysler Imperial (HT)	Dark red	8.2
Paradise (HT)	Mauve blend	8.8
Queen Elizabeth (GR)	Medium pink	9.1
Cherish (F)	Medium pink/light pink	8.0
Sun Flare (F)	Medium yellow	7.8
Olé (GR)	Orange-red	7.9
Party Girl (MINIATURE)	Pale yellow blend	8.0
Holy Toledo (MINIATURE)	Apricot blend	8.5

F—Floribunda GR—Grandiflora HT—Hybrid Tea

THE FRAGRANCE OF ROSES

The fragrance of roses is as varied as roses themselves. Blossom aroma from various roses has been compared to the smell of honey (R. multiflora), cloves (R. rugosa alba, among others), green apples (the wichuraiana climbers May Queen and New Dawn), lemons (Paul's Lemon Pillar and Typhoo Tea), myrrh (Constance Spry) and licorice (Sun Flare). Other roses are said to smell like violets, lilies-of-the-valley, raspberries and even wine. Some claim that the spicy damask gives off the "true-rose" scent; it is the major source of attar of roses. Some roses have scented foliage; the leaves of the Sweet Briar (R. eglanteria) are said to smell sweetly of pippin apples, especially after rain. Other rose leaves have been described as "peppery." The moss on many moss roses is pine-scented, an interesting foil to the heady centifolia perfume most of them possess.

> Toward the roser gan I go
> And when I was not fer therfro
> The savour of the roses swote
> Me smoot right to the herte root
> As I hadde al enbawned be.
> "THE RAMAUNT OF THE ROSE," TRANSLATED BY CHAUCER

The Importance of Fragrance

Fragrance is often sacrificed by rose breeders in their search for other desirable characteristics such as hardiness and disease resistance. It is a heavy price to pay—one of the reasons humans have loved roses for so long is because of their wonderful fragrance. Many old herbals inform us that the scent of roses comforts the heart and dispels depression, a supposition that modern aromatherapy seems to confirm. Research has shown that smell has a direct effect on the parts of the brain that regulate fear and anxiety and that pleasant scents soothe and can reduce blood pressure. Researchers also tell us that memories of smells can last a lifetime, while visual memories begin to fade in a few months. Why then should we plant roses that do not delight noses as well as eyes?

Fragrant Hybrid Teas

The James Alexander Gamble Medal of the American Rose Society has been awarded to eight Hybrid tea roses for a high fragrance rating. They are:

1961 **Crimson Glory**	Dark red	7.2
1962 **Tiffany***	Orchid pink	8.3
1965 **Chrysler Imperial***	Crimson red	8.2
1966 **Sutter's Gold***	Golden yellow	6.5
1968 **Granada***	Red/yellow	8.6
1970 **Fragrant Cloud**	Orange-red	8.1
1974 **Papa Meilland**	Dark red	7.4
1986 **Double Delight***	Red/white bicolor	9.0

*All-America Rose Selection

In 1979 the Floribunda rose Sunsprite (deep yellow, 8.9) received the award.

A Dozen Other Fragrant Roses

Detecting fragrance is subjective; a rose that smells sweet to one person may have little perfume for another. Fragrance itself also varies; a blossom that smells good in the morning sometimes has no scent by late afternoon. Generally, roses are the most fragrant on warm, sunny days when the ground is moist. Catalogs sometimes use words such as "fresh," "soft" and "light fragrance" as euphemisms for no fragrance. The following roses are all fragrant (some more so than others) and all have received an ARS general quality rating of "Good" or better:

Amber Queen* (F)	Apricot blend	7.5
Angel Face* (F)	Rose-lavender	8.3
Apricot Nectar* (F)	Pink-apricot	8.1

*All-America Rose Selection
F—Floribunda GR—Grandiflora HT—Hybrid Tea

Dolly Parton (HT)	Orange-red	7.4
Electron* (HT)	Rose-pink	8.0
Folklore (HT)	Orange blend	8.3
Iceberg (F)	White	8.9
Mister Lincoln* (HT)	Deep red	9.1
Perfume Delight* (HT)	Medium pink	7.8
Pink Peace (HT)	Dusty pink	7.5
Sheer Bliss* (HT)	White/pink center	7.6
Sonia (GR)	Pink blend	8.1

*All-America Rose Selection
F—Floribunda GR—Grandiflora HT—Hybrid Tea

Fragrant Climbers

Climbers grow anywhere from 6 to 20 feet tall. Lacking tendrils, they do not really climb but need to be tied to a trellis or have other means of support. A number of good varieties are of questionable hardiness in the North. Rosa banksiae lutea (9.0) is a highly rated rose with yellow flowers. It can grow 20 feet tall but is best in regions with mild winters. Although it has little fragrance, it also has few thorns and many flowers. Another tender climber (8 feet tall), Mermaid (7.1; 1917) has single, lemon-yellow flowers, recurrent bloom, fierce thorns and a sweet perfume. Also tender with pale yellow flowers, Paul's Lemon Pillar (7.5; 1915) has a fine citrus scent. (Paul's Scarlet Climber [7.7; 1916] is scentless but very hardy; it is a parent of the popular Blaze.) The favorite white-flowered climber in England, Mme. Alfred Carriere (6.5; 1879) is a profuse bloomer with vigorous growth, shade tolerance and fragrance; unfortunately it is hardy only from Philadelphia south. Ten other climbers with fragrance and an ARS rating of "Good" or better are:

1923 **Lawrence Johnston** (8.0)—This rose can grow 20 feet or more and produces large, semidouble golden flowers. Fragrance is present but not outstanding. It is generally vigorous and disease-resistant, although with R. foetida in its ancestry it is prone to blackspot, especially in the South.

1930 **New Dawn** (7.7)—This pale pink-flowered climber (12 to 15 feet) is a sport of the old Dr. W. Van Fleet (7.5; 1910) and is similar except that New Dawn is a repeat bloomer. New Dawn, with its light apple scent, is a fine rose and the world's first patented plant; it is the parent of many other climbers, such as Aloha, Blossomtime, Coral Dawn, Parade and Rhonda.

1931 Shot Silk (7.8)—Shot Silk grows to about 15 feet and has dark green glossy foliage. Flowers are bright pink with a yellow base and very fragrant.

1945 City of York—An excellent, hardy rose with fragrant white flowers and glossy leaves, it can reach 20 feet in height. A rating has not yet been established although this rose won the ARS National Gold Medal Certificate in 1950. May bloom again in autumn.

1951 Blossomtime (8.1)—Blossomtime makes a tall shrub or small climber, growing about 6 to 8 feet tall. Medium pink flowers are large and sweet-smelling. It is a repeat bloomer.

1955 Dortmund (9.2)—Described as a fragrant shrub rose by ARS, Dortmund is a vigorous (but only slightly scented) rose that is suitable for growing as a climber since it reaches 8 feet or more in height. It has true and bright red single flowers with a white eye, recurrent bloom and dark, glossy leaves.

1956 Alchymist (8.2)—Classified as a shrub rose by ARS, it has vigorous upright growth reaching 8 feet or more in height. Large flowers, which open flat like some vintage roses, are apricot-colored and fragrant. Foliage is glossy with bronze tones; bloom is nonrecurrent.

1958 Don Juan (8.5)—Another descendant of New Dawn, Don Juan has velvety dark red flowers; dark, glossy foliage; recurrent bloom and a rich perfume. It grows 8 to 10 feet tall and is probably best in areas with mild winters.

1963 Viking Queen (7.5)—A hardy rose, developed at the University of Minnesota, Viking Queen has medium to deep pink fragrant flowers and recurrent bloom. Leaves are dark and glossy and canes will grow 12 to 15 feet tall.

1976 America (8.8)—A highly rated, coral-flowered climber that grows 9 to 12 feet high. Fragrance is strong thanks to Fragrant Cloud, a parent. This rose was an All-America Rose Selection in 1976.

In areas where mildew is not a problem try Crimson Glory (7.2; 1946). This rose has velvety, deep red flowers and the rich, clove-rose scent of the Hybrid tea of the same name.

Fragrant Miniature Roses

Probably originating in China, the ancestors of modern miniatures were pretty much ignored in the West until rediscovered growing on a Swiss windowsill in the early part of this century. Today there is much enthusiasm for these small plants, which permit city dwellers and others with limited space to enjoy roses. Some catalogs list varieties that are said to do well in partial shade both indoors and out, although like their larger cousins, most miniatures need ample sunshine. As a whole, miniatures are not noted for fragrance (and fragrance is hard to detect in a tiny rose), but the following all smell sweet:

1953	Cinderella	White, pink edges	8.6
1960	Baby Betsy McCall	Light pink	8.1
1975	Beauty Secret*	Medium red	9.2
1978	Heidi (Moss)	Medium pink	7.8
1981	Pacesetter*	White	7.8
1982	Little Jackie*	Orange blend	7.9
1984	Sweet Chariot	Mauve blend	7.7
1986	Sachet	Mauve	7.7
1986	Winter Magic	Lavender/gray	7.4
1989	Church Mouse	Taupe/yellow	not established

*Award of Excellence Winner

A quarterly "Miniature Rose Bulletin" is available from the American Rose Society, PO Box 30,000, Shreveport, LA 71130 for $5 per year.

Horticulturists suggest growing roses indoors in a potting mixture of 80 percent soil and 20 percent peat moss.

THE COLORS OF ROSES

The American Rose Society recognizes 17 color classifications, but these categories cannot begin to describe the many shades and combinations to be found in modern roses. The roses that ancient Greeks and Romans knew were mainly red and pink; it wasn't until yellow roses arrived from the East in the eighteenth century that all the shades of coral and apricot and the yellow/pink blends that so delight rose lovers today began to appear. Despite the variety, however, many are not satisfied and catalogs continue to praise their newest "blue" rose. Although present-day blue roses are really lavender roses (and many are not rated very highly), a blue rose may not be too far in the future. Researchers have been able to transplant a gene from a corn plant into a petunia, thereby changing the petunia's pigment-making chemistry, and a gene has been cloned that produces blue petunias. Scientists hope to transfer these "blue genes" into roses, carnations and mums.

Colorfast Roses

Some roses, like some people, need sunscreens to preserve their complexions. A walk through a rose garden recently revealed crops of freckles on the blossoms of Simplicity and Apricot Nectar, while nearby varieties remained spotless. Exhibitors sometimes set up special shading devices to prevent color from fading and freckling on roses they plan to show. Robert Whitaker, a consulting rosarian in the Tenarky district, lists some of his favorite roses for color stability. The roses below either keep their original color or their color change is a pleasant one. (The list originally appeared in *The American Rose,* February 1989.)

Hybrid Teas for Color Stability: Olympiad, Double Delight, Folklore, Lolita, Milestone, Mon Cheri, Color Magic, Red Masterpiece, White Masterpiece, Century Two, Miss All-American Beauty, Swarthmore

Floribundas: Showbiz, Summer Fashion, French Lace, Iceberg, Europeana, Evening Star, Impatient, Playboy

Grandifloras: Gold Medal, White Lightnin', Prima Donna, Prominent

Miniatures: Chattem Centennial, Fancy Pants, Snow Bride, Minnie Pearl, Red Beauty, Acey Deucy, Cheer Up, Magic Carrousel, Green Ice

HINTS FOR GROWING ROSES

- Roses should be planted when dormant and the best time depends on where you live. Spring planting is safest in the coldest states, and winter planting best in the South. In some states (New Jersey, Maryland) late fall planting (November) can be quite successful; roots become established before winter, often resulting in earlier and better spring bloom.

- Roses seem to do best in soils that are neither too acid nor too alkaline; a pH of 6.5 is considered optimum. Good drainage is essential—roses will not tolerate soggy soil.

- Plant roses away from tree roots, especially deciduous trees with invasive roots. Choose a site where the sun shines at least six hours a day. (Some shrub and vintage roses are tolerant of more shade.)

- Prune roses in the spring, except for ramblers, which should be pruned after they have bloomed. Cut back to live wood; be sure all cuts are close to a bud. Do not prune newly planted roses during the first growing season.

- Roses may be fertilized after pruning and once or twice during the growing season, but not after mid-August in the North. To encourage dormancy it is also a good idea not to cut late fall flowers. Clean up old rose leaves in fall and spring to help keep diseases from spreading.

- Some roses do not need winter protection in most parts of the country. Many species roses, old roses and shrub roses as well as some climbers, miniatures and floribundas are quite cold-resistant. Check with your local extension service about the best methods of winter protection for your area.

ALL-AMERICA ROSE SELECTIONS' SUGGESTED PLANTING TIMES AND SPACING

Region	Planting Time	Hybrid Tea/ Grandiflora Spacing (in Feet)	Floribunda Spacing (in Feet)
Northeast	April–early May	1½–2	1½–2
Eastern Seaboard	March–early April	2½–3	2–3
North-Central	April–early May	2–2½	2–2½
Subtropical	December–January	3–4	2½–3½
Mid-South	December–January	2½–3	2–3
South-Central	late January–February	2½–3	2–3
Southwest	late December–January	3–4	2½–3½
Pacific Southwest	January–February	3–4	2½–3½
Pacific Northwest	February–March	3–4	2½–3½

Rose Diseases

The two most serious diseases that affect roses are blackspot and mildew. Both are caused by fungi. Blackspot is characterized by circular black spots with fringed margins that appear on leaves; mildew produces a white powdery film that can cover leaves, buds and young shoots.

Blackspot is generally not a problem in semiarid sections of the country where mildew is of more concern. To control disease, plant roses where there is good air circulation and avoid wetting leaves when watering. Clean up dead leaves on which fungi can overwinter. Apply fungicides when necessary.

Disease-Resistant Roses

According to studies conducted on roses throughout the country and compiled by Mr. Lincoln Atkiss of Newton Square, Pennsylvania, the following roses were found to be resistant to blackspot and mildew. (Results were published in the *American Rose Annual,* 1978.):

HYBRID TEAS MOST RESISTANT TO BLACKSPOT:

Tropicana	Proud Land
First Prize	Duet
Miss All-American Beauty	Peace
Mister Lincoln	Electron
Tiffany	Pascali
Portrait	Sutter's Gold
Pristine	Granada
Pink Peace	Carla

FLORIBUNDAS/GRANDIFLORAS MOST RESISTANT TO BLACKSPOT:

Queen Elizabeth	Sonia
Prominent	Carrousel
Rose Parade	Angel Face
Razzle Dazzle	Sunsprite
Gene Boerner	Betty Prior
Europeana	The Fairy
Montezuma	Pink Parfait
First Edition	Redgold
Ivory Fashion	

Frau Dagmar Hartopp (hybrid rugosa, 8.9) is also reported to have a very high resistance to blackspot, as is the shrub rose Carefree Beauty (7.5).

HYBRID TEAS MOST RESISTANT TO MILDEW:

Tiffany	Proud Land
Pristine	Mister Lincoln
Miss All-American Beauty	Tropicana

Futura
Pascali
Peace
Seashell
Pink Peace

Chicago Peace
Portrait
Royal Highness
Double Delight
Fragrant Cloud

FLORIBUNDAS/GRANDIFLORAS MOST RESISTANT TO MILDEW:

Queen Elizabeth
Europeana
Rose Parade
Charisma
Sarabande
Saratoga
Cathedral

Sunsprite
Prominent
Razzle Dazzle
First Edition
Evening Star
Pink Parfait
Sonia

THE MOST OVERALL DISEASE-RESISTANT VARIETIES:

Tropicana
Queen Elizabeth
Prominent
Miss All-American Beauty
Pristine
Peace

Tiffany
Cathedral
Fragrant Cloud
Pascali
Pink Peace
Europeana

Other disease resistant varieties include Mister Lincoln, Portrait, Electron, Gene Boerner, and Charisma. Two new roses that are said to have excellent disease resistance are Class Act, a white Floribunda, and the pink Grandiflora Tournament of Roses.

Insect Pests of the Rose

> Oh rose, thou art sick
> The invisible worm
> That flies in the night
> In the howling storm
>
> Has found out thy bed
> Of crimson joy,
> And his dark secret love
> Does thy life destroy.
> WILLIAM BLAKE, "THE SICK ROSE"

Why did roses develop protective thorns? We can only speculate about the ancient predators that may have been deterred by rose barbs; certainly thorns do little today to guard against the army of insects that seem to prefer the rose above all other plants. Twelve of the worst pests of roses (there are others!) are:

Aphids—Tiny green or pink insects that cluster on growing tips and suck plant juices.

Fuller rose beetle—Gray-brown nocturnal beetle (⅓ inch), eats leaf margins, doing the most damage in the larval stage. Can be a serious pest in California and the South.

Japanese beetle—Roses seem to be the favorite fare of these large metallic-green/bronze colored insects (miniature roses, being closer to the ground, seem less bothered.) Milky spore treatments will control the grubs in the lawn before they turn into rose attacking beetles; birds such as starlings are also helpful. Once beetles have emerged, hand-picking seems to be the only environmentally safe recourse.

Leaf roller—Small greenish caterpillar that eats leaves and bores holes in buds. Pupates inside a rolled-up leaf.

Rose beetle—Small, oval metallic pest that bores into buds and eats holes in flowers.

Rose chafer—Light brown beetle (¼ inch) with long spiney legs; damages flowers (especially white ones) and eats leaves in early summer.

Rose curculio—Red beetle with long black snout. Adults and white larvae feed on buds and flowers.

Rose leafhopper—Tiny light-colored insects that feed on the undersides of leaves. A second generation appears in the fall.

Rose midge—Tiny brownish yellow fly whose eggs hatch into minute white maggots that cause death of buds and young shoots. This pest seems to be making a comeback in many areas.

Rose scale—White- or gray-scale insects that suck plant juices and prefer older canes.

Spider mite—A scourge in hot, dry weather, tiny mites inhabit the undersides of leaves; their fine webs are often visible. Severe leaf drop can occur if numbers are large; washing the undersides of leaves weekly with a water wand helps keep them at bay.

Thrips—Another small pest that likes hot, dry weather, thrips have dark bodies with four feathery wings; yellow young are nearly invisible. Thrips attack young leaves and buds and seem to prefer (like the rose chafer) white flowers. Their presence should be suspected if white rose buds fail to open.

Companion Plants for Roses

Roses, especially the older varieties and modern "shrub" types, can be combined attractively with other shrubs or even placed in a perennial border. Vintage roses and herbs are natural companions; roses were once useful plants as well as ornamental ones. The following shrubs are particularly suited to planting with roses:

WITH ALL ROSES:

Deutzia spp. (DEUTZIA)
Fothergilla spp. (FOTHERGILLA)
Hydrangea paniculata and H. paniculata grandiflora
 (PANICLE AND PEE GEE HYDRANGEA)
Philadelphus spp. (MOCK ORANGE)
Rhodotypos scandens (JETBEAD)*
Viburnum spp. (VIBURNUM)

WITH PINK AND RED ROSES:

Buddleia spp. (BUTTERFLY BUSH)
Kolkwitzia amabilis (BEAUTYBUSH)
Weigela florida varieties (WEIGELA)

WITH YELLOW AND ORANGE ROSES:

Kerria japonica (KERRIA, JAPANESE ROSE)*
Potentilla fruticosa (SHRUBBY CINQUEFOIL)*
Pyracantha spp. (FIRETHORN)*

*Members of the Rose family.

Perennials to Plant with Roses

Consider flower colors if roses and perennials are to bloom at the same time. Gray-leaved perennials such as Iris, Betony, Lavender and

Nepeta are especially handsome with pink/red and white roses. Ten more companions for roses are:

Aquilegia (COLUMBINE)
Astilbe (ASTILBE)
Campanula (BELLFLOWER)
Chrysanthemum parthenium (FEVERFEW)
Dianthus (PINK, CARNATION)
Geranium spp. (HARDY GERANIUM, CRANESBILL)
Gypsophila (BABY'S BREATH)
Hosta (HOSTA)
Limonium (SEA-LAVENDER)
Paeonia (PEONY)

ALL-AMERICA ROSE SELECTIONS ACCREDITED PUBLIC ROSE GARDENS

It is not surprising that rose growers cannot agree on the perfect rose; a star performer in Pennsylvania could well be a dud in California. Some roses are quite disease resistant generally but are subject to troubles in certain regions. Two examples are Tropicana, which is prone to mildew in the West, and the yellow climber Lawrence Johnson, which is prone to blackspot in the South. Some rose blossoms have trouble opening in cool, foggy climates; gardeners in such regions should plant varieties with fewer petals to insure good bloom. The United States is a big country, with many climate zones as well as quite a bit of variation within zones. Happily for rose growers, there are a number of AARS Accredited Public Rose Gardens located throughout the country where one can view yearly award-winning roses before they are available on the market and see how they, and many other varieties, perform in the local climate and soils.

Alabama
(Fairhope): Fairhope City Garden
(Mobile): Battleship Memorial Park
(Mobile): David A. Hemphill Park
(Theodore): Bellingrath Gardens

Arizona
(Glendale): Sahaura Historical Ranch Rose Garden
(Phoenix): Valley Garden Center Rose Garden
(Tucson): Gene Reid Park Rose Garden

Arkansas
  (Little Rock): Arkansas State Capitol Garden

California
  (Citrus Heights): Fountain Square Garden
  (Corona del Mar): Rogers Gardens
  (DeLano): Bella Rosa Winery Garden
  (LaCanada): Descanso Garden
  (Los Angeles): Exposition Park Garden
  (Oakland): Morcom Amphitheater of Roses
  (Pasadena): Tournament of Roses Wrigley Garden
  (Pasadena): Rose Bowl Garden
  (Riverside): Fairmount Park
  (Sacramento): Capitol Park
  (San Diego): Inez Parker Memorial Garden
  (San Francisco): Golden Gate Park
  (San Jose): San Jose Municipal Garden
  (San Marino): Huntington Botanical Gardens
  (Santa Barbara): A. C. Postel Memorial Garden
  (Westminster): Westminster Civic Center Garden
  (Whittier): Pageant of Roses Garden

Colorado
  (Littleton): War Memorial Garden
  (Longmont): Longmont Lions Club Memorial Garden

Connecticut
  (Norwich): Norwich Memorial Garden
  (West Hartford): Elizabeth Park Garden

District of Columbia:
  George Washington University

Florida
  (Lake Buena Vista): Walt Disney World
  (Largo): Sturgeon Memorial Garden
  (Winter Haven): Florida Cypress Gardens

Georgia
  (Athens): Elizabeth B. Turner Memorial Garden
  (Atlanta): Greater Atlanta Garden, Piedmont Park
  (Thomasville): Rose Test Garden

Hawaii
>   (Kula): University of Hawaii Maui Agricultural Research
>   Center

Illinois
>   (Alton): Nan Elliott Memorial Garden, Moore Park
>   (Evanston): Merrick Park Rose Garden
>   (Glencoe): Bruce Krasberg Garden, Chicago Botanical Garden
>   (Libertyville): Lynn Arthur Rose Garden
>   (Peoria): George Luthy Memorial Botanical Garden
>   (Rockford): Sinnissippi Garden
>   (Springfield): Washington Park Botanical Garden
>   (Wheaton): Cantigny Gardens

Indiana
>   (Fort Wayne): Lakeside Park

Iowa
>   (Ames): Iowa State Horticultural Gardens
>   (Bettendorf): Bettendorf Park Board Municipal Garden
>   (Cedar Rapids): Noelridge Park Garden
>   (Davenport): VanderVeer Park Municipal Garden
>   (Des Moines): Greenwood Park Garden
>   (Dubuque): Dubuque Arboretum Rose Garden
>   (Muscatine): Weed Park Memorial Garden
>   (State Center): State Center Public Rose Garden

Kansas
>   (Topeka): E.F.A. Reinisch Garden

Kentucky
>   (Louisville): Kentucky Memorial Rose Garden

Louisiana
>   (Baton Rouge): Louisiana State University Rose Test Garden
>   (Many): Hodges Gardens
>   (Shreveport): American Rose Center (Here the American
>   Rose Society is creating a 118-acre garden that will be the
>   largest park in the U.S. devoted mainly to roses.)

Maine
>   (Portland): Deering Oaks Municipal Rose Garden

Maryland
>   (Wheaton): Brookside Botanical Gardens

Massachusetts
(Boston): James P. Kelleher Rose Garden
(Westfield): Stanley Park of Westfield

Michigan
(East Lansing): Michigan State University Horticulture Garden
(Lansing): Frances Park Memorial Garden

Minnesota
(Minneapolis): Lyndale Park Municipal Rose Garden

Mississippi
(Hattiesburg): Hattiesburg Area Public Rose Garden

Missouri
(Cape Girardeau): Capaha Rose Display Garden
(Kansas City): Laura C. Smith Municipal Rose Garden
(St. Louis): Anne Lehmann Rose Garden
(St. Louis): Gladney Rose Garden

Montana
(Missoula): Missoula Memorial Rose Garden

Nebraska
(Boys Town): AARS Constitution Rose Garden
(Lincoln): Lincoln Municipal Garden, Antelope Park
(Omaha): Memorial Park Rose Garden

Nevada
(Reno): Reno Municipal Rose Garden

New Hampshire
(North Hampton): Fuller Gardens

New Jersey
(E. Millstone): R. W. VanderGoot Garden, Colonial Park
(Lincroft): L. C. Bobbink Memorial Garden, Thompson Park
(Tenafly): J. D. Lissemore Garden, Davis Johnson Park
(Union): Brookdale Park Rose Garden

New Mexico
(Albuquerque): Prospect Park Rose Garden

New York
 (Bronx): Bechtel Memorial Rose Garden, New York Botanical Garden
 (Brooklyn): Cranford Memorial Garden, Brooklyn Botanic Gardens
 (Buffalo): Joan Fuzak Memorial Garden, Erie Marina
 (Canandaigua): Sonnenberg Gardens
 (Flushing): Queens Botanical Garden
 (New York): United Nations Rose Garden
 (Old Westbury): Old Westbury Gardens
 (Rochester): Maplewood Rose Garden
 (Schenectady): Central Park Garden
 (Syracuse): Mills Memorial Rose Garden, Thorndon Park

North Carolina
 (Ashville): Biltmore Estate
 (Clemmons): Tanglewood Park Garden
 (Fayetteville): Fayetteville Rose Garden
 (Raleigh): Raleigh Municipal Rose Garden
 (Winston-Salem): Reynolds Rose Gardens, Wake Forest University

Ohio
 (Akron): Stan Hywet Hall and Gardens
 (Bay Village): Cahoon Memorial Rose Garden
 (Columbus): Columbus Park of Roses
 (Mansfield): C. E. Nail, Sr., Memorial Rose Garden

Oklahoma
 (Muskogee): J. E. Conrad Municipal Garden, Honor Heights Park
 (Oklahoma City): Sparks Garden, Will Rogers Park
 (Tulsa): Tulsa Municipal Rose Garden

Oregon
 (Coos Bay): Shore Acres State Park
 (Corvallis): Corvallis Rose Garden, Avery Park
 (Eugene): George Owen Memorial Rose Garden
 (Portland): International Rose Test Garden

Pennsylvania
 (Allentown): Malcolm W. Gross Memorial Rose Garden
 (Hershey): Hershey Rose Gardens

(Kennett Square): Longwood Gardens
(Philadelphia): Morris Arboretum Rose Garden
(West Grove): Robert Pyle Memorial Rose Garden

South Carolina
(Orangeburg): Edisto Memorial Gardens

South Dakota
(Rapid City): Memorial Park Garden

Tennessee
(Chattanooga): Warner Park Rose Garden
(Memphis): Memphis Municipal Rose Garden

Texas
(Austin): Mabel Davis Rose Garden, Zilker Botanical Gardens
(Dallas): Samuel-Grand Municipal Garden
(El Paso): Municipal Rose Garden
(Ft. Worth): Ft. Worth Botanic Garden
(Houston): Houston Municipal Rose Garden
(Tyler): Tyler Municipal Garden
(Victoria): Victoria Rose Garden

Utah
(Fillmore): Territorial Statehouse State Park Rose Garden
(Nephi): Nephi Memorial Rose Garden
(Salt Lake City): Municipal Rose Garden, Sugar House Park

Virginia
(Alexandria): American Horticultural Society, River Farm
(Arlington): Bon Air Memorial Rose Garden
(Norfolk): Bicentennial Rose Garden, Norfolk Botanical Gardens

Washington
(Bellingham): Fairhaven Park Garden
(Chehalis): Chehalis Municipal Rose Garden
(Seattle): Woodland Park Rose Garden
(Spokane): Rose Hill, Manito Park

West Virginia
(Huntington): Ritter Park Rose Garden
(Moundsville): Prabupada's Palace Rose Garden

Wisconsin
> (Hales Corners): Boerner Botanical Gardens
> (Madison): Olbrich Botanical Gardens All-American Display
> Rose Garden

ROSE FACTS AND FANCIES

The Language of Roses

Although plants have served as symbols throughout human history, some societies elevated florigraphy (the language of flowers) into a sophisticated method of communication. The Middle East, which also gave the world the beautiful flower carpets called "Oriental rugs," may have been the first region to develop this custom. Florigraphy spread throughout Europe and reached another pinnacle of development in Victorian times when it became the rage to send complicated floral messages and decipher them with the many floral dictionaries of the period. People who send and receive roses today correctly understand the flower as a symbol of love. Years ago, however, the "language of flowers" was a lot more complicated:

> **Red rose**—*I love you.* Red roses also stand for respect and
> courage.
> **Red rosebud**—*You are pure and lovely.*
> **White rose**—*I am worthy of you.* White roses also stand for
> purity, reverence, humility and secrecy. Long ago a white
> rose could also stand for refusal.
> **White rosebud**—*Too young for love.*
> **Red and white roses together**—*Unity.*
> **A faded rose**—*Beauty is fleeting.*
> **Fully opened rose placed over buds**—*Secrecy.*
> **Yellow rose**—*Jealousy; a decrease of love or I love another.*
> Recently rose growers declare that yellow roses stand for
> gladness but can also say "try to care."
> **Pink rose**—*Grace, gentility and gratitude.*

Different varieties of roses had their own special meanings: Rosa mundi could express a wish for variety, a centifolia or Provence rose declares "My heart is in flames," while La France (the world's first Hybrid tea) says "Meet me by moonlight."

The Taste of Roses: Rose-Petal Sandwiches

Put a layer of Red Rose-petals in the bottom of a jar or
covered dish, put in 4 oz. of fresh butter wrapped in waxed
paper. Cover with a thick layer of rose-petals. Cover closely
and leave in a cool place overnight. The more fragrant the roses
the better. Cut bread into thin strips (or circles or hearts),
spread each with the perfumed butter and place several petals
from fresh Red Roses between the slices, allowing edges to
show.

MRS. M. GRIEVE, *A MODERN HERBAL*, 1931

Other Facts and Fancies

- Roses probably originated in Asia about 60 million years ago.
- The oldest fossil rose, 40 million years old, was found in
  Florissant, Colorado.
- A Minoan fresco painted about 1500 B.C. is the earliest known
  painting of a rose.
- Homer wrote (in the *Iliad*) that Hector's helmet and Achilles'
  shield were decorated with roses when they dueled at Troy.
- The word *rosa* comes from the Greek word *rodon,* which
  means "red."
- An emblem of Venus, the rose was a compulsory badge worn
  by prostitutes as a mark of disgrace in ancient times.
- Once scorned by Christianity, which connected it with
  Roman debauchery, the rose became the symbol of Mary in
  the Middle Ages, a talisman against witchcraft and the
  inspiration for the great rose windows of Europe's Gothic
  cathedrals.
- Early rosary beads were often fashioned from a paste made of
  pulverized rose petals.
- The Golden Rose, an award given by the pope to those who
  have given outstanding service to the church, is blessed on
  Rose Sunday, the fourth Sunday in Lent. At first (the award
  has been recorded since 1096 but is believed to have been
  given much earlier) the rose was a single flower of red-tinted

gold, but later it was enlarged and embellished with gems. Some winners include the queens of Belgium and Italy and an American, M. G. Caldwell, who helped establish Catholic University.

- In feudal times in England tenants sometimes paid a symbolic rent of one red rose. This custom was also practiced in colonial America.

- According to the American Rose Society, Columbus's dejected crew fished a rose branch, covered with red fruit, from the sea on October 11, 1492. The rose told them land was near, and gave new hope to the men who were about to discover the "New World."

- The yellow flowers of Rosa foetida (called the Austrian Briar Rose, although it originated in Asia) have an unpleasant odor. This rose is important, however, because it is responsible for the golden shades in many modern roses. Unfortunately, Persian yellow roses also brought high susceptibility to blackspot.

- Rose petals were believed to calm the nerves and dispel depression and once were used to treat stomach and pulmonary disorders and to heal pimples.

- Rose hips (fruit) are very rich in Vitamin C. Rosa rugosa and R. canina produce some of the best edible hips.

- Strawberries, raspberries, blackberries, cherries, plums, apples, pears, peaches and apricots all belong to the great rose family. Recently, researchers have found that ellagic acid, found in many of these fruits, can block the action of several different cancer-causing chemicals.

- Most modern florists remove thorns from cut roses, a practice that significantly shortens (by 1 to 3 days) vase life.

- Roses with small, glossy leaves generally have the longest vase life. Lavender roses and yellow roses tend to have short vase lives; sweetheart roses usually last longer than Hybrid teas.

- The rose is the national floral emblem of England, Ireland and the United States.

- The original White House architect, James Hoban, decorated the building's stately Ionic columns with roses.

- The rose has appeared on 150 different postage stamps in 42 different countries.
- Today there are more than 20,000 varieties of roses.
- About 40 million rose plants are grown for garden use in the U.S. annually, and another 20 million are grown for the cut-flower industry. The main U.S. production areas are located in Texas, California, Arizona and Pennsylvania.

SOURCES FOR ROSES

Antique Rose Emporium
Rt. 5, Box 143
Brenham, TX 77833
(Old roses)

Carroll Gardens
PO Box 310
444 E. Main St.
Westminster, MD 21157

Donovan's Roses
PO Box 37800
Shreveport, LA 71133-7800

Emlong Nurseries, Inc.
Stevensville, MI 49127

Heritage Rosarium
211 Haviland Mill Rd.
Brookeville, MD 20833
(Old roses)

High Country Rosarium
1717 Downing St.
Denver, CO 80218
(Old roses)

Hortico Roses, Inc.
RR 1
Waterdown, Ontario, Canada
LOR 2HO

Howertown Rose Nursery
Rt. 3, Box 36
Northampton, PA 18067

Inter-State Nurseries
PO Box 208
Hamburg, IA 51640-0208

Jackson and Perkins
1 Rose Lane
Medford, OR 97501

Kraus Nurseries Ltd.
Carlisle, Ontario, Canada LOR 1HO

Lowe's Own Root Nursery
6 Sheffield Rd.
Nashua, NH 03062
(Old roses)

Pickering Nurseries
670 Kingston Rd.
Pickering, Ontario LIV IA6
Canada
(Old roses)

Roses by Fred Edmunds
6235 S.W. Kahle Rd.
Wilsonville, OR 97070

Roses of Yesterday and Today
802 Browns Valley Rd.
Watsonville, CA 95076
(Old roses)

Wayside Gardens
1 Garden Lane
Hodges, SC 29695

SOURCES FOR MINIATURES

Jackson and Perkins
1 Rose Lane
Medford, OR 97501

McDaniel's Miniature Roses
7523 Zemco St.
Lemon Grove, CA 92045

Mini-Roses
POBox 4255, Station A
Dallas, TX 75208

Moore Miniature Roses
Sequoia Nursery
2519 E. Noble Ave.
Visalia, CA 93277

Nor'East Miniature Roses, Inc.
58 Hammond St.
Rowley, MA 01969
PO Box 473
Ontario, CA 91762

Pixie Treasures
4121 Prospect Ave.
Yorba Linda, CA 92686

Oregon Miniature Roses
8285 S.W. 185th Ave.
Beaverton, OR 97007

Rosehill Farm Miniature Roses
Gregg Neck Rd.
Galena, MD 21635

Tiny Petals Nursery
489 Minot Ave.
Chula Vista, CA 92010

Wee Gems Mini Roses
2197 Stewart Ave.
St. Paul, MN 55116

Beverly Dobson publishes a Combined Rose List, which contains information on all known roses in commerce and cultivation and where to find them. Send $15.00 to Beverly R. Dobson, 215 Harriman Road, Irvington, NY 10533.

2

Annuals, Perennials, Bulbs and Grasses

ANNUALS

Annuals for the Shade

Many annuals require full sun. The following will tolerate partial shade (Begonia, Browallia, Coleus and Impatiens are especially shade-tolerant):

Begonia x semperflorens-cultorum (WAX BEGONIA)
Browallia spp. (BUSH VIOLET)
Cleome hasslerana (SPIDER FLOWER)
Coleus hybrids (COLEUS, FLAME NETTLE)
Impatiens wallerana and **I. balsamina** (IMPATIENS AND BALSAM)
Lobelia erinus (EDGING LOBELIA)
Mimulus hybrids (MONKEY FLOWER)
Nemophila menziesii (BABY BLUE EYES)
Nicotiana alata (FLOWERING TOBACCO, JASMINE TOBACCO)
Salvia spp. (BLUE OR MEALY CUP SAGE AND SCARLET SAGE)

Torenia fournieri (WISHBONE FLOWER, BLUEWINGS)
Viola tricolor and **V. x wittrockiana** (JOHNNY-JUMP-UP AND
PANSY)

Ageratum, Forget-Me-Not and Sweet Alyssum will also grow in light
shade. Shade-happy plants for hanging baskets include Fuchsia and Thunbergia (Black-Eyed Susan Vine).

THESE ANNUALS ENJOY PLENTY OF MOISTURE:

Browallia (BUSH VIOLET)
Cleome (SPIDER FLOWER)
Impatiens (IMPATIENS)
Lobelia (EDGING LOBELIA)
Mimulus (MONKEY FLOWER)
Mirabilis (FOUR O'CLOCK)
Myosotis (FORGET-ME-NOT)*
Nicotiana (FLOWERING TOBACCO)
Torenia (BLUEWINGS)
Viola (PANSY)

*M. sylvatica is a biennial.

Seeds That Will Germinate in Cool Soil

Attention, early birds! Many seeds should be started indoors or sown
in the garden after the soil warms up. The following, however, can be
planted outdoors before the last frost, as soon as the ground can be
worked:

IN THE VEGETABLE GARDEN:

Allium (ONION, LEEK)
Beta (BEET, SWISS CHARD)
Brassica (KALE, KOHLRABI)
Lactuca (LETTUCE)
Pisum (PEAS)
Raphanus (RADISH)
Spinacia (SPINACH)

Calendula officinalis (POT MARIGOLD)
Centaurea cyanus (BACHELOR'S BUTTON)
Consolida ambigua (ROCKET LARKSPUR)
Gypsophila elegans (ANNUAL BABY'S BREATH)
Lathyrus odoratus (SWEET PEA)
Lobularia maritima (SWEET ALYSSUM)
Nigella damascena (LOVE-IN-A-MIST)
Papaver spp. (ICELAND POPPY AND CORN POPPY)
Phlox drummondii (ANNUAL PHLOX)
Reseda odorata (MIGNONETTE)

Annuals That Need Light to Germinate

Not all seeds should be covered with soil. Light enhances germination in a number of species, often those with tiny seeds. Place seeds of the following on top of the planting medium and do not cover:

Antirrhinum (SNAPDRAGON)
Ageratum (FLOSSFLOWER, AGERATUM)
Begonia (BEGONIA)
Browallia (BUSH VIOLET)
Clarkia (GODETIA)
Coleus (COLEUS, FLAME NETTLE)
Helichrysum (STRAWFLOWER)
Impatiens (IMPATIENS)
Lobularia (SWEET ALYSSUM)
Nicotiana (FLOWERING TOBACCO)
Petunia (PETUNIA)
Portulaca (PORTULACA)
Reseda (MIGNONETTE)
Salvia (SCARLET SAGE)

Other annuals, such as Celosia, Cleome, Cosmos, Mimulus, Gerbera and Torenia, prefer at least some light for germination; barely cover them at planting time. Some perennials also need light, including Columbine, Chamomile, Digitalis and Lychnis.

Annuals That Drape or Trail

Most annuals can be grown in containers; the following will gracefully spill over edges and borders. The American Horticultural Society recommends them as ideal for hanging baskets and window boxes:

Browallia species (BUSH VIOLET)—white, lilac, purple
Dianthus barbatus (SWEET WILLIAM)—white, pink, rose, red, purple
Impatiens wallerana (IMPATIENS)—white
Lobularia maritima (SWEET ALYSSUM)—white
Pelargonium peltatum (IVY GERANIUM)—reds and whites
Petunia x hybrida (PETUNIA)—many colors
Portulaca grandiflora (MOSS ROSE)—many colors
Sanvitalia procumbens (CREEPING ZINNIA)—yellow to orange petals, dark centers
Tropaeolum majus (NASTURTIUM)—yellow, orange, bronze
Verbena x hybrida (GARDEN VERBENA)—yellow, orange, bronze
Viola tricolor (JOHNNY-JUMP-UP)—yellows, purples, violet blue

Annuals for Fragrance

Today we have bigger and brighter annuals, but our great-grandparents' annual flower beds were sweeter smelling. Unfortunately, some modern hybrids of once fragrant plants such as Sweet Pea, Verbena and Nicotiana have lost much of their scent, although good-smelling, old-fashioned varieties can still be found. Annuals for fragrance include:

Artemisia annua (SWEET ANNIE)—Sweetly aromatic leaves and branches are perfect for wreath making.
Centaurea moschata (SWEET SULTAN)—Plant about 2 to 3 feet tall; large, thistlelike flowers in yellow, white, pink or purple; Asian native; there are several cultivars.
Cosmos atrosanguineus (BLACK COSMOS)—Small maroon flowers are thought by many to smell like chocolate; foliage is reddish. Mexican native.
Heliotropium arborescens (HELIOTROPE)—A perennial in its native Peru; has purple (varying to white) flowers that some say smell like vanilla or apples, others think it smells like another common name—Cherry-Pie.

Lathyrus odoratus (SWEET PEA)—Many of today's colorful cultivars do not possess that old-time fragrance.

Lobularia maritima* (SWEET ALYSSUM)—Low-growing, frost tolerant and self-sowing; the tiny flowers are delicately scented.

Matthiola longipetala (EVENING STOCK OR PERFUME PLANT)—The subspecies bicornis has very fragrant pink or purple flowers that open in the evening; the annual cultivar of M. incana is also fragrant.

Mirabilis jalapa (FOUR O'CLOCK, BEAUTY OF THE NIGHT)—Another plant with sweet-smelling flowers that open in late afternoon; colors may be red, pink, yellow or white.

Nicotiana alata (FLOWERING TOBACCO)—Tall plant with fragrant white flowers; also called Jasmine Tobacco; only the tall evening bloomer is fragrant; bright day-blooming cultivars have lost the perfume.

Pelargonium graveolens (ROSE GERANIUM)—Actually a tender, woody plant with sweet-scented leaves and small rose-colored flowers; needs sun and some pruning to keep it bushy.

Reseda odorata (MIGNONETTE)—A Victorian favorite; plant the old-fashioned whitish flowered Mignonette (instead of newer and brighter hued cultivars) for best fragrance.

Tropaeolum majus (NASTURTIUM)—Some cultivars of this brightly flowered (and edible) plant are sweetly fragrant.

*Two older AAS winners that are fragrant are Sweet Alyssum 'Royal Carpet' (1953) and 'Rosie O'Day' (1961).

Garden Volunteers: Annuals That Reseed Easily

Many annuals and biennials are prolific reseeders, which explains why you sometimes have Sweet Alyssum and Cornflowers popping up in unexpected places. While this can be a nuisance, many gardeners welcome at least a few volunteers. Some seedling plants are smaller than their parents and tend to peter out after a few years; other plants seem to reseed indefinitely. Remember that hybrids (such as most of the new All-America Selections (AAS) winners and other plants purchased at garden centers) will not "come true" from seed; only open-pollinated plants will do so. Be careful not to mistake tiny plants for weeds in the spring.

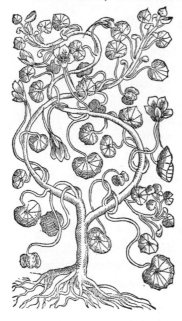

Tropaeolum sp. (Nasturtium). Though native to cool South American highlands, frost-tender Nasturtiums are grown as annuals in most gardens. Plants contain mustard oil and leaves and flowers may be added to salads.

FIFTEEN SELF-SOWERS:

Anthemis (GOLDEN MARGUERITE) B or (SHORT-LIVED) P
Calendula (POT MARIGOLD) A (HARDY)
Cleome (SPIDER PLANT) A
Centaurea (BACHELOR'S BUTTON, CORNFLOWER) A
Coreopsis (COREOPSIS) A and P
Cosmos (COSMOS) A
Dianthus (SWEET WILLIAM) B
Digitalis (FOXGLOVE) B or P
Hesperis (DAME'S ROCKET) B or P
Lobularia (SWEET ALYSSUM) A
Lunaria (HONESTY OR MONEY PLANT) B
Nicotiana (FLOWERING TOBACCO) A
Portulaca (PORTULACA, ROSE MOSS) A
Rudbeckia (CONEFLOWER) A, B, P
Viola (JOHNNY-JUMP-UP) A or (SHORT-LIVED) P

A—Annual   B—Biennial   P—Perennial

Perennials such as Aquilegia (Columbine), Feverfew (Chrysanthemum) and Phlox are also proficient self-sowers, although like all hybrids, hybrid Columbine and Phlox will not produce seedlings that resemble parents. Phlox seedlings generally mature into magenta-flowered plants.

*Annuals for Beginners: "A Chapter of Flower Gossip"** *

Several correspondents have asked me to give a list of a dozen kinds of the annuals that will be most likely to give satisfaction under amateur culture. I would suggest:

- Phlox drummondi, a free and constant bloomer, requiring very little care. This plant comes in a wonderful variety of colors, and never fails to please.
- Calliopsis, another "stand-by" that deserves a place in all gardens. Its rich yellows and browns will be found extremely effective in masses.
- Verbena, an old favorite which is again coming into popularity. Being of low-growing habit it is admirably adapted to places near the path, or under the windows of the dwelling, where it can be looked down upon.
- Portulaca, another plant of low and spreading habit. Particularly adapted to hot and sunny locations where most other plants would fail. Comes in a great variety of colors. An all-season bloomer.
- Sweet-pea. Of course these will be found in all gardens. Perhaps the most popular flower we have at the present time.
- Aster, a close rival of the sweet-pea. No garden can afford to be without it. The very best flower we have for cutting. The best variety for this purpose is the "branching" class, with flowers borne on long stalks.
- Larkspur, an old favorite. You will surely be pleased with a bed of it.
- Mignonette. Not a showy flower, but so delightfully fragrant that it should be given a place in all collections.
- Ten-weeks stock, the "gillyflower" of our grandmother's garden. A profuse bloomer, and deliciously sweet. Good for cutting. Continues in bloom until heavy frost.
- Nasturtium. This flower is another important member of the "stand-by" class. It is equally fine for cutting and for the decoration of the garden. Be sure to include it in your list this spring.

*By Eben E. Rexford, *Hearth and Home,* January 1916.

- Cosmos, a flower of recent introduction that deserves general attention. Excellent for cutting, as well as outdoor show. But be sure to order the early kind, as the large-growing variety will not come into bloom until so late in the season that frost is pretty sure to injure it before it becomes effective.

- Nicotiana, a comparatively new flower, but one that will find a place in all gardens as soon as its merits become better known. It is admirably adapted to massing, and in addition to its ornamental features it is delightfully fragrant. It is also valuable for cutting.

I can most confidently recommend every one of the above to the amateur gardener. Try them all.

Uncommon Annuals

Tired of Impatiens and Marigolds? A dozen less usual annuals to try are:

Asperula orientalis (ANNUAL WOODRUFF)—This Eurasian native grows about a foot tall and produces a profusion of small blue flowers and attractive seed heads. Sun or partial shade.

Clarkia unguiculata* (FAREWELL-TO-SPRING, GODETIA)—Erect, to 3 feet tall (as opposed to sprawling types like C. amoena), this Clarkia has pink/salmon or purple flowers. There are double-flowered cultivars.

Coreopsis tinctoria* (CALLIOPSIS)—Important dye plant much grown in the nineteenth century; yellow and bronze daisylike flowers. Full sun and light, sandy soils. 'Nana' is a low-growing cultivar.

Dyssodia tenuiloba* (DAHLBERG DAISY, GOLDEN-FLEECE)— Golden flowers, long period of bloom and beautiful feathery foliage make this low-growing native a fine edging or rock garden plant. Full sun; good drainage. Likes cool weather but tolerates heat; reseeds when happy.

Layia platyglossa* (TIDY TIPS)—Yellow daisy-type flowers with white tips, this California native likes full sun and reseeds readily.

*U.S. native.

Linaria maroccana (TOADFLAX)—Snapdragon flowers in shades of purple, red, pink, orange, yellow and white; reseeds readily. Native to Morocco; likes full sun. Cousin to the beautiful but invasive L. vulgaris (Butter and Eggs).

Linum grandiflorum 'Rubrum' (RED FLAX)—Bushy plants, about one foot tall, with narrow gray-green leaves and deep rose flowers. There are blue and scarlet flowered cultivars; N. African native.

Nemesia strumosa (NEMESIA)—S. African native that likes cool, dry summers; full sun or partial shade. Long-flowering and brightly colored Nemesias grow 1 to 2 feet tall (there are lower-growing cultivars) and are excellent in containers and rock gardens as well as borders.

Nemophila menziesii* (BABY BLUE EYES)—Low-growing plant with sky blue flowers with white centers. Reseeds in many locations; tolerates partial shade. N. maculata (Five Spot or Buffalo Eyes) grows 6 feet tall and has white flowers with purple spots.

Phacelia campanularia* (CALIFORNIA BLUEBELL)—A desert native with gray-green leaves and bell-shaped bright blue (rarely white) flowers in spring. Needs full sun. P. tanacetifolia (Fiddleneck or Bee Food) is cultivated in some areas as a honey plant. Phacelia probably best in the West and South.

Trachymene coerulea (BLUE LACE FLOWER)—Compound leaves and showy pale blue flowers, Blue Lace Flower grows about 2 feet tall. Native of Australia.

Verbesina encelioides* (BUTTER DAISY, GOLDEN CROWNBEARD)—Grows 2 to 3 feet tall, producing gray-green leaves and large, deep yellow flowers. Grown by Jefferson at Monticello.

*U.S. native.

SOURCES FOR UNUSUAL SEEDS

J. L. Hudson, Seedsman
PO Box 1058
Redwood City, CA 94064

Thomas Jefferson Center for
Historic Plants, Monticello
PO Box 316
Charlottesville, VA 22902

SOURCES FOR FLOWER SEEDS

W. Atlee Burpee and Co.
Warminster, PA 18974

Gurney Seed and Nursery Co.
Yankton, SD 57079

J. Harris Company
Moreton Farm
Rochester, NY 14624

J. W. Jung Seed Company
Randolph, WI 53956

Nichols Garden Nursery,
1190 N. Pacific Highway
Albany, OR 97321

Park Seed Company
Cokesbury Rd.
Greenwood, SC 29647

Pinetree Garden Seeds
New Gloucester, ME 04260

Clyde Robin Seed Company
PO Box 2366
Castro Valley, CA 94546

R. H. Shumway Seedsman, Inc.
628 Cedar St.
Rockford, IL 61101

Stokes Seeds, Inc.
737 Main St.
Buffalo, NY 14240

Thompson and Morgan, Inc.
PO Box 1308
Jackson, NJ 08527-0308

Otis Twilley Seed Co. Inc.
PO Box 65
Trevose, PA 19047

PERENNIALS

Perennials for Beautiful Foliage

Most gardeners select perennials for their beautiful flowers. It makes more sense (especially in small gardens) to consider carefully the appearance of a plant's leaves. Even perennials with long flowering periods are without blossoms for much of the growing season, and a number of the most floriferous ones are undistinguished in form and leaf. When planning a garden, choose at least some plants for good foliage first and experiment with interesting foliage combinations. Here are ten perennials that would be attractive without flowers, though they all happen to have appealing bloom:

Alchemilla vulgaris (LADY'S MANTLE)—Partial shade; rounded and creased gray-green leaves, which appear very early in spring, catch dew and waterdrops. Dainty clusters of chartreuse flowers are produced in late spring.

Astilbe spp. (ASTILBE, FALSE SPIREA)—Partial shade; sun is tolerated if shallow roots receive adequate moisture. Reddish young shoots expand into neat, dark green, compound leaves that contrast well with the bolder foliage of Bergenia or Hosta. Plumes of tiny flowers (pink, red, purple, white) appear in summer.

Baptisia australis (FALSE INDIGO)—Drought-resistant and pest-resistant native American with compound, blue-green foliage and blue flowers in spring. Three to 4 feet tall, False Indigo also produces silvery seed pods for dried arrangements. Sun or light shade. Drawback: frost blackens foliage.

Bergenia cordifolia (BERGENIA)—Very hardy, with large evergreen leaves with a reddish blush; foliage turns purple-bronze in winter. Rose or purplish flowers in spring. Grows in sun or shade; prefers partial shade and moist, well-drained, limy soil. 'Bressingham White' is a white-flowered cultivar; B. stracheyi is a compact species suitable for rock gardens.

Dicentra eximia (FRINGED BLEEDING HEART) and D. formosa (Western Bleeding Heart)—These two U.S. natives have delicate, fernlike blue-green foliage that does not die down in summer like some species of Dicentra do. Both long-flowering plants produce pink flowers; there are also white varieties.* D. formosa's foliage is somewhat larger and it requires some shade; D. eximia is more tolerant of sun. There are a number of cultivars and named varieties.

Epimedium spp. (BARRENWORT)—Partial shade; likes organic matter and some moisture in the soil but will stand some drought when established. Compound, dainty and nearly evergreen leaves are heart-shaped and mottled; often rose-tinted in spring and reddish hued in the fall. Yellow, red or white flowers in early spring; usually not troubled by pests including deer.**

Heuchera sanguinea (CORAL BELLS)—A free-flowering plant for the front of a sunny border, this native of the American

---

*Garden writers have called the white-flowered form of Dicentra formosa "a fairy in the night garden," because the glistening blooms shine so brightly. See R. Cumming and R. Lee, *Contemporary Perennials,* (New York: Macmillan, 1960) 145.

**Alchemilla, Astilbe, Bergenia and Peony are also deer-resistant.

Southwest has many cultivars; flower colors are red, pink and white. Heart-shaped leaves, often two or more inches broad, have various patterns on dark green backgrounds in summer and turn reddish bronze in autumn.

Hosta spp. (HOSTA)—This shade lover with its bold (or diminutive) foliage is an obvious choice in spite of its appeal for deer. Elegant, large, ribbed leaves come in various shapes and shades of green (some are variegated); other small-leaved Hostas are suitable for rock gardens. H. plantaginea has large, shiny, pale green leaves and fragrant white flowers in late summer-fall. Hostas (and Epimediums, too) tolerate root competition from large trees well.

Paeonia spp. (PEONY)—Common garden Peonies with their deep green lobed foliage and large fragrant flowers are mostly offspring of Asian P. lactiflora. The new maroon shoots of many varieties are handsome among blooming spring bulbs and fall color may be red or gold. Plant in a sunny spot.

Pulmonaria saccharata (LUNGWORT)—New leaves and lavender-blue (pink in bud) flowers appear in early spring, blooming along with cobalt blue Siberian Squill. Long, dark green, persistent leaves are silver-spotted and remain attractive (especially in shaded sites where Pulmonaria is happiest) all season. Flower color and spotting is variable; P. angustifolia's leaves are all green.

Long-Blooming Perennials

Gardeners appreciate annuals because of their nonstop bloom all summer. Most perennials, in contrast, bloom for several weeks at the most. (Some, like Oriental Poppy, are in flower for only a few days.) The following perennials bloom for 6 weeks or more:

Anchusa azurea (ITALIAN BUGLOSS)
Chrysogonum virginianum (GREEN AND GOLD, GOLDENSTAR)*
Corydalis lutea (CORYDALIS)
Coreopsis spp. (TICKSEED)*

*U.S. native.

Myosotis scorpioides (Forget-Me-Not). Both this perennial species and the biennial M. sylvatica like partly shady, moist conditions. M. scorpioides var. semperflorens is noted for its long season of bloom.

Dicentra eximia (FRINGED BLEEDING HEART) and D. formosa
    (Western Bleeding Heart)*
Gaillardia aristata (BLANKETFLOWER)*
Geranium sanguineum (CRANESBILL)
Gypsophila repens (TRAILING BABY'S BREATH)
Hemerocallis (DAYLILY)—The cultivar Stella de Oro is noted
    for its very long period of bloom.
Heuchera sanguinea (CORALBELLS)*
Lamium maculatum (DEAD NETTLE)
Linum perenne (COMMON BLUE FLAX)
Myosotis scorpioides semperflorens (FORGET-ME-NOT)
Nepeta x faassenii (CATMINT)
Viola cornuta (TUFTED PANSY)

*U.S. native.

Tall Perennials

The following perennials are suitable for planting at the back of flower borders, or in the center of flower beds that are to be viewed from all sides. They all grow 4 feet or more; flowering times and flower color are noted.

Aconitum napellus (MONKSHOOD)—Summer; blue to violet

Aruncus dioicus (GOATSBEARD)—Late spring-early summer; white; dioecious; the pistillate (female) plants are more attractive

Cimicifuga spp. (BUGBANE)—Summer; white

Delphinium spp. (DELPHINIUM)—Early summer (sometimes a second flowering in fall); blue, purple, white, pink; short-lived perennial

Digitalis purpurea (FOXGLOVE)—Early summer; purple, pink, white, yellow, apricot; biennial or short-lived perennial

Echinops exaltatus (GLOBE THISTLE)—Summer; blue

Echinops sphaerocephalus (Globe Thistle). Bold accent plant with thistlelike leaves and metallic blue flowers that dry well when cut early.

Helenium autumnale (SNEEZEWEED)—Late summer; yellow or orange

Liatris spicata (BLAZING STAR)—Summer; mauve; there are also lower-growing species and cultivars

Lilium spp. and hybrid (LILY)—Spring-fall (depending on variety); white, gold, orange, pink

Sanguisorba spp. (BURNET)—Fall; white (S. obtusa has pink flowers)

Thalictrum rochebrunianum (MEADOW RUE)—Mid to late summer; lavender. T. speciosissimum (Dusty Meadow Rue) has gray-green leaves and produces lightly fragrant yellow flowers in early summer

Thermopsis caroliniana (CAROLINA LUPINE)—Early summer; yellow

Veronicastrum virginicum (CULVER'S ROOT)—Late summer; white

Tall-growing annuals and biennials include Alcea (Hollyhock), Cleome (Spider Plant), Cosmos, some Dahlias and Sunflower.

Uncommon Perennials

Frederick McGourty grows perennials—the usual and the unusual—at Hillside Gardens in Norfolk, Connecticut, and writes extensively on the subject. His latest book, *The Perennial Gardener,* appeared in 1989. Below are his favorite uncommonly grown perennials:

Alchemilla conjuncta (DWARF LADY'S MANTLE)
Allium cernuum (NODDING ONION OR LADY'S LEEK)*
Artemisia lactiflora (WHITE MUGWORT)
Astilbe 'Sprite' (ASTILBE)—Clear pink flowers
Aster 'Alma Potschke'—Mildew-resistant, 3½ feet, pink-red
Campanula ** **glomerata 'Crown of Snow'** (CLUSTERED BELLFLOWER)
Dicentra eximia 'Alba' (FRINGED OR WILD BLEEDING HEART)
Filipendula palmata 'Nana' (DWARF MEADOWSWEET)

*An American native with white or rosy-lilac flowers in summer, Lady's Leek was described by Capt. Meriwether Lewis of the Lewis and Clark Expedition (see p. 413).
**A neglected genus in many gardens. There are about 300 species of Campanula; many are fine border and rock garden subjects.

Phlox maculata 'Omega'—Mildew-resistant, 3½ feet, white
  flowers with pink centers

Sanguisorba canadensis (CANADIAN BURNET)—White flower
  spikes; compound leaves; once used as a woundwort;
  "Sanguisorba" means "to stop bleeding"

Perennials for the Blue Garden

English herbaceous borders have enchanted the gardening world for
seventy years; for almost as long some gardeners have sought to create
the one (or two) color garden. White has probably been the most popular
garden theme; surely gardens that feature blue flowers must be second.
Green or brown are the rarest flower colors found in nature; the next least
common is blue. Cobalt blue found in Siberian Squill and the sky blue
found in Forget-Me-Not and some Delphiniums are rarer still; most
flowers called blue are really lavender or purple. Here are thirty perennials for the Blue Garden:

Aconitum spp. (MONKSHOOD)—Fall

Adenophora spp. (LADYBELLS)—Summer

Ajuga spp. (BUGLEWEED)—Spring

Allium caeruleum—Spring

Amsonia spp. (BLUESTAR)*—Steel-blue, spring

Anchusa spp. (BUGLOSS)—True blue, spring-summer

Baptisia australis (WILD INDIGO)*—Spring

Brunnera macrophylla (SIBERIAN BUGLOSS)—True blue, spring

Campanula persicifolia (PEACH-LEAVED BELLFLOWER)—Summer;
  there are many other blue-flowered species

Catananche caerulea (CUPID'S DART)—Summer

Centaurea montana (MOUNTAIN BLUET)—Cornflower blue,
  spring; the annual Bachelor's Button or Cornflower is C.
  cyanus

Ceratostigma plumbaginoides (LEADWORT)—Cobalt-blue,
  summer-fall

Echinops spp. (GLOBE THISTLE)—Silvery steel-blue, summer

Eupatorium coelestinum (MIST FLOWER, HARDY
  AGERATUM)*—Summer-fall

*U.S. native.

Geranium himalayense (GERANIUM)—Summer
Limonium latifolium (SEA-LAVENDER)—Summer
Linum perenne (BLUE FLAX)—Sky blue, summer
Lobelia siphilitica (GREAT BLUE LOBELIA)*—Deep blue, summer
Mertensia virginica (BLUEBELLS)*—True blue, spring
Penstemon spp. (BEARDTONGUE)*—Among the blue-flowered
    species are P. strictus and P. unilateralis
Perovskia atriplicifolia (RUSSIAN SAGE)—Summer
Phlox divaricata (BLUE PHLOX)*—Spring
Platycodon grandiflorus 'Mariesii' (BALLOON
    FLOWER)—Summer
Polemonium caeruleum (JACOB'S LADDER)*—Spring-summer
Pulmonaria spp. (LUNGWORT)—Some varieties very blue,
    spring
Salvia spp. (SAGE)—There are many beautiful blue-flowered
    species and cultivars; S. azurea* is one
Scabiosa spp. (PINCUSHION FLOWER)—Colors range from barely
    blue to deep lavender, summer
Stokesia laevis (STOKES ASTER, AMERICAN
    CORNFLOWER)*—Bright, metallic blue, late summer
Tradescantia x andersoniana (SPIDERWORT)*—Several cultivars
    have medium or sky-blue flowers, summer
Veronica spp. (SPEEDWELL)—Some cultivars have gentian-blue
    flowers, summer

*U.S. native.

Many other perennials have blue or purple/lavender flowers: Lupine, Clematis, Columbine, Primrose, Pansy and Violet come quickly to mind, and who can forget the beautiful but not always easily tamed Gentian? Many herbs, too, in addition to Sage have blue flowers: Rosemary, Lavender and Catmint (Nepeta x faassenii) are three; Borage may have purple flowers or the sky blue flowers of its relative, Forget-Me-Not. Some annuals and woody plants with blue flowers:

Annuals: Ageratum, Borago (Borage), Browallia, Heliotropium, Ipomoea (Morning Glory), Nemophila (Baby Blue Eyes), Nigella (Love-in-a-Mist), Salvia farinacea, Torenia (Wishbone Flower), Trachymene (Blue Lace Flower), Verbena (Garden Verbena)

Woody Plants: Buddleia, Caryopteris (Bluebeard), Ceanothus spp., Hibiscus syriacus (Rose of Sharon), Hydrangea macrophylla, Lithodora diffusa, Plumbago, Syringa, Wisteria

Color analysts tell us that the color blue inspires devotion, love and loyalty (as in the expression "true blue"). Blue is quiet, cool, restful, mysterious. Landscapers remind us that yellows and pinks are busy stand-outs in the garden; blue recedes and provides depth to a planting. The great English gardener, Gertrude Jekyll advised including yellow flowers in a blue border; the two colors are complements and green, the color of most foliage, lies between them on the color wheel. Other gardeners enjoy combining blue and white.

Blue Gardens to Visit

Georgia
(Augusta): Pendleton King Park and Sunken Blue Garden

New Jersey
(Swainton): Leaming's Run Botanical Gardens

New York
(Canandaigua): Sonnenberg Gardens (blue and white garden)

Rhode Island
(Bristol): Blithewold Gardens and Arboretum (blue and yellow garden)

Some universities with blue and white colors have a garden with a blue and white theme; the President's Garden at the University of Connecticut is such a garden.

"Work-Free" Perennials for the New York City Area

Robert S. Hebb composed the following list when he was associated with New York's Cary Arboretum, and it originally appeared in the *New York Times*. He now directs one of the nation's newest botanical gardens, the Lewis Ginter Botanical Garden in Richmond, Virginia, (visitors are welcome) and is working on what will be one of the largest displays of perennials in America.

Aconitum carmichaelii (MONKSHOOD)
Cimicifuga racemosa (BUGBANE, SNAKEROOT)

Filipendula rubra 'Venusta' (QUEEN OF THE PRAIRIE)
Hemerocallis (DAYLILY)
Hibiscus moscheutos (HARDY HIBISCUS)
Hosta (PLANTAIN LILY)
Iris sibirica (SIBERIAN IRIS)
Paeonia (PEONY)
Papaver orientale (ORIENTAL POPPY)
Platycodon grandiflorus 'Mariesii' (MARIE'S OR DWARF
     BALLOON FLOWER)
Rudbeckia fulgida 'Goldsturm' (RUDBECKIA)
Sedum 'Autumn Joy'

Outstanding Perennials for the South

Allan M. Armitage and Raymond Kessler of the University of
Georgia in Athens continue to evaluate a number of perennials for use
in Southern gardens. Plants that thrive in this area must withstand
drought, high temperatures and high humidity. In their publication *1988
Sixth Annual Report on the Performance of Perennial Plants in the Horticulture Gardens* plants were rated on a scale of 1 to 5, with 5 standing for
excellence.

A DOZEN TOP PERFORMERS:

Aster x frikartii (MICHAELMAS DAISY)—Light blue flowers,
     yellow centers, long flowering period. The cultivar
     'Monch' out-performed the species; best summer flowering
     aster.
Astilbe taquetii (FALSE GOAT'S BEARD)—Pink-purple flowers
     bloom four weeks. Cultivar tested was 'Superba.'
Ceratostigma plumbaginoides (LEADWORT)—Bright blue
     flowers for 18 weeks during hot, dry time of year.
     Longevity is 4 to 5 years.
Coreopsis grandiflora (TICKSEED)—23 weeks of bright yellow
     flowers; outstanding perennial for the South. Cultivar
     tested was 'Early Yellow.'
Dictamnus albus (GAS PLANT)—Fragrant white flowers for one
     month; strong, long-lived, pest-free.
Gaillardia aristata (BLANKET FLOWER)—22 weeks of
     yellow/dark orange bloom. Cultivar 'Goblin' is more
     compact and performs better than the species.

Geranium sanguineum (CRANESBILL)—This Cranesbill is the most durable and dependable geranium for southern climates. Fine foliage; lilac flowers produced for nine weeks. G. sanguineum 'Album' is somewhat smaller (white flowers) but also top rated.

Hemerocallis Stella de Oro (DAYLILY)—Yellow flowers for six weeks; low maintenance.

Heuchera sanguinea 'White Cloud' (CORALBELLS)—Excellent cultivar that produces eight weeks of abundant white flowers. Dense mounds of rounded, bright green leaves.

Iberis sempervirens (CANDYTUFT)—White flowers for 11 weeks. Excellent heat and drought tolerance, low maintenance; outstanding for southern gardens.

Limonium altaica (STATICE)—Pale blue flowers; this evergreen statice flowers for 12 weeks.

Phlox x chattahoochee (CHATTAHOOCHEE PHLOX)—This pale blue-flowered Phlox, which blooms for seven weeks, has lustrous dark green leaves. One of the best plants in the garden. P. divaricata 'Fuller's White' (Woodland Phlox) was also given a top score.

SOME POOR RISKS FOR SOUTHERN GARDENS INCLUDE:

Bergenia cordifolia (BERGENIA)
Convallaria majalis (LILY-OF-THE-VALLEY)
Dianthus alpinus (ALPINE PINK)*
Papaver orientale (ORIENTAL POPPY)

*Cheddar Pink (D. gratianopolitanus) was rated highly.

Perennials for the Shade

There are many degrees of shade. Some garden areas receive sunshine for only an hour or two each day; others, such as those situated under an open tree, will get intermittent sun throughout the day. Still other sites receive no direct sun at all—light here can also vary from semidarkness to very bright. A number of perennials thrive in shady spots; in fact, to be at their best, many require it. Listed below are twenty perennials that do well in partial shade or bright light with little direct sun:

Aconitum spp. (MONKSHOOD, WOLFSBANE)
Alchemilla spp. (LADY'S MANTLE)

Aruncus spp. (GOATSBEARD)—Likes moist soil.

Asarum (WILD GINGER)—Half to deep shade.

Astilbe (ASTILBE)—Moist (but not wet) soil is necessary.

Aquilegia spp. (COLUMBINE)—Full sun tolerated, light shade preferred.

Bergenia cordifolia (BERGENIA)—Prefers moist soil.

Brunnera macrophylla (SIBERIAN BUGLOSS)—Will survive nearly anywhere but best in moist soil/partial shade.

Cimicifuga spp. (BUGBANE, SNAKEROOT)—Soil should be rich and moist; tolerates fairly heavy shade.

Convallaria majalis (LILY-OF-THE-VALLEY)

Corydalis lutea (CORYDALIS)

Dicentra spp. (BLEEDING HEART)

Epimedium (BARRENWORT)—Adapts to fairly heavy shade.

Helleborus spp. (HELLEBORE, CHRISTMAS/LENTEN ROSE)

Hosta spp. (HOSTA)—Some cultivars tolerate fairly heavy shade but may not flower.

Macleaya spp. (PLUME POPPY)

Mertensia spp. (BLUEBELLS)—Leaves die down after flowering.

Primula spp. (PRIMROSE)—Needs moist organic soil.

Tiarella cordifolia (FOAMFLOWER)—There are several garden cultivars of this U.S. native. Foliage turns attractive colors in the fall.

Tradescantia virginiana (SPIDERWORT)—Thrives in sun or shade.

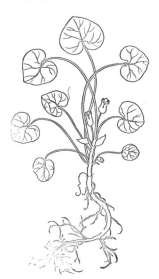

Asarum sp. (Wild Ginger). Low-growing Wild Gingers are native throughout the North Temperate zone and are excellent for half- to deeply shaded gardens. Soil should be moist.

Epimedium sp. (Barrenwort). A choice perennial for partial shade, Epimedium has few pests and deer avoid it.

Ground covers such as Ajuga, Lamium, Vinca and Pachysandra also perform well in shade, as do many wildflowers (in addition to the ones listed above) and Ferns. See "Wildflowers for Woodland Gardens," pages 365–367, and "Annuals for the Shade," pages 38–39.

Perennials for Damp Ground

Some plants, such as Purple Loosestrife, Forget-Me-Not, Yellow Flag and Japanese Iris will thrive in soggy conditions; others, like Astilbe, need better drainage. Several will also perform well in ordinary garden soil.

Astilbe spp. (ASTILBE)—Partial shade
Bergenia cordifolia (BERGENIA)—Partial shade
Iris kaempferi (JAPANESE IRIS)—Sun or light shade
Iris sibirica (SIBERIAN IRIS)—Sun*
Lysimachia clethroides (GOOSENECK LOOSESTRIFE)—Sun or
    partial shade
Lythrum salicaria (PURPLE LOOSESTRIFE)—Sun or partial shade;
    plant a sterile cultivar
Myosotis scorpioides (FORGET-ME-NOT)—Partial shade
Primula spp. (PRIMROSE, COWSLIP)—Partial shade
Thalictrum spp. (MEADOW RUE)—Sun or light shade
Trollius spp. (GLOBEFLOWER)—Sun or partial shade

*I. pseudacorus (European Yellow Flag) is another Iris for moist ground.

Native Plants for Moist Sites

Palustris means "marsh loving." Tolerance for standing water varies; Wild Calla and Marsh Marigold grow in open, wet sites in ponds and streams, while plants such as Cardinal Flower and Wild Iris prefer the water's edge. Many (Monarda, Liatris, Lobelia, Sanguisorba) also do well in borders.

Arisaema triphyllum (JACK-IN-THE-PULPIT)—Partial shade
Aster novae-angliae (NEW ENGLAND ASTER)—Sun
Calla palustris (WILD CALLA)—Full sun or light shade
Caltha palustris (MARSH MARIGOLD)—Sun or partial shade
Chelone spp. (TURTLEHEAD)—Partial shade
Cimicifuga racemosa (BUGBANE)—Partial shade
Clintonia borealis (BEAD-LILY)—Shade
Erythronium americanum (TROUT LILY)—Partial shade
Eupatorium spp. (JOE-PYE WEED, BONESET)—Sun
Gentiana spp. (BOTTLE GENTIAN, FRINGED GENTIAN)—Sun
Helenium autumnale (SNEEZEWEED)—Sun
Hibiscus moscheutos (ROSE MALLOW)—Sun or light shade
Iris versicolor (WILD IRIS, BLUE FLAG)—Sun or partial shade
Liatris spicata (BLAZING STAR, GAYFEATHER)—Sun
Lobelia spp. (CARDINAL FLOWER, GREAT BLUE LOBELIA)—Partial
   shade
Monarda didyma (BEE BALM, OSWEGO TEA)—Partial shade
Sanguisorba canadensis (CANADIAN BURNET)—Sun or partial
   shade
Sisyrinchium angustifolium (BLUE-EYED GRASS)—Sun
Symplocarpus foetidus (SKUNK CABBAGE)—Light shade
Vernonia spp. (IRONWEED)—Sun

Aquatic and Bog Plants

Advice from *American Agriculturist*, May, 1883:

A moist or springy place in one's grounds, instead of being regarded as a misfortune, a trouble to be remedied by draining, may often be turned to good account. There are many pleasing and showy plants that will grow in such places, and will flourish nowhere else. If by excavation a permanent pool or lakelet can be secured, then a large number of beautiful aquatics may be grown such as a collection of the various water lilies

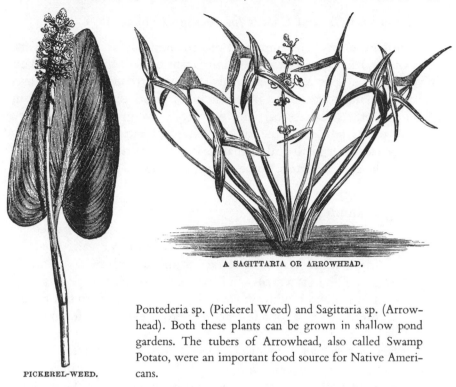

A SAGITTARIA OR ARROWHEAD.

PICKEREL-WEED.

Pontederia sp. (Pickerel Weed) and Sagittaria sp. (Arrow-head). Both these plants can be grown in shallow pond gardens. The tubers of Arrowhead, also called Swamp Potato, were an important food source for Native Americans.

and others, while moisture-loving plants can occupy the margin. The various species of Sarracenia (Pitcher Plant), with the California Darlingtonia (Cobra Plant) would make an attractive group in such a locality. The Golden Club (Orontium), the Arrowheads (Sagittaria), the Swamp Loosestrife (Decodon), the Pickerel-weed (Pontederia), the Lizard's-tail (Saururus), and many other inhabitants of our marshes, would form an interesting and showy collection. Such plants would be quite new to most persons, as few, save botanists and anglers, ever see them in their native haunts. Of the Arrowheads, a curious collection of forms could be made, as few plants present such a variety of shapes in their leaves. Those who have never seen a clump of our native Lizard's-tail, would be surprised at the graceful beauty of its flower clusters* and there are few more charming shades of blue than that presented by our Pickerel-weed.

*White and fragrant and also called Swamp Lily or Water Dragon.

Perennial Ground Covers for Sun and Shade

Shrubby plants* are employed most commonly as ground covers; many of them are evergreen and are important parts of the garden design throughout the year. Some perennials can also provide interesting and effective ground cover. This group includes plants that "disappear" in winter and others that are partially or wholly evergreen. The majority of these plants produce some type of seasonal interest and most are especially useful in small-scale situations or where bold effects are not needed in the colder months. Some perennials to use as ground covers are:

Aegopodium podagraria (GOUTWEED, BISHOP'S WEED)—Sun or partial shade; may become a nuisance as common names suggest. Gardeners are most familiar with the variegated form, which can be effective in difficult spots.

Ajuga spp. (BUGLEWEED)—Sun or shade; tolerant of poor soils. Blue, pink or white flowers in spring; some varieties have bronze foliage; others tend to remain evergreen for much of the winter.

Asarum spp. (WILD GINGER)—Deep shade; some species evergreen. Several species are U.S. natives. A. europaeum, with leathery, evergreen leaves, is the landscape star of the genus although slow to become established.

Ceratostigma plumbaginoides (LEADWORT)—Sun; bronze-green leaves turn even redder in fall; cobalt-blue flowers in late summer and early fall. New leaves are slow to appear in spring.

Chamaemelum nobile (CHAMOMILE)—Sun; will tolerate a little shade. Aromatic, fernlike leaves; small, white daisylike flowers in summer. Will carpet sandy, well-drained soils and tolerate heat and drought.

Convallaria majalis (LILY-OF-THE-VALLEY)—Shade or sun; will, like Ajuga, prosper under trees. Fragrant white flowers are a plus in spring. Foliage does not appear as early as Sweet Woodruff in spring.

Coronilla varia (CROWN VETCH)—Sun; pink- and white-

---

*Pachysandra and Vinca are listed as subshrubs by some; Ivy is a woody vine. See "Shrubby Gound Covers for Sun and Shade," pages 260–261. Hosta also makes a bold and elegant ground cover in partial shade where evergreen foliage is not required. Leaves come in many sizes, shapes and colors; lavender or white flowers (some are fragrant) are produced in summer or fall.

flowered member of the legume family, useful for erosion control on steep banks and hillsides.

Epimedium spp. (BARRENWORT)—Shade; tolerant of dry conditions once established. Red, yellow or white flowers in spring. Outstanding, semievergreen leaves are tinged with rose in spring and sometimes turn crimson in fall. Spreads slowly but worth the wait.

Gallium odoratum (SWEET WOODRUFF)—Moist soil and light shade preferred; will also do well in sunnier sites. Fresh green starlike leaves appear very early in spring; white flowers are a bonus.

Lamiastrum galeobdolon (YELLOW ARCHANGEL)—Shade; green or variegated leaves and bright yellow flowers in spring; similar to Lamium.

Lamium maculatum (DEAD NETTLE)—Shade; several attractive variegated cultivars perform well even in dry shade. 'Beacon Silver' has pink flowers and the slightly more vigorous 'White Nancy' has white flowers.

Liriope spp. (LILYTURF)—Sun or shade; these Asian natives form a grasslike ground cover with the added attraction of white or lilac summer flowers. Hardy north to parts of zone 6.

Lysimachia nummularia (MONEYWORT, CREEPING JENNY)—Shade-loving, sun-tolerant, bright yellow summer flowers; inclined to be invasive and weedy.

Sedum spp. (SEDUM)—Sun loving plants with attractive succulent leaves; some like the evergreen Golden Carpet (S. acre) make good ground covers in sunny, dry spots. The cultivar 'Minus' is smaller and less invasive.

Dale Chapman's Ground-Cover Favorites

Dale Chapman, a chemical engineer by training, has been raising ground covers in southern Connecticut for many years.* Some of his favorites are listed on the following pages.

*Dale Chapman, Quality Groundcover Plants, RR 1, Box 15, Hampton, CT 06247-9702, (203) 455-9706. 'Green Sheen' won an Award of Horticultural Merit at the 1990 New England Flower Show.

Ajuga reptans 'Burgundy Glo'—A variegated variety with burgundy/white foliage and blue flowers. A bit more fragile and not as hardy as some Ajugas; best in sunny locations. Very showy.

Ajuga reptans 'Gaiety'—Dark purple leaves, blue flowers. Likes more sun than the average Ajuga.

Asarum europaeum (EUROPEAN WILD GINGER)—Deep, shiny green leaves; for shade only. Soil must not get too dry.

Euonymus fortuni 'Colorata' (WINTERCREEPER)—Very hardy; green foliage turns purple in the fall. Stands up to salt well and may be planted near roads.

Euonymus fortuni 'Silver Queen' (WINTERCREEPER)— Prostrate form; 3.8 inch leaf; the nicest of the silver-edged plants.

Hedera helix 'Baltica' (ENGLISH IVY)—This is a very hardy form of English Ivy with light-veined evergreen leaves.

Pachysandra terminalis 'Green Sheen' (SHINY-LEAVED JAPANESE SPURGE)—Low-growing, dark green and glossy new cultivar. Introduced by Mr. Chapman.

Pachysandra terminalis 'Silver Edge'—A variegated Japanese Spurge; brightens a shady spot.

Vinca minor 'Blue Bowles' (PERIWINKLE, MYRTLE)— Free-flowering. Euonymus fortuni 'Colorata' and Vinca minor are the hardiest ground covers for southern New England. There are also red-flowered, white-flowered, double-flowered and silver-edged Periwinkles.

American Native: Iris

All regions of America are blessed with beautiful native Irises and many prefer them to the more gardenesque bearded moderns commonly grown. The Dwarf Iris (I. verna), with lightly fragrant blue flowers, is native from Pennsylvania south; Dwarf Crested Iris (I. cristata) is also found from the Mid-Atlantic states south and west to Missouri. Of the two, the latter is more tolerant of soils and growing conditions and is quite hardy in New England. Taller Iris versicolor or Blue Flag (also with rose flowers, or rarely white) is native to the North and North Central states, ranging south into Pennsylvania. Several species of southern Irises have hybridized naturally; this group, known as Louisiana Irises, has been further hybridized by horticulturalists and today has a special society of devotees: Society for Louisiana Irises. According to the Society, Louisiana

Irises are hardy in parts of the North, and several cultivars (Ann Chowning, Clara Goula, Easter Tide) are eligible for the Dykes Medal.* Another group of native hybrids, the Pacific Coast Irises, adorn the hills above the Pacific in California and Oregon. Like other American natives, they were largely ignored at home until British growers fell in love with them, created new varieties (a Pacific Iris variety called No Name won England's top Iris award in 1967) and finally attracted the attention of American gardeners. Although "at home" in the Northwest, Pacific Irises can be successful in other parts of the country, including the Northeast. (They are least successful in the South.) With all the beautiful natives available, surely there is an American Iris for your garden?

AWARD-WINNING IRISES

The genus Iris is large (about 200 species) and widespread. The tall, bearded Iris of our gardens, which originated in Eurasia, has many hundreds of named varieties and color range has increased dramatically since the 1920s. With beautiful colors and ease of cultivation, it is not surprising that Iris has many devotees. The most coveted of varietal awards is the Dykes Medal, established by the British Iris Society to honor William R. Dykes, an author *(The Genus Iris)* and leading hybridizer. Listed below are the Dykes Medal Award Winners (there are also special awards for Siberian, Japanese, Louisiana and Pacific Irises). No awards were given in years missing from list.

1927 San Francisco*	1942 Great Lakes
1929 Dauntless	1943 Prairie Sunset
1932 Rameses	1944 Spun Gold
1933 Coralie	1945 Elmohr
1935 Sierra Blue	1947 Chivalry
1936 Mary Geddes	1948 Ola Kola
1937 Missouri	1949 Helen McGregor
1938 Copper Lustre	1950 Blue Rhythm
1939 Rosy Wings	1951 Cherie
1940 Wabash	1952 Argus Pheasant
1941 The Red Douglas	1953 Truly Yours

*Some of the early winners, like this blue and white Iris, were none too hardy.

*Eligible for the Mary Swords DeBaillon Medal for Louisiana Iris are Acadian Miss, Black Gamecock, C'est Magnifique, Count Pulaski, Delta Dawn, Full Eclipse, Mary's Charlie, Monument, President Hedley and Rhett.

1954 Mary Randall	1972 Babbling Brook
1955 Sable Night	1973 New Moon
1956 First Violet	1974 Shipshape
1957 Violet Harmony	1975 Pink Taffeta
1958 Blue Sapphire	1976 Kilt Lilt
1959 Swan Ballet	1977 Dream Lover
1961 Eleanor's Pride	1978 Bride's Halo
1962 Whole Cloth	1979 Mary Frances
1963 Amethyst Flame	1980 Mystique
1964 Allegiance	1981 Brown Lasso**
1965 Pacific Panorama	1982 Vanity
1966 Rippling Waters	1983 Ruffled Ballet
1967 Winter Olympics	1984 Victoria Falls
1968 Stepping Out	1985 Beverly Sills
1970 Skywatch	1986 Song of Norway
1971 Debby Rairdon	1988 Titan's Glory

**One of the shorter or "border bearded" Irises, which also has smaller flowers.

American Iris Society members voted for their favorite Irises at the 1988 symposium. The top ten winners were:

1. **Beverly Sills** (M)—36 inches tall; flower color pink
2. **Victoria Falls** (E-L)—40 inches; blue with white spots
3. **Stepping Out** (M-L)—38 inches; white, blue-violet plicata
4. **Vanity** (E-L)—36 inches; pink
5. **Song of Norway** (M-L)—38 inches; light blue, blue beards
6. **Mary Frances** (M)—38 inches; blue-orchid
7. **Laced Cotton** (M-L)—34 inches; white
8. **Going My Way** (M)—37 inches; white, blue-violet plicata
9. **Mystique** (E-L)—36 inches; light blue/blue-purple
10. **Copper Classic** (L)—30 inches; burnt orange

E—Early   M—Midseason   L—Late

1987 AIS AWARD OF MERIT FOR SIBERIAN IRIS

Siberian Irises also have awards and winners:

Dance Ballerina Dance	**Harbor Mist**
Omar's Cup	

Runners-up:

King of Kings   **Creme Chantilly**
Dancing Nanou   **Lavender Bounty**
Kismet

TIPS FOR IRIS GROWERS

Divide clumps of bearded Iris every 3 to 5 years for best bloom; remember they like good drainage and plenty of sun. Clean up and burn dead bearded-Iris leaves in the fall and spring to help control Iris borer. Plant plenty of yellows and light blues for best visual results; lavenders add sparkle. There are many shorter-growing bearded Irises to choose from, including early-blooming dwarfs. Beardless Japanese (I. kaempferi, which also has numerous named varieties) and Siberian (I. sibirica, extra hardy) Irises don't require frequent division; many beardless Irises also do well in moist spots.

American Iris Society
J. Stayer, Secretary
7414 E. 60th St.
Tulsa, Oklahoma 74145

IRIS SOCIETIES

Society for Louisiana Irises
Box 40175, USL
Lafayette, LA 70504

Society for Pacific Coast Native Iris
c/o Adele Lawyer
4333 Oak Hill Road
Oakland, CA 94605

Species Iris Group of North America
Florence Stout, Secretary
150 N. Main St.
Lombard, IL 60148

SOURCES FOR IRISES

Adamgrove
Rt. 1, Box 246
California, MO 65018
(Irises and Daylilies, catalog $1.00)

Aitken's Salmon Creek Garden
608 N.W. 119 St.
Vancouver, WA 98685 (Display garden open to visitors; catalog and map $1.00)

Bois d'Arc Gardens
PO Box 485
Houma, LA 70361
(504) 868-5422
(Specializing in Louisiana Iris)

Cal Dixie Iris Gardens
14115 Pear St.
Riverside, CA 92504
(Please enclose two first-class
stamps with catalog request)

Clean Shaven Iris
George C. Bush
1739 Memory Lane Extension
York, PA 17402
(717) 755-0557
(Featuring Japanese, Siberian and
species Iris; send stamp for price
list)

Ensata Gardens
9823 E. Michigan Ave.
Galesburg, MI 49053
(Specialists in Japanese Iris; price
list and culture sheet on request)

Garden of the Enchanted
Rainbow
Jordan and Bernice Miller
Rt. 4, Box 439B
Killen, AL 35645
(Send stamp for price list)

Grandview Iris Gardens
HC 86
Box 91
Bayard, NE 69334
(Send stamp for catalog)

Kirkland Iris Garden
725 20th Ave. West
Kirkland, WA 98033
(Median and Dwarf Irises;
catalog on request)

Newburn's Iris Gardens
1415 Meadow Dale Dr.
Lincoln, NE 68505
(Over 1,000 varieties of tall,
bearded Irises; many older
varieties)

Portable Acres
2087 Curtis Dr.
Penngrove, CA 94951
(Pacific Coast Irises; free list for
SASE)

Rancho de la Flor de Lis
PO Box 227
Cerrillos, NM 87010
(catalog $1.00; over 4,000
varieties grown)

Schreiner's Gardens
3661 Quinaby Road N.E.
Salem, OR 97303
($2.00, deductible from first
order, for full-color catalog)

Where to Visit the Irises

Colorado
(Boulder): Longs Iris Gardens
(Denver): Denver Botanic Gardens

Missouri
(St. Louis): Missouri Botanical Gardens

New Jersey
(Montclair): Presby Memorial Iris Garden (over 75,000 Irises)

New York
(Brooklyn): Brooklyn Botanic Garden

Tennessee
(Memphis): Memphis Botanic Garden

Texas
(Abilene): McMurry College Iris Garden

Many other botanical gardens will have an Iris display garden.

Peonies and Daylilies

GOLD MEDAL PEONIES

Peonies, like many Irises, are hardy plants that can last for generations. Named for Paeon, physician to the Greek gods, Peonies were long thought to have medicinal and magical properties. Peony seeds, in particular, were made into necklaces to protect children from witchcraft and the Devil. Western America is home to several native species and the European P. officinalis is an ancestor of some of our modern cultivars. It is the hardy Siberian/Chinese native P. lactiflora, however, that figures most prominently in the herbaceous Peonies we grow today. P. suffruticosa, the shrubby Tree Peony, is also an Asian native. The following Peonies have been awarded the American Peony Society's Gold Medal for excellence (a few of the earlier varieties are no longer available, but many Gold Medal winners are still in commerce):

1923 Mrs. A. M. Brand	1943 Elsa Sass
1933 A. B. Franklin	1946 Hansina Brand
1933 Mrs. J. V. Edlund	1946 Golden Glow
1934 Harry F. Little	1948 Mrs. Franklin D. Roosevelt
1941 Nick Shaylor	1949 Doris Cooper

1956 Red Charm	1981 Bowl of Cream
1956 Miss America	1982 Westerner
1957 Kansas	1983 Chinese Dragon (TREE
1959 Moonstone	PEONY)
1971 Miss America	1984 Dolorodell
1972 Nick Shaylor	1985 Burma Ruby
1973 Age of Gold	1986 Coral Charm
1974 Walter Mains	1987 Norma Volz
1975 Bu-te	1988 Paula Fay
1980 Cytherea	1989 High Noon (TREE PEONY)

In some years the Gold Medal was not awarded. It will be noted that both Miss America and Nick Shaylor were awarded the medal twice, which emphasizes their high quality.

SOME FRAGRANT PEONIES AVAILABLE TODAY

Peonies can be delightfully fragrant or have little or no scent. The following varieties are all fragrant. Numbers appearing after some names are ratings once given that variety by the American Peony Society (10 was the highest score; ratings have been discontinued for some time).

Ala Mode—White, single, early
Bu-te—White, midseason/late
Cheddar Gold—White (yellow center), midseason
Edulis Superba—Bright pink, tufted center, early
Festiva Maxima (9.3)—White with crimson marks, early, 1851
Florence Nicholls—White, double, midseason
Karl Rosenfeld (8.8)—Bright red, late midseason, 1908
Le Cygne (9.9)—White tinged ivory, midseason, 1907
Miss America—White, early
Mons. Jules Elie (9.2)—Rose-pink, double, early, 1888
Moonstone—Pink, midseason
Mrs. Franklin D. Roosevelt—Pink, double, midseason, 1933
Nancy Nicholls—Pink (fluted edges), double, late midseason
Philippe Rivoire (9.2)—Red, early midseason, 1911
Pink Lemonade—Pink/yellow/cream blend, midseason
Port Royale—Deep red, midseason
Sarah Bernhardt (9.0)—Soft pink, double, late, 1906
Vivid Rose—Deep pink, double, late

TIPS FOR GROWING PEONIES

Peonies like good drainage and plenty of sun. Plant Peonies in the fall. They respond to liberal fertilizing. The ants that are sometimes found on buds and flowers are not thought to be harmful. Some reasons Peonies may fail to bloom:

- Plants receive too much shade.
- Old plants need division. (Divide in fall.)
- New plants were too recently planted, planted too late in the season or divisions of old plants were made too late in fall.
- Plants were set too deep. (Growth "eyes" should be about 1½ inches below soil level.)
- Buds were hurt by a late freeze in the spring.
- Plants attacked by Botrytis or Phytophthora.

American Peony Society
Greta M. Kessenich, Secretary
250 Interlachen Road
Hopkins, MN 55343

AWARD-WINNING DAYLILIES

The orange Daylily, an immigrant from the East and a common roadside plant in many parts of the country, is a tough survivor. The same cannot be said about many of today's more refined and tender hybrids, but for summer flowers in many shades of apricot, pink and gold it is not too high a price to pay. Dr. Arlow B. Stout did much to develop the modern Daylily, and the Stout Medal, the highest varietal award a Daylily can receive, was named in his honor. (The American Hemerocallis Society gives out six other annual awards; among them are awards for fragrance, double-flowered Daylilies, miniatures and "All Americans" that are outstanding in all parts of the country.) Stout Medal winners include:

1950 **Hesperus**	1957 **Ruffled Pinafor**
1951 **Painted Lady**	1958 **High Noon**
1952 **Potentate**	1959 **Salmon Sheen**
1953 **Revolute**	1960 **Fairy Wings**
1954 **Dauntless**	1961 **Playboy**
1955 **Prima Donna**	1962 **Betsy Ross**
1956 **Naranja**	1963 **Multnomah**

1964 Frances Fay	1977 Green Glitter
1965 Luxury Lace	1978 Mary Todd
1966 Cartwheels	1979 Moment of Truth
1967 Full Reward	1980 Bertie Ferris
1968 Satin Glass	1981 Ed Murray
1969 May Hall	1982 Ruffled Apricot
1970 Ava Michelle	1983 Sabie
1971 Renee	1984 My Belle
1972 Hortensia	1985 Stella de Oro
1973 Lavender Flight	1986 Janet Gayle
1974 Winning Ways	1987 Becky Lynn
1975 Clarence Simon	1988 Martha Adams
1976 Green Flutter	1989 Brocaded Gown

1988 POPULARITY POLL

The top ten Daylilies in the 1988 nationwide popularity poll were (height can vary quite a bit in the various parts of the country):

1. Fairy Tale Pink—24 inches tall; pink

2. Brocaded Gown—26 inches; lemon cream, green throat

3. Barbara Mitchell—20 inches; flesh pink

4. Becky Lynn—20 inches; rose

5. Martha Adams—19 inches; pink

6. Betty Woods—26 inches; Chinese yellow

7. Joan Senior—25 inches; near white

8. Ruffled Apricot—28 inches; apricot

9. Stella de Oro—11 inches; gold

10. Golden Scroll—19 inches; tangerine

DAYLILY HARDINESS

Some Daylilies do best in a particular climate. In general, dormant Daylilies (which lose their leaves after frost) grow best in northern states and evergreen Daylilies are best in southern gardens; those with semievergreen foliage enjoy the widest range. The American Hemerocallis Society warns that there are more southern cultivars on the national popularity poll because the Society has more members in the South than the North. The regional popularity polls (the United States is divided into 15 regions by AHS) will be of more help in selecting Daylilies for your garden. Here are the top five (1987) from some of the regions:

Region 1 (IA, MN, NE, ND, SD): Brocaded Gown, Dance Ballerina Dance, Condilla, Fairy Tale Pink, Joan Senior

Region 3 (DE, MD, NJ, PA, VA, WV): Fairy Tale Pink, Joan Senior, Ruffled Apricot, Pardon Me, Stella de Oro

Region 4 (CT, ME, MA, NH, NY, RI, VT): Stella de Oro, Ruffled Apricot, Fairy Tale Pink, Joan Senior, Betty Woods

Region 6 (NM, TX): Ono, Seductress, Fairy Tale Pink, Becky Lynn, Jerome

Region 12 (FL): Betty Woods, Becky Lynn, Midnight Magic, Sebastian, Seductress

FRAGRANT DAYLILIES

Gardeners familiar with the species Lemon Lily (Hemerocallis lilioasphodelus or flava) know that Daylilies can be deliciously fragrant. The following cultivars have won the Ernest Plouf Consistently Very Fragrant Award (all are reputedly hardy in the North):

1979 **Willard Gardner**	1984 **Siloam Mama**
1980 **Tender Love**	1985 **Siloam Double Classic**
1981 **Frozen Jade**	1986 **Hudson Valley**
1982 **Siloam Double Rose**	1987 **Evening Bell**
1983 **Ida Miles**	1988 **Chorus Line**

Fragrance, however, can be subjective; what is fragrant to one person may not be to another. Plants also vary; not every individual of a fragrant species will be uniformly fragrant, and perfume can be affected by where a plant grows and the time of day. Andy Moore, an expert in Daylily fragrance, who gardens in Tennessee, lists his favorite cultivars below. Note that Ida Miles is the only EP Award Winner he considers very fragrant:

H. flava	**Hyperion**
H. citrina	**Star Dreams**
Ida Miles	**So Sweet**
Panned Gold	**Erlianna**
Oriental Princess	**Judge Orr**

American Hemerocallis Society
Elly Launius, Executive Secretary
1454 Rebel Dr.
Jackson, MS 39211

DAYLILY DISPLAY GARDENS

Listed below are a dozen American Hemerocallis Society board approved gardens in various parts of the country that are open to visitors:

Alpine Valley Gardens
2627 Calistoga Rd.
Santa Rosa, CA 95404
(707) 539-1749

American Horticultural Society
River Farm
7931 E. Blvd. Dr.
Alexandria, VA 22308
(703) 768-8882

Berkshire Garden Center
Rts. 83 & 102
Stockbridge, MA 01262
(413) 298-5530

Birmingham Botanical Gardens
2612 Lane Park Rd.
Birmingham, AL 35223
(205) 879-1227

Busse Gardens
Rt. 2, Box 238
Cokato, MN 55321
(612) 286-2654

Caprice Farm Nursery
15425 S.W. Pleasant Hill Rd.
Sherwood, OR 97140
(503) 625-7241

Coker Arboretum
Univ. of N. Carolina
Chapel Hill, NC 27514
(919) 962-3775

Denver Botanic Gardens
909 York St.
Denver, CO 80206

Jedi Daylily Garden
Rt. 1, Box 69
Flomaton, AL 36441
(205) 296-3189

Los Angeles Arboretum
Arcadia, CA 90011

Minnesota Landscape Arboretum
Chaska, MN 56007

U.S. National Arboretum
24th & R St. N.E.
Washington, DC 20002
(202) 475-4815

SOURCES FOR PEONIES AND DAYLILIES

American Daylily & Perennials
PO Box 7008
The Woodlands, TX 77387
(Color catalog $3.00, deductible with first order)

W. Atlee Burpee & Company
Warminster, PA 18974
(Small selection but some fine old Peony varieties)

Brand Peony Farm and Nursery
Box 842
St. Cloud, MN 56301

Busse Gardens
Rt. 2, Box 238
Cokato, MN 55321
(Small-flowered Daylilies and
others; catalog $2.00, deductible
from first order)

Caprice Farm Nursery
15425 S.W. Pleasant Hill Rd.
Sherwood, OR 97140
(Daylilies, Peonies, Japanese Iris
and Hosta; color catalog $1.00,
deductible from first order)

Cordon Bleu Farms
PO Box 2033
San Marcos, CA 92069
(Daylilies plus Spuria and
Louisiana Iris; color catalog
$1.00)

Gilbert H. Wild and Son, Inc.
Sarcoxie, MO 64862
(Peonies and Daylilies
exclusively; catalog $2.00)

Golden Glow Gardens
115 Sligo Rd.
Cumberland Center, ME 04021
(Daylilies, Peonies and others;
catalog $1.00)

Granville Hall
Rt. 6, Box 7365
Gloucester, VA 23061
(Peonies, including some old
favorites)

J. W. Jung Seed Co.
Randolph, WI 53957
(Several old Peonies)

Louisiana Nursery
Box 43
Opelousas, LA 70570
(Daylily catalog $2)

Springlake Ranch Gardens
Joan and Luke Senior
Rt. 2, Box 360
DeQueen, AR 71832
(Daylilies; price list for two
stamps)

The Country Greenery
Box 200
Glen Mills, PA 19342
(Modern Daylilies, miniatures;
list sent on request)

The Klehm Nursery
Route 5, Box 197
S. Barrington, IL 60010
(Peonies; color catalog $4.00,
money refunded with first order)

The Reath Nursery
Box 251
Vulcan, MI 49892
(Peonies; catalog $1)

White Flower Farm
Litchfield, CT 06759-0050
(Informative catalog $5.00,
refundable; free catalogs to active
customers)

Hostas

RECOMMENDED HOSTAS

Another Asian import that has captured American hearts is Hosta, Plantain Lily or, as the Victorians knew it, Funkia. Once classified with Daylilies (Hemerocallis), Hostas were also placed in several other genera (including Funkia) before they were finally named in honor of Austrian botanist and physician N. T. Host. These hardy plants thrive in almost all regions of the country; there are tiny Hostas for rock gardens, sweet-smelling Hostas for the fragrance garden, Hostas for sun and Hostas for shade. Many have attractive yellow fall color. Noted for their fine performance in shady gardens, most Hostas need a fairly rich and moisture retentive soil. Several can cope with abundant sun in northern gardens (in the South, Hosta requires shade); in general, Hostas with golden leaves need filtered sun while those with bluer foliage like a bit more shade. Here are ten cultivars recommended by Peter Ruh, grower of Hosta and former vice-president of the American Hosta Society:

Antioch*—Leaves with gold or cream colored edges; lavender flowers. Grows in sun or shade; plant larger in shade.

August Moon*—Gold-leaved Hosta with lavender-tinged white flowers in late summer. Will take morning sun.

Francee*—Heart-shaped dark green leaves with narrow white margins; lavender flowers in late summer. Likes part sun, part shade. Clumps about 1½ feet tall and slightly wider.

Golden Tiara*—Heart-shaped leaves with gold margins; lavender flowers. Plant about one foot tall.

Honeybells—Fragrant pale lavender flowers and large, ribbed light green leaves. An old favorite; does well in sun.

Kabitan—This small to medium-size cultivar from Japan has pale yellow lance-shaped leaves with green margins and purple flowers. Partial shade.

Krossa Regal*—Large, blue-green leaves; lavender flowers on stalks that grow 5 or more feet tall. Clumps may grow 2 feet tall.

Pearl Lake*—Heart-shaped blue-green leaves; lavender flowers produced in spring.

Piedmont Gold*—Large plant with gold-colored leaves and white flowers. Part sun, part shade.

*AHS award winner.

Royal Standard—Fragrant white flowers in late summer; green leaves are thick and glossy. Sun or shade.

HOSTAS WITH LATIN NAMES

Although the species is the basic unit of plant classification, botanists also recognize subspecies, varieties and forms. The latter terms are names given to plants created by Mother Nature often for very specific environmental niches and can sometimes be found after the species name in taxonomic guides. Humans, too, have long been in the business of creating new plants, called "cultivars," which *Hortus Third* defines as a special variety of a plant that has originated—and persisted—under cultivation. Most Hosta cultivars are now given descriptive English names such as August Moon or Honeybells. Before 1959, however, new Hosta cultivars were given Latin names that were listed after the species in single quotation marks, such as in Hosta fortunei 'Albomarginata.' To confuse matters further, a number of Hostas listed as species are now thought to be old hybrids. Growers and botanists alike often disagree on a particular plant's proper name. In short, you can't always be sure of what you will get when you order a Hosta, but that is no reason not to order them! Eight commonly offered Hostas with Latin names are:

Hosta fortunei 'Albomarginata'—Large green leaves with white margins and lavender flowers. H. fortunei, said to have pointed green leaves with wavy edges, is listed by a few growers although some say that the species alone does not exist.

Hosta lancifolia (NARROW-LEAVED PLANTAIN LILY)—Dark green glossy leaves; violet (fading lighter) late summer flowers. Some suppliers list an 'Albomarginata' that often is another Hosta and not lancifolia.

Hosta plantaginea (AUGUST LILY)—Old-time favorite with glossy, heart-shaped yellow/green leaves and fragrant white flowers in late summer. Can take morning sun, then full shade. 'Royal Standard', also fragrant, is a plantaginea cultivar.

Hosta sieboldiana—A large-leaved species native to Japan with a blue cast to leaves and relatively short flowering stalks. Variegated cultivars are listed in addition to 'Elegans' and 'Frances Williams.'

Hosta tardiflora—A small species native to Japan with narrow, glossy, green leaves. Pale purple flowers are produced in the fall.

Hosta undulata—A variegated plant, found in cultivation only, and believed by some to be a garden hybrid and not a true species. Sharp-pointed leaves are striped white/cream; lavender flowers appear in summer. May be the most widely grown variegated Hosta; several cultivars are listed.

Hosta ventricosa (BLUE PLANTAIN LILY)—Attractive green heart-shaped leaves and dark violet flowers in late summer. This species is a Chinese native. 'Aureo-marginata' is variegated with cream-edged leaves.

Hosta venusta—Often growing less than a foot high, H. venusta is native to Korea and has tiny oval leaves and lavender flowers which bloom in summer.

SOURCES FOR HOSTAS

Englerth Gardens
2461 22nd St.
Hopkins, MI 49328
(616) 793-7196

Hatfield Gardens
22799 Ringgold Southern Rd.
Stoutsville, OH 43154
(614) 474-5719

Homestead Division
Sunnybrook Farms Nursery
9448 Mayfield Rd.
Chesterland, OH 44026
(216) 729-9838

Charles Klehm Nursery
Rt. 5, Box 197
Penny Rd.
S. Barrington, IL 60010
(708) 551-3720

Savory's Greenhouse/Gardens
5300 Whiting Ave.
Edina, MN 55435
(612) 941-8755

The Wonderful World of Lilies

Within the garden's peaceful scene
Appear'd two lovely foes,
Aspiring to the rank of queen,
The Lily and the Rose.
              COWPER

Lilies are hardy perennials found throughout the world. They range from easy to grow (Asiatic and fragrant Trumpet hybrids) to the fairly difficult Japanese Oriental hybrids. Lilies do best in light, sandy soil where good air circulation allows foliage to dry off early in the morning. Botrytis, a fungus disease, may develop on leaves that stay wet; aphids also spread the virus diseases that plague most Lilies. As a group, the Martagons (hybrids derived from Balkan country natives) are most resistant to virus, along with Regal Lily (L. regale), L. henryi and several others. Susceptible Lilies include Gold-Banded Lily (L. auratum) and the beautiful native Americans Canada Lily (L. canadense) and Turk's Cap (L. superbum). Tiger Lilies (L. lancifolium) often harbor the virus and spread it to others without becoming diseased themselves. Sacred Madonna Lily (L. candidum) is native to the Mediterranean region; our Easter Lilies are cultivars of L. longiflorum, a Japanese native.

North American Lily Society's 1989 Popularity Poll, voted upon by membership:

Hall of Fame: Black Beauty

1. White Henri
2. Casa Blanca
   Gold Eagle
3. Red Velvet
   Tiger Babies
4. Star Gazer
   Thunderbolt
5. Corsica
   Unique
6. Chinook
   Connecticut King
   Journey's End

7. Crete
8. Sally
   L. speciosum 'Uchida'
9. Apricot Supreme
   Black Dragon
   Everest
   Schellenbaum
10. L. canadense (species)
    Enchantment
    Doeskin
    Jolanda
    Louise

SOURCES FOR LILIES

B & D Lilies
330 "P" St.
Port Townsend, WA 98368

Borbeleta Gardens, Inc.
15980 Canby Ave.
Faribault, MN 55021

Russell Graham
4030 Eagle Crest Rd. NW
Salem, OR 97304 (species Lilies only)

Vandenberg's
Black Meadow Rd.
Chester, NY 10918

Leslie Woodriff
1100 Griffith Rd.
McKinleyville, CA 95521

Ferns for the Shady Garden

Ferns have graced the earth for 400 million years and continue to do so with amazing diversity. They are perfect for shaded "green" or "quiet" gardens, excellent ground covers under shrubs such as Rhododendrons and beautiful around ponds or when interplanted with other shade lovers such as Astilbe, Primula and Cimicifuga. (Bold-leaved Hosta makes an excellent companion for many Ferns, but may not be a wise choice where deer browse.) Most of the following need acid (many other Ferns prefer limy sites), water-retentive soils and dappled but not dense shade. The following ten easy-to-grow species are all native except Japanese Painted Fern.

Adiantum pedatum (MAIDENHAIR FERN)—Grows 2 feet tall and has dainty fronds with black stems. There are several dwarf cultivars.

Athyrium goeringianum 'Pictum' (JAPANESE PAINTED FERN)—Related to attractive but invasive U.S. native A. felix-femina* (Lady Fern), this Japanese cultivar has gray leaves and maroon stems. Enlivens dark corners.

Dryopteris marginalis (MARGINAL SHIELD FERN)—Leathery, semievergreen fronds that grow about 2½ feet tall; sori (little dots that bear spores usually found on the undersides of leaves) arranged close to leaf margins. Dark green; many classic beauties in this genus.

Matteuccia pensylvanica (OSTRICH FERN)—Can grow 6 feet tall though it is generally shorter on sites that are only average in soil moisture or are south of its optimum range. Fronds were thought to resemble ostrich plumes; also produces attractive fertile fronds. Spreads by runners. Edible fiddleheads.

Osmunda cinnamomea (CINNAMON FERN)—Handsome fuzzy fiddleheads in spring grow into elegant, tall (4 feet) fronds. Showy cinnamon-colored fertile fronds form in center of clump. Will tolerate rather wet conditions.

---

*Two other attractive but invasive Ferns are Sensitive Fern (Onoclea sensibilis) and Hay-scented Fern (Dennstaedtia punctilobula). The former, called Sensitive because it succumbs to early frosts, tolerates wet soils and produces handsome fertile fronds that are attractive in dried winter bouquets. Hay-scented Fern will thrive on poorer and drier soils; it is capable of invading well-established plantings of Pachysandra. The common name refers to the sweet scent of dried leaves.

Osmunda claytoniana (INTERRUPTED FERN)—Another fern that grows about 4 feet tall; brown, spore-bearing areas "interrupt" some of the green central fronds. Prefers low, wet ground. Royal Fern (O. regalis) is an Osmunda that tolerates dry, rocky conditions as well as moister sites; it ranges from Canada south to Florida and Texas. Royal Fern has reddish new foliage, yellow fall color and grows 4 feet tall.

Polystichum acrostichoides (CHRISTMAS FERN)—Individual leaflets look like tiny stockings on this handsome dark green evergreen fern. Tolerates sun but needs damp soil. Good rock garden Fern.

Polystichum braunii (BRAUN'S HOLLY FERN)—Native to the North country, Braun's Holly Fern has glossy green fronds and a stately appearance though it (like Christmas Fern) grows only 1 to 2 feet tall. Leaflets almost rectangular in shape, becoming smaller at both the base and tips of fronds.

Thelypteris noveboracensis (NEW YORK FERN)—Another fern that tolerates sun (it likes ample soil moisture but can survive in drier sites); has lacy, pale green fronds and grows 2 feet tall. Delicate and graceful; like Braun's Holly Fern above, leaflets become much smaller toward base of fronds.

Woodwardia virginica (VIRGINIA CHAIN FERN)—A tall (3 to 4 or more feet), glossy-leaved Fern that thrives in soggy, sunny sites. Netted Chain Fern (W. areolata) is smaller and has yellow fall color.

SOURCES FOR FERNS AND OTHER NATIVE PLANTS

Carroll Gardens
Box 310
Westminster, MD 21157

Fancy Fronds
1911 4th Ave. W.
Seattle, WA 98119

Conley's Garden Center
145 Townsend Ave.
Boothbay Harbor, ME 04538

Gardens of the Blue Ridge
Box 10
Pineola, NC 28662

Native Gardens
Rt. 1, Box 494
Greenback, TN 37742

Rice Creek Gardens
1315 66th Ave. N.E.
Minneapolis, MN 55432

Shady Oaks Nursery
700 19th Ave. N.E.
Waseca, MN 56093

Siskiyou Rare Plant Nursery
2825 Cummings Rd.
Medford, OR 97501

Sunny Border Nursery
1709 Kensington Rd.
Kensington, CT 06037

Andre Viette Nursery
Box 16, Fisherville VA 22939

American Fern Society, Inc.
James D. Caponetti, Treasurer
Department of Botany
University of Tennessee
Knoxville, TN 37996-1100

GARDEN PLANT SOCIETIES

Several of the following national organizations also have regional societies; addresses change often. For additional groups devoted to annual plants, see "Houseplant Societies," page 192.

American Daffodil Society, Inc.
1686 Grey Fox Trail
Milford, OH 45150

American Dahlia Society
159 Pine St.
New Hyde Park, NY 11040

American Fern Society, Inc.
Dept. of Botany
Univ. of Tennessee
Knoxville, TN 37996-1100

American Hemerocallis Society
1454 Rebel Dr.
Jackson, MS 39211

American Hosta Society
5300 Whiting Ave.
Edina, MN 55435

American Peony Society
250 Interlachen Rd.
Hopkins, MN 55343

Marigold Society of America, Inc.
PO Box 112
New Britain, PA 18901

National Wildflower Research
Center
PO Box 9415
Austin TX 78766-9974

National Chrysanthemum Society
5012 Kingston Dr.
Annandale, VA 22003

The American Iris Society
6518 Beachy Ave.
Wichita, KS 67206

The North American Lily
Society, Inc.
PO Box 272
Owatonna, MN 55060

SOURCES FOR PERENNIALS

Kurt Bluemel
2740 Greene Lane
Baldwin, MD 21013
(301) 557-7229 (Catalog $2.00)

Bluestone Perennials
7211 Middle Ridge Rd.
Madison, OH 44057
(800) 852-5243 (Free catalog)

Busse Gardens
Rt. 2, Box 238
Cokato, MN 55321
(612) 286-2654
(Catalog $2.00, deducted from
first order)

Carroll Gardens
PO Box 310
Westminster, MD 21157
(800) 638-6334
(Catalog $2.00)

Garden Place
6780 Heisley Rd.
Box 388
Mentor, OH 44061
(216) 255-3705
(Catalog $1.00)

Lamb Nurseries
E. 101 Sharp Ave.
Spokane, WA 99202
(509) 328-7956 (Free catalog)

Milaeger's Gardens
4838 Douglas Ave.
Racine, WI 53402
(414) 639-2371
(Catalog $1.00, refundable)

Andre Viette Farm Nursery
Route 1, Box 16
Fishersville, VA 22939
(703) 943-2315
(Catalog, $2.00)

Wayside Gardens
1 Garden Lane
Hodges, SC 29695
(800) 845-1124
(Color catalog $1.00)

White Flower Farm
Litchfield, CT 06759
(800) 888-7756
(Three handsome catalogs, $5.00
per year, refundable)

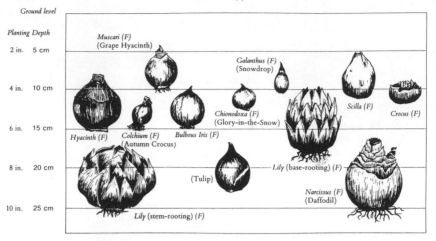

Fall Planted (F)

Ground level

Planting Depth

2 in.   5 cm

4 in.   10 cm

6 in.   15 cm

8 in.   20 cm

10 in. 25 cm

Muscari (F)
(Grape Hyacinth)

Galanthus (F)
(Snowdrop)

Chionodoxa (F)
(Glory-in-the-Snow)

Scilla (F)

Crocus (F)

Hyacinth (F)

Colchium (F)
(Autumn Crocus)

Bulbous Iris (F)

(Tulip)

Lily (base-rooting) (F)

Narcissus (F)
(Daffodil)

Lily (stem-rooting) (F)

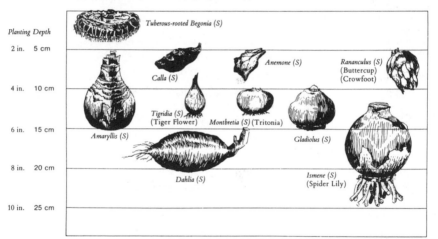

Spring Planted (S)

Planting Depth

2 in.   5 cm

4 in.   10 cm

6 in.   15 cm

8 in.   20 cm

10 in. 25 cm

Tuberous-rooted Begonia (S)

Calla (S)

Anemone (S)

Rananculus (S)
(Buttercup)
(Crowfoot)

Tigridia (S)
(Tiger Flower)

Montbretia (S) (Tritonia)

Amaryllis (S)

Gladiolus (S)

Dahlia (S)

Ismene (S)
(Spider Lily)

Courtesy of the University of Connecticut Cooperative Extension Service.

BULBS

Tulips

Many flowers have enslaved human beings, perhaps none more than Tulips. Native to the Old World, especially central Asia, they probably entered Europe via Turkey sometime in the sixteenth century. Holland in particular has loved Tulips; it was the Dutch who gave us both the wild speculation in bulbs known as "Tulipomania" and the great seven-

teenth-century floral paintings that often featured Tulips. The love for
Tulips remained; the Dutch are still leading hybridizers and growers. The
English were also smitten with this genus and a look at the many Tulip
motifs in Pennsylvania German art shows that Tulips were loved in the
New World, too.

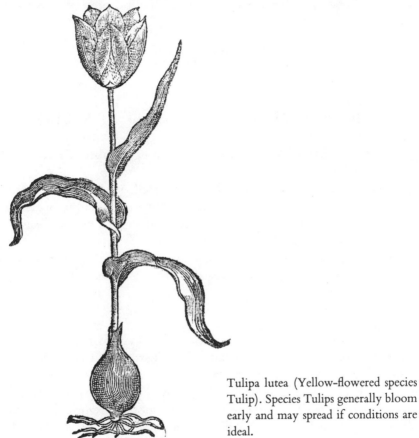

Tulipa lutea (Yellow-flowered species
Tulip). Species Tulips generally bloom
early and may spread if conditions are
ideal.

TULIP CLASSIFICATION

Tulips are classified according to their size, time of bloom and
flower characteristics. In addition to the Species or Botanical Tulips, the
following categories are recognized:

EARLY BLOOMERS (MOST SPECIES TULIPS ARE EARLY BLOOMERS):

Single Early Tulips—12 to 15 inches tall; some are fragrant
Double Early—10 to 12 inches; some are fragrant

MIDSEASON BLOOMERS:

Mendel Tulips—18 to 20 inches tall
Triumph Tulips—Rarely more than 20 inches high; result of
    crosses between Single Early and Late Tulips
Darwin Hybrids—24–28 inches tall; achieved by crossing
    T. fosterana with Late (Darwin) Tulips; often with red-
    orange colors

LATE BLOOMERS:

Darwin Tulips—Tall (30 to 36 inches) with the widest color
    range
Lily-flowered—24 inches; flowers pointed and shaped like a
    lily
Cottage Tulips—Single flowers, often egg-shaped; 25 to 26
    inches
Rembrandt or Broken Tulips—Flecked or striped in color, a
    condition caused by a virus; height varies. Tulip-Breaking
    Virus (TBV) is the most serious of the lily virus diseases.
    Do not plant Broken Tulips near Lilies.
Parrot Tulips—24 inches; unusual colors and feathered flowers
Double Late or Peony Tulips—20 to 24 inches; double
    flowers

SPECIES TULIPS

Before horticulturists gave us the many hybrids there were only species Tulips, and many are available to gardeners today. Most are considerably smaller than the modern hybrids and flower earlier. Some are fragrant. Unlike their hybridized cousins, the species will often naturalize if they are happily situated in a sunny spot with good drainage (a rock garden is ideal). Smaller Tulips are a good bet in areas where deer browse. Tulip foliage is a favorite of Eastern deer, but the smaller leaves of most species are not the attraction the larger-leaved hybrids are. A few Tulips still recognized as species have also been hybridized; among them are T. kaufmanniana (Water-Lily Tulip) and fosterana and greigii with their scarlet hues. The first two may have mottled or striped leaves; greigii always does. Others to try include:

Tulipa batalinii—4 to 6 inches high with soft yellow flowers
    (may be flushed apricot) and narrow gray-green leaves.
    There are several named varieties:

Tulipa clusiana—Commonly called Lady, Peppermint Stick or Candy-stripe Tulip and native to Afghanistan and Iran, this species has become naturalized in parts of southern Europe. Grows 8 to 10 inches tall; flowers are red on the outside, cream on the inside.

Tulipa kolpakowskiana—Flowers are deep yellow with pink or olive blush on the outside petals. Narrow gray-green leaves. Very hardy; 8 inches tall; from Turkestan.

Tulipa marjolettii—With flowering stems that may reach 2 feet, this mid- to late-season bloomer produces creamy yellow flowers (fading to white) with pink trim.

Tulipa praestans—This 8 to 10 inch tall Tulip from central Asia produces orange/red flowers, often several to a stem in early spring. Leaves are fairly broad and gray-green.

Tulipa pulchella—Small (4 inches), early-blooming species from Asia Minor with crimson/purple flowers and a white-margined blue basal blotch. Cultivars available with white, pinkish or violet flowers.

Tulipa saxatilis—A native of Crete, saxatilis grows 6 to 8 inches tall and has rosy-lilac flowers with a yellow basal blotch. Fragrant. Narrow green leaves.

Tulipa sylvestris—Bright yellow, fragrant flowers late in season and spreading to form large colonies, but according to *Hortus Third,* often rather shy of bloom. Several cultivars flower more freely. Native to Europe, North Africa and Iran. Gray-green straplike leaves.

Tulipa tarda—A midseason native of Turkestan, tarda is easy to grow and spreads readily. Six inches tall, it produces clusters of starlike yellow/white flowers that cover the ground.

Tulipa turkestanica—Another Tulip from Turkestan, this one produces early clusters of graceful white flowers with golden basal blots.

Hortus Third notes the fragrant species Tulips:

T. patens
T. primulina
T. saxatilis
T. suaveolens
T. sylvestris

Summer-Blooming Bulbs

It is hard to imagine spring without the flowering bulbs; much less well-known are the late spring/summer and fall flowering bulbous plants that can add interest to the garden. Most of the following require excellent drainage:

Allium spp. (ONION)—A. christophii (Stars of Persia) has ornamental lilac flowers; A. giganteum has 4-inch umbels covered with bright lilac flowers and grows 4 or more feet tall and A. thunbergii has purple flowers in fall.

Alstroemeria aurantiaca (PERUVIAN LILY)—Native to the Andes, this plant grows 3 to 4 feet tall and produces red-striped orange flowers in summer. Long-lasting as cut flowers.

Belamcanda spp. (BLACKBERRY LILY)—B. chinensis has orange flowers with red dots in July and August and likes full sun; B. flabellata, which blooms later, has yellow flowers and enjoys partial shade and moist soil. Both have shiny black seeds that remain when the pod splits.

Camassia spp. (CAMASS)—These western U.S. natives do well in eastern gardens and produce white, blue or blue-violet flowers. The bulbs were once an important food for native Americans; blooms in late spring.

Colchicum autumnale (AUTUMN CROCUS)—Leaves appear in spring, but pink/purple (or white) flowers do not bloom until autumn. Source of the drug colchicine.

Cyclamen hederifolium (BABY CYCLAMEN)—Attractive markings on leaves; rose-pink or white flowers with a darker eye in late summer-fall.

Galtonia candicans (SUMMER HYACINTH)—A large plant with gray-green leaves and fragrant white flowers in summer and fall. A long-lasting cut flower.

Leucojum autumnale (SNOWFLAKE)—White (may be rose-tinged) small bells on 4 to 6 inch stems in late summer through fall. Grasslike leaves. Taller L. aestivum has green-trimmed white flowers and blooms in the spring.

Tigridia pavonia (TIGER FLOWER)—There are many cultivars of these South and Central American natives with spotted flowers in red, yellow, white and rose. Bulbs are eaten in some countries; store indoors during winter north of zone 7.

Triteleia spp. (BRODIAEA) (Triplet Lily)—Western U.S. natives with grassy leaves and clusters of small flowers. Various species bloom at various times; B. hyacinthina (Wild Hyacinth) has white or lilac flowers and blooms in summer. Provide winter mulch north of zone 7.

Zephyranthes spp. (FAIRY LILY, RAIN LILY)—Summer blooming Z. citrina has fragrant yellow flowers; Z. candida, white and pink, blooms in the fall.

Bulbs listed above are all relatively hardy. The following summer and autumn bloomers are tender and will need to be dug before frost and stored inside:

Acidanthera bicolor (PEACOCK ORCHID)—White flowers with brown trim; very fragrant. A member of the Iris family in spite of the name.

Gladiolus spp. (SWORD LILY)—G. byzantinus and cultivars are especially recommended.

Ixia maculata (AFRICAN CORN LILY)—Cream flower with purple throat; other Ixias have red, pink, yellow or orange flowers. Good cut flower.

Pancratium maritimum (SEA DAFFODIL)—Large, very fragrant white flowers and handsome gray-green leaves. Grows 1½ feet tall.

Polianthes tuberosa (TUBEROSE)—Thought to be Mexican natives but no longer known in the wild, Tuberoses produce very fragrant white blossoms in summer and fall. Grows about 3½ feet tall.

Sparaxis spp. (WANDFLOWER)—African natives with colorful flowers. S. grandiflora has yellow or purple blooms; S. tricolor and its hybrids are brightly multicolored.

Tritonia spp. (MONTBRETIA)—South African native that grows 3 feet tall and resembles its relatives Gladiolus, Ixia and Sparaxis. Blooms in late summer. Flowers may be 4 inches in diameter and colored red, orange, gold and yellow.

American Native: Triplet Lily

Over 100 years ago the newspaper *Rural New Yorker* recommended Triteleia laxa or Triplet Lily to its readers as quoted on the following page.

Triplet Lily is a native of California; it has not yet been introduced into the East to any extent. Wherever it has been cultivated it has at once passed into popularity. The bulb is about one inch deep, and the same in thickness, in shape resembling that of the crocus; it is astonishing the magnificent large flowers such a small bulb will produce. Growing naturally, it is found five or six inches below the surface of the ground. The flower stem grows about two feet high, each stem producing from five flowers to two dozen. The trumpet shaped flowers are from two to three inches long, and from one to two inches in diameter at the mouth. In color they are a handsome purple, inclined more to the shade of what is known as Victoria blue. The flowers diffuse a delicate fragrance.

Hardy Bulbs for Small Gardens

The following plants all grow to a height of 15 inches or less. Flowering times and flower color are noted (see also the Species Tulips and American Daffodil Society–recommended Miniature Daffodils, pages 95–96):

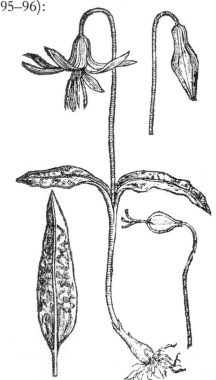

Erythronium sp. (Dog-tooth Violet). Also called Trout Lily, Fawn Lily and Adder's Tongue, these small lilies are native in many parts of North America. The attractive and often mottled leaves disappear in summer.

Allium moly (LILY LEEK)—Bright yellow flowers in spring. Other small Alliums have pink or purple flowers; some are summer blooming.

Chionodoxa luciliae (GLORY-OF-THE-SNOW)—Blue star-shaped flowers with white centers; blooms with Scilla sibirica in early spring. There are also varieties with pink or white flowers.

Colchicum autumnale (AUTUMN CROCUS)—Pink flowers appear in the fall; there is a white cultivar. C. 'Roseum Plenus' has double rose flowers in fall.

Crocus spp. (CROCUS)—Not all of this genus blooms in the spring; C. speciosus (violet-blue), C. kotschyanus (rosy-lilac with yellow throat) and others are fall blooming.

Eranthis spp. (WINTER ACONITE)—Sweet-smelling yellow flowers may bloom through the snow. Attractive foliage goes dormant in summer.

Erythronium spp. (TROUT LILY, DOG-TOOTH VIOLET)—Close to 10 species are available, many (including a yellow-flowered native American, E. americanum) with beautifully mottled leaves. Other species have pink or white flowers.

Fritillaria meleagris (GUINEA HEN FLOWER)—Sometimes called Checkered Lily because of its checkered veining; colors are bronze, purple or white. Blooms in spring.

Galanthus nivalis (SNOWDROP)—Very early blooming white flowers; there are several cultivars, including one with double flowers.

Ipheion uniflorum (SPRING STARFLOWER)—Flowers white (with bluish tinge) to blue; 'Wisley Blue' is white/violet. Foliage has onionlike odor when bruised; flowers are fragrant.

Muscari spp. (GRAPE HYACINTH)—Several species of these spring bloomers bearing clusters of purple-blue (or white) flowers resembling tiny grapes are available. M. armeniacum is fragrant.

Puschkinia scilloides (STRIPED SQUILL)—Pale bluish flowers with darker stripe bloom in the spring.

Scilla sibirica (SIBERIAN SQUILL)—Deep blue flowers in early spring; the several cultivars include 'Alba' (white). Naturalizes readily. Sometimes listed as a Scilla, and called Spanish Squill, relative Endymion hispanicus grows 15 to 20 inches tall and has white, pink or blue bell-like flowers in mid- to late spring.

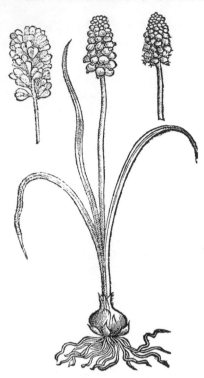

Muscari sp. (Grape Hyacinth). Easy-to-grow members of the Lily family, Grape Hyacinths may be blue, white or (rarely) yellow. Several species are fragrant.

Star-of-Bethlehem (Ornithogalum umbellatum), a biblical plant that grows about 8 inches tall, has narrow leaves and white flowers (green trim) in late spring but naturalizes so readily that it may become a weedy pest. O. nutans is taller, with silvery gray-green flowers and better behavior.

Bulbs to Avoid

Bulbs in the wild are threatened for many reasons; not least among them is commercial collecting. Recently the World Wildlife Fund and the National Resources Defense Council issued the following list of bulb species that gardeners may wish to avoid. Many of these species are still collected from the wild:

AMARYLLIS FAMILY

Galanthus (SNOWDROP): G. elwesii can always be assumed to be of wild origin. G. nivalis is widely propagated and safe to buy.

Leucojum (SUMMER SNOWFLAKE): L. vernum and L. aestivum are suspect.

Narcissus, especially N. triandrus var. albus, N. asturiensis and
  N. cylamineus: Be cautious about all small species.
Sternbergia species

LILY FAMILY

Chionodoxa, especially C. sardensis, C. tmoli and C. luciliae.
Erythronium, except for 'Pagoda,' which is a propagated
  hybrid.
Fritillaria: Use caution when buying F. persica 'Adiyamen' and
  · F. imperialis; avoid others.
Lilium: Exercise caution with L. martagon.
Scilla species: Be cautious; many are still collected in Turkey.
Trillium, especially T. grandiflorum.
Tulipa: Many tulips that have been called "botanical" are really
  small cultivars and safe to buy; avoid T. praecox.

ORCHID FAMILY

Bletilla striata
Pleione species
Cypripedium, especially C. acaule.

PRIMROSE FAMILY

Cyclamen: Buy only from those few U.S. dealers who
  propagate their stock.

BUTTERCUP FAMILY

Anemone: Blue or mixed stock of A. blanda may be from the
  wild.
Eranthis, especially the popular yellow-flowered E. hyemalis
  and E. cilicica.

Catching Yellow Fever: Daffodils

The American Daffodil Society (ADS) encourages the planting of
Narcissus, a hardy, cheerful and carefree genus of the Amaryllis family.
Native to the Old World, and perhaps named for the Greek god,*

---

*Some authorities believe the genus was named for the Narcissus of mythology; others do
not.

Daffodils arrived on American shores with the first colonists. Some eighteenth-century plantings still survive. There are only about 26 species of Narcissus, but today we have 20,000 cultivars that the ADS places in 12 divisions, depending on size and flower characteristics. Mary Lou Gripshover, executive director of the ADS, recommends the following inexpensive ($2.25 or under) and readily available varieties:

TRUMPETS: DIVISION 1

Yellow self: Viking, Banbridge, Arkle, Golden Rapture, Carrickbeg, Olympic Gold
Yellow/white: Preamble, Jet Set, Ivy League
White self: Queenscourt, Cantatrice, Perseus
Reversed Bi-Color: Chiloquin, Honeybird, Lunar Sea

LARGE CUP: DIVISION 2

Yellow self: Golden Aura, Amber Castle, Camelot, Symphonette, Tristram
Yellow and Red or Orange: Bunclody, Vulcan, Shining Light, Resplendent, Loch Stac
White and Yellow: Chapeau, Festivity, Tudor Minstrel
White and Red or Orange: Bit-o-Gold, Ringleader, Avenger, Irish Rover
White and Pink: Passionale, Romance, Coral Ribbon, Tullycore, Violetta, Propriety, Roseworthy
White self: Fastidious, Polar Circle, Wedding Bell, Broomhill
Yellow and white: Daydream, Bracken Hill, Cloud Nine

SMALL CUP: DIVISION 3

Yellow and Colored Cup: Perimeter, Ardour
White and Yellow: Old Satin, Aircastle, Woodland Prince, Eminent
White and Red or Orange: Merlin, Corofin, Palmyra
White and Pink: Gossamer
White self: Verona

DOUBLES: DIVISION 4

One bloom to a stem: Acropolis, Unique
More than one bloom to a stem: Cheerfulness, Yellow Cheerfulness

TRIANDRUS HYBRIDS: DIVISION 5 (MORE THAN ONE FLOWER PER STEM; LATE-BLOOMING)

White/white: Tresamble
Yellow/yellow: Liberty Bells

CYCLAMINEUS HYBRIDS: DIVISION 6 (USUALLY ONE FLOWER PER STEM WITH SWEPT-BACK PETALS; VERY EARLY)

Yellow/yellow: Charity May
Yellow/orange: Beryl
White/yellow: Dove Wings, Joybell, Early Entry
White/white: Jenny

JONQUIL HYBRIDS: DIVISION 7 (FLOWERING STEM WITH TWO TO SIX FLOWERS, OFTEN CLUSTERED; FRAGRANT)

Yellow/yellow: Sweetness, Quail, Trevithian, Oregon Gold
Yellow/orange: Stratosphere (being changed to Y-Y)
Yellow/white: Pipit, Dickcissel, Chat
Yellow/red: Suzy
White/white: Dainty Miss

TAZETTA HYBRIDS: DIVISION 8 (FLOWERS SMALL AND IN CLUSTERS; FRAGRANT; MANY ARE TENDER)

White/yellow: Geranium
White/white: Silver Chimes

POETICUS HYBRIDS: DIVISION 9 (WHITE, FLAT CUPS, FRAGRANT; THE LAST DAFFODILS TO BLOOM)

Actaea, Perdita, Cantabile

SPECIES AND WILD FORMS AND HYBRIDS: DIVISION 10

Tenby Daffodil, Albus Plenus Odoratus, Jonquilla, Poeticus Recurvus

Split Corona Daffodils and Miscellaneous make up Divisions 11 and 12.

SOME MINIATURES ON THE ADS-APPROVED LIST OF MINIATURES:

April Tears (YELLOW-YELLOW)
Baby Moon (YELLOW-YELLOW)

Bagatelle (YELLOW-YELLOW)
Bebop (WHITE-YELLOW)
Bobbysoxer (YELLOW-YELLOW/YELLOW/ORANGE)
Chit Chat (YELLOW-YELLOW)
Clare (YELLOW-YELLOW)
Hawera (YELLOW-YELLOW)
Little Beauty (WHITE-YELLOW)
Little Gem (YELLOW-YELLOW)
Minnow (WHITE-YELLOW)
Pixie's Sister (YELLOW-YELLOW)
Small Talk (YELLOW-YELLOW)
Stafford (YELLOW-ORANGE)
Sundial (YELLOW-YELLOW)
Sun Disc (YELLOW-YELLOW)
Tete-a-Tete (YELLOW-YELLOW)

FRAGRANT DAFFODILS

In addition to some of the species Daffodils (such as jonquilla and poeticus) fragrant Daffodils are most often found in the following ADS divisions:

Division 7—Jonquilla; multiflowered, usually yellow
Division 8—Tazetta; this division includes the tender forcing
　　cultivars
Division 9—Poeticus

Some Division 3 Daffodils that have been called scented are Benvarden, Dunley Hall, Merlin, Irish Nymph, and Pixies Pool.

1988 POPULARITY POLL

The top dozen (the number directly after the name refers to the division):

	Year Introduced
Tete-a-Tete (12), Yellow-yellow	1949
Accent (2), White-pink	1960
Festivity (2), White-yellow	1954
Stratosphere (7), Yellow-orange	1968
Daydream (2), Yellow-white	1960
Foundling (6), White-Pink	1969

	Year Introduced
Gull (2), White-green eye	1979
Ceylon (2), Yellow-orange	1943
Ice Follies (2), White-white	1953
Quail (7), Yellow-yellow	1974
Silver Chimes (8), White-white	1916
Sweetness (7), Yellow-yellow	1939

WISTER AWARD

Only two Daffodils have received the recently established Wister Award for excellence: Stratosphere and Accent.

TIPS FOR DAFFODIL GROWERS

Plant bulbs in the early fall. Tops of bulbs should be 4 inches below the surface in heavy soils; 8 inches in sandy soil and where summers are hot. Plant miniatures 2 inches deep (where winters are cold, plant deeper). Daffodils are happy in sun or half-shade. Do not cut foliage until it begins to die down after blooming. Daffodil bulbs are toxic and are not bothered by rodents. Daffodils usually do well when planted among shallow-rooted ground covers such as Vinca; less well when planted with more vigorous growers such as Ivy and Pachysandra.

American Daffodil Society, Inc.
Mrs. Paul Gripshover, Executive Director
1686 Gray Fox Trail
Milford, OH 45150

Narcissus sp. (Daffodil). Daffodils are care-free and long-lived and their bulbs are not eaten by rodents. Do not remove leaves until they have died down in late spring.

SOURCES FOR DAFFODILS

Bonnie Brae Gardens
1105 S.E. Christensen Rd.
Corbett, OR 97019

The Daffodil Mart
Route 3, Box 794
Gloucester, VA 23601
(804) 693-3966

Hatfield Gardens
22799 Ringgold Southern Rd.
Stoutsville, OH 43154
(614) 474-5719
Specializing in Daffodils,
Daylilies, Hostas

Grant Mitsch
Novelty Daffodils
PO Box 218
Hubbard, OR 97032
(503) 651-2742

Mary Mattison van Schaik
RR 1, Box 181
Cavendish, VT 05142-9725
(802) 226-7338

SOURCES FOR BULBS

W. Atlee Burpee Co.
300 Park Ave.
Warminster, PA 18974

Peter De Jager Bulb Co.
Box 2010
188 Asbury St.
S. Hamilton, MA 01982

R. Graham Gardens
4030 Eagle Crest Rd. N.W.
Salem, OR 97304
(Carries several species of
Erythronium)

John D. Lyon, Inc.
143 Alewife Brook Parkway
Cambridge, MA 02140

McClure and Zimmerman*
108 W. Winnebago
PO Box 368
Friesland, WI 53935

Michigan Bulb Co.
1950 Waldorf N.W.
Grand Rapids, MI 49550

Oregon Bulb Farms
39391 S.E. Lusted Rd.
Sandy, OR 97055

John Scheepers, Inc.
63 Wall St.
New York, NY 10005

Smith & Hawken*
25 Corte Madera
Mill Valley, CA 94941

Van Bourgondien
245 Farmingdale Rd.
Babylon, NY 11702

Van Engelen, Inc. (Wholesale)
307 Maple St.
Litchfield, CT 06759

Wayside Gardens
1 Garden Lane
Hodges, SC 29695

White Flower Farm
Litchfield, CT 06759

*Firm claims to sell only commercially
propagated bulbs.

GRASSES AND SEDGES

Decorative Perennial Grasses and Sedges

Grasses are fashionable right now (in the garden—not the lawn) and why not? They are undemanding and disease-free. Maintenance consists of cutting old foliage back to the ground once in early spring. Colors can be as vivid as those found in other perennials: from the bright red or blue foliage of Japanese Blood Grass and certain Fescues to the showy pink or purple plumes of Fountain Grass. Most gardeners, however, appreciate Grasses for their subtle color changes throughout the seasons. When other perennials have vanished for the winter, Grasses are still an attractive part of the landscape. The swishing and fluttering of their leaves and flower heads add sound and movement to the garden. Some are tolerant of poor soils and air quality; others like wet spots near ponds and pools. Many tolerate partial shade. The taller species make good screens (see "The 'New American' Garden," page 384). The following species are all low to medium in height:

Briza media (QUAKING GRASS)—Graceful Eurasian about 2 feet tall that has become naturalized in the Northeast. Tolerates light shade but not drought. The perennial (media) and annual (B. maxima and minor) Quaking Grasses all have showy, open flower panicles and are useful for naturalizing.

Carex morrowii (JAPANESE SEDGE)—Reddish brown sedge that grows 2 feet tall. 'Aurea-variegata,' a shade lover, is smaller (15 inches), evergreen, and has green and cream leaves. There are several other attractive species of Carex.

Chasmanthium latifolium (SEA OATS, SPANGLE GRASS)—American native with large nodding panicles; grows 3 to 4 feet tall and is best in partial shade. Bronze fall color is especially beautiful; seed heads will retain their green color when dried in flower arrangements.

Deschampsia caespitosa (TUFTED HAIR GRASS)—3 to 4 feet tall with fine, arching leaves and delicate purple-tinged flowers in summer. Several cultivars have yellow plumes. Native to North America and Eurasia. Sun or shade.

Festuca ovina glauca (BLUE FESCUE)—Introduced from Europe, this Fescue grows 10 inches tall, prefers cool climates and has slender, silvery blue leaves. There are several other blue-leaved Fescues; F. amethystina (Large Blue Fescue) is said to tolerate warmer weather.

Imperata cylindrica (JAPANESE BLOOD GRASS)—This grass grows 1 to 2 feet tall and has arresting red leaves throughout the season. Requires moist but well-drained soil; sun or light shade.

Molina caerulea 'Variegata' (PURPLE MOOR GRASS)—Beautiful Eurasian Grass with striped leaves and purplish flower plumes that bloom all summer. Grows 2 to 3 feet tall in sun or partial shade; likes a water-retentive soil.

Panicum virgatum (SWITCH GRASS)—Native to the American prairie, drought-resistant sun-loving Switch Grass can grow to 7 feet tall; variety 'Rubrum' is lower growing with red-tinged leaves and crimson fall color. There are several other named varieties.

Pennisetum alopecuroides (CHINESE FOUNTAIN GRASS)—Grows 3½ feet tall with showy pinkish plumes in late summer and yellow fall color. Other Pennisetums have purple or pale-colored flowers and are lower growing.

Stipa pennata (FEATHER-GRASS)—Handsome fine-leaved Eurasian Grass with feathery white flowers in summer. S. gigantea is twice as tall (6 feet) as pennata, has large flowers that turn from green/purple to yellow and tolerates drought.

RIBBON GRASS

Ribbon grass (Phalaris arundinacea 'Picta') is a rather coarse perennial grass that can grow 4 feet tall. It is popular because of its attractive variegated leaves and its tolerance of poor soils and wet sites; it may be quite invasive in light, sandy soils, however, and foliage needs to be cut

Briza sp. (Quaking Grass). Quaking Grasses may be annual or perennial and all are handsome in the garden and in bouquets.

back in midsummer to keep it looking good. Native to both North America and Eurasia.

MORE NATIVE GRASSES

America is rich in beautiful native grasses; in addition to the several natives listed above, the following perennials also deserve mention (except for the two shade-lovers noted, these grasses will thrive under sunny, dry conditions):

Andropogon spp. (BLUESTEM)—Big Bluestem (A. gerardii), which grows 5 feet tall, has bluish stems and red-orange fall color; lower-growing Little Bluestem or Broom-Beardgrass (A. scoparius) is most attractive in fall with its rosy tan color and delicate fluffs of seed.

Bouteloua spp. (GRAMA GRASS)—B. curtipendula (Sideoats Grass) grows 2½ feet tall and has graceful leaves and summer flowers. B. gracilis (Blue Grass) is a little shorter; its interesting flowers are thought by some to resemble mosquito larvae; hence another name, Mosquito Grass. Suitable for the rock garden.

Elymus spp. (WILD RYE)—There are many species of this beautiful grass (also called Lyme-Grass); it can be invasive. Several species have very blue foliage and attractive flower spikes.

Eragrostis spectabilis (PURPLE LOVE GRASS, TUMBLE GRASS)—Bright purple flowers in late summer. Occurs on sandy soils and dry road banks; cats are fond of chewing the flower heads. Grows 1 to 3 feet tall; flower panicles taller.

Hystrix patula (BOTTLEBRUSH GRASS)—Hystrix grows 2 to 4 feet tall and has showy flowers and a long blooming period. Prefers partial shade; moist soil in sun. Grows wild in rich, low woods.

Milium effusum (WOOD MILLET)—An elegant and graceful grass for shade, Wood Millet grows 2 feet tall and has delicate panicles of pale spikelets and broad, thin leaves. Variety 'Aureum' is bright yellow. Needs adequate moisture; prefers limy soils.

Sorghastrum avenaceum (INDIAN GRASS)—A tall graceful grass (5 to 6 feet), Indian Grass has golden flowers and fluffy seed heads. Withstands drought as does Bluestem, Grama Grass, Wild Rye and Purple Love Grass.

Extension Bulletin on Ornamental Grasses

Cornell University Extension Service offers a bulletin, "Ornamental Grasses for the Home and Garden," by Mary Hockenberry and Robert Mower. The bulletin describes over 30 grasses with tips on siting and culture and contains an identification key to 41 grasses. (Order Bulletin #64, enclose a check for $2.50 and mail your request to Cornell Distribution Center, Research Park, Ithaca, NY 14850). The following lists are from the bulletin:

PERENNIAL GRASSES FOR WATER GARDENS

Alopecurus pratensis 'Aureus' (YELLOW FOXTAIL)
Arundo donax and A. d. 'Versicolor' (GIANT REED)
Calamagrostis epigeous (FEATHER REED GRASS)
Carex buchananii (LEATHERLEAF SEDGE)
Carex morrowii 'Expallida' (JAPANESE SEDGE GRASS)
Deschampsia caespitosa (TUFTED HAIR GRASS)
Glyceria maxima 'Variegata' (VARIEGATED MANNAGRASS)
Miscanthus sinensis (EULALIA GRASS)
Miscanthus sinensis 'Zebrinus' (ZEBRA GRASS)
Molinea caerulea 'Variegata' (PURPLE MOOR GRASS)
Panicum virgatum (SWITCH GRASS)
Spartina pectinata 'Aureo-marginata' (CORD GRASS)

PERENNIAL GRASSES FOR SHADY LOCATIONS

Calamagrostis epigeous (FEATHER REED GRASS)
Carex pendula (PENDULOUS SEDGE GRASS)
Carex spp. (SEDGES)
Chasmanthium latifolium (NORTHERN SEA OATS)
Deschampsia caespitosa (TUFTED HAIR GRASS)
Festuca gigantea (GIANT FESCUE)
Hystrix patula (BOTTLEBRUSH GRASS)
Luzula spp. (WOODRUSHES)
Melica altissima 'Atropurpurea' (PURPLE MELIC)
Milium effusum 'Aureum' (MILLET GRASS)
Molinea caerulea 'Variegata' (PURPLE MOOR GRASS)
Stipa pennata (FEATHER GRASS)

Grasses for Dried Arrangements

Cut grass flowers as soon as they appear and dry them in a cool, dry location with good air circulation for a week to ten days. The earlier the flowers are cut, the less chance they will shatter.

Agrostis nebulosa (CLOUD GRASS) A
Briza media (QUAKING GRASS) P
Bromus spp. (BROME GRASS) A
Eragrostis spp. (LOVE GRASS) A or P
Imperata brevifolia (SATIN TAIL) P
Phleum pratensis (TIMOTHY) A
Rhynchelytrum repens (RUBY GRASS) A or P*
Setaria italica (FOXTAIL MILLET) A
Stipa pennata; Stipa spp. (FEATHER GRASS) P
Uniola paniculata (SEA OATS) P

A—Annual   P—Perennial
*Beautiful grass with red flowers, fading to pink or silver, and purple-tinged upper leaves.

Where to Visit the Grasses

According to John Averett of the National Wildflower Research Center, the native prairie was once the largest ecosystem in the United States, stretching from Minnesota to as far south as Texas. This sea of grass rippled over 250 million acres; less than half of 1 percent remains. Some organizations, like the National Wildflower Research Center, are recreating prairies; others have preserved bits and pieces of the original.

Illinois
> (Morris): Goose Lake Prairie State Park. Tall-grass prairie remnant.

Iowa
> (Manson): Kaslow Prairie. Native grasses and wildflowers.
> (Guthrie Center): Sheeder Prairie.
> Cayler and Hayden Prairies are also located in Iowa.

Kansas
> (Manhattan): Konza Prairie Research Center. Most of the area is closed to the public but there is a self-guided trail several miles long that is open. Tall grass (and some short grass). Call (913) 532-6620 for information.

Nebraska:

Large portions of the state are grasslands; Bluestem prairies in the east and mixed tall and short grasslands in the western Sandhills. The Ogallala National Grassland is located in Dowes/Sioux counties.

Pennsylvania

(Butler): Jennings Nature Preserve. An area formed at the end of the Pleistocene, Jennings Preserve contains grasses but is best known for wildflowers, especially Blazing Stars, at their best the last two weeks of July and the first two weeks of August.

South Dakota

(Leola): Samuel H. Ordway Jr. Memorial Prairie. One of the largest preserves in South Dakota. There are a number of others.

Wisconsin

(Madison): University of Wisconsin-Madison Arboretum maintains several restored prairies. Curtis Prairie is the oldest restored tall-grass prairie in the world.

SOURCES FOR GRASSES

Kurt Bluemel
2740 Greene Lane
Baldwin, MD 21013

Garden Place
Box 388
Mentor, OH 44061

Hatfield Gardens
22799 Ringgold Southern Rd.
Stoutsville, OH 43154

Hortico, Inc.
RR 1, Robson Rd.
Waterdown, ON (Canada)
LOR 2

Limerock Ornamental Grasses
RD 1
Port Matilda, PA 16870

Milaeger's Gardens
4838 Douglas Ave.
Racine, WI 53402 (A small selection of native prairie grasses.)

Prairie Nursery
PO Box 365
Westfield, WI 53964

Surry Gardens
Box 145
Surry, ME 04684

Andre Viette Nursery
Box 16
Fisherville, VA 22939

Wayside Gardens
1 Garden Lane
Hodges, SC 29695

Selecting Turfgrass

There are no bargains in grass seed. A cheap mixture is not only composed of inferior seed, but often more of it will be needed to seed an area that a high quality mix would cover using less seed. Read labels carefully. The most commonly used turfgrasses in the cool regions of the country are Kentucky Bluegrass (Poa pratensis), the Fescues (Festuca), and Perennial Ryegrass (Lolium). Although Kentucky Bluegrass is probably the most important, and sometimes special-situation lawns consisting solely of Bluegrass varieties are created, most home owners are best served by a blend such as the one below, recommended by the Cooperative Extension Service of the University of Connecticut in Storrs (call your Extension Service for recommended blends and seeding times for your area).

Improved Kentucky Bluegrass—at least 2 varieties	40–60%
Fine-leaf Fescues consisting of one or more varieties (no less than 20% of any one variety)	40–60%
Turf-type perennial Ryegrass (use no more than 20% if there is any slope)	20% or less

Sunny or light-partial-shade blend (turfgrass will not grow in dense shade) recommended for most home lawns. Seed at the rate of 3 to 4 pounds/1000 square feet.

Use the following blend for seeding during periods of the year other than optimum time or on steep slopes when rapid establishment is desired:

Fine-leaf Fescues	50–60%
Improved Kentucky Bluegrass (2 varieties)	20–30%
Turf-type perennial Ryegrass	15–20%

Seed at the rate of 4 pounds/1000 square feet.

Note: Bluegrass germinates slowly; warmth and moisture hasten germination. Fescues tolerate dry soils and shade better than Kentucky Bluegrass. Perennial Ryegrass germinates quickly, as does common annual Ryegrass; the latter is recommended for quick, temporary lawns or cover. The best pH range for most turfgrasses is 5.8–6.5; mower settings between 2½–3 inches help to develop strong root systems.

What Are Improved Kentucky Bluegrasses?

Many new turfgrass cultivars are introduced each year; so far there are more than three hundred Kentucky Bluegrass cultivars alone. Each variety has its virtues, mainly disease resistance, but homeowners should be aware that each new variety usually has drawbacks as well. Generally the new varieties are for those who desire perfect lawns and are willing to spend the time this requires. The following ten Bluegrass cultivars were developed for shade tolerance. Look for them in mixtures developed for shady lawns.

America	Merit
A-34 Bensun	Midnight
Bristol	Nugget
Eclipse	Ram 1—Somewhat drought tolerant
Glade	Victa—Somewhat drought tolerant

Shade mixtures should also contain significant amounts of the Fescues, which are shade-tolerant grasses to begin with. The Lawn Institute recommends the following as among the best:

Arid	Koket
Banner	Mirage
Cindy	Mustang
Era	Rebel II
Falcon	Reliant
Gala	SR 3000
Hounddog	Titan
Jamestown	Valda

Low-Maintenance Kentucky Bluegrass Cultivars

If you want a manicured green carpet surrounding your home and are willing to water and fertilize regularly, the high-maintenance new cultivars may be for you. If you are less zealous about lawn care, or need to curtail summer water use, low-maintenance varieties will be the better choice. These grasses, many developed years ago, generally withstand drought better and need less nitrogen fertilizer; in fact, some are more disease-prone under intensive care. Nick Christians, of the Horticulture Department at Iowa State University, has compiled the following list of low-maintenance Bluegrass cultivars that have performed well with restricted fertilizer and water in field trials at Ames; the first four are among the best.

Kenblue	Piedmont
South Dakota Common	Victa*
S-21	Monopoly
Argyle	Mosa*
Plush*	Ram 1*
Vanessa*	Harmony
Parade*	Barblue*
Wabash	Kimona

*Cultivars that do well under both low- and high-maintenance conditions.

Help from the Lawn Institute

The Lawn Institute has prepared a number of fact sheets to help home owners with turf problems. Located in Tennessee, a state where both northern/cool grasses and southern/warm grasses (the latter being predominantly Bermudagrasses, St. Augustinegrass and Zoysia) can be grown, this organization also selects top cultivars of the year for special recognition and will recommend grasses for your area. Fact sheets that deal with problem situations such as "Getting Lawn Grasses and Woody Ornamentals to Live Together" are also available. For information write to The Lawn Institute, County Line Road, Box 108, Pleasant Hill, TN 38578. Enclose a self-addressed stamped envelope.

Rating the Turfgrasses

University of California's Cooperative Extension Service has published a leaflet (#2589, "Selecting the Best Turfgrass"), which compares various grasses with regard to a number of things such as disease and heat tolerance:

HEAT TOLERANCE

Zoysiagrass—most tolerant
Hybrid Bermudagrass
Common Bermudagrass
St. Augustinegrass
Tall Fescue

Creeping Bentgrass
Kentucky Bluegrass
Perennial Ryegrass
Colonial Bentgrass
Red Fescue—least tolerant

DROUGHT TOLERANCE

Hybrid Bermudagrass—most tolerant
Zoysiagrass
Common Bermudagrass
St. Augustinegrass
Tall Fescue
Red Fescue
Kentucky Bluegrass
Perennial Ryegrass
Creeping Bentgrass
Colonial Bentgrass—least tolerant

COLD TOLERANCE (WINTER COLOR PERSISTANCE)

Creeping Bentgrass—most tolerant
Kentucky Bluegrass
Red Fescue
Colonial Bentgrass
Perennial Ryegrass
Tall Fescue
Zoysiagrass
Common Bermudagrass
Hybrid Bermudagrass
St. Augustinegrass—least tolerant

NITROGEN REQUIREMENT

Creeping Bentgrass—most required
Hybrid Bermudagrass
Perennial Ryegrass
Kentucky Bluegrass
Colonial Bentgrass
Common Bermudagrass
St. Augustinegrass
Tall Fescue

Red Fescue
Zoysiagrass—least required

DISEASE INCIDENCE

Creeping Bentgrass—most prone
Colonial Bentgrass
Kentucky Bluegrass
Red Fescue
Perennial Ryegrass
St. Augustinegrass
Hybrid Bermudagrass
Tall Fescue
Zoysiagrass
Common Bermudagrass—least prone

SHADE TOLERANCE

Red Fescue—most tolerant
St. Augustinegrass
Zoysiagrass
Creeping Bentgrass
Colonial Bentgrass
Tall Fescue
Kentucky Bluegrass
Perennial Ryegrass
Hybrid Bermudagrass
Common Bermudagrass—least tolerant

ESTABLISHMENT RATE (TIME NEEDED TO COVER)

Perennial Ryegrass—fastest
Tall Fescue
Common Bermudagrass
Red Fescue
Colonial Bentgrass
Creeping Bentgrass
Kentucky Bluegrass
Hybrid Bermudagrass
St. Augustinegrass
Zoysiagrass—slowest

3

Herbs

THE CULINARY HERBS WE GROW TODAY ARE THE remnants of a vast array of food, medicinal and magical plants used by people since time began. Their history goes back many thousands of years. Medicine gave the science of botany its start; long before people studied plants for their own sake they examined them for the healing or magic they might possess. Some scoff today at the elaborate directions for harvesting that many old herbals gave, yet our ancestors recognized that the potency of plants was highly variable even if they did not fathom the exact cause. The early herbals were mixtures of medical, magical and botanical lore, often illustrated beautifully by artists who rendered the plants more exactly than they were described in words. Only quite recently have these herbals given way to manuals of flora alone, as the eighteenth-century housewife's herb garden and stillroom gave way to the apothecary shop.

"Herb" has several definitions. One is "a flowering plant whose stem above ground does not become woody." The second definition, "such a plant when valued for its medicinal properties, flavor, scent, or the like,"* is the one most of us think of first. This definition could include many plants in addition to the common herbs grown for flavor and

*The Random House Dictionary of the English Language, 2nd ed., unabridged, 1987.

garnish today; the dye plants as well as plants once, but no longer, used medicinally would all qualify as suitable herb-garden subjects.

Most of us no longer count on herbs to heal our cuts or deter misfortune. But their magic remains. Herbal plants are beautiful. They delight the nose as well as the eye, many are drought-resistant with fuzzy leaves that don't appeal to predators. Many (like Fennel, Dill, Mint, Tansy and Thyme) are thought to attract beneficial insects. All of them possess an ancient history of human use. The daily work performed by citizens of a modern technological nation bear little resemblance to the chores of our distant ancestors. The food we eat would hardly be recognized by people from the past; many of the modern roses and irises we plant in our gardens would amaze them as well. They would recognize most herb plants, however, and welcome a cup of mint tea. The herbs we grow offer us a link with our past, a sense of continuity, a tribute to those that lived long before recorded history.

Illustrators of Leonard Fuchs's herbal, *De Historia Stirpium* (1542). Fuchs gave special recognition to his artists by publishing their portraits in the back of his book. Here are Albrecht Mayer making the drawings, Heinrich Füllmaurer preparing the woodblocks and Rudolph Speckle, the master cutter.

PARSLEY, SAGE, ROSEMARY AND THYME

The herbs we grow belong to a number of different plant families (the Lily family gives us Chives and Garlic, the Compositae or Daisy family is represented by Chamomile, Costmary and Tarragon), but two great families stand out—the Mint (Labiatae) and the Parsley (Umbelliferae). Members of the Mint family have cheered the human heart for thousands of years. They are not powerful medicinals but they have long provided comfort and enhanced well-being without producing the harmful side effects that users of Cannabis and Nicotiana experience. The herbalist Culpeper (1616–1654) said of Mint, "Being smelled into, it is comfortable for the head and memory, and a decoction when used as a gargle, cures the mouth and gums when sore." Other members of the family, like Sage and Rosemary, were also believed to strengthen the memory and the stimulating effect many of these herbs produce was thought to help nervous complaints, digestive disorders and even the common cold. The flavor of Mint is still popular in medicines, toothpastes, teas and cordials. The aroma of Mint, Sage, Melissa and others still comforts and refreshes.

MEMBERS OF THE MINT FAMILY GROWN IN HERB GARDENS:

Hyssopus (HYSSOP)
Lavandula (LAVENDER)
Marrubium (HOREHOUND)
Melissa (LEMON BALM)
Mentha (MINT)
Monarda (BERGAMOT, BEE BALM)
Nepeta (CATNIP)
Ocimum (BASIL)
Origanum (MARJORAM)
Rosmarinus (ROSEMARY)
Salvia (SAGE)
Satureja (SAVORY)
Stachys (BETONY; LAMB'S EARS)
Teucrium (GERMANDER)
Thymus (THYME)

The other great family of herb garden plants is the Parsley family, or Umbelliferae, named for the shape of its umbrellalike flowers. More important as food plants than the Mints, members of this family include Carrot, Parsnip and Celery. Also in the family are the poisonous "Hemlocks" (Cicuta and Conium); good reason to avoid eating any members of the Parsley family that cannot be positively identified. Among the Umbelliferae found in our herb gardens:

Anethum (DILL)
Angelica (ANGELICA)
Anthriscus (CHERVIL)
Carum (CARAWAY)
Coriandrum (CORIANDER)
Cuminum (CUMIN)
Foeniculum (FENNEL)
Levisticum (LOVAGE)
Myrrhis (SWEET CICELY)
Petroselinum (PARSLEY)
Pimpinella (ANISE)

HERBS FOR SUNNY, DRY SITES

A number of herbs on this list are native to warm, dry regions and have the gray foliage that often indicates a preference for sunny sites and poor soils and a tolerance of drought. Savory likes a richer (but dry) soil; Borage, Rue and Marjoram like a little more moisture than others listed. Some herbs for a sunny, well-drained site are:

Borago officinalis (BORAGE) A
Hyssopus officinalis (HYSSOP) P—Tolerates a little shade
Lavandula species (LAVENDER) P
Marrubium vulgare (HOREHOUND) P—Tender
Origanum dictamnus (DITTANY OF CRETE) P—Tender; not hardy north
Origanum majorana (SWEET MARJORAM) P—Tender
O. vulgare (WILD MARJORAM, OREGANO) P
Rosmarinus officinalis (ROSEMARY) P—Tender
Ruta graveolens (RUE) P
Salvia species (SAGE) P—Tender
Santolina chamaecyparissus (LAVENDER COTTON) P—Tender
Satureja spp. (SAVORY) A and P
Thymus species (THYME) P

A—Annual   P—Perennial

"Not every soil can bear all things" (Virgil). Some herbs, such as Sweet Woodruff, Sweet Cicely, Tansy, Angelica, Dill, Basil, Lovage, Chervil and most Mints, favor slightly acid soils. Most of the herbs listed above, however, prefer the limy soils of their native lands. A soil test will determine the pH of your herb plot, and the addition of ground limestone can bring the pH up to the 6.5–7.5 level enjoyed by many herbs.

HERBS FOR A SHADY GARDEN

Many favorite herbs are happiest in full sun; here are a dozen to try in partial shade. Most of the following appreciate soils on the moist side, although Lemon Balm, which also likes a limy soil, does well in a fairly dry garden. Angelica and Lovage can reach 6 feet and Comfrey half that height; others are lower-growing.

Alchemilla vulgaris (LADY'S MANTLE) P
Allium schoenoprasum (CHIVES) P
Angelica officinalis (ANGELICA) B, P
Anthriscus cerefolium (CHERVIL) A
Galium odoratum (SWEET WOODRUFF) P
Lamium spp. (DEAD NETTLE, ARCHANGEL) P*
Levisticum officinale (LOVAGE) P
Melissa officinalis (LEMON BALM) P
Mentha sp. (MINT) P
Myrrhis odorata (SWEET CICELY) P
Petroselinum sativum (PARSLEY) B
Symphytum officinale (COMFREY) P

A—Annual   P—Perennial   B—Biennial
*Dead Nettles were once used medicinally as well as for culinary purposes.

Bee Balm, Costmary and Tarragon will also tolerate some shade.

HERBS FOR LIMITED SPACE

Herbs such as Angelica and Lovage grow 4 or more feet tall and are not suitable for small herb gardens. Some low-growing herbs (starred plants make good ground covers) are:

Ajuga reptans* (BUGLEWEED) P
Alchemilla vulgaris (LADY'S MANTLE) P

Allium schoenoprasum (CHIVES) P
Anthriscus cerefolium (CHERVIL) A—hardy
Asarum canadense* (WILD GINGER) P
Calendula officinalis (POT MARIGOLD) A—hardy
Chamaemelum nobile* (CHAMOMILE) P
Crocus sativus (SAFFRON CROCUS) P
Galium odoratum* (SWEET WOODRUFF) P
Hyssopus officinalis (HYSSOP) P
Lavandula angustifolia 'Compacta' and 'Nana' (DWARF
    LAVENDER) P
Marrubium vulgare (HOREHOUND) P—tender
Petroselinum sativum (PARSLEY) B
Salvia officinalis 'Compacta' (SAGE) P
Satureja montana (WINTER SAVORY) P
Symphytum grandiflorum* (DWARF COMFREY) P
Teucrium chamaedrys* (GERMANDER) P
Thymus serpyllum* (CREEPING LEMON THYME) and T. vulgaris
    (Garden Thyme) P
Tropaeolum minus (DWARF NASTURTIUM) A
Viola odorata* (SWEET VIOLET) P—tender

A—Annual   B—Biennial   P—Perennial
*Small native plants suitable for a shady, woodland herb garden include Ginseng, Bloodroot and Goldthread. Native American Wild Ginger was an Indian medicinal plant as well as a tea plant.

HERBS FOR LOW HEDGES AND EDGING

Buxus sempervirens 'Suffruticosa' (Edging Box) is a traditional edging plant used to define patterns in formal herb gardens. Its dark green foliage contrasts attractively with many of the gray-green herbs. Other herbs (several, such as Lavandula and Santolina, have dwarf forms) to use as low hedges or edging include:

Alchemilla (LADY'S MANTLE)
Hyssopus (HYSSOP)
Lavandula (LAVENDER)
Myrtus communis 'Compacta' (MYRTLE)
Rosmarinus (ROSEMARY)
Santolina spp. (SANTOLINA)
Teucrium (GERMANDER)
Thymus (THYME)

WINTER WINDOWSILL HERBS

The coming of winter doesn't have to mean the end of fresh herbs. The following plants can be grown on a sunny windowsill. Provide adequate humidity and cool temperatures for best results.

Allium (CHIVES)
Laurus (SWEET BAY)*
Marrubium (HOREHOUND)
Mentha (PEPPERMINT)
Ocimum (BASIL)—Select a small variety; Opal Basil is also suitable. Some cuttings will root in water; plants may get leggy if not enough light is available, but the flavor will be fine.
Origanum (SWEET MARJORAM)
Petroselinum (PARSLEY)
Rosmarinus (ROSEMARY)*—Blue flowers a bonus in winter.
Satureja (SAVORY)
Thymus (THYME)

*Good year-round houseplants.

GROWING HERBS FROM SEED

Some herbs are difficult, if not impossible, to raise from seed, yet seed merchants continue to offer them for sale. Do not attempt to grow the following from seed:

Artemisia (TARRAGON)—Culinary Tarragon does not set seed. Seed sold as Tarragon is useless as a flavoring.
Lavandula (LAVENDER)—Seed does not grow true to type.
Mentha x piperita (PEPPERMINT)—Peppermint is a sterile hybrid. All Mints are best raised from cuttings.
Origanum (SWEET MARJORAM)—Much of the Origanum sold is O. vulgare or Wild Marjoram
Rosmarinus (ROSEMARY)—Very low germination rate.
Thymus (THYME)—English Thyme cannot be raised from seed.

Below are ten herbs that may be raised from seed (remember that germination rates will average only 50 to 60 percent):

Anethum (DILL)
Anthriscus (CHERVIL)
Borago (BORAGE)
Coriandrum (CORIANDER)
Melissa (LEMON BALM)
Ocimum (BASIL)
Petroselinum (PARSLEY)
Rumex (GARDEN SORREL)
Salvia (SAGE)
Satureja (WINTER SAVORY)

HERBS FOR THE TEA GARDEN

Some commonly grown herbs also make interesting teas; do not steep more than several minutes and expect a pale color. Drink these and all herbal teas in moderation.

Foeniculum vulgare (FENNEL)—This herb makes a licorice-flavored tea that was given to children and adults for stomach ache and indigestion. Since the time of the ancient Greeks (and perhaps earlier) dieters have used Fennel tea and chewed Fennel seeds to suppress the appetite.*

Galium odoratum (SWEET WOODRUFF)—Use dried leaves to make a sweet, vanilla-flavored tea once thought to be a mild aphrodisiac. Cleavers, also a Galium, has long been thought (like Fennel) to be a slimming herb.

Melissa officinalis (LEMON BALM)—Melissa makes a tea with a hint of citrus and combines well with other teas; try it with Mint or Rosemary. Long thought to stimulate the appetite and help digestion.

Mentha suaveolens (APPLE MINT)—Many Mints make good teas, but Apple Mint is especially recommended by herbalists. Mint teas were thought to spur the appetite. Pliny remarked that Peppermint "stirred up the mind and taste to a greedy desire of meat." Also thought to aid digestion.

---

*William Coles (1657): "Both the seeds, leaves and roots of our Garden Fennel are much used in drinks and broths for those that are grown fat, to abate their unwieldiness and to cause them to grow more gaunt and lank."

Nepeta cataria (CATNIP)—Soothing Catnip tea was once a favorite in many parts of England before the introduction of tea from China. Comforts those with colds and fever.

Ocimum basilicum (BASIL)—There are many kinds of Basil (including lemon-scented 'Citriodorum') and most kinds make a fragrant, delicious tea once given for depression and nausea. Add a few Basil leaves to flavor regular tea.

Petroselinum crispum (PARSLEY)—Make pleasant Parsley tea from freshly dried sprigs (one minute in the microwave); the tea is said to be a good source of iron. Drink in moderation.

Rosmarinus officinalis (ROSEMARY)—Spicy Rosemary tea once was thought to revive a failing memory. Add a little lemon or honey. Drink in moderation only; some think this old culinary herb belongs on the "questionable" list.

Salvia officinalis (SAGE)—Fine tea in its own right (it is said the Chinese accepted it eagerly when introduced into their country); also an ancient medicinal tea. Sage tea is reputed to ease headaches and sore throats and improve appetites and failing memories.

Thymus vulgaris (GARDEN THYME)—Thyme makes a strong, zesty tea; T. citriodorus (Lemon Thyme) is lemon-scented. Thyme tea has been recommended for many ailments, from sore throat to depression and hangovers.

Drying Herbs

Microwave—Several minutes
Oven—overnight (with pilot on)
Air—About 10 days. Lay herbs on clean paper (single layer) and put in a dry, warm, *shady* place.

North American Teas

The glossy leaves of an Asian shrub, Camellia sinensis, gives us commercial tea, the world's most important caffeine beverage. (This genus also gives us the beautiful ornamental shrub of southern climates, C. japonica.) Long before Asian tea was exported, people in other parts of the world brewed tea from native plants, and native teas continued to be brewed where Asian tea was scarce, such as in colonial America. Native Americans and colonists alike put the leaves, bark and berries of many native plants into the teapot to brew drinks that could give pleasure as well as relieve pain.

Betula nigra (BLACK BIRCH)—Dried, powdered bark of this tree was (and still is) used as a healthful and agreeable drink.*

Ceanothus americanus (NEW JERSEY TEA)—Considered one of the best substitutes for tea during the American Revolution; sometimes called "Liberty Tea."

Eupatorium perfoliatum (BONESET)—A medicinal, bitter tea that was sometimes flavored with Mint and served to those suffering from fever and colds.

Gaultheria procumbens (TEABERRY, MOUNTAIN TEA)—Aromatic Wintergreen makes a sweet, pink tea though leaves must be steeped for some time. Old-time remedy for colds and fever, the drink was also called "Pioneer Tea."

Ilex vomitoria (YAUPON HOLLY)—Leaves contain considerable caffeine (the berries are toxic) and were roasted and brewed into tea by Indians and colonists.

Ledum groenlandicum (LABRADOR TEA)—Fragrant leaves of this evergreen shrub make a rose-colored tea used by many tribes and trailblazers.

Lindera benzoin (SPICEBUSH)—Simmer leaves and twigs 5 or more minutes to make this spicy brew.

Monarda didyma (BEE BALM OR OSWEGO TEA)—A minty tea used by Native Americans and eighteenth-century colonists.

Rhus glabra (SMOOTH SUMAC)—Berries were gathered by native Americans and colonists to make a lemon-flavored tea.

Solidago odora (SWEET GOLDEN ROD)—The fragrant leaves of this Goldenrod made an anise-flavored beverage known to Pennsylvania Germans as "Blue Mountain Tea."

Viburnum cassinoides (WITHEROD)—A drink known as "Appalachian Tea" is prepared from this handsome shrub.

*Black Birch Tea is used as a vitamin supplement, a treatment for arthritis and other ailments, as well as for a refreshing drink.

Herbal Teas to Avoid

Many people turn to herbal teas in an effort to lead healthier life-styles and avoid caffeine found in other beverages. This is commendable if one keeps in mind that many plants contain substances that may be harmful if consumed in quantity, and some plants found in herbal blends are known to be toxic. Ten plants that are best avoided in teas because all contain harmful chemicals are:

Acorus calamus (SWEET FLAG)
Chamaemelum (CHAMOMILE) and Matricaria (Sweet False Chamomile)—These two closely related herbs may cause allergic reactions in sensitive people.
Echium spp. (VIPER'S BUGLOSS)*
Lobelia (INDIAN TOBACCO)—This plant is found in teas promoted to help smokers quit. All Lobelias are toxic and contain alkaloids similar to nicotine.
Mentha pulegium (PENNYROYAL)
Sassafras (SASSAFRAS)
Senecio spp. (RAGWORT, TANSY RAGWORT, GROUNDSEL)*
Symphytum (COMFREY)
Tanacetum (TANSY)
Tussilago (COLTSFOOT)

*Consumption of these plants in herbal teas is associated with an incurable liver disease.

Tanacetum vulgare (Tansy). Reputed to deter pests, especially ants, Tansy is no longer recommended for the teapot.

A Cook's List

Culinary uses for some favorite herbs:

Anethum (DILL)—Use fresh leaves on poached fish, all kinds of salads, many soups and cheeses, beans, beets and cabbage. Seeds are used as a pickling spice, in breads, gravies, soups and vegetable dishes. Leaves lose much of their flavor when dried.

Angelica (ANGELICA)—Place leaves in water used to poach seafood. Stems may be cooked or prepared with sugar like rhubarb; roots sometimes candied.

Anthriscus (CHERVIL)—Add a few young leaves to salads. Use to flavor fish dishes and soup.

Artemisia (TARRAGON)—Use in egg dishes, with fish and chicken and in sauces such as tartar and bearnaise. Cut up a few fresh leaves in a salad, use dried leaves in salad dressing. Use in mushroom soup, tomato soup and fish chowders.

Borago (BORAGE)—Use the young leaves and flowers in salads; garnish drinks with flowers. Old herbalists wrote that Borage banishes gloom and melancholy.

Foeniculum (FENNEL)—Use a few young leaves in salads. Leaves also flavor fish and soups. Lightly steam stems to eat as a fresh vegetable. Fennel seed is also much used in salads, shrimp boil, beef stew and cakes and cookies.

Mentha spp. (MINT)—Make a Mint sauce for lamb. Sprinkle a little on peas. Use in eggplant dishes as did ancient Romans. Make Mint tea. Garnish drinks and fruit salads.

Ocimum (BASIL)—Sprinkle fresh Basil leaves on fresh tomato slices. Use fresh or dried Basil in spaghetti sauce. Sprinkle on omelets. Bake with carrots. Use with fatty fish (such as tuna). Make pesto!

Origanum (SWEET MARJORAM AND OREGANO)—O. majorana is the culinary marjoram. O. heracleoticum is thought by many to be the culinary Oregano. O. vulgare, or Wild Marjoram, widely advertised as oregano, has little flavor. Use in tomato dishes and sauces, in omelets and on pizza. Good on green beans. Rub on meat before roasting and sprinkle on minestrone, tomato juice and salads.

Rosmarinus (ROSEMARY)—Rosemary was thought to improve

the memory (as was Sage) and it became an emblem of fidelity worn at weddings and funerals. Use Rosemary with meat (excellent with lamb) and poultry and add to water when cooking cauliflower, peas and spinach. Chop a few fresh leaves into potato dishes and scrambled eggs; try a fresh leaf in a fruit cup.

Salvia (SAGE)—Use in stuffings and with cheeses. Excellent with pork (a must in sausages) and duck. Put a little Sage in a beef stew.

Thymus (THYME)—Thyme is a must in stuffings and clam chowder; use also with eggplant, mushrooms, onions, potatoes, squash and beets. Sprinkle a little on fish before cooking. Use in cream cheese and cottage cheese.

Origanum vulgare (Wild Marjoram). A hardy, variable and often weedy species. O. majorana, a tender perennial, is the culinary herb Marjoram.

HERBES DE PROVENCE

Make this savory mixture to use in stews, soups, dressings and dips:

3 tablespoons each of basil, marjoram, savory and thyme
1½ teaspoons rosemary
½ teaspoon each of fennel seed and sage

Mix well. Makes about ½ cup.

ROSEMARY CHICKEN

Mix cornflake crumbs with generous amounts of grated Parmesan cheese and Rosemary. Dip chicken breasts (bone in) in lemon juice (or wine or water) and roll in cornflake mixture until well coated. Bake, uncovered, at 350 F degrees for one hour.

Basil Varieties

Most gardeners are familiar with Purple or Dark Opal Basil, often grown as an ornamental, and many have noticed that garden centers sometimes offer several types of green-leaved Basil. Actually, there are over one hundred species of Basil, although Ocimum basilicum is the Basil usually grown in gardens. However, there are many varieties of O. basilicum in cultivation. Fox Hill Farm of Parma, Mich., sells over twenty types of Basil:

Bush Basil—O. basilicum 'Minimum,' a small, 18-inch tall cultivar.

Camphor Basil—A nonculinary species, Camphor Basil is a 4-foot shrub native to Africa. Use for repelling moths.

Cinnamon Basil—Variety of O. basilicum; grows 2 feet tall and has a cinnamon flavor. Good dessert herb.

Dark Opal—Vivid purple Basil developed at the University of Connecticut about 30 years ago. Listed as O. basilicum 'Purpurascens' in *Hortus Third,* use this Basil to brighten salads.

Festival Sweet—Fox Hill's Basil Festival Basil. Check with the Farm for this year's Festival date.

Fine-Leaf—Perhaps a variety of O. basilicum 'Minimum,' this Basil grows about 2 feet tall and has a delicate, sweet flavor. A bit more tolerant of frost than other Basils; best for pot culture.

Genovese—Variegated (green/purple) variety of O. basilicum.

Holy Basil—A sacred species native to India; sharp clove scent. Grows about 2 feet tall.

Ka Prou—A variety native to Thailand.

Lemon Basil—Thought by some to be a hybrid although it produces true from seed. Two feet tall with strong lemon flavor. *Hortus Third* lists 'Citriodorum,' a lemon-scented variety of O. basilicum.

Lettuce Leaf—Large, wavy leaves are produced by this variety of O. basilicum.

Licorice—Open-branched variety of O. basilicum that grows to 2½ feet; flavor similar to French Tarragon.

Nano Compatto—Vero Basil. Compact plant that grows about a foot tall and has a strong anise-clove undertone in its flavor.

Peruvian—A New World Basil?

Piccolo Verde—Fino Basil. The O. basilicum variety said to be the authentic pesto Basil. Light, sweet, with a touch of anise.

Purple Ruffles—Wavy purple foliage of excellent color and flavor.

Silver Fox—Variegated leaf with a silver edge developed at Fox Hill Farm.

Spicy Globe—Very small (10 inches tall) and spicy.

Thrysiflora—A very sweet Basil with a pyramidal growth habit.

Tiny Leaf Purple—Short and small with purple leaves.

Tree Basil—A nonculinary fiber plant.

Read more about Basils in Marilyn Hampstead's (founder of Fox Hill Farm) paperback, *The Basil Book,* available from Fox Hill Farm. See "Sources for Herbs," pages 154–155.

CARROTS WITH BASIL

Scrape carrots and cut into pennies. Put in a casserole with a little water and plenty of basil. Dot with a small amount of margarine. Cover and bake 45 minutes at 350 F degrees. Check midway and add a little more water if necessary.

Risky Basil?

Like many of our other culinary herbs, Basil once had other important uses. It was thought to aid digestion, cure earaches, combat fungus infections, aid in childbirth and increase the flow of milk. It was used to treat those with nervous ailments and was highly regarded for its ability to calm patients without sedating them. Some used Basil to perfume the body. Others used it specifically to repel flies. However, some physicians sounded cautionary notes hundreds of years ago when they claimed Basil hurt the stomach, dulled the eyes and even brought on madness. More recently, researchers inform us that Basil contains estragole, a natural pesticide that, if consumed excessively, may cause cancer.[*] (Comfrey also contains a natural pesticide, symphytine, and a daily cup of Comfrey tea should be avoided.) When considering this new information, I note that bacon, peanut butter, raw mushrooms, diet cola, wine and beer are also

---

[*]Based on research by B. Ames et al. and R. Wilson and E. Crouch, *Science,* 17 April 1987.

on the risky list. Since I am willing to forego most of those things, perhaps it's safe to eat a little Basil now and then. In general, all herb teas should be enjoyed in moderation, as should regular tea and coffee, not to mention ethyl alcohol.

Ocimum sp. (Basil). Basils are native to the warm regions of the Old World. They have been used medicinally, to repel insects and for flavoring food.

DIOSCORIDES'S GARDEN: A GREEK MEDICINE KIT

Dioscorides, a first-century Greek physician, collected plants in many countries during the years he was physician to the Roman army. His *De Materia Medica* remained the authority in medicinal botany for many centuries. The National Herb Garden in Washington, D.C., grows over 70 plants in their Dioscorides Garden. Some of the most familiar are:

Achillea ptarmica (SNEEZEWORT)
Aloe vera (BURN PLANT)
Anchusa tinctoria (DYER'S ALKANET)
Anethum graveolens (DILL)
Artemisia campestris (ARTEMISIA)
Brassica rapa (TURNIP)
Colchicum autumnale (AUTUMN CROCUS)
Conium maculatum (POISON HEMLOCK)
Coriandrum sativum (CORIANDER)
Crocus sativus (SAFFRON CROCUS)

Dipsacus fullonum (COMMON TEASEL)
Euphorbia spp. (SPURGE)
Foeniculum vulgare (FENNEL)
Gladiolus communis (GLADIOLI, CORN FLAG, SWORD LILY)
Hedera helix (IVY)
Inula helenium (ELECAMPANE)
Lilium candidum (MADONNA LILY)
Marrubium vulgare (HOREHOUND)
Melissa officinalis (MELISSA, BALM)
Nerium oleander (OLEANDER)
Ocimum basilicum (BASIL)
Origanum spp. (WINTER SWEET AND POT MARJORAM)
Ricinus communis (CASTOR-OIL PLANT)
Ruta graveolens (RUE)
Papaver somniferum (OPIUM POPPY)
Piper nigrum (BLACK PEPPER)
Plantago psyllium (PLANTAIN, FLEAWORT)
Platanus orientalis (ORIENTAL SYCAMORE OR PLANE)
Sambucus ebulus (DWARF ELDERBERRY)
Saponaria officinalis (SOAPWORT)
Smilax sp. (GREENBRIER)
Vinca minor (PERIWINKLE)
Vitex agnus-castus (CHASTE TREE)
Zingiber officinale (GINGER)

Although not on the National Herb Garden list, G. M. Fosler and J. R. Kamp, in their extension bulletin "Daylilies for Every Garden" (University of Illinois College of Agriculture), list Hemerocallis flava (Lemon Lily) as a plant mentioned in *De Materia Medica*. Daylily petals were eaten as painkillers in ancient China.

University of California's Chinese Medicinal Herb Garden

This garden, planted on the Berkeley campus in 1987, was designed with the cooperation of staff from the Guangzhou Garden of Traditional Chinese Medicine, Guangzhou, People's Republic of China. It is the first garden of its kind in the United States and contains over 100 species of medicinal plants. Among them are:

Aconitum carmichaelii (MONKSHOOD)
Acorus gramineus (GRASSY-LEAVED SWEET FLAG)

Agrimonia pilosa var. japonica (AGRIMONY)
Allium fistulosum (JAPANESE BUNCHING ONION), A. sativum
    (GARLIC) and A. tuberosum (GARLIC CHIVE, CHINESE CHIVE)
Aloe vera (BURN PLANT)
Artemisia vulgaris (MUGWORT)
Aster tataricus (TARTARIAN ASTER)
Belamcanda chinensis (BLACKBERRY LILY)
Catharanthus roseus (ROSE OR MADAGASCAR PERIWINKLE)
Chelidonium majus (CELANDINE)
Chrysanthemum indicum (CHRYSANTHEMUM)
Clematis chinensis (CLEMATIS)
Coriandrum sativum (CORIANDER, CHINESE PARSLEY)
Datura stramonium (THORN APPLE)
Dianthus chinensis (RAINBOW PINK)
Ephedra sinica (EPHEDRA)
Epimedium grandiflorum (EPIMEDIUM, BARRENWORT)
Euphorbia pekingensis (SPURGE)
Foeniculum vulgare (FENNEL)
Gomphrena globosa (GLOBE AMARANTH)
Gossypium arboreum (TREE COTTON)
Lemna minor (COMMON DUCKWEED)
Levisticum officinale (LOVAGE)
Lilium brownii
Lobelia chinensis (LOBELIA)
Mentha haplocalyx (MINT)
Ophiopogon japonicus (DWARF LILYTURF)
Papaver somniferum (OPIUM POPPY)
Piper nigrum (BLACK PEPPER)
Plantago asiatica (PLANTAIN, RIBWORT)
Platycodon grandiflorus (BALLOON FLOWER)
Polygonum cuspidatum (JAPANESE KNOTWEED)
Rheum officinale (RHUBARB)
Sanguisorba officinalis (GREAT BURNET, BURNET BLOODWORT)
Saxifraga stolonifera (STRAWBERRY GERANIUM)*
Smilax sp. (GREENBRIER, CATBRIER)
Zingiber officinale (GINGER)

*A familiar houseplant for hanging baskets, native to eastern Asia, and hardy outdoors fairly far north, especially with some protection.

Among the trees in this medicinal garden are: Gingko biloba, Magnolia quinquepeta and Morus alba (White Mulberry).

HERBS OF THE BIBLE

And Isaiah said, take a lump of figs. And they took and laid it on the boil and he recovered.

(2 KINGS 20:7)

James A. Duke, in his book *Medicinal Plants of the Bible,* lists 142 species of plants mentioned in the Bible that were known to have medicinal value. Few biblical references actually describe an herbal cure, as does the reference above, but without doubt the healing qualities of many plants were well known. Ten herbs commonly grown today that are mentioned in the Bible are:

Anethum graveolens (DILL)—Thought to be the biblical Anise.
Artemisia spp. (WORMWOOD)
Coriandrum sativum (CORIANDER)
Crocus sativus (SAFFRON)
Cuminum cyminum (CUMIN)
Laurus noblis (BAY)
Marrubium spp. (HOREHOUND)—Much confusion surrounds the biblical word "Hyssop," which is identified as Origanum by some. Marrubium seems a more likely candidate.
Mentha longifolia (HORSEMINT)
Ruta graveolens (RUE)
Salvia judaica (SAGE)—Believed to be the inspiration for the seven-branched menorah.

FIVE BITTER HERBS OF PASSOVER

There is much disagreement over the "bitter herbs." Moldenke believes they were probably Lactuca (Lettuce), Cichorium (Chicory), Taraxacum (Dandelion), Rumex (Sorrel) and perhaps Mint or Watercress. Another list includes:

Armoracia (HORSERADISH)—Used in Greek cuisine of 1000 B.C., though some authorities do not believe this plant was known to the ancient Hebrews.
Coriandrum (CORIANDER)—One of the most ancient herbs; mentioned in the Old Testament (Exodus 16:31, Numbers 11:7).
Lactuca (LETTUCE)—No longer known in the wild, this widely grown salad plant has many varieties.

Marrubium (HOREHOUND)—Name thought to be derived from marrob, a Hebrew word meaning "bitter juice."

Urtica (NETTLE)—These widely distributed plants have been used as potherbs, in medicinal products and to make dyes and fibers.

PLANTS OF THE DRUIDS

The early Celtic priests known as Druids were part magician, astronomer, witch doctor and perhaps even metalworkers. There is little doubt they possessed much knowledge of plant medicinals and trees and plants that played a vital role in ritual.

Seven Sacred Plants:

Aconitum (WOLFSBANE)
Anomene (PULSATILLA)
Hyoscyamus (HENBANE)
Primula (PRIMROSE)
Trifolium (CLOVER)
Verbena (VERVAIN)
Viscum (MISTLETOE)—chief herb

Seven Important Trees:

Betula (BIRCH)
Corylus (HAZEL)
Fagus (BEECH)
Ilex (HOLLY)
Quercus* (OAK)
Sorbus (MT. ASH)
Taxus (YEW)

*It is generally thought that the oak was the chief sacred tree of the Druids (some say the name "druid" means "wise man of the oak") and that religious rituals were performed in oak groves. "Magic" wands, used in prophecy, were made of yew, mountain ash or hazel.

Verbena hastata (Blue Vervain, Simpler's Joy). An attractive native perennial, Blue Vervain was also used medicinally. V. officinalis, the European Vervain, is an ancient medicinal and magic plant.

PLANTS THAT REPEL DEMONS

Our ancestors believed that what today we call bad "luck" was the work of evil spirits. They depended on plants, the great providers of food and medicine, also to protect them from demons and witches and even thunder and lightning. Among those considered powerful talismans against evil:

Allium* (ONION AND GARLIC)—Vampires, beware!

Artemisia (MUGWORT)—Even believed to protect against sore eyes.

Hypericum** (ST. JOHN'S WORT)—Hang in home to ward off thunder and evil spirits.

Rosa (ROSE)—Prayer beads (Rosaries) were named for the rose and often made from the dried paste of rose petals.

Rosmarinus (ROSEMARY)—A sprig under your pillow protects from evil dreams.

Ruta** (RUE)—Keeps away plague as well as the devil.

Sempervivum (HOUSE LEEK)—Charlemagne ordered them planted on rooftops throughout his empire to protect householders against lightning.

Verbascum (MULLEIN)—Planted by monks in the Middle Ages to deter evil spirits.

Vinca (PERIWINKLE)—Protects home from evil and promotes harmonious relationships.

Viscum (MISTLETOE)—Protects against witches and opens all locks.

*Believed to be the "Moly" used by Ulysses to protect himself from the wiles of Circe. Some claim Ulysses also carried Mullein.
**Much used by exorcists in the sixteenth century.

Allium moly (Lily Leek). Southern Europeans believed this yellow-flowered spring bloomer brought good luck.

Sempervivum sp. (Houseleek). Another plant once used as a charm, Houseleek was put on roofs to ward off lightning.

The peach tree (China) and the holly tree also allegedly protected against demons and witchcraft.

OLD STREWING HERBS

Several hundred years ago it was the custom to cover floors with straw in winter and herbs and flowers in summer. This practice continued into the seventeenth century. Both royal households and humbler quarters used strewing herbs to discourage infection and vermin and make rooms smell good. (Other plants, like rushes and swordgrass, were arranged along walls; floor herbs were replaced by straw mats and then carpets and tapestries replaced wall rushes.) Thomas Tusser, in his book *Five Hundred Points of Good Husbandry* (1577), lists 20 plants to strew on floors. Among the favorites:

Acorus calamus (SWEET FLAG, SWEET SEDGE)
Chamaemelum nobile (CHAMOMILE)
Chrysanthemum balsamita (COSTMARY)
Filipendula ulmaria (MEADOWSWEET)—A favorite of Queen
    Elizabeth.
Foeniculum vulgare (FENNEL)
Hyssopus officinalis (HYSSOP)
Mentha spicata and M. pulegium (SPEARMINT AND
    PENNYROYAL)
Origanum spp. (MARJORAM)
Rosmarinus officinalis (ROSEMARY)
Tanacetum vulgare (TANSY)
Teucrium chamaedrys (GERMANDER)

THE GREAT WOUNDWORTS

Many plants have been used throughout history to arrest bleeding and promote healing. Modern science has verified that some of them do have astringent qualities and possible antibiotic action. Eleven famous woundworts are:

Achillea millefolium (YARROW)—Named for Achilles, who used the plant to cure his battle wounds.

Alchemilla vulgaris (LADY'S MANTLE)—Once considered one of the best wound herbs, the generic name of this member of the Rose family is derived from the word alchemy.

Arnica montana (ARNICA)—Sometimes grown in rock gardens, this golden-flowered member of the Daisy family has long been a remedy for wounds and sores.

Centaurium erythraea (CENTAURY)—Leaves and flowers made an antiseptic medication for "fresh or old wounds and ulcers." Also used to treat snakebite and fever.

Hypericum perforatum (ST. JOHN'S WORT)—Long thought to cure sores and stop bleeding.

Prunella vulgaris (SELFHEAL, HEAL-ALL)—Other common names for this herb are "Sicklewort" and "Hook-Heal."

Sanguisorba officinalis (BURNET)—Another member of the great Rose family, Burnet was also called "Bloodwort." The name Sanguisorba means "blood stopping."

Solidago virgaurea (EUROPEAN GOLDENROD)—The name Solidago comes from the Greek and means "to make solid or whole." Stem, leaves and flowers were crushed and applied to stop bleeding and prevent infection.

Stachys officinalis (BETONY)—Sometimes called "Woundwort," Betony leaves were used as poultices.

Symphytum officinale (COMFREY)—Other common names are "Healing Herb" and "Boneset"; poultices made from leaves and roots.

Vinca spp. (PERIWINKLE)—Common Periwinkle and Madagascar Periwinkle (put in the genus Catharanthus by some) have long been used in wound healing. Drugs from the latter plant are used today in chemotherapy.

Ten other plants employed for the same purposes were Agrimony, Foxglove, Germander, Herb Robert, Horehound, Lythrum, Madonna Lily,

Plantain, Sage and Solomon's Seal. There are others! Sometimes mixtures of herbs were used.

Alchemilla vulgaris (Lady's Mantle). Roundish gray leaves that catch the dew and delicate chartreuse flowers make this old healing herb a handsome garden subject.

HERBAL REMEDIES AND APHRODISIACS

Herbal Cold Remedies

The local flora, until recently humanity's only drugstore, provided us with relief from our various ills. Hundreds of plants were described in old herbals and Native American lore as being effective against that ancient scourge, the common cold, and it is certain that some of them were. The following plants turn up regularly on lists and in recipes of plants that once brought comfort to those afflicted with coughs and colds; some of them are used today in modern preparations.

Althaea officinalis* (MARSH MALLOW)—Root used.
Borage officinalis (BORAGE)—Flowers/leaves used.
Ephedra sp. (EPHEDRA)—Branches used in Chinese medicine for thousands of years; source of modern drug ephedrine, now made semisynthetically.
Glechoma hederacea (GROUND IVY)—Flowers/leaves used.
Inula helenium (ELECAMPANE)—Root used.
Marrubium vulgare (HOREHOUND)—Flowers/leaves used.

*Officinalis or officinale indicates that the plant was recognized as an important medicinal.

Pinus sp. (PINE)—Europeans and Native Americans both used pine needles and buds to make cold medications.

Prunus serotina and P. virginiana (WILD BLACK CHERRY AND CHOKECHERRY)—Native American remedy; bark used; Cherry was also used in ancient Egypt, Greece and Rome.

Sambucus nigra (EUROPEAN ELDER)—Flowers used.

Symphytum officinale (COMFREY)—Whole plant used.

Thymus sp. (THYME)—Entire plant used.

Tilia sp. (LINDEN, LIME, BASSWOOD)—Flowers used.

Tussilago farfara (COLTSFOOT)—Name comes from tussis, a cough; all parts of the plant used.

Verbascum sp. (MULLEIN)—Flowers used.

Viola sp. (SWEET VIOLET AND HEARTSEASE OR WILD PANSY)—Flowers used.

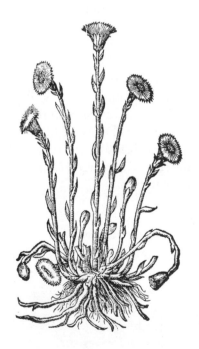 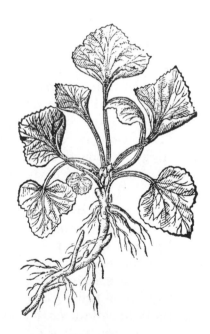

Tussilago farfara (Coltsfoot). Golden flowers appear before the leaves in early spring. Coltsfoot was once used to prepare a popular cough remedy.

Symphytum officinale (Common Comfrey). Comfrey was formerly recommended as a tea for pulmonary complaints and as an external dressing for wounds and broken bones. Common Comfrey is a large perennial; there is a variegated cultivar.

Baldness Remedies

Old remedies for baldness were chuckled at for years, but lately American Cyanamid and Upjohn, among others, have brought new antibaldness drugs to market. These drugs (Minoxidil and Viprostol) increase blood flow to the skin. The following plants have long been used in preparations to promote the growth of hair. Some, like Savin (Juniperus sabina) and Nettles, were known to increase the flow of blood.

Achillea (YARROW)
Adiantum (MAIDENHAIR FERN)
Anagallis (PIMPERNEL)
Artemisia (SOUTHERNWOOD)*
Juniperus (SAVIN)
Petroselinum (PARSLEY)
Ruta (RUE)
Salvia (SAGE)
Tilia (LINDEN)
Urtica (NETTLE)

*Southernwood (A. abrotanum) was also known as "Lad's Love" because it was once used in an ointment that young men applied to promote the growth of a beard.

Aphrodisiacs

People in every culture throughout history have made note of favorite aphrodisiacs; the use of Mandrake as an aphrodisiac is mentioned in the Bible. Modern medicine has tended to discount most claims although recently several libido-boosting substances (including yohimbine, a drug derived from the bark of an African tree) have been the subjects of serious scientific research. At least some of the following plants, all thought at one time to be aphrodisiacs, will provide good nutrition, if nothing more.

Allium spp. (ONION AND LEEK)
Apium graveolens (CELERY)
Asparagus officinalis (ASPARAGUS)
Coriandrum sativum (CORIANDER SEEDS)—Many other seeds and nuts were recommended as aphrodisiacs, including Sesame, Anise, Dill, Chestnuts, Hazelnuts* and Pine Nuts.
Galium odoratum (SWEET WOODRUFF)
Ipomoea batatas (SWEET POTATO)**
Mentha spp. (MINT)—Mint was thought to be an aphrodisiac since ancient times, as were other members of the Mint family, such as Catnip, Savory and Basil.
Panax spp. (GINSENG)
Pastinaca sativa (PARSNIP)
Persea americana (AVOCADO)
Phoenix dactylifera (DATE PALM)
Polygonatum multiflorum (SOLOMON'S SEAL)
Vanilla planifolia (VANILLA ORCHID)—The family name Orchidaceae means "testicles" in Greek; an orchid is one ingredient of the Indian aphrodisiac salep.
Zingiber officinale (GINGER)

*Hazelnuts are a good source of zinc, thought to be a libido enhancer in both sexes.
**Shakespeare knew this one, and has Falstaff exclaim, "Let the sky rain potatoes!"

Anaphrodisiacs

What to do if aphrodisiacs worked too well? The following plants were used in preparations to cool ardor:

Angelica (ANGELICA)—Besides dispelling lust in the young, the candied stems of this versatile herb were thought to quench a desire for alcohol.

Cannabis (HEMP)
Coffea arabica (COFFEE)*
Humulus lupulus (HOP)
Lavandula (LAVENDER)—A Victorian favorite.
Nymphaea alba (WHITE WATER LILY)
Ruta graveolens (RUE)
Vitex agnus-castus (CHASTE TREE)

*New research from the University of Michigan tells us that coffee drinking and sexual activity may be "positively correlated."

Angelica archangelica (Angelica). This Eurasian species was highly thought of as a magical, medicinal and culinary plant. North America's native Angelica is A. atropurpurea.

PLANT AROMAS

For thousands of years herbalists have known that certain plant aromas could affect people and scents were used to calm the agitated and energize the depressed. Now science is taking a new look at this ancient "aroma therapy" in an effort to find safe products to relieve distress. Although most of this research is top secret, a few tantalizing hints have been reported.

Fragaria (STRAWBERRY)—Fragrance of the fruit calms and reduces anxiety.

Lavandula (LAVENDER)—Aroma said to calm nerves and relieve headaches, though Lavender is stimulating to some people.

Malus (APPLE)—The smell of spiced Apples is reported to be calming enough to reduce blood pressure.

Mentha (MINT)—Stimulates the depressed. Since ancient times Mint, the perfume of strength, was thought to strengthen nerves as well as sinews.

Rosa (ROSE)—Smell of the flowers calms and comforts.

A NATIVE-AMERICAN MEDICINE KIT

Red Thunder Cloud of Northbridge, Massachusetts, a master herbalist from the Catawba Nation of South Carolina (and the last of his tribe to speak his native tongue) learned native American herbal medicine from his mother and his tribe's medicine man. In July 1988 he led an herb walk along the Fenton River in northeastern Connecticut, instructing those with him on the uses of various plants encountered and sprinkling tobacco on some of the great medicinals as an offering. Here are a dozen note-worthy plants and their uses:

Aralia (WILD SARSAPARILLA)—Good for many afflictions including boils, blisters, burns and stomach trouble.

Asarum (WILD GINGER)—The root of this plant was used by native Americans as a cold remedy.

Erigeron (FLEABANE)—Fleabane tea was also employed to relieve colds and to rub on stiff joints.

Impatiens (JEWELWEED)—Used for treating poison ivy and other rashes.

Monotropa (INDIAN-PIPE)—Sacred to native Americans, Indian-Pipe was used to break fevers and as an eye lotion.

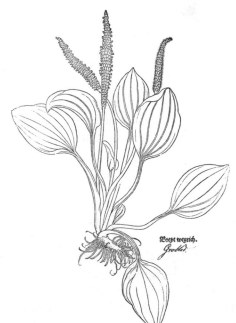

Plantago major (Common Plantain; White Man's Foot). Eurasian plant once used to heal many ailments, Common Plantain is now naturalized throughout the world.

Parthenocissus (VIRGINIA CREEPER)—Believed to be beneficial to liver and kidneys.

Phytolacca (POKEWEED)—Various parts of the plant were used to ease cramps, decongest nasal passages and stimulate the immune system.

Plantago (PLANTAIN)—An important medicinal (in many cultures), native Americans used Plantain for burns, cuts, bruises, bites and stings and to promote fertility.

Polygonatum (SOLOMON'S SEAL)—Used to treat boils and other skin afflictions.

Prunus (WILD CHERRY AND CHOKECHERRY)—The bark was used to make a brew that was used to treat fever, colds and asthma.

Urtica (NETTLE)—Stinging nettles were used to treat many ills, among them ulcers and burns.

Viola (VIOLET)—Was thought to help the body fight the beginning stages of stomach cancer. (Red Clover* and Mayapple roots were also employed against cancer.)

*It was believed that a tea made from Red Clover blossoms could strengthen the immune system. Red Clover (Trifolium pratense) is not a U.S. native. Many European plants (including Common Plantain, called "White Man's Foot" by native Americans) arrived in the New World very early and quickly were welcomed into the Native American pharmacology.

Trifolium pratense (Red Clover). Red Clover tea was prescribed for pulmonary complaints, and poultices made from it were used to treat skin cancers.

North American tribes used hundreds of plants in the preparation of various remedies; twenty other species employed were:

Allium canadense (WILD GARLIC)

Apocynum spp.* (INDIAN HEMP, RHEUMATISM ROOT)

Arisaema (JACK-IN-THE-PULPIT OR INDIAN TURNIP)

Asclepias tuberosa (BUTTERFLY WEED OR PLEURISY-ROOT)

Betula nigra (BLACK BIRCH)

Cimicifuga racemosa (BLACK COHOSH OR SQUAW-ROOT)

Cypripedium calceolus var. pubescens (YELLOW LADY'S SLIPPER OR NERVE-ROOT)

Eupatorium (BONESET AND JOE-PYE WEED)

Hamamelis virginiana (WITCH HAZEL)

Hedeoma (AMERICAN PENNYROYAL OR SQUAW MINT)

Lobelia inflata* (INDIAN TOBACCO)

Mitchella (PARTRIDGE-BERRY OR SQUAW-BERRY)

Panax quinquefolius (AMERICAN GINSENG)

Polygala senega (SENECA SNAKEROOT)

Populus tremuloides (QUAKING ASPEN) and P. x gileadensis (Balm-of-Gilead)

Salix spp.** (WILLOW)

Sambucus spp. (ELDERBERRY)

Sarracenia (PITCHER-PLANT)

Ulmus rubra (SLIPPERY ELM)

Veratrum viride* (AMERICAN HELLEBORE, ITCHWEED OR INDIAN POKE)

*These plants, in particular, are dangerous. Never use wild plants for medicinal purposes.
**Willows are native to the Old World as well as America and have been important as a source of salicin, the forerunner of aspirin, since ancient times.

AMERICAN NATIVE: JEWELWEED

Where would gardeners be without Impatiens to add color to a shady corner? The much-planted Impatiens of our gardens is I. wallerana; old-fashioned garden Balsam, a close relative, is I. balsamina. Several native Impatiens are found in our flora and their soft, juicy stems have long been known as a poison-ivy remedy. Both species, I. capensis (Spotted Jewelweed or Touch-Me-Not) and I. pallida (Pale Jewelweed) are tall annuals of shaded, moist sites with nectar-bearing orange or yellow flowers that attract hummingbirds. Children enjoy touching ripe fruits that "explode," expelling seeds in all directions, hence the name "Touch-Me-Not." Perhaps the name "Jewelweed" comes from the small, bright flowers, or maybe from the way leaves turn silvery when touched with water. A leaf placed beneath water changes into molten silver. Native Americans employed the herb against poison ivy (which is often found growing near Jewelweed); could it have been effective? The *AMA Handbook of Poisonous and Injurious Plants* claims that about ten minutes are required for poison ivy's phenolic compound allergen to penetrate skin and recommends washing with running water. The use of soap is not necessary and may even increase the chance of getting a reaction. It seems quite possible that liberal application of Jewelweed's apparently nonirritating sap could reduce the chances of getting a severe reaction after contact with the ivy leaf.

HERBS FOR THE DYE GARDEN

The National Herb Garden in Washington, D.C., features 10 different herb gardens. The following are the plants grown in the Dye Garden (the Latin tinctorius means belonging to dyers):

Achillea millefolium (YARROW)
Agrimonia eupatoria (AGRIMONY)
Alcea rosea (HOLLYHOCK)
Alchemilla vulgaris (LADY'S MANTLE)
Allium cepa (ONION)
Anchusa officinalis (ALKANET)
Anemone pulsatilla (PASQUEFLOWER)
Anthemis tinctoria (GOLDEN MARGUERITE)
Arctostaphylos uva-ursi (BEARBERRY)
Asperula tinctoria (DYER'S WOODRUFF)
Baptisia australis (BLUE FALSE INDIGO)
Baptisia tinctoria (WILD INDIGO)
Calendula officinalis (POT MARIGOLD)
Carthamus tinctorius (SAFFLOWER)
Centaurea cyanus 'Blue Boy' (BACHELOR'S BUTTON)
Chelidonium majus (CELANDINE)
Chenopodium album (LAMB'S QUARTERS)
Convallaria majalis (LILY-OF-THE-VALLEY)

Coreopsis tinctoria (CALLIOPSIS)
Crocus sativus (SAFFRON CROCUS)
Cytisus scoparius (SCOTCH BROOM)
Dipsacus sativus (FULLER'S TEASEL)
Filipendula ulmaria (QUEEN-OF-THE-MEADOW)
Galium mollugo (WHITE BEDSTRAW)
Galium verum (YELLOW BEDSTRAW)
Genista tinctoria (DYER'S BROOM)
Helianthus annuus (SUNFLOWER)
Hypericum perforatum (ST. JOHN'S WORT)
Indigofera tinctoria (INDIGO)
Inula helenium (ELECAMPANE)
Iris pseudacorus (YELLOW FLAG)
Isatis tinctoria (DYER'S WOAD)
Mahonia aquifolium (OREGON GRAPE)
Myrica pensylvanica (BAYBERRY)
Phytolacca americana (POKE)
Pteridium aquilinum (BRACKEN)
Reseda luteola (WELD)
Rubia tinctorum (MADDER)
Rumex obtusifolius (BROAD DOCK)
Ruta graveolens (RUE)
Sambucus canadensis (AMERICAN ELDERBERRY)
Sanguinaria canadensis (BLOODROOT)
Solidago spp. (GOLDENROD—ESPECIALLY S. CANADENSIS)
Tagetes tenuifolia 'Lulu' (MARIGOLD)
Tanacetum vulgare (TANSY)
Urtica dioica (STINGING NETTLE)
Verbascum thapsus (MULLEIN)

HERBS FOR COMPANION PLANTING

I have noticed that Japanese beetles do not visit my Tansy plants, yet it is hard to believe that even a large planting of Tansy near the Raspberries would have much effect on the army of beetles that descend on the berry patch each summer. Still, herb merchants and cooperative extension services alike offer the public lists of pest-repelling herbs to plant among the vegetable plants. In fairness to the latter, most extension services clearly note that their lists are for reference only and are not based on research.

Basil—Plant with tomatoes to improve flavor and repel flies. Do not plant near Rue.

Borage—Deters Tomato Worms. Companion plant for Tomatoes, Squash and Strawberries.

Catnip—Deters Flea Beetles.

Garlic—Plant close to Roses to repel Aphids. Also repels Japanese beetles and generally improves the health of Roses and Raspberries.

Horseradish—Discourages Potato Bugs.

Hyssop—Good companion for Cabbage and Grapes; do not plant near Radishes. Deters Cabbage Moths.

Mint—Improves the health of Tomatoes and Cabbage. Deters White Cabbage Moths.

Pennyroyal—Repels the Carrot Fly.

Pot Marigold—Plant among Tomatoes to discourage Tomato Worm and other garden pests.

Rosemary—Plant near Cabbage, Beans and Carrots to repel Cabbage Moth, Bean Beetle and Carrot Fly.

Rue—Said to deter Japanese Beetles from Roses and Raspberries.

Sage—Companion with Rosemary, Cabbage and Carrots to discourage Cabbage Moth and Carrot Fly. Do not plant near Cucumbers.

Summer Savory—Plant next to Beans and Onions to improve growth and flavor and repel Bean Beetles.

Southernwood—Deters the Cabbage Moth.

Tansy—Plant around fruit trees, Roses and Raspberries. Deters flying insects, Japanese Beetles, Cucumber Beetles, Squash Bugs and Ants.

Thyme—Discourages Cabbage Worms.

Wormwood—Helps to keep animals out of the garden and improves the growth and flavor of Cabbage.

HERBS THOUGHT TO ATTRACT BENEFICIAL INSECTS

Scientists are working on chemical scents that will attract beneficial insects to crop fields. Meanwhile, the 15 plants listed on the following page are among those that may attract helpful insects to a garden (the Parsley family is well represented).

Achillea (YARROW)
Anethum (DILL)
Coriandrum (CORIANDER)
Cuminum (CUMIN)
Daucus (CARROT, QUEEN ANNE'S LACE)
Foeniculum (FENNEL)
Helianthus (SUNFLOWER, JERUSALEM ARTICHOKE)
Mentha (MINT)
Pastinaca (PARSNIP)
Petroselinum (PARSLEY)
Salvia (SAGE)
Tagetes (MARIGOLD)
Tanacetum (TANSY)
Thymus (THYME)
Tropaeolum (NASTURTIUM)

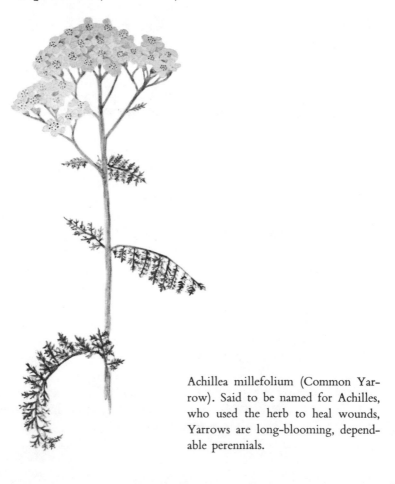

Achillea millefolium (Common Yarrow). Said to be named for Achilles,
who used the herb to heal wounds,
Yarrows are long-blooming, dependable perennials.

Beneficial Insects

It's a jungle out there in the insect world, with Lacewings, Stink-bugs, Assassin bugs and others attacking and making meals of other insects. Many gardeners are eager to enlist these good bugs in their backyard war against pests that attack vegetable and flower plants. Does it help to order cartons of beneficial insects to release in your garden? It isn't easy to establish high populations of beneficial insects on the home grounds according to Dr. Milton Savos, Professor Emeritus of Entomology at the University of Connecticut. Most successful biological control programs involve very large outdoor areas or enclosed spaces such as greenhouses.* Still, gardeners should remember that not every insect seen patrolling the garden should be dispatched. Three allies that may be worth installing in your yard:

> **Ladybugs**—Everyone's favorite, this attractive insect eats soft-bodied pests such as aphids. Not easy to keep from straying; Ladybugs are often collected while dormant and are programmed to migrate upon awakening.
>
> **Praying mantis**—Eats anything that moves (including kin), unfortunate because youngest mantises are often devoured by older siblings as they hatch. These insects are attracted to yards that feature tall grass.
>
> **Trichogrammas**—Tiny wasps that lay eggs in the eggs of many insect pests. Many other wasps also attack garden pests.

In Defense of Wasps

Most gardeners appreciate the good work birds do in keeping insect pests in check. Many can also appreciate bats and spiders for the same reason. Few gardeners are happy, however, to see that wasps have taken up residence on their property, yet these creatures are just as helpful as any insects one might order from a beneficial insect supplier. Unlike honeybees, which feed their larvae pollen, wasps feed their young partially chewed insects. Providing "insectburgers" to nests full of hungry larvae results in the destruction of many insects around the wasp nest. Paper wasps, for example, relish hornworms and, according to Professor

---

*Encarsia formosa has been successful in controlling white fly in greenhouses.

Carl Rettenmeyer of the Connecticut State Museum of Natural History, southern farmers take advantage of this by encouraging them to build nests along fence posts to control tobacco hornworm. Like honeybees, wasps are very unlikely to sting unless extremely provoked. Gardeners should appreciate them for the friends that they are.

SOURCES FOR BENEFICIAL INSECTS

Mellinger's Nursery
2310 W. South Range Rd.
North Lima, OH 44452

Peaceful Valley Farm Supply
11173 Peaceful Valley Rd.
Nevada City, CA 95959

Natural Gardening Research
Center
Highway 48
PO Box 149
Sunman, IN 47041

Unique Insect Control
5504 Sperry Dr.
Citrus Heights, CA 95621

Necessary Trading Company
PO Box 603
New Castle, VA 24127

HERBS ANIMALS LOVE (AND HATE)

Everyone knows that cats like Catnip and moths dislike cedar but these are not the only plants that can attract and deter animals and insects. All animals respond in one way or another to the plants around them, many reacting quite strongly to certain plants. Here are some special plants and the creatures they attract or deter:

> **Angelica** (ANGELICA)—A chemical in this plant is a powerful attractant to Mediterranean fruit flies.
> **Euphorbia** (GOPHER PURGE)—Many Euphorbias are poisonous to grazing animals, and their roots deter moles and voles. Other plants reputed to discourage moles are Fritillaria and Castor Bean. Some claim Daffodil bulbs deter gophers.
> **Laurus** (BAY)—Bay leaves will repel roaches.
> **Melissa** (LEMON BALM)—Melissa means "bee" in Greek; this plant is favored by bees but its aroma repels cats. Cats are also said to dislike Rue.
> **Mentha** (MINT)—American Pennyroyal deters insects; mice also dislike the smell of mint.

Nepeta (CATNIP)—Attractive to cats but said to repel rats. Among the other plants that some (not all) cats find appealing are Baby Blue Eyes, Boxwood, Cat Thyme (Teucrium marum), Cranberry Bush (Viburnum opulus), Dittany of Crete, Silver Vine (Actinidia), Trumpet Creeper (Campsis) and Valerian.

Pimpinella (ANISE)—Said to be a potent mouse bait and bear bait. Used on lures to attract certain fish.

Tanacetum (TANSY)—Tansy is often planted as an ant repellent. Other plants reputed to repel ants are Sage, Black Walnut and Southernwood. Ground-up Citrus peel, placed in fire-ant colonies, has been effective in destroying them.

Valeriana (VALERIAN)—The smell of this plant is loved by rats as well as cats. Were the Pied Piper of Hamelin's clothes stuffed with Valerian? Some horses also like the aroma.

Moth Repellents

Acorus (SWEET FLAG)
Artemisia (SOUTHERNWOOD AND WORMWOOD)
Juniperus (RED CEDAR)
Lavandula (LAVENDER)
Rosmarinus (ROSEMARY)
Santolina (LAVENDER COTTON)
Thymus (THYME)

Catmints

A number of Nepetas are sold as "Catnip" although only one, Nepeta cataria, is of much interest to cats. N. cataria, or true Catnip, is a gray-green perennial; the small white flowers may be dotted with pale purple spots. Many of the other Catmints produce blue flowers. It is said that Catnip is easily rooted from cuttings taken in the early spring; I know from experience that it is not easily rooted if cuttings are taken later in the season. Where to plant Nepeta? Some recommend sun; some recommend shade; there is also disagreement about whether moist or dry soils are best. The grayish, fuzzy foliage of the Catmints suggests that sun and well-drained soils are preferred. I grow long-flowering Nepeta x faassenii, a sterile blue-flowered hybrid, in a partially shaded garden where soil is on the dry side. It seems more than content with these conditions.

Nepeta cataria (Catnip). Catnip has gray-green leaves, purple-spotted white flowers and likes a well-drained site. There is a lemon-scented cultivar.

WHEN DOES AN HERB BECOME A WEED?

Many plants have made the trip from "a plant valued for medicinal, savory or aromatic qualities" to "a plant of no value, usually of rank growth . . . that tends to choke out more desirable plants."* A number of once-valued plants escaped from colonial gardens in the East and now blossom along roadsides and in fields in many parts of America. While it is true that these immigrants displace native American plants, it is also true that some are a bright and pleasing addition to the summer landscape. Here are ten Old World "herbs," now called "wildflowers" (or "weeds") in many parts of America:

Achillea millefolium (YARROW)—Astringent properties arrest bleeding; leaves chewed to relieve toothache.
Chrysanthemum leucanthemum (OX-EYE DAISY)—Once used to relieve coughs and asthma and externally for skin ailments.
Cichorium intybus (CHICORY)—Salad herb, pot herb and (roasted roots) coffee substitute.

*Webster's Ninth New Collegiate Dictionary, 1985.

Glechoma hederacea (GROUND IVY)—This little member of the Mint family was once used for many ailments and to clarify beer.

Hypericum perforatum (ST. JOHN'S WORT)—An old remedy for sores and wounds.

Linaria vulgaris (TOADFLAX, BUTTER AND EGGS)—Golden snapdragonlike flowers were made into lotions for skin diseases.

Prunella vulgaris (SELFHEAL, HEAL-ALL)—A Mint family member used to treat cuts.

Saponaria officinalis (BOUNCING BET, SOAPWORT)—A cleanser and old remedy for bruises. Crushed root or leaves in water will produce a soapy lather.

Taraxacum officinale (DANDELION)—Once a plant of many uses, still used today by some as a salad green.

Verbascum thapsus (MULLEIN)—Used to treat the pulmonary complaints of people and cattle.

Impatiens capensis (Jewelweed). An old-time poison ivy remedy that attracts hummingbirds.

The Purple Tide

"New American" gardens that feature Purple Loosestrife (Lythrum salicaria) are actually quite un-American, for this immigrant has invasive qualities that seem guaranteed to place it in a league with Dandelion. Granted it is a beautiful plant that creates summer color in hard-to-plant moist spots and water meadows. Its flowers attract native bumblebees as well as honeybees. It also has a long and versatile herbal history, once used as a medicinal (wound healer and cure for dysentery), a cosmetic (hair dye) and a magic plant (garlands were hung around the necks of oxen in the ancient world to calm them). Nevertheless, Purple Loosestrife arrived on American shores without its many Old World insect predators to help keep it in check. It now covers vast stretches of land in the East, crowding out native plants such as Cattail that provide food and shelter for native waterfowl. Some defend it by saying that we are all a nation of immigrants (so why not a beautiful immigrant plant?) and extermination campaigns might do more harm than good. Others deplore the loss of valuable native species that Lythrum displaces. A number of cultivars exist (some tolerant of drought as well as wet conditions, and some

Lythrum salicaria (Purple Loosestrife). Beautiful in moist meadows but invasive and harmful to native plants and animals.

reputed to be sterile*) and many catalogs offer Purple Loosestrife for sale. Garden writers sing its praises. But should we plant it? Joe Pye Weed, New England Aster and Ironweed are American native alternatives to the magenta tide of Loosestrife; the pinks and purples they bring to low, moist areas are more interesting and to many more beautiful as well.

THE LANGUAGE OF HERBS

Achillea (YARROW)—War

Angelica (ANGELICA)—Inspiration

Anthriscus (CHERVIL)—Sincerity

Artemisia (WORMWOOD)—Absence

Borago (BORAGE)—Bluntness

Chamaemelum (CHAMOMILE)—Fortitude; energy in adversity

Coriandrum (CORIANDER)—"Never judge solely on appearances"

Foeniculum (FENNEL)—Strength; courage; long life; worthy of praise

Hyssopus (HYSSOP)—Cleanliness

Laurus (BAY)—Constant and unchanging

Lavandula (LAVENDER)—Distrust; refusal ("I like you only as a friend")

Melissa (BALM)—Fun; pleasantry; sympathy

Mentha (MINT)—Strength; virility; virtue; warmth of feeling

Ocimum (BASIL)—Animosity

Origanum (MARJORAM)—Marjoram means "joy of the mountain" and was the herb of happiness to early Greeks and Romans; it stood also for innocence and blushes

Petroselinum (PARSLEY)—Festivity

Rosmarinus (ROSEMARY)—Remembrance

Ruta (RUE)—Disdain

Salvia (SAGE)—Esteem; domestic virtue; long life; wisdom

Tanacetum (TANSY)—Dislike; refusal

Thymus (THYME)—Courage; activity; grace; elegance; domestic virtues

---

*Although several sterile cultivars are advertised, most are questionable and may produce seed. A few states have passed laws making it illegal to grow L. salicaria, but do allow the planting of noninvasive cultivars. Minnesota has outlawed even these because of fear they could mutate into an invasive form, especially if grown near the wild species.

THE ORIGINS OF HERBS

Herbal plants have been in use for so long that pinpointing their exact source of origin is very difficult.

Angelica (ANGELICA)—Northern Hemisphere, New Zealand
Anethum (DILL)—Southwest Asia, Europe
Anthriscus (CHERVIL)—Southeast Europe, Russia, western Asia
Artemisia (TARRAGON)—Southern Europe, Asia, U.S. West
Borago (BORAGE)—Europe, north Africa
Calendula (POT MARIGOLD)—Southern Europe
Coriandrum (CORIANDER)—Southern Europe, Asia Minor
Foeniculum (FENNEL)—Southern Europe
Hyssopus (HYSSOP)—Southern Europe to central Asia
Laurus (BAY)—Mediterranean region
Lavandula (LAVENDER)—Europe, Mediterranean region to India
Levisticum (LOVAGE)—Southern Europe
Marrubium (HOREHOUND)—Mediterranean region, Europe, Asia
Melissa (LEMON BALM)—Southern Europe
Mentha (MINT)—Temperate regions of Europe
Myrrhis (SWEET CICELY)—Europe
Nepeta cataria (CATNIP)—Eurasia
Ocimum (BASIL)—Tropical Africa, India
Origanum (SWEET MARJORAM)—North Africa, southwestern Asia
Origanum (POT MARJORAM, OREGANO)—Europe to central Asia
Petroselinum (PARSLEY)—Europe, western Asia
Rosmarinus (ROSEMARY)—Mediterranean region, Portugal, Spain
Ruta (RUE)—Mediterranean region to western Asia
Salvia officinalis (SAGE)—Spain to western Asia Minor
Satureja (SAVORY)—Mediterranean region
Tanacetum (TANSY)—Europe, Asia
Thymus (THYME)—Europe, Asia

Herb Gardens to Visit

Many restorations and period homes have adjacent herb gardens to visit. Large botanical gardens often feature herb gardens as well. A sampling of herb gardens follows:

Alabama
   (Mobile): Oakleigh

Arkansas
   (Little Rock): Arkansas Territorial Restoration

California
   (Berkeley): University of California's Chinese Medicinal Herb
      Garden
   (San Marino): Huntington Botanical Gardens

Colorado
   (Denver): Denver Botanic Gardens

Connecticut
   (Old Saybrook): General William Hart House

District of Columbia
   (Washington): U.S. National Arboretum, The National Herb
      Garden—features ten different herb gardens

Florida
   (Gainesville): Kanapaha Botanical Gardens—nine special gar-
      dens including the South's largest herb garden

Georgia
   (Augusta): Pendleton King Park—contains a Blue Garden and
      a touch-and-smell herb garden

Indiana
   (Madison): Dr. William Hutching's Medicinal Herb Garden

Iowa
   (Des Moines): Des Moines Botanical Center

Massachusetts
   (Sturbridge): Old Sturbridge Village

New Jersey
   (Middletown): Eighteenth Century Herb Garden

New York
   (Brooklyn): Brooklyn Botanic Garden

North Carolina
   (Winston-Salem): Old Salem

Ohio
   (Bates): Hale Homestead and Village

Oregon
(Portland): Aurora Colony

Pennsylvania
(Fort Washington): Hope Lodge

Vermont
(Shelburne): Shelburne Museum Garden

Virginia
(Williamsburg): Colonial Williamsburg

Washington
(Seattle): Drug Plant Gardens, University of Washington

Wisconsin
(Eagle): Old World Wisconsin

SOURCES FOR HERBS

Caprilands Herb Farm
Silver St.
Coventry, CT 06238
(203) 742-7244
Herb plants shipped starting in April
Send SASE for herb list

Fox Hill Farm
444 W. Michigan Ave.
Parma, MI 49269-0009
(517) 531-3179

Goodwin Creek Gardens
PO Box 83
Williams, OR 97544
(503) 488-3308
Culinary herbs and native American herbs
Send $1.00 (refundable) for catalog

Merry Gardens
Camden, ME 04843
(207) 236-9064
Send $1.00 for catalog

Milaeger's Gardens
4838 Douglas Ave.
Racine, WI 53402-2498
(414) 639-2371
Catalog $1.00 (refundable)

Nichols Garden Nursery
1190 QR Pacific
Albany, OR 97321
(503) 928-9280
Herb seeds and plants, free catalog

Sandy Mush Herb Nursery
Rt. 2
Surrett Cove Rd.
Leicester, NC 28748
(704) 683-2014
Large inventory, informative
catalog/handbook $4.00,
refundable

Taylor's Herb Gardens
1535 Lone Oak Rd.
Vista, CA 92084
(619) 727-3485
Send $1.00 for catalog

Wayside Gardens
1 Garden Lane
Hodges, SC 29695
(800) 845-1124

Well-Sweep Herb Farm
317 Bethel Rd.
Port Murray, NJ 07865
(201) 852-5390
Send $1.00 for plant list
Plants shipped during growing
season

Wrenwood
Rt. 4, Box 361
Berkeley Springs, WV 25411
(304) 258-3071
Catalog $1.50

4

Houseplants

EVEN WITH GOOD CARE AND LARGE, MODERN windows, few plants are really content when grown inside homes. Yet they have survived and decorated our habitations for thousands of years. We know that Greeks and Romans grew plants inside their villas. Probably, even long before recorded history, plants were brought inside when indoor light first became available. The earliest "houseplants" were undoubtedly important medicinal or food plants or those used in connection with religious celebrations like the pots of herbs, grains and flowers grown for the ancient god of vegetation called Adonis by the Greeks. Today we grow plants for psychological and aesthetic reasons, although recently another good reason has been discovered: Plants help purify indoor air.

There are many misconceptions about houseplants. Desert Cacti are assumed to like it hot and dry; in reality they prefer summers with regular watering (outdoors if possible) and winters in cold rooms with just enough water to stay alive. Small wonder most of them never bloom. Fortunately, many plants adapt more readily to surroundings deemed comfortable by human standards, although some can do this much better than others. Success with indoor gardening (as with outdoor gardening) requires that you consider your site carefully and then buy the right plant for it. The best indoor gardener cannot make an orchid happy in blazing sunlight or a geranium prosper in semidarkness.

Do not be afraid to move a plant that is not thriving. Indoor light changes with the seasons, just as outdoor light does. A southern window may be just right for a plant in winter, but a poor choice for the same plant in summer. Watering, too, should depend on the season, the temperature and the location of a plant; hanging baskets generally need water sooner than plants kept on tables or on the floor. In addition to being attractive, grouping indoor plants together increases surrounding humidity, which is beneficial to all.

Houseplants are not able to communicate as effectively as house cats, but they will convey their needs if they are noticed. Look closely at them. Turn over leaves and look for pests; use a magnifier if necessary. Sponge leaf tops or mist those that like misting. Touch the soil and lift pots (if possible) to determine moisture content. Water them with room-temperature water. Like all living things, plants need care that is informed and flexible. Determining what is best for your houseplants is not difficult; if you succeed they will reward you with flowers, fragrance and lush and healthy growth.

GROWING CONDITIONS

East Side, West Side, North Side, South Side

The direction windows face is only one factor that determines the amount of light entering a room. Window size, the time of year, time of day and outdoor plantings that may block light are all important. Still, generalizations can be made. North windows are usually almost sunless. North window plants like bright light but not direct sunlight. Eastern windows enjoy cool morning sun. When in doubt, try east; eastern exposures are favored by the greatest number of houseplants. Western windows are hotter and brighter, and some plants may need to be protected from hot summer sun. Southern windows are quite sunny in winter but less so in summer; plants that would not thrive on a southern windowsill in winter might do well there in the summer. On the other hand, sun lovers might need to be moved to a sunnier location. Many plants that like southern exposures will also thrive in western exposures and vice versa. If possible, place pots in larger outer pots to keep roots cool. Available light is only one consideration, however; plants also need the proper temperature, humidity and soil moisture for optimum health. Ten plants for each exposure are listed on the following page:

PLANTS FOR EAST WINDOWS:

Araucaria (NORFOLK ISLAND PINE)
Begonia (BEGONIA)
Epiphyllum (ORCHID CACTUS; ALSO OTHER JUNGLE CACTI, SUCH
    AS CHRISTMAS CACTUS)
Episcia (FLAME VIOLET)
Gardenia (GARDENIA)
Nephrolepis (BOSTON FERN)
Saintpaulia (AFRICAN VIOLET)
Sinningia (GLOXINIA)
Strelitzia (BIRD OF PARADISE)
Streptocarpus (CAPE PRIMROSE)

PLANTS FOR WEST WINDOWS:

Ceropegia (STRING OF HEARTS, ROSARY VINE)
Codiaeum (CROTON)
Coleus (COLEUS)
Crassula (JADE PLANT)
Ficus (RUBBER PLANT)
Hoya (WAX PLANT)
Hypoestes (POLKA DOT, FRECKLE FACE)
Jasminum (JASMINE)
Persea (AVOCADO)
Sansevieria (SNAKE PLANT)—This plant will grow almost
    anywhere but is happiest where it gets some sun.

PLANTS FOR SOUTH WINDOWS:

Acalypha (CHENILLE PLANT)
Beaucarnea (PONY TAIL PLANT)
Citrus (ORANGE, LEMON)
Echeveria (ECHEVERIA)
Euphorbia (CROWN OF THORNS)
Justicia (SHRIMP PLANT)
Kalanchoe (KALANCHOE)
Myrtus (MYRTLE)
Pelargonium (GERANIUM)
Sedum (JELLYBEAN PLANT, BURRO'S TAIL)

PLANTS FOR NORTH WINDOWS:

Aucuba (GOLD DUST PLANT)
Chlorophytum (SPIDER PLANT)—Variegated plants do well with some sun.
Dieffenbachia (DUMB CANE)
Dizygotheca (FALSE ARALIA)
Fatshedera (IVY TREE)—'Variegata' needs more light than all-green plants.
Maranta (PRAYER PLANT)
Peperomia (PEPEROMIA)
Schefflera (UMBRELLA TREE)
Tolmiea (PIGGYBACK PLANT)
Vriesea (FLAMING SWORD)—A number of Bromeliads will thrive in bright light.

Houseplants for the Twilight Zone

No plant likes a really dark corner, although a few plants, such as Parlor Palm and Horsehead Philodendron, actually prefer a low-light environment. Others listed below will do well in north windows or low-light situations at some distance from a window, although some may prefer brighter conditions. None requires direct sun. When you move a plant that prefers bright light into a darker environment, do not expect much growth. Be especially careful not to overwater (low light reduces the need for water), and fertilize sparingly if at all.

Aglaonema modestum (CHINESE EVERGREEN)—Mist often.
Aspidistra elatior (CAST IRON PLANT)—Tolerates dry air.
Chamaedorea elegans (PARLOR PALM)—Mist if room is heated.
Cissus rhombifolia (GRAPE IVY)—Appreciates misting but will survive in dry surroundings.
Dracena draco (DRAGON TREE)—Tolerates dry air. Many Dracenas will adapt to poor light; most enjoy misting.
Howea forsteriana (SENTRY PALM)—Mist or sponge leaves occasionally if room is heated.
Monstera deliciosa (SWISS CHEESE PLANT)—Mist if room is heated.
Philodendron bipennifolium (HORSE HEAD PHILODENDRON)—Mist if room is heated. P. scandens (Heart Leaf Philodendron) is also quite shade-tolerant.

Scindapsus aureus (POTHOS)—Mist if temperatures are high; variegation may fade in very low light.

Syngonium (NEPHTHYTIS, ARROWHEAD VINE)—Likes average warmth and occasional misting.

Ferns do not like the dark conditions many think they do; most kinds prefer east or north windows. Moist air is also appreciated.

Plants That Tolerate Heat and Dry Air

Few houseplants like high temperatures and dry air, although this combination appeals to one of their main pests, spider mites. Plants like Aspidistra (Cast Iron Plant) tolerate low humidity but like cool rooms. Many Cacti and other succulents, contrary to popular belief, also like cool rooms—especially in winter. Some may survive other conditions, but they will not be at their best nor will they flower. The following may grow in a room with your woodstove, though most would probably benefit if room humidity were increased:

Beaucarnea recurvata (PONY TAIL PLANT)—Bright light; some sun.

Billbergia nutans (QUEEN'S TEARS)—Bright light; some sun.

Cissus rhombifolia (GRAPE IVY)—Tolerates low light.

Chlorophytum (SPIDER PLANT)—Adapts to sun or shade.

Dracena draco (DRAGON TREE)—Will tolerate low light.

Dracena surculosa (GOLD DUST DRACENA)—Will tolerate low light.

Euphorbia milii (CROWN OF THORNS)—Likes sun; needs some protection from hot summer sun.

Peperomia obtusifolia (BABY RUBBER PLANT)—Bright light or partial shade.

Plectranthus (SWEDISH IVY)—Bright light or partial shade.

Sansevieria (SNAKE PLANT)—Obliging almost anywhere.

Victorian Houseplants

Victorian homes tended to be cold and drafty—especially at night. It was often too hot in some of the rooms in the daytime, and gas fumes and smoke from coal fires caused the ferns that Victorians loved great distress. (As a result, the more sensitive ferns were grown in conservatories or protective glass cases.) Nevertheless, Victorians loved houseplants, and their bay windows and sun porches were full of them. Some favorites:

Abutilon (FLOWERING MAPLE)
Agave (CENTURY PLANT)
Aspidistra (CAST IRON PLANT)
Chlorophytum (SPIDER PLANT)
Citrus (LEMON PLANT)
Clivia (KAFIR LILY)
Ficus (RUBBER PLANT)
Fuchsia (FUCHSIA)
Heliotropium (HELIOTROPE)*
Howea (KENTIA PALM)
Jasminum (POET'S JESSAMINE)
Nephrolepis (SWORD FERN)**
Pandanus (SCREW PINE)
Selaginella (CREEPING MOSS)
Zantedeschia (CALLA LILY)

*Raise new cuttings every year to keep it flowering.
**Other ferns, such as Maidenhair and Holly Fern, were also popular.

Plants That Need Frequent Watering

Overwatering kills more houseplants than underwatering. When a plant droops we often water it, although sometimes an apparently wilted plant may actually be suffering from too much water. Not everyone is aware that plant roots need air as well as water, that most plants need less water when resting than during active growth periods (early spring through summer) and that many plants benefit from a partial drying out between waterings. Remember that soils dry out faster when temperatures are high and water needs are higher when flowers and buds appear. Moisture-loving species naturally require more water, and, in general, flowering plants like moist (not drenched) soils when in flower. Here are some plants with above-average water requirements (room temperature water is best); keep soil moist at all times:

Acalypha (CHENILLE PLANT)
Acorus (SWEET FLAG)
Azalea (AZALEA)
Anthurium (ANTHURIUM)
Camellia (CAMELLIA)
Chamaedorea (PARLOR PALM)—Other Palms also need moist soil.
Cyclamen (CYCLAMEN)
Cyperus (UMBRELLA PLANT)

Dionaea (VENUS FLY TRAP)
Ferns—Most ferns need moist soil and humid air.
Gardenia (GARDENIA)
Helxine (BABY'S TEARS)
Hibiscus (HIBISCUS)
Jasminum (JASMINE)
Sinningia (GLOXINIA)
Zebrina (INCH PLANT)

The following are among those plants that like evenly moist soil during the growing season, but appreciate a rest at cooler temperatures with less water in winter. Reduce watering in winter for these unless flowering or unless room temperatures are high:

Abutilon (FLOWERING MAPLE)
Aeschynanthus (LIPSTICK PLANT)
Aglaonema (CHINESE EVERGREEN)
Aphelandra (ZEBRA PLANT)
Araucaria (NORFOLK ISLAND PINE)
Brunfelsia (YESTERDAY, TODAY AND TOMORROW)
Chlorophytum (SPIDER PLANT)
Codiaeum (CROTON)
Coleus (COLEUS)
Columnea (GOLDFISH PLANT)
Dracaena (DRACAENA)
Episcia (FLAME VIOLET)
Fatsia (JAPANESE FATSIA)
Fittonia (FITTONIA)
Fuchsia (FUCHSIA)
Hedera (IVY)
Impatiens (IMPATIENS)
Justicia (SHRIMP PLANT)
Maranta (PRAYER PLANT)
Pellionia (PELLIONIA)
Philodendron (PHILODENDRON)
Plectranthus (SWEDISH IVY)
Spathiphyllum (SPATHE FLOWER)
Syngonium (NEPHTHYTIS)
Tolmiea (PIGGYBACK PLANT)

Plants That Need Less Frequent Watering

Overwatering the following plants will prove especially harmful. Let soil dry between waterings; just a little for plants such as Saintpaulia and Pilea, more for Beaucarnea, Crassula and Kalanchoe. Many listed below also enjoy a cool winter rest during which watering is further reduced, but do not let plants kept in warm rooms (or plants in flower) become too dry.

Beaucarnea (PONY TAIL PLANT)
Begonia (BEGONIA)
Ceropegia (STRING OF HEARTS)
Citrus (CITRUS)
Crassula (JADE PLANT)
Dieffenbachia (DUMB CANE)—Likes high humidity.
Euphorbia (CROWN OF THORNS)
Ficus (FIG)—Trailing types need more water.
Hoya (WAX PLANT)
Kalanchoe (KALANCHOE)
Myrtus (MYRTLE)
Oxalis (OXALIS)
Pandanus (SCREW PINE)
Pelargonium (GERANIUM)
Peperomia (PEPEROMIA)
Pilea (ALUMINUM PLANT)
Rhipsalis (CHAIN CACTUS)
Saintpaulia (AFRICAN VIOLET)
Sansevieria (SNAKE PLANT)
Schlumbergera (CHRISTMAS CACTUS)
Scindapsus (POTHOS)
Strelitzia (BIRD OF PARADISE)

Many recommend keeping the soil of African Violet (Saintpaulia) constantly moist; my Violets appear happier if water is withheld until soil begins to dry. Most Bromeliads need water only when compost dries (keep the center "vases" filled with water), and desert Cacti need watering when soil begins to dry in summer and a cool rest with reduced water in winter.

SIGNS OF OVERWATERING

Some of the following may also be symptoms of other problems:

- Leaves turn yellow.
- Leaves may appear limp and wilted.
- Leaves and/or stems may have soft, discolored areas.
- Leaves may exhibit brown or yellow edges or tips.
- Leaves curl and drop. (This will occur from all over the plant. Underwatering usually results in lower leaves falling first.)
- Flower buds turn yellow and/or drop.
- Plant is not growing or growing very slowly.
- Roots are brown and dead.
- Green slime appears on clay pots. (This is a definite sign of overwatering or blocked drainage holes.)

Houseplants That Will Grow in Water

Many indoor gardeners have discovered that Pothos and Acorus will grow nicely in tap water; last winter several of my Impatiens cuttings bloomed happily in water for many months. According to Tok Furuta of UCLA (Riverside) Extension Service, a number of plants can be grown in tap water. Use stones or coarse gravel for support if you wish, but do not add soil or organic matter. Charcoal may be added to keep the water sweet. Plants to grow in water include:

Aglaonema modestum (CHINESE EVERGREEN)
Cissus rhombifolia (GRAPE IVY)
Crassula argentea (JADE PLANT)
Dieffenbachia sp. (DUMB CANE—ALL KINDS)
Dracaena sanderiana (RIBBON PLANT)
Fatshedera lizei (IVY TREE)*
Hedera helix (ENGLISH IVY)
Philodendron bipennifolium (HORSE HEAD OR FIDDLE LEAF PHILODENDRON)
Philodendron scandens (COMMON HEART-LEAF PHILODENDRON)

*The genus x Fatshedera is a hybrid, the result of a cross between Fatsia (Japanese Fatsia) and Hedera (Ivy). Easy-to-grow Ivy Tree can be grown as a climber or as a shrub.

Sansevieria sp. (SNAKE PLANT)
Scindapsus aureus (POTHOS, DEVIL'S IVY)
Syngonium podophyllum (NEPHTHYTIS)
Tolmiea menziesii (PIGGYBACK PLANT)
Tradescantia fluminensis (WANDERING JEW)
Zebrina pendula (SILVERY INCH PLANT)

BLOOMS, FRAGRANCE, FOLIAGE AND DECORATION

Long-Blooming Houseplants

The following are treasured for long periods of bloom; most will flower off and on throughout the year if conditions are right. Fertilizer with a high potassium content (usually labeled potash) will help promote flowering. Plants in bloom generally need more water than resting plants, but remember that too much water—and too much fertilizer—kills plants.

Abutilon (CHINESE LANTERN)—Members of the Mallow family along with Hibiscus, Abutilons are shrubby plants with maplelike leaves, hence another common name—Flowering Maple. Abutilons like cool conditions (especially in winter) and lots of light but no direct, hot sun. Prune back in spring or late summer.

Anthurium (FLAMINGO FLOWER)—Exotic red flowers makes this plant special. Likes warm, humid conditions and bright light. For best results keep moist with room-temperature water and mist often. 'Southern Blush' is a new dwarf plant with pink blooms.

Begonia (BEGONIA)—Wax Begonia (B. semperflorens) and the Elatior hybrids (B. x hiemalis) are noted for flowers. Begonias must have plenty of light; a few hours east or west window winter sun is ideal. Moist air is appreciated. Let soil dry out a bit between waterings.

Brunfelsia (YESTERDAY, TODAY AND TOMORROW PLANT)—So-called because its fragrant flowers change from purple to lavender to white. Will bloom all year if light is adequate. Likes average warmth and some sun, but protect from hot summer sun. Keep well watered when in flower.

Euphorbia (CROWN OF THORNS)—Like its relative Poinsettia, Crown of Thorns has small yellowish flowers surrounded by colorful bracts. Blooms most when days are short; likes a warm, sunny room though temperatures that are too hot may discourage flowers.

Hibiscus (HIBISCUS)—This tropical shrub has glossy leaves (there is a variegated variety) and bright single or double flowers that may be white, pink, red, yellow or apricot. Grow in a sunny window (shade from hot summer sun) and keep well watered. Likes warmth; avoid drafts and large temperature swings. Mist. May be rested for a short time in winter or kept in bloom.

Impatiens (IMPATIENS)—Cuttings of these garden favorites may be brought indoors where they will blossom all winter. Needs good light; a few hours a day sun in winter is necessary for best flowering. Let soil dry out between waterings. Prefers a cool room.

Justicia (SHRIMP PLANT)—Bracts (not flowers) make this plant colorful and they can last year round if plant is well cared for. Likes warm and sunny conditions but should not be placed in strong summer sun. Keep soil moist; appreciates a cool (but sunny) rest with reduced watering in winter after the small white flowers have stopped appearing. Cut back in spring to keep bushy.

Pelargonium (GERANIUM)—Likes a cool room and ample direct sun. P. zonale, with reddish rings on leaves and small flowers, is especially floriferous. Soil should dry out between waterings.

Saintpaulia (AFRICAN VIOLET)—Needs good light (not bright sun), moist soil, warm room. Try an east window. Probably the easiest of all to keep in bloom throughout the year if you have a good variety. Some cultivars are shy about blooming; ask about whether a plant you like is a good bloomer.

Winter-Blooming Houseplants

In addition to the plants listed above, a number of others will flower during winter months; some like Citrus, Osmanthus and the miniature Sinningias may bloom throughout the year.

Barleria (PHILIPPINE VIOLET)
Citrus (CALAMONDIN ORANGE)
Columnea (GOLDFISH PLANT)
Cyclamen (CYCLAMEN)
Euphorbia (POINSETTIA)
Hippeastrum (AMARYLLIS)
Hoya (HOYA)
Jasminum (WINTER JASMINE)
Kalanchoe (KALANCHOE)
Kohleria (TREE GLOXINIA)
Lachenalia (CAPE COWSLIP)
Osmanthus (SWEET OLIVE)
Pentas (EGYPTIAN STAR CLUSTER)
Reinwardtia (YELLOW FLAX)
Rosmarinus (ROSEMARY)
Schlumbergera (CHRISTMAS CACTUS)
Sinningia (SINNINGIA)
Streptocarpus (CAPE PRIMROSE)
Tetranema (MEXICAN FOXGLOVE, MEXICAN VIOLET)
Zantedeschia (WHITE CALLA LILY)

Holiday Bloomers

Poinsettia, Kalanchoe and Christmas Cactus are three popular plants that are often purchased during the December holidays. Christmas Cactus likes a cool room with good light but little or no direct sun. Poinsettia and Kalanchoe like warmer rooms and more sun, but should be protected from hot summer rays. All should receive a rest period with infrequent watering after flowering; prune Poinsettia and Kalanchoe if necessary and put in a shady spot. Move into brighter light and resume regular watering in spring. To encourage holiday flowering, restrict light in the fall so that plants receive about 14 hours of darkness each night for approximately eight weeks. Christmas Cactus will also produce buds without light restriction if night temperatures are kept between 50 and 55 degrees F. When buds appear, light restriction (and/or cool nights) may be discontinued.

Short-Lived Houseplants

Jade Plants and Christmas Cacti can last for generations. Other potted plants commonly found in flower shops and garden centers (especially during holiday times) remain attractive for only a short time—some not much longer than many cut flowers. It is possible, but not easy, to maintain several of the following as houseplants, and dedicated gardeners might even achieve a second round of flowering. Most, however, should be discarded after blossoms fade:

Aphelandra (ZEBRA PLANT)
Calceolaria (SLIPPER FLOWER, POCKETBOOK PLANT)
Chrysanthemum—Some kinds may be planted in the garden.
Cineraria
Cyclamen
Euphorbia (SCARLET PLUME AND POINSETTIA)
Exacum (PERSIAN VIOLET)
Rhododendron (AZALEA)—Most large-flowered Azaleas are not
    hardy enough to be planted outdoors in the north. Azaleas
    can last for years if growing conditions are met; bright
    light (no direct sun), cool temperatures and plenty of
    moisture.
Schizanthus (POOR MAN'S ORCHID)

Bulbs to Grow Indoors

Gardeners who enjoy watching commonly advertised bulbs such as Amaryllis and Paperwhite Narcissus bloom indoors may wish to experiment with other species. Some, like the tender Amaryllis and Paperwhite, require little more than planting, while others, such as the hardy, spring-blooming bulbs, will need an extended cold period for root development.* Garden catalogs often note varieties recommended for forcing. Some to try are:

Anemone coronaria (FLORIST'S ANEMONE)—Does not need long
    cold period.
Crocus (CROCUS)—Needs an eight-week cold period. Yellow
    does not seem to force well. Varieties to try:
    Peter Pan—White
    Pickwick—Lilac/dark lilac stripes
    Purpurea Grandiflora—Purple

---

*Plant in pots and place pots in the refrigerator. After cold period, place in a cool room indoors, where pot will get bright light and then some sun. When buds form move to desired location; flowers will last longer in a shady, cool spot. See "Sources for Bulbs," page 98.

Remembrance—Violet

Freesia (FREESIA)—Tender plants that do not need a long cold period. Wonderful fragrance.

Hyacinthus (HYACINTH)—Very reliable; needs an eight-week cold period. May also be grown in water.

   Amsterdam—Rose red

   Anne Marie—Pink

   Blue Jacket—Dark Blue

   Carnegie—White

   Ostara—Light violet blue

Muscari (GRAPE HYACINTH)—Excellent for forcing; needs cold period of about eight weeks.

Narcissus (DAFFODIL)—Needs 10- to 12-week cold period.

   Barrett Browning—White/flat ruffled orange cup

   Cragford—White/orange cup; multiflowered

   Fortune—Yellow/orange

   Golden Harvest—Yellow

   Ice Follies—White/lemon yellow crown

   King Alfred (Introduced in 1899)—Pure yellow

   Mt. Hood—White

   Tete-a-Tete—(Miniature) yellow flowers produced in pairs

Tulipa (TULIP)—Needs a cold period of 12 or more weeks; more of a challenge than others. Best for forcing indoors are the early (and shorter) varieties.

   Bellona—Yellow, fragrant

   Couleur Cardinal—Red

   Diana—White

   General DeWet—Orange, fragrant

Houseplants for Fragrance

The following plants (with the possible exceptions of Brunfelsia and Carissa, which like warm rooms) are not for overheated rooms:

Brunfelsia calycina (YESTERDAY, TODAY AND TOMORROW PLANT)

Carissa grandiflora (NATAL PLUM)

Cestrum nocturnum (NIGHT BLOOMING JASMINE)—Sap and white fruit is toxic.

Citrus spp. (CALAMONDIN ORANGE AND DWARF LEMON)

Gardenia jasminoides (GARDENIA)

Hoya spp. (WAX PLANT)

Jasminum polyanthum (PINK JASMINE)
Myrtus communis (MYRTLE)
Osmanthus fragrans (SWEET OLIVE)
Rosa chinensis 'Minima' (MINIATURE ROSE)*
Stephanotis floribunda (MADAGASCAR JASMINE)
Tulbaghia fragrans (TULBAGHIA)

*Not all miniature roses are fragrant!

Don't overlook Pelargonium (Scented Geraniums) and Rosemary for fragrance, although they will get leggy indoors without plenty of light. Some varieties of Spathiphyllum (try 'Regency' or 'Viscount') are said to be fragrant. Fragrant flowers are even produced by a couple of old standbys, Corn Palm (Dracaena fragrans) and some Snake Plants (Sansevieria), although they rarely bloom in most homes.

Houseplants with Variegated Foliage

It seems as though nearly every green-leaved houseplant has a variegated form: Swedish Ivy, Jade Tree, Strawberry Geranium, Spider Plant and even Lady Palm (Rhapis) can be found with decorative leaf markings. Ten other easy-to-grow variegated plants are:

Aucuba japonica 'Variegata' (GOLD DUST PLANT)—Yellow spots; plant needs cool temperatures. Does well in semishade but variegation fades without sufficient light.

Begonia cv. 'Lucerna' (SPOTTED ANGEL WING)—White spots on upper leaf surfaces; reddish beneath. Average room temperature best. Keep in a bright spot that gets some winter sun. Let soil dry out a bit between waterings. There are many variegated Begonias.

Coleus blumei (COLEUS)—Leaves of all colors; best in a spot that is sunny but cool. Water regularly.

Dracaena marginata 'Tricolor'—Green, pink and cream stripes; needs average warmth and bright light (but not direct sun). Likes humidity; keep potting soil moist. Another Gold Dust Plant, a Dracaena with yellow-spotted leaves, (D. surculosa) is said to tolerate dry air.

Hypoestes phyllostachya (FRECKLE FACE, POLKA DOT)—Pink spots; foliage becomes all green without adequate sunshine. Likes warmth and moisture; water sparingly in winter.

Neoregelia spectabilis (FINGERNAIL PLANT)—This Bromeliad has shocking pink leaf tips and silver markings on the undersides of leaves. Most Bromeliads like warmth and bright light but not direct sun. Keep center "cups" filled with water; enjoys misting.

Pilea cadierei (ALUMINUM PLANT)—Silvery markings on quilted leaves. Enjoys cool to average temperatures and semishade. Let soil dry out a little between waterings; water less in winter.

Sansevieria trifasciata (SNAKE PLANT)—Gold-edged swordlike leaves with beautiful banding; taken for granted because of its toughness. Likes average warmth; tolerates shade (though it prefers some sun). Water sparingly, especially in winter.

Tradescantia spp. (WANDERING JEW)—Several species have colorful cultivars. T. 'Laekenensis' has white stripes and purple edging. Other varieties have pink trim. Bright light needed for good color. Likes average to cool temperatures; let soil dry out between waterings.

Zebrina pendula 'Purpusii' (INCH PLANT)— Maroon/silver/green streaks on top of leaf; underside violet. 'Quadricolor' has metallic green leaves striped with pink, green and white. Some direct sun necessary for good color. Many say this plant, which looks like a Tradescantia, is not easy to grow without a greenhouse. Mine does well in a west window above a sink, a convenient spot to locate a plant that appears to like humid and moist conditions.

Houseplants for Hanging Baskets

Hanging pots are a good solution for those who find themselves out of windowsill space, and there are many plants that are especially attractive when grown in this manner. Flowering plants are best grown in east, west or, in the case of real sun lovers, south windows. Grow foliage plants where light is not as plentiful. Don't neglect them; hanging plants tend to be overlooked and because of their position nearer the ceiling they sometimes require watering sooner than plants grown closer to the floor.

FOR FOLIAGE:

Asparagus (ASPARAGUS FERN)
Callisia (STRIPED INCH PLANT)
Ceropegia (STRING OF HEARTS, ROSARY VINE)
Chlorophytum (SPIDER PLANT)
Cissus (GRAPE IVY AND KANGAROO VINE)
Cyanotis (TEDDY BEAR VINE)
Ficus (CREEPING FIG)
Hedera (IVY)
Nephrolepis (BOSTON FERN)
Oplismenus (BASKET GRASS)
Pellionia (SATIN PLANT, RAINBOW VINE)
Peperomia (PEPEROMIA)
Philodendron (HEARTLEAF PHILODENDRON)
Pilea (CREEPING JENNY AND CREEPING CHARLIE)
Plectranthus (SWEDISH IVY)
Rhipsalis (MISTLETOE CACTUS AND CHAIN CACTUS)
Saxifraga (STRAWBERRY GERANIUM, MOTHER OF THOUSANDS)
Scindapsus (DEVIL'S IVY, POTHOS)
Sedum (BURRO'S TAIL)
Senecio (STRING OF BEADS)
Tolmiea (PIGGYBACK PLANT)
Tradescantia (WANDERING JEW)
Zebrina (INCH PLANT)

FLOWERING PLANTS:

Aeschynanthus (LIPSTICK VINE)
Begonia (BEGONIA)
Campanula (ITALIAN BELLFLOWER, FALLING STARS)
Columnea (COLUMNEA)
Epiphyllum (ORCHID CACTUS)
Episcia (LACE FLOWER, FLAME VIOLET)
Hoya (WAX PLANT)
Jasminum (WINTER JASMINE)
Manettia (FIRECRACKER PLANT)
Pelargonium (GERANIUM)
Schlumbergera (CHRISTMAS CACTUS)
Streptocarpus 'Good Hope' (CAPE PRIMROSE)

FAVORITE HOUSEPLANTS

Something Old: Hoya lacunosa

Hoyas, choice members of the Milkweed family, are Asian natives named for a British gardener, Thomas Hoy. Probably first to reach European shores, and still the most commonly grown indoors, Hoya carnosa (Wax or Honey Plant) is an attractive trailer or climber with clusters of pink flowers and succulent leaves that may be green or variegated. This Hoya can be a fairly large and vigorous plant, one reason I have resisted bringing it home to my jungle, largely composed of once-irresistible young things now run amuck. Walking through a greenhouse several winters ago, though, proved to be my undoing. Hoya lacunosa caught my eye (or should I say nose?) and I was hooked. This small Indonesian native with neat, pointed leaves, was covered with dainty white clusters that resembled tiny doilies and exuded an intoxicating fragrance. Closer inspection revealed waxy, star-shaped flowers with fringed petals, decorated with glistening drops of honey. A bit worried about the fussy smaller Hoyas I had read about, I brought it home to a west window. It has thrived in a hanging pot, flowering nearly all year long, even though some books say it is a summer bloomer. If you have a window that gets some sun, but is not too sunny, this species makes an excellent hanging plant. Let soil dry out a bit between waterings and resist the urge to repot for as long as possible. Most important: never remove the little spurs on which Hoya flowers appear, for new flowers are formed on the same stalks.

Something New: Streptocarpus 'Good Hope'

Streptocarpus 'Good Hope,' another plant for hanging baskets, was recently given to me by a son. Although there are more than 100 species in the genus, (a relative of African Violet), I was familiar with only the long-leaved Streptocarpus or Cape Primrose. 'Good Hope' has much smaller, oval, velvety leaves and grows a bushy 8 to 10 inches tall. What makes it special are the masses of perky lilac flowers, with purple-spotted white throats, that dance above the leaves on 4- to 6-inch flowering stalks. Streptocarpus likes average room temperatures and bright light. Mine grows in a west window over a sink and seems to thrive with some direct sun and the extra humidity. This is a cheerful plant, a generous bloomer and easy to grow. It will quickly become a favorite of yours.

Windowsill Orchids

Many gardeners in the North consider orchids fragile tropicals and are easily intimidated by this aristocratic genus. In reality, many are tough, fairly easy to grow, and some actually require cold temperatures in order to bloom. It is important to learn the origin of the orchid you want to grow; orchids are found high in the Himalayas as well as in tropical forests. In general, they require humid conditions (many people set pots on a pebble tray) but must not be overwatered. Orchids need plenty of light but never direct summer sun and most need a 10-to 15-degree nighttime temperature drop year round. In winter, daylight may need to be supplemented with artificial light. In summer put your orchids outdoors in a shady spot; orchids need good air circulation all year.

Orchid. As with other houseplants, the most common cause of failure with orchids is overwatering.

Cattleya violacea* (CATTLEYA)—Among the easiest orchids to grow, Cattleyas are the common corsage orchid. Compact C. violacea, native to South America, has bright fuchsia flowers with white and yellow trim. Likes a little sun and warm temperatures. There are many new Cattleya hybrids; 'Scheherazade' is an American Orchid Society award winner.

Coelogyne cristata* (COELOGYNE)—Native to the Himalayas, C. cristata has large white flowers with yellow centers in winter. Considered a difficult genus, C. cristata is probably the best Coelogyne for beginners. This orchid prefers cool temperatures year round; buds will not form in the fall unless plant receives a cold period.

Laelia pumila* (LAELIA)—A tiny plant that produces large rose purple flowers (with yellow throats) in the fall. There are several cultivars including a white variety. Easy to grow in average temperatures; native to Brazil.

Lycaste aromatica* (LYCASTE)—Named for a mythological Greek princess, this orchid has apricot-yellow flowers with a spicy lemon scent in the spring. Leaves are deciduous which means they die down periodically; plant should be rested and watering reduced during this time. Likes fairly warm conditions. Native to Central America.

Miltonia roezlii* (PANSY ORCHID)—Orchid from Columbia with large flat white flowers with purple and yellow trim. There is a pure white cultivar. J&L Orchid growers claim the flowers of M. roezlii have "the fragrance of roses." Blooms in the winter and spring; prefers average temperature conditions.

Neofinetia falcata* (NEOFINETIA)—Native to China and Japan, this orchid has large fragrant white flowers which become pale yellow-orange. Needs cool to average conditions.

Odontoglossum grande (TIGER ORCHID)—Winter flowers are few but large; to 6 inches across in shades of brown and yellow. This orchid, native to Mexico and Guatemala, is another orchid for the unheated "sun porch" (but keep out of direct sun). One of the easiest orchids to grow.

Oncidium ornithorhynchum* (DOVE ORCHID)—Small rosy lilac flowers are produced on slender branching stems. This

*Fragrant.

Mexican/South American native is fairly easy to grow and likes average growing conditions. Let compost surface dry between waterings. There are a number of new Oncidium hybrids; most are easier to grow than the species.

Paphiopedilum spp. (ASIAN LADYSLIPPER)—Once classified in the same genus (Cypripedium) as the Ladyslippers of North American woods, Paphiopedilum is much easier to grow. Flowers are long-lasting. Try a north window; keep potting mixture moist but not soggy. P. insigne has green leaves; flower colors are predominantly yellow/green/brown. P. callosum has mottled leaves and green/white/purple flowers with rose petal tips.

Phalaenopsis spp. (MOTH ORCHID)—Sprays of flowers (which can be white, pink, yellow or red) were thought to resemble the insect. The hybrids are said to be easier to grow than the species; likes a bit more light than Paphiopedilum. Many Moth Orchids will bloom several times a year and some tolerate low humidity. Do not overwater.

Plants for Terrariums

Native woodland plants used in terrariums need a dormant period. If you want to keep your terrarium or bottle garden for more than a year, place it in a cool place to rest for several months. Even better would be carefully to return native plants to the woodlands and replace with fresh plants. Tropical terrariums do not need a rest period. Terrariums should have good light but no direct sun. A north window is ideal. If you want flowering plants to flower, provide additional light via fluorescent lighting, which will not produce much heat.

NATIVE PLANTS FOR TERRARIUMS:

Antennaria (PUSSY'S TOES)
Chimaphila (PIPPSISSEWA AND SPOTTED WINTERGREEN)
Coptis (GOLDTHREAD)
Fragaria (WILD STRAWBERRY)
Galium (SWEET WOODRUFF)*

*European native, sometimes found naturalized.

Goodyera (RATTLESNAKE PLANTAIN)
Hepatica (HEPATICA, LIVERLEAF)
Lycopodium (CLUB MOSS)
Mitchella (PARTRIDGE BERRY)
Polygala (FRINGED POLYGALA)
Polypodium (ROCK POLYPODY)
Pyrola (WINTERGREEN)
Vaccinium (SMALL CRANBERRY)
Viola (VIOLET)

Various Mosses, Shelf Fungi and Lichens also thrive in terrariums, as do certain carnivorous plants such as Sundews. Seedling evergreens may also be grown in a terrarium for a while.

Goodyera pubescens (Rattlesnake Plantain). Decorative leaves make this native orchid a terrarium favorite, though plants should not be collected from the wild unless habitats face destruction.

TROPICAL PLANTS FOR TERRARIUMS:

Acorus (ACORUS)
Adiantum (MAIDENHAIR FERN)
Calathea (PEACOCK PLANT)
Cyrtomium (HOLLY FERN)
Dracena (DRACENA)
Ficus (CREEPING FIG)
Fittonia (FITTONIA)
Helxine (BABY'S TEARS)
Maranta (PRAYER PLANT)
Peperomia (PEPEROMIA)
Philodendron (PHILODENDRON)
Pteris (TABLE FERN)
Selaginella (CREEPING MOSS)
Sonerila (SONERILA)
Zebrina (INCH PLANT, WANDERING JEW)

Small Bromelids and Crotons can also make good terrarium subjects. Flowering plants to try include small African Violets, Begonia, Episcia, Malphighia and Sinningia. Remember that the most successful terrariums combine plants that enjoy similar amounts of moisture, heat and light.

PREPARING A TERRARIUM

First place a layer of fine gravel (obtainable at pet stores) in your container to insure good drainage. Many then advise sprinkling the gravel with a little charcoal (also obtainable at aquarium supply shops). Soil may be added next; use a sterilized mix sold in garden centers. After planting, water lightly and cover. Soil should be moist but not wet. Ideally, it should be several months before additional water is needed. If you have overwatered and heavy condensation persists during the daytime, remove the cover for a while to allow evaporation to take place.

Indoor Trees

A number of houseplants would become large trees if grown outdoors in their native lands. Norfolk Island Pine grows 200 feet tall on Norfolk Island, Rubber Plant is a large forest tree in India and Malaya and Umbrella Tree (Schefflera) reaches 40 feet in Australia and parts of Asia. Fortunately these plants, when grown as a kind of modified bonsai, can adapt to living room or office life. If you decide to invest in a large specimen, be sure to buy from a reputable dealer. Plants that have been inadequately prepared for indoor life have a high rate of failure. Do not attempt to promote rapid growth; beginners often overfeed and overwater large plants with unhappy results. Ten of the easiest-to-maintain indoor trees are:

Araucaria heterophylla (NORFOLK ISLAND PINE)—This conifer slowly grows about 5 feet tall. It is not difficult to grow but it does need bright light (no direct summer sun) and temperatures on the cool side. Keep it well watered in summer; reduce waterings in winter. Will enjoy a shady spot outdoors in summer. Loss of lower branches will occur with age, but this will be hastened by winter overwatering and overheated rooms.

Brassaia actinophylla (UMBRELLA TREE OR SCHEFFLERA)— Handsome umbrellalike leaves; plant will reach 6 or more feet, growing about a foot a year if repotted and well tended. This plant likes high humidity and moderate warmth. It requires good light but not direct sun. Water and mist often in summer, water less frequently in winter.

Dracaena fragrans (CORN PALM)—Corn Palm, which reaches 20 feet tall in its native Upper Guinea, also makes a treelike houseplant that grows 5 or more feet tall. Corn Palm's stout trunk is topped with a crown of broad leaves, which may be plain green or striped depending on the variety. Dracaenas like warmth and moist soil. Corn Palm will grow in a shaded spot; mist leaves if air is dry.

Dracaena marginate (MADAGASCAR DRAGON TREE)—Easy to grow, this Dracaena also matures into a treelike houseplant that will grow under shady conditions and reach 5 feet in height. Leaves are narrower than those of Corn Palm and may also be all green or variegated. Keep soil moist (reduce watering a little in winter) and mist if air is dry, or set on a tray of wet stones. This Dracaena tolerates lower winter temperatures than most Dracaenas.

Ficus benjamina (WEEPING FIG)—One of the most graceful indoor trees, with glossy leaves and an arching habit. Can reach 6 feet; fairly slow grower. Ficus is not as demanding as some species (Brassaia, for example). Weeping Fig likes a bright spot and average warmth. Do not overwater; soil should dry out some between waterings.

Ficus elastica (RUBBER PLANT)—There are several varieties of this old standby available: 'Decora' has broad leaves, 'Doescheri' and 'Variegata' are variegated. Rubber Plant thrives with a little morning or winter sun. Variegated types, which are harder to grow, need bright light for good color. Let soil dry out between waterings. Ficus likes average warmth (a little cooler in winter if possible) and an occasional leaf sponging. Growing tip of F. elastica may be cut to encourage branching; an an overgrown plant may be cut back to within 6 inches of the soil in spring.

Ficus lyrata (FIDDLELEAF FIG)—Like Rubber Plant, this Fig can grow 8 to 10 feet tall, but the growing tip can be removed to encourage branching. The large, fiddle-shaped leaves are striking; provide bright light and let the soil dry out between waterings.

Howea forsteriana (KENTIA PALM) and H. belmoreana (Sentry Palm)—These two easy-to-grow, graceful palms are both native to Lord Howe Island, Australia. Kentia is a larger tree in the wild and tends to be a little faster-growing, although Palms in general are slow growers. These trees like cool temperatures (60 to 65 degrees F) and good light but no sun. Keep soil moist but not soggy. Reduce water a little in winter. Mist—especially if the room is heated and temperatures exceed the optimum.

Podocarpus macrophyllus (SOUTHERN YEW OR BUDDHIST PINE)—A slow-growing evergreen that can grow 6 to 8 feet or more indoors but will grow over 40 feet tall in its native Japan. Podocarpus needs bright light (some sun is recommended) and cool temperatures. Let the soil dry out a bit between waterings, especially in winter—and especially if the plant's wintertime temperatures are kept at the optimum cool levels.

Rhapsis excelsa (BAMBOO PALM, LADY PALM)—Attractive, reedlike Palm, probably native to China, which (slowly) reaches about 5 feet in height. R. humilis (Reed Palm) is similar but grows taller and the leaves are more finely divided. Like Howea, Rhapsis likes temperatures on the cool side, bright light (Howea will tolerate lower light levels) and moist soil. If you can rest the plant during the winter at a cool temperature, reduce watering. Under warm conditions, mist frequently.

USEFUL AND MISCELLANEOUS HOUSEPLANTS

Plants That Clean the Air

Plants produce carbon dioxide during respiration, but they also "exhale" considerable amounts of oxygen which makes them good companions for humans. Masses of large-leaved plants will naturally produce more oxygen than only a few plants with tiny leaves, and new foliage is thought to produce more of the gas than older leaves. Recently, researchers* have discovered that plants can also take in other gases, such as formaldehyde, benzene, nitrogen dioxide and carbon monoxide, and reduce the levels of these pollutants in the surrounding atmosphere. The following plants, among the ones that were tested, were the most effective in reducing harmful air pollutants. It is probable that many other untested species have the same ability.

Aglaonema (CHINESE EVERGREEN)
Aloe vera (ALOE)
Brassaia (MINI-SCHEFFLERA)
Chlorophytum (GREEN SPIDER PLANT)
Dracaena spp. (DRACAENA)
Philodendron scandens subsp. oxycardium (COMMON
    HEART-LEAF PHILODENDRON)
Philodendron domesticum (ELEPHANT'S EAR)
Philodendron selloum (LACY TREE PHILODENDRON)
Sansevieria (SNAKE PLANT)
Scindapsus aureus (GOLDEN POTHOS)
Spathiphyllum (SPATHE FLOWER)
Syngonium podophyllum (NEPHTHYTIS)

Snake Plant and Spider Plant are especially efficient in removing formaldehyde; the Philodendrons and Pothos are also effective. Aloe seemed to remove formaldehyde better than Philodendron at low formaldehyde concentrations. Elephant's Ear and Pothos can also remove benzene and carbon monoxide from the air. It is suggested that washed gravel be used to cover soil surface of potted plants if large numbers of them are grown in the home; this will discourage the growth of molds.

*B. C. Wolverton and R. C. McDonald, NASA, National Space Technology Laboratories.

Plants for the Office

Many offices are even less hospitable to plants than the average home. Light is often inadequate, the air too dry and temperatures too high. The shut down of heating, cooling and ventilation systems at night and over weekends and holidays adds to the stress. Many plants (such as most Ferns) are usually doomed under such conditions. Listed below are a dozen rugged plants for the office (see also "Plants That Tolerate Heat and Dry Air," page 160):

Aechmea (URN PLANT)—Likes bright light; keep cups watered.

Beaucarnea (PONY TAIL PLANT)—Do not overwater; likes some sun.

Chlorophytum (SPIDER PLANT)—Grows in sun or shade.

Cissus (GRAPE IVY)—The most tolerant vine.

Dracaena (DRAGON TREE)—Tolerates low light, heat and dry air.

Euphorbia (AFRICAN MILK TREE)—Likes sun or partial shade.

Ficus (RUBBER PLANT)—Do not overwater.

Philodendron (HEART-LEAF PHILODENDRON)—Tolerates shade.

Plectranthus (SWEDISH IVY)—Avoid direct sunlight.

Sanseviera (SNAKE PLANT)—Grows nearly anywhere.

Spathiphyllum (SPATHE FLOWER)—Keep soil moist.

Yucca (YUCCA)—Keep soil dry.

AN AMERICAN NATIVE: TOLMIEA MENZIESII

Tolmiea, or Piggyback Plant, is a plant particularly appropriate for a doctor's office. One of the very few North American natives grown as houseplants, Tolmiea is easy to grow and appeals to children. Its name honors not one but two physicians: The genus, Tolmiea, is named for Dr. W. F. Tolmie, a plant collector and surgeon of the Hudson Bay Company at Fort Vancouver, who died in 1886, and Dr. Archibald Menzies,* another physician/plant enthusiast who lived from 1754 to 1842. Piggyback is a relative of Foam-Flower (Tiarella), which graces eastern and central woodlands in spring, and once was placed in the same genus by some. This undemanding plant with its fuzzy, bright green heart-shaped leaves grows 6 to 12 inches tall and will thrive in a sunless spot. It is not grown for the rather homely brownish flowers that might

---

*Several other plants were named in Dr. Menzies's honor, including Delphinium menziesii, Pseudotsuga menziesii (Douglas Fir) and a favorite native garden annual, Baby Blue Eyes (Nemophila menziesii).

be produced. The big attraction (and why it is also commonly known as Mother of Thousands and Youth-on-Age) are the plantlets that form at the base of each mature leaf and appear to ride upon them. Plantlets are easy to root; the plant itself is attractive in a hanging basket. On second thought, it may not be the best selection for a doctor's office: Tolmiea prefers a cool and humid atmosphere. Special enemies are hot, dry air and mealybugs.

Plants for Children

Some of these plants are very easy to grow, others more difficult. All are sure to fascinate. "Action" plants like Mimosa and Maranta have special appeal for the very young. For flowers, try bulbs such as Paper-white Narcissus and Hyacinth or a plant almost sure to put on a display at a special time of the year, like Christmas Cactus. Plants that flower continually, like Wax Begonias or African Violets, may soon be taken for granted.

Cephalocereus senilis (OLD MAN CACTUS)—While young, this cactus is covered with long, silvery hair that may be brushed (very gently) with a soft brush to remove dust and dirt. (Be careful of the short spines under the "hair.") Needs plenty of sun. Will tolerate summer heat; water when soil begins to dry out. Provide cool temperatures and reduce watering during winter rest period.

Chlorophytum comosum (SPIDER PLANT)—This unfussy plant does well almost anywhere, produces attractive plantlets ("spiders") on long wiry runners, tolerates overwatering and, perhaps best of all, has been identified by scientists as being particularly effective in removing indoor air pollutants.

Kalanchoe daigremontiana (GOOD-LUCK PLANT)— Easy-to-grow plant interesting for the lavish production of baby plantlets on leaves. K. tomentosa, sometimes called Panda-Bear Plant, has furry leaves, soft to touch. Both plants enjoy sun. Let soil dry out between waterings.

Lithops lesliei (LIVING STONES)—Easy-to-grow plant that illustrates the concept of camouflage. Needs some sun and a winter rest period. Water when soil is dry during the summer, keep cooler and drier in winter if possible. If the plant flowers, old leaves may die but new ones will eventually appear (withhold water until they do).

Maranta leuconeura (PRAYER PLANT)—Leaves fold upward at night as if saying prayers; they open in the morning. This easy-to-grow plant needs partial shade, warmth and high humidity. Keep soil moist (reduce watering in winter); mist often. Use room-temperature water for both.

Mimosa pudica (SENSITIVE PLANT)—Folds up its leaves when touched during the day and naturally at night. Likes average warmth, some sunlight and regular watering. Reduce water in winter.

Psilotum nudum (WHISK FERN)—Not a Fern at all, but thought to be one of the world's most primitive plants—its ancestors may have been one of the first plants to invade the land. If it has sandy, moist soil and good light it will put forth many delicate green branches (leaves are unrecognizable scales) and yellow spore balls.

Sedum rubrotinctum (JELLYBEAN PLANT, CHRISTMAS CHEER)—Leaves, which resemble the candy in shape, turn red in the sun. Enjoys a sunny windowsill. Let soil dry out between waterings; water less in winter. Like Lithops, Sedums appreciate a cool, dry winter rest period.

Senecio rowleyanus (STRING OF BEADS)—Leaves of this succulent resemble beads on a chain; best in a hanging pot. Easy-to-grow; likes some sunshine and temperatures on the cool side. Let soil dry out a bit between waterings; reduce watering further during plant's winter rest period.

Tolmiea menziesii (PIGGYBACK PLANT)—Easy-to-grow; gets its name from the small plantlets that form at bases of leaves and can be rooted. Likes cool-to-average temperatures and bright light. Will tolerate shade. Keep soil moist. Can be grown in plain tap water.

Plants from the Produce Department

Children also enjoy growing their own plants from easily obtained grocery-store produce. Seeds, tubers and even leaves will often yield interesting—and sometimes beautiful—houseplants. Some to try are:

Ananas (PINEAPPLE)—Native to tropical America, the Pineapple is a Bromeliad and likes warmth and humidity. Pineapples like more sun than most Bromeliads; they enjoy misting but do not overwater. To grow a Pineapple from the grocery store fruit, cut off the top leaves together with a small bit of the fruit. Let the cutting dry for a day and then plant (leaves up) and water regularly. You should notice new leaf growth in about a month. There are several variegated Pineapples available as houseplants.

Citrus (CITRUS FRUITS)—Plants from seed will produce handsome, glossy leaves though they will rarely blossom or fruit. Plant the largest, best-looking seeds you can find and be prepared to wait several weeks. Plants like high humidity; air in the average home is too dry for Citrus, which also requires plenty of sunshine and temperatures on the cool side. Let the soil dry out a bit between waterings. Select one of the commercially available varieties if you want flowers and fruit: Calamondin Orange (C. mitis), Otaheite Orange (C. x limonia) and Dwarf Lemon (C. limon 'Meyer').

Helianthus (JERUSALEM ARTICHOKE)—Not from Jerusalem and not an artichoke, the crunchy tubers of this American native can sometimes be found in produce departments. If one of the white tubers is planted outside, a towering perennial plant will result; although a sunflower, Jerusalem Artichoke produces only small yellow flowers but it grows with abandon almost anywhere and edible tubers may be dug from fall into winter.

Mangifera (MANGO)—A handsome tree that grows 90 feet tall in tropical regions, Mango will reach 4 or more feet indoors. The young plant has attractive reddish leaves and needs little pruning. Scrape fruit off a fresh, ripe Mango pit. Some let it dry off a day, extract the seed from the pit and plant. Others soak the pit in water for several days (change water daily) and plant the whole pit in potting soil. Be sure to plant eye up; give the pot a good soaking. After the young Mango appears, make sure it gets plenty of sun. Mango also needs warmth and moisture, but let the soil dry out a bit between waterings. Mango is somewhat tolerant of dry air.

Persea (AVOCADO)—Growing an Avocado tree from the pit found in the fruit was quite a fad several years ago. Easy to germinate and fast growing, Avocado can make a fairly attractive plant if grown in a sunny spot. Make sure to use a pit from a ripe Avocado. Using toothpicks, suspend pit pointed end up on the edge of a small glass of water so that just the bottom of the pit is moistened. Add a tiny amount of water daily to make sure that the very bottom of the pit stays wet. Change the water if it becomes discolored. After the root appears, plant in soil, leaving the top third of the pit above the soil level. Pits may be placed directly in the soil if you leave one-third of it exposed (Avocado needs light to germinate), and remember to keep the soil moist, but you will miss seeing the new root emerge. Pinch to encourage branching.

Also try Taro, often available in specialty food departments, which produces a big plant with lush, tropical leaves and Sweet Potato (if an untreated one can be found), which will produce an interesting vine. The Rare Pit and Plant Council (see "Houseplant Societies," page 192) gives instructions on how to grow seeds and tubers of many other exotic plants, such as Black Sapote, Carob, Litchi, Loquat, Tamarillo, Tamarind and Malanga. Also available from them is a list of when the various fruits and tubers are likely to be found in the markets.

PESTS AND POISONS

Common Pests of Houseplants

Keep a new plant away from your other indoor plants until you are sure it is disease- and pest-free. Check plants that have summered outside carefully before bringing them indoors in the fall. Purchase an insecticidal soap (or make your own*) to combat insects that cannot be washed away or handpicked.

Aphids—Small, soft-bodied (usually green) sucking insects that like to congregate at growing tips. If the plant is small, rinse them off at the sink. Gently crush with fingers. Try a soap spray if infestation is large.

Fungus Gnats—Generally these tiny, slim, black flies do little damage since their larvae feed on fungi and organic matter

---

*Three tablespoons of Ivory Liquid to a gallon of tepid water. After spraying foliage, wait several hours and then respray with plain water. Repeat daily for a week to 10 days.

in potting soil. A few types feed on plant roots. An application of lime water to the soil will discourage them.

Mealybugs—Highly visible sucking insects that look like white cottony masses that move around. Easy to handpick or rinse off with water; use wet cotton swabs instead of fingers to remove insects if you wish.

Scale—Not as common a pest as others mentioned here, scale often goes unrecognized. These insects are hidden (and immobile) under hard outer shells. There are several types of scale. Like Mealy Bugs (which are scale insects without hard outer shells), they can be handpicked or branches covered with them can be pruned back.

Spider Mites—Look for them with a magnifier on the undersides of leaves. If you wait until you notice webs, the infestation is serious. These tiny relatives of spiders may be reddish, green, tan or colorless, and they like warm, dry conditions. Periodic washing of leaves will discourage them; use soap solution if necessary. Repeat applications will be necessary as eggs are not easily killed.

Whitefly—These relatives of aphids often come indoors on favorite plants such as Geranium or Fuchsia in the fall. Adults look like tiny white moths and do little damage. Nymphs, which look like tiny circles, suck plant juices and can cause considerable damage. Take plant back outside and spray with water. Apply insecticidal soap. Adults can also be trapped; coat a yellow-painted board with petroleum jelly. Whiteflies will be attracted to it and become stuck.

Poisonous Houseplants

Listed by common names:

Aloe—Latex under the leaf surface is toxic.
Amaryllis—Bulb is poisonous.
Azalea—Azalea and Rhododendron have toxic leaves; honey that is made from the flower nectar is also toxic.
Caladium*

---

*Chewing on the leaves of this plant can produce intense pain of mouth, lips and throat but no systemic poisoning in humans. Swelling in the throat could hamper breathing.

Clivia—Ingestion of a fair amount is needed to produce nausea.

Crown of Thorns**

Dieffenbachia*—Eating leaves can render you speechless; hence the common name Dumb cane.

Elephant's Ear*

English Ivy—Berries and leaves are toxic.

Hydrangea—Flower bud is poisonous.

Jerusalem Cherry—Fruit is toxic; immature fruit believed to be most dangerous, especially to children.

Jessamine (CESTRUM SPP.)—Fruit and sap are poisonous.

Lantana—Immature fruit is toxic.

Lords-and-Ladies*

Oleander—Whole plant is very toxic; so are water in which flowers are placed and smoke from burning.

Philodendron*—Can cause a contact dermatitis.

Poinsettia**

Pothos—Eating the plant can cause diarrhea, especially in children; pothos can also cause dermatitis.

*Chewing on the leaves of this plant can produce intense pain of mouth, lips and throat but no systemic poisoning in humans. Swelling in the throat could hamper breathing.
**Crown of Thorns and Poinsettia are Euphorbias, many of which produce a poisonous latex. Poison-control centers receive many inquiries about Poinsettias during the holidays and the data is inconclusive. Ingestion of this plant often produces no symptoms at all; occasionally it produces vomiting.

The Rochester (New York) Poison Control Center receives many inquiries concerning ingestion of plants by children one year of age or younger. The following plants are listed by frequency of inquiry:

1. Philodendron*

2. Jade Plant

3. Wandering Jew

4. Swedish Ivy

5. Spider Plant

6. Dieffenbachia* and Rubber Plant

7. Asparagus Fern

8. Aloe*

*Considered harmful.

9. String-of-Pearls

10. Pothos*

*Considered harmful.

HOUSEPLANTS POISONOUS TO CATS

Fortunately, the poisoning of cats by plants isn't very common, but cat lovers should be aware that most plants listed as dangerous to humans are also poisonous to cats. Bored indoor cats are more likely to sample houseplants or floral arrangements than are cats who spend time outdoors where there is grass to chew on and life is more exciting. Listed below are a dozen plants sometimes found inside homes that are toxic to cats (people should beware as well):

Abrus (ROSARY PEA)—This plant is common in Florida and Hawaii; attractive red seeds (with black tips) are often made into jewelry. Cats may also be tempted by seeds of Castor Bean, Black Locust, Mescal Bean or Wisteria. All could be dangerous.

Convallaria (LILY-OF-THE-VALLEY)*

Dieffenbachia (DUMB CANE)

Euphorbia (CROWN OF THORNS, POINSETTIA)

Hedera (ENGLISH IVY)

Hippeastrum (AMARYLLIS)—The bulb is especially dangerous; bulbs of Daffodil are also toxic.

Nicotiana (TOBACCO)—Marijuana is also toxic to cats.

Philodendron (PHILODENDRON, ELEPHANT'S EAR)

Rheum (RHUBARB)—Leaves and upper stems are dangerous.

Solanum (JERUSALEM OR WINTER CHERRY)**

Strelitzia (BIRD OF PARADISE)

Taxus spp. (YEW)—Extremely toxic to cats.

*Convallaria affects the cardiovascular system and can be life-threatening. Other plants that interfere with cardiovascular functioning are Foxglove, Oleander, Monkshood, Larkspur and Hydrangea as well as Apple seeds and the pits of Cherry, Peach, Apricot and Almond.

**Another Solanum, Potato (especially green parts and uncooked sprouts) should be avoided.

Remember that dyes used to color grasses and other dried materials can harm animals. Also keep Kitty out of the Alfalfa sprouts! For additional lists of toxic plants see "Poisonous Houseplants," pages 187–188, and "Toxic Garden Plants," pages 425–426.

EDIBLE PLANTS FOR CATS

June E. Tuttle of the Cornell University Feline Health Center* suggests a nontoxic garden for cats. The following plants would be especially welcome to cats that are kept indoors. Be sure to use chemically untreated seed; some chemicals migrate into the growing plants and could be harmful. Five plants for kitty gourmets (Ms. Tuttle says cats will eat some of the foliage and leave the flowers for you to enjoy):

Nepeta cataria (CATNIP)
Petroselium crispum (PARSLEY)
Poa pratensis (KENTUCKY BLUEGRASS)—Oats may be substituted.
Tagetes spp. (DWARF MARIGOLD)
Zinnia spp. (DWARF ZINNIA)

HOUSEPLANTS THAT ARE CONSIDERED NONTOXIC

African Violet	**Gardenia**
Aluminum Plant	**Gloxinia**
Baby's Tears	**Hoya**
Boston Fern	**Kalanchoe**
Bridal Veil	**Lipstick Plant**
Burro's Tail	**Peperomia**
Christmas Cactus	**Piggyback Plant**
Coleus	**Prayer Plant**
False Aralia	**Schefflera (Umbrella Tree)**
Fuchsia	**Snake Plant**

LORE AND MORE

Origins of Favorite Houseplants

The American windowsill, like America itself, contains individuals whose ancestors came from every corner of the globe:

Abutilon (FLOWERING MAPLE)—South America
Aglaonema (CHINESE EVERGREEN)—Southeast Asia, Philippines

---

*Cornell Feline Health Center publishes a newsletter for cat fanciers, "Perspective on Cats," $15/year. Write to: Cornell University College of Veterinary Medicine, Ithaca, NY 14853.

Aloe (BURN PLANT)—Mediterranean region
Aphelandra (ZEBRA PLANT)—Brazil
Araucaria (NORFOLK ISLAND PINE)—Norfolk Island, near New
    Zealand
Aucuba (GOLD DUST PLANT)—Himalayas to Japan
Chlorophytum (SPIDER PLANT)—South Africa
Cissus (GRAPE IVY)—Mexico to South America
Coleus (COLEUS)—Old World tropics, Java
Crassula (JADE TREE AND SILVER DOLLAR PLANT)—Africa
Dieffenbachia (DUMB CANE)—South America
Dracaena (DRACAENA)—Old World tropics, Africa
Euphorbia (POINSETTIA)—Mexico
Fatsia (FATSIA)—Japan
Fuchsia (FUCHSIA)—South America
Hedera (IVY)—Europe
Howea (SENTRY PALM)—Australia (Lord Howe Island)
Hoya (WAX PLANT)—South China to Australia
Hypoestes (POLKA DOT, FRECKLE FACE)—Madagascar
Justicia (SHRIMP PLANT)—Mexico
Lithops (LIVING STONES)—South Africa
Maranta (PRAYER PLANT)—Central and South America
Monstera (SWISS CHEESE PLANT)—Central America
Pelargonium (GERANIUM)—South Africa
Peperomia (PEPEROMIA)—South America
Philodendron (PHILODENDRON)—South America
Pilea (ALUMINIUM PLANT)—Vietnam
Plectranthus (SWEDISH IVY)—Australia, Old World tropics
Saintpaulia (AFRICAN VIOLET)—East Africa
Sansevieria (SNAKE PLANT)—Africa
Saxifraga (STRAWBERRY GERANIUM)—China and Japan
Schefflera (UMBRELLA TREE)—Australia
Schlumbergera (CHRISTMAS CACTUS)—Brazil
Sedum (SEDUM)—Cosmopolitan genus (which includes Burro's
    Tail and Jelly Bean Plant); natives of the North
    Temperate Zone and mountains of the tropics
Scindapsus (POTHOS, DEVIL'S IVY)—South Pacific (Solomon
    Islands)
Streptocarpus (STREPTOCARPUS)—South Africa
Syngonium (NEPHTHYTIS)—Central America
Tolmiea (PIGGYBACK PLANT)—North America
Tradescantia (WANDERING JEW)—South America

HOUSEPLANT SOCIETIES

African Violet Society of
America
Box 3609
Beaumont, TX 77704

American Begonia Society
P.O. Box 56
Rio Dell, CA 95562-0056

American Fuchsia Society
County Fair Building
9th Ave. and Lincoln Way
San Francisco, CA 94122

American Gloxinia and Gesneriad
Society
Box 493
Beverly Farms, MA 01915

American Hibiscus Society
Drawer 1540
Cocoa Beach, FL 32931

American Ivy Society
Box 520
West Carrolton, OH 45449

American Orchid Society
6000 S. Olive Ave.
W. Palm Beach, FL 33405

Cactus and Succulent Society of
America, Inc.
2631 Fairgreen Ave.
Arcadia, CA 91006

Cymbidium Society of America,
Inc.
6881 Wheeler Ave.
Westminster, CA 92683

Gardenia Society of America
Box 879
Atwater, CA 95301

Hoya Society International, Inc.
PO Box 54271
Atlanta, GA 30308

Indoor Citrus and Rare Fruit
Society
176 Coronado Ave.
Los Altos, CA 94022

Indoor Gardening Society of
America, Inc.
Robert D. Morrison,
Membership Secretary
5305 S.W. Hamilton St.
Portland, OR 97221

International Aroid Society*
Box 43-1853
S. Miami, FL 33143

International Carnivorous Plant
Society
Fullerton Arboretum
California State University
Fullerton, CA 92634

International Tropical Fern
Society
8720 S.W. 34th St.
Miami, FL 33165

International Geranium Society
1442 N. Gordon St.
Hollywood, CA 90028

*Aroids include plants such as Calla Lily, Spathe Flower, Philodendron, Pothos, Dieffen-bachia, Chinese Evergreen, Monstera, Jack-in-the-Pulpit and Skunk Cabbage, all members of the Araceae or Arum family.

Palm Society, Inc.
Box 368
Lawrence, KS 66044

Peperomia Society
5240 W. 20th St.
Vero Beach, FL 32960

Rare Pit and Plant Council
303 E. 37th St.
New York, NY 10016

The Terrarium Association
57 Wolfpit Ave.
Norwalk, CT 06851

SOURCES FOR HOUSEPLANTS

Buell's Greenhouses, Inc.
PO Box 218
Eastford, CT 06242
(203) 974-0623
Offers a wide variety of
Gesneriads* as well as other
houseplants
Catalog $0.25; enclose SASE
with $0.45 postage

Burk's Nursery
PO Box 1207
Benton, AR 72015-1207
Specialists in rare Haworthias
(Wart Plant/Star Cactus/Cushion
Aloe)
Write for free list

Davidson-Wilson Greenhouses
Box 168
Crawfordsville, IN 47933
(317) 364-0556
Zonal Geraniums and other
houseplants

Glasshouse Works
10 Church Street
Box 97
Stewart, OH 45778
(614) 662-2142
Ivies, Gesneriads* and other
houseplants
Catalog $1.50

Greenlife Gardens
101 County Line Rd.
Griffin, GA 30223
(404) 228-3669
Specializes in Christmas Cactus
and other succulents
Catalog $2.00

Hausermann Orchids
2N134 Addison
Villa Park, IL 60181
(312) 543-6855

Highland Succulents
Eureka Star Route
Gallipolis, OH 45631
(614) 256-1428
Cacti and succulents; rare species
Catalog $2.00

*Gesneriads, noted for long flowering seasons, include African Violets, Lipstick Plant, Columnea, Streptocarpus, Kohleria and Episcia. Gesneriad seed may be ordered from Park Seed Co., Greenwood, SC 29647-0001.

J & L Orchids
20 Sherwood Rd.
Easton, CT 06612
(203) 261-3772
Miniature orchids, fragrant
orchids
Catalog $1.00

Kartuz Greenhouses, Inc.
1408 Sunset Dr.
Vista, CA 92083
(619) 941-3613
Specializes in Gesneriads*
Catalog $2.00

Lauray of Salisbury
Undermountain Rd., Rt. 41
Salisbury, CT 06068
(203) 435-2263
Good selection of houseplants,
including Hoyas and Moth and
Ladyslipper Orchids
Catalog $2.00

Logee's Greenhouses
55 North St.
Danielson, CT 06239
(203) 774-8038
Many hard-to-find plants; large
selection of Begonias
Catalog $3.00

Louisiana Nursery
Rt. 7, Box 43
Opelousas, LA 70570
(318) 948-3696
Sells Magnolias and other woody
outdoor plants as well as a good
selection of indoor plants
Catalog $3.50

Rainbow Gardens
1444 E. Taylor St.
Vista, CA 92084
(619) 758-4290
Specializes in Jungle Cacti
(Christmas Cactus, Chain Cactus)
and other tropical rain forest
plants; several Orchids
Catalog $2.00

Shady Hill Gardens
821 Walnut St.
Batavia, IL 60510
(312) 879-5665
Over 1,100 different varieties of
Geraniums including zonals and
scented Geraniums
Catalog $2.00

Weiss' Gesneriads
2293 S. Taylor Rd.
Cleveland Heights, OH 44118
Many Gesneriads* with fancy
foliage
Free catalog

*Gesneriads, noted for long flowering seasons, include African Violets, Lipstick Plant, Columnea, Streptocarpus, Kohleria and Episcia. Gesneriad seed may be ordered from Park Seed Co., Greenwood, SC 29647-0001.

5

Trees and Shrubs

THE WOODY PLANTS

Trees have been esteemed by humans since earliest times. Providers of food and shelter, they also inspired awe, and groves were among the first places of worship. Pliny writes that Romans once considered trees the temples of the deities. Until recent times, much of the earth was covered with forest giants, so long lived in contrast to human beings that they must indeed have inspired reverence in our ancestors. The word paradise comes from the Persian *pardes,* which means a park planted with trees, and among the Persians tree planting was a sacred occupation. Vestiges of tree worship linger on today in various holiday traditions. Trees were important in the first gardens we have records of and they are no less appreciated today. Recent research reveals that hospital patients improve faster if they have a view of trees. In addition, the woody plants have always provided our medical arsenals with many valuable drugs, and they continue to do so.

Trees, earth's oldest living inhabitants, are also vital to the health of our planet. Attention today is focused on the destruction of tropical forests because they are among the last remnants of the vast forests that once covered temperate zones as well as tropics. Long appreciated as sources of food, fuel and building material, trees only recently have been appreciated for the roles they play in climate control and the preservation of air and water quality. The planting of trees is being encouraged by many organizations as a means of addressing the threat of global warming.

Aside from their many other roles, the woody plants are also the bones of our landscapes. They do not disappear with the first frosts, as do herbaceous plants, but are with us for all seasons. They occupy space, of course, but they also create space around them—which may be difficult to manage if proper thought has not been given to their selection. Some gardeners select a plant for pretty flowers alone, flowers that may last for only a few days or weeks. Others buy a small, attractive plant at the nursery with no idea of that plant's rate of growth or ultimate size. Often overlooked are questions such as: How will the tree or shrub appear in ten years? In twenty years? Will someone care what it looks like in forty years?

Based on a quick drive through our landscapes, a visitor from another planet might conclude that the only woody plants available to our gardeners were Dogwood, Rhododendron, Yew, Forsythia, Cherry and Maple. These are fine plants, but there are many other excellent woody plants that should be in our gardens but are rarely planted. Besides being more interesting, a varied landscape is insurance against a barren view should one species fall victim to a new pest or disease. Some of our woody favorites are under attack today by agents both known and unknown. As environments change, what we plant must change too if we are to maintain our gardens without the use of limited resources (like water) or excessive use of harmful pesticides.

A Word about Sex

Most people who plant American Holly would be disappointed if the red berries did not appear, yet not all gardeners realize Ilex opaca is a dioecious plant. This means that male flowers and female flowers are produced on different trees. If red fruit is desired, a female tree must be planted (there must also be a male tree in the vicinity so pollination can occur.) Monoecious plants produce male and female flowers on the same plant. It is important to know if a tree or shrub is monoecious or dioecious if fruit is desired. Ginkgo, another fine dioecious tree, produces bad-smelling fruit that many find objectionable. In this case, only the male tree should be planted. Some common dioecious plants are:

Aucuba japonica (JAPANESE AUCUBA)—Attractive red fruits will develop on pistillate (female) plants if staminate (male) plant is nearby.

Acer rubrum (RED MAPLE)—Pistillate trees are more colorful because of bright red young fruits. Not all Maples are dioecious.

Celastrus spp. (BITTERSWEET)—The American species is usually dioecious.

Chionanthus (FRINGE TREE)—Staminate flowers somewhat larger; only pistillate plants develop the purple fruit that is attractive in late summer but may not be wanted.

Fraxinus americana (WHITE ASH)—Reseeds readily; therefore staminate trees may be desired. Blue Ash is not dioecious.

Ginkgo biloba (GINKGO OR MAIDENHAIR TREE)—Only plant staminate trees to avoid objectionable fruit.

Gymnocladus dioica (KENTUCKY COFFEE TREE)—Female trees have fragrant flowers but produce messy pods.

Hippophae rhamnoides (SEA BUCKTHORN)—Only pistillate plants produce the showy and persistent orange fruit.

Ilex (HOLLY)—Pistillate plants produce the showy fruit.

Juniperus (JUNIPER)—Pistillate plants produce silver-blue fruit.

Lindera (SPICEBUSH)—Chiefly dioecious with yellow spring flowers more effective on staminate plants; both sexes should be planted for the attractive red fruit.

Myrica (BAYBERRY)—Only females produce the silver berries.

Nyssa sylvatica (PEPPERIDGE TREE)—Birds like the blue-black fruit.

Phellodendron amurense (CORKTREE)—Very hardy tree from Asia with attractive bark and bright yellow fall color. Female trees produce black, pea-size fruits that persist into winter but smell like turpentine.

Populus (POPLAR, ASPEN, COTTONWOOD)—Fruits are a nuisance.

Rhus (SUMAC)—Rhus has excellent red fall color; some species have showy red fruit on pistillate plants.

Ribes alpinum (MOUNTAIN CURRANT)—Scarlet fruit is found on female shrubs. Not all Currants are dioecious.

Salix discolor (PUSSY WILLOW)—Both sexes produce the attractive silvery early spring buds, but staminate plants go on to produce beautiful yellow catkins (pistillate catkins are not showy.) All Willows are dioecious.

Skimmia japonica (JAPANESE SKIMMIA)—Staminate plants have larger fragrant flowers; pistillate plants produce the red fruit. Not all Skimmias are dioecious.

Taxus spp. (YEW)—Red fruits can be attractive but seeds are toxic.

A Word about Hardiness

Many plants grow throughout several temperature zones and appear to thrive equally well in all. Others will survive (often requiring special attention) in several zones but will be at their best in one or two. Adventuresome gardeners have always experimented with plants that are native to other temperature zones and have often been pleasantly surprised. Others, like some of our first settlers, have watched with dismay as treasured plants brought from Europe succumbed in the New England winter. It is generally good practice to purchase plants from nearby nurseries; young trees raised in northern nurseries will be hardier than the same species imported from milder climates. In addition, one will be less likely to acquire unwanted pests, as North Dakota recently did when gypsy moths were inadvertently introduced into the state on an East Coast Elm planted by President Bush. Plants today may be stressed by drought, acid rain and/or other pollutants in the air, and pests are standing by ready to take advantage of these stresses. Selecting a species that is right for your hardiness zone and local site is more important now than ever before.

Indicator Plant Examples*

Following are names of representative persistent plants listed under the coldest zones in which they normally succeed. Such plants may serve as useful indicators of the cultural possibilities of each zone.

*From the USDA Pub. #1475, *USDA Plant Hardiness Zone Map.*

Zone	Botanical Name	Common Name
°F Below −50 °C Below −45.6 **1**	Betula glandulosa Empetrum nigrum Populus tremuloides Potentilla pensylvanica Rhododendron lapponicum Salix reticulata	Dwarf Birch Crowberry Quaking Aspen Pennsylvania Cinquefoil Lapland Rhododendron Netleaf Willow
°F −50 to −40 °C −45.6 to −40 **2**	Betula papyrifera Cornus canadensis Elaeagnus commutata Larix laricina Potentilla fruticosa Viburnum trilobum	Paper Birch Bunchberry Dogwood Silverberry Eastern Larch Bush Cinquefoil American Cranberrybush
°F −40 to −30 °C −40 to −34.5 **3**	Berberis thunbergii Elaeagnus angustifolia Junipercus communis Lonicera tatarica Malus baccata Thuja occidentalis	Japanese Bayberry Russian Olive Common Juniper Tatarian Honeysuckle Siberian Crab Apple American Arborvitae
°F −30 to −20 °C −34.5 to −28.9 **4**	Acer saccharum Hydrangea paniculata Juniperus chinensis Ligustrum amurense Parthenocissus quinquefolia Spiraea x vanhouttei	Sugar Maple Panicle Hydrangea Chinese Juniper Amur River Privet Virginia Creeper Vanhoutte Spirea
°F −20 to −10 °C −28.9 to −23.3 **5**	Cornus florida Deutzia gracilis Ligustrum vulgare Parthenocissus tricuspidata Rosa multiflora Taxus cuspidata	Flowering Dogwood Slender Deutzia Common Privet Boston Ivy Japanese Rose Japanese Yew
°F −10 to 0 °C −23.3 to −17.8 **6**	Acer palmatum Buxus sempervirens Euonymus fortunei Hedera helix Ilex opaca Ligustrum ovalifolium	Japanese Maple Common Box Winter Creeper English Ivy American Holly California Privet

(Continued)

Zone	Botanical Name	Common Name
°F 0 to 10 °C −17.8 to −12.3 **7**	Acer macrophyllum Rhododendron Kurume hybrids Cedrus atlantica Cotoneaster microphylla Ilex aquifolium Taxus baccata	Bigleaf Maple Kurume Azalea Atlas Cedar Small-leaf Cotoneaster English Holly English Yew
°F 10 to 20 °C −12.3 to −6.6 **8**	Arbutus unedo Choisya ternata Olearia haastii Pittosporum tobira Prunus laurocerasus Viburnum tinus	Strawberry Tree Mexican Orange New Zealand Daisy Bush Japanese Pittosporum Cherry-laurel Laurestinus
°F 20 to 30 °C −6.6 to −1.1 **9**	Asparagus setaceus Eucalyptus globulus Syzygium paniculatum Fuchsia hybrids Grevillea robusta Schinus molle	Asparagus Fern Tasmanian Blue Gum Australian Bush Cherry Fuchsia Silk Oak California Pepper Tree
°F 30 to 40 °C −1.1 to 4.4 **10**	Bougainvillea spectabilis Cassia fistula Eucalyptus citriodora Ficus elastica Ensete ventricosum Roystonea regia	Bougainvillea Golden Shower Lemon Eucalyptus Rubber Plant Ensete Royal Palm

*Cold-Hardiness Ratings for Some Additional Woody Plants**

Botanical and Common Names	Zone
Abeliophyllum distichum (WHITE FORSYTHIA)	5b
Acer platanoides (NORWAY MAPLE)	4
Aesculus x carnea (RED HORSECHESTNUT)	4
Araucaria araucana (MONKEYPUZZLE)	7b
Arctostaphylos uva-ursi (BEARBERRY)	2b
Aristolochia durior (DUTCHMAN'S PIPE)	4b

*From the USDA Pub. #1475, *USDA Plant Hardiness Zone Map.*

Botanical and Common Names	Zone
Aucuba japonica (JAPANESE AUCUBA)	7b
Bauhinia variegata (PURPLE ORCHID TREE)	9b
Berberis darwinii (DARWIN BARBERRY)	8
Betula pendula (EUROPEAN WHITE BIRCH)	3
Bouvardia 'Coral' (CORAL BOUVARDIA)	9
Butia capitata (PINDO PALM)	8b
Camellia reticulata (RETICULATA CAMELLIA)	9
Camellia sasanqua (SASANQUA CAMELLIA)	7b
Carya illinoinensis 'Major' (PECAN)*	5, 6
Casuarina equisetifolia (AUSTRALIAN PINE)	9b
Ceanothus impressus (SANTA BARBARA CEANOTHUS)	8
Cedrus deodara (DEODAR CEDAR)	7b
Cercis chinensis (CHINESE REDBUD)	6b
Chamaecyparis lawsoniana (LAWSON CYPRESS)	6b
Chamaecyparis pisifera (SAWARA CYPRESS)	5
Cinnamomum camphora (CAMPHOR TREE)	9
Cistus laurifolius (LAUREL ROCKROSE)	7
Cistus x purpureus (PURPLE ROCKROSE)	8
Cornus alba (TATARIAN DOGWOOD)	3
Cornus kousa (JAPANESE DOGWOOD)	5b
Cunninghamia lanceolata (CUNNINGHAMIA)	7
Cytisus x praecox (WARMINSTER BROOM)	6
Elaeagnus multiflora (CHERRY ELAEAGNUS)	5
Elaeagnus pungens (THORNY ELAEAGNUS)	7
Eriobotrya japonica (LOQUAT)	8
Euonymus alatus (WINGED EUONYMUS)	3b
Euphorbia pulcherrima (POINSETTIA)	10
x Fatshedera lizei (BOTANICAL WONDER)	8
Forsythia ovata (EARLY FORSYTHIA)	4b
Forsythia suspensa (WEEPING FORSYTHIA)	5b
Fremontodendron mexicanum (FLANNEL BUSH)	9
Ginkgo biloba (GINKGO, MAIDENHAIR TREE)	5
Hibiscus rosa-sinensis (CHINESE HIBISCUS)	9b
Hibiscus syriacus (SHRUB ALTHEA)	5b
Hypericum 'Hidcote' (HIDCOTE ST. JOHNSWORT)	6
Iberis sempervirens (EVERGREEN CANDYTUFT)	5
Ilex crenata 'Convexa' (CONVEXLEAF JAPANESE HOLLY)	6b
Jacaranda acutifolia (GREEN EBONY)	10

*The Pecan will grow in both zones 5 & 6; it will bear fruit only in zone 6.

Botanical and Common Names	Zone
Juglans regia (ENGLISH OR PERSIAN WALNUT)	6b
Juniperus horizontalis (CREEPING JUNIPER)	3
Koelreuteria paniculata (GOLDENRAIN TREE)	6
Laburnum x watereri (WATERER LABURNUM)	5b
Lagerstroemia indica (CRAPEMYRTLE)	7
Mahonia aquifolium (OREGON HOLLYGRAPE)	5b
Malus x arnoldiana (ARNOLD CRABAPPLE)	4
Melia azedarach (CHINABERRY)	7b
Metasequoia glyptostroboides (DAWN REDWOOD)	5b
Myrtus communis (TRUE MYRTLE)	8b
Nandina domestica (HEAVENLY BAMBOO)	7
Nerium oleander (OLEANDER)	8b
Olea europaea (COMMON OLIVE)	9
Osmanthus heterophyllus (HOLLY OSMANTHUS)	7
Picea abies (NORWAY SPRUCE)	3
Pieris japonica (JAPANESE ANDROMEDA)	6
Pinus mugo var. mughus (MUGO PINE)	3
Pinus radiata (MONTEREY PINE)	7b
Pinus strobus (EASTERN WHITE PINE)	3b
Prunus yedoensis (YOSHINO CHERRY)	6
Rhaphiolepis indica 'Rosea' (INDIAN HAWTHORN)	8
Rhododendron 'America' (HYBRID RHODODENDRON)	5
Rhododendron 'Loderi King George' (HYBRID RHODODENDRON)	8
Rhododendron mollis hybrids (MOLLIS AZALEA)	5
Rhododendron prinophyllum (ROSEUM) (ROSESHELL AZALEA)	4
Rhododendron 'Purple Splendor' (HYBRID RHODODENDRON)	7
Rhododendron southern Indian hybrids (INDIAN AZALEA)	8b
Rosa rugosa (RUGOSA ROSE)	3
Schinus terebinthifolius (BRAZILIAN PEPPER TREE)	9b
Sequoia sempervirens (REDWOOD)	8
Sequoiadendron giganteum (GIANT SEQUOIA)	7
Stewartia pseudocamellia (JAPANESE STEWARTIA)	6
Syringa vulgaris (COMMON LILAC)	3b
Ulmus americana (AMERICAN ELM)	2
Viburnum burkwoodii (BURKWOOD VIBURNUM)	5b
Zelkova serrata (JAPANESE ZELKOVA)	5b

A Pruning Primer

Keep the natural shape of the plant in mind when pruning. Also keep in mind the mature size a plant will ultimately reach when selecting plants for your sites. By choosing low growers—and slow growers—the need for continual pruning to keep plants in bounds will be greatly reduced or eliminated.

Flowering plants should be pruned at different times of the year, depending upon when and where the flower buds form. Prune the following immediately after flowering:

Beautybush
Camellia
Chokeberry (ARONIA)
Deutzia
Firethorn
Flowering Quince
Forsythia
Honeysuckle
Hydrangea macrophylla—Cut out all blooming canes after flowers fade; leave new shoots that may appear at base.
Kerria*
Lilac—Remove spent flowers; cut off one or two of the oldest canes at the ground (you can remove up to one-third of these older branches if shrub needs renewing).
Mock Orange
Spirea—Spring blooming.
Viburnum
Weigela
Winter jasmine

*Others claim good results if Kerria is pruned between late November and early March.

Prune the following during the dormant season. Most are summer-flowering shrubs that produce their flowers on growth of the same season:

Abelia
Butterflybush
Beautyberry (CALLICARPA)
Hydrangea arborescens (HILLS OF SNOW)
Hypericum
Privet
Potentilla

Rose of Sharon
Scotch Broom
Spiraea 'Anthony Waterer'
Tamarix
Vitex (CHASTE TREE)

Also prune the following "bleeders" (so-called because their sap flows freely when limbs are cut during the growing season) while they are dormant:

Birch
Elm
Flowering Dogwood
Grape
Maple
Walnut
Yellow-wood

General rules for pruning: (1) Prune spring flowering shrubs right after bloom and summer flowering ones in late winter/early spring; (2) Make cuts about one-eighth of an inch above a node or bud or flush with a remaining branch.

REJUVENATE AN OVERGROWN FLOWERING SHRUB

Remove about one-third of the oldest wood by cutting it off as close to the ground as possible. Following this system, the shrub should be renewed in three years. After this, an annual removal of one or two older limbs (at ground level) and some trimming of newer branches should be enough. Keeping shrub wood young is important if you are growing Kerria or Dogwood for green, red or yellow twigs. New growth is more colorful in these plants.

TREE PRUNING

It was once recommended that tree branches be cut as close to the trunk as possible. No more! Cut limbs just outside the branch collar (see page 205), which will expose only branch wood; do not make cuts flush with the trunk. Aim for the minimum surface to heal. Wound dressings are not necessary and in some cases may be harmful. Tree cavities are better left alone; cleaning them out could destroy the natural barrier to decay that the tree has produced. Large cavities may be covered to support callus growth.

Besides producing ugly trees, "topping" is often detrimental to tree health. Reduce the height of trees by proper pruning or select lower-growing species.

BRANCH PRUNING

Cut living and dying branches (A) as close as possible to the branch collar (B).

- Do not remove the branch collar (C).

- Do not leave stubs (D).

- Do not paint the cuts.

Most trees can be pruned anytime, but if possible avoid pruning when leaves are forming or falling.

Pruning in the dormant period and after leaves mature is good.

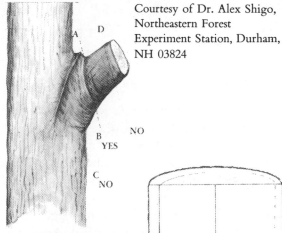

Courtesy of Dr. Alex Shigo, Northeastern Forest Experiment Station, Durham, NH 03824

DO NOT MAKE FLUSH CUTS!

Here is an inside view of pruning cuts that removed the collar—a flush cut—left, and a proper cut, right.

Flush cuts and wound dressings stimulate a large callus that rolls inward and prevents wound closure. Flush cuts start over 14 serious tree problems!

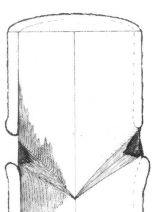

DEAD BRANCH REMOVAL IS A HEALTH TREATMENT!

But, do not remove the ring of living wood that surrounds the dead branch. Dead wood is an energy source for the fungi that grow into trees.

INJECTIONS, done properly, can benefit trees.

Holes should be small, shallow, and at the tree base.

If holes are not closed after one growing season, do not continue to inject.

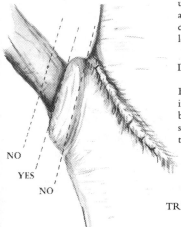

TREE TOPPING INJURES MATURE TREES

Young trees can be topped to regulate size and shape.

Proper early pruning can regulate tree height and make later topping unnecessary.

If you think your mature tree needs topping; maybe you need a new tree, especially if it is under a power line.

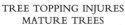

A = Stem stub.
B = Branch Bark Ridge.

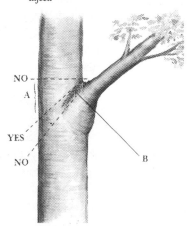

TREES

Fine Trees for Your Garden

Four of the following trees are native to the United States; most are free of serious pests and disease and will not grow too large for the average yard. Several are listed in the Garden Club of America's *Plants That Merit Attention.* Anyone about to add a tree to the landscape should consult Volume I: *Trees,* edited by Janet M. Poor. This book lists 143 species of attractive and disease-resistant trees, many of them rarely planted, which deserve better recognition. It is hoped that if greater demand is generated for these plants, American landscapes might become more varied and interesting. Call your local extension agent to discuss the trees that might be the best choice for your locale.

Acer ginnala (AMUR MAPLE), USDA zones 3–8, 10–25 feet high—Dense and compact, this maple has fragrant yellow flowers and brilliant red (early) fall color. Grows in wide range of soils and pH; tolerates shearing into hedges, container growing and drought.

Amelanchier laevis (SHADBLOW), USDA zones 4–7, 10–25 feet high—Delicate white flowers in spring and soft red color in fall. Edible fruits attract birds. There is a pink-flowered variety. This species flowers with new leaves; A. arborea, which can grow taller, flowers before leaves appear. A hybrid between them (x grandiflora) is thought to be the best tree Amelanchier by Garden Club of America. Grows in sun and partial shade, neutral or acid soils. Can tolerate drought but not air pollution. U.S. native.

Aesculus carnea 'Briotii' (RUBY HORSE CHESTNUT), USDA zones 5–8, 30–50 feet high—Smaller than ordinary Horse chestnut, with showy red flowers; there is a double-flowered form. Resistant to leaf-scorch. Variety 'Rosea' has pink flowers.

Chionanthus virginicus (WHITE FRINGE TREE), USDA zones 5–9, 15–25 feet high—Airy, white fragrant flowers in late spring and yellow fall color. Female tree has blue-black fruit. Prefers sun and moist, acid soil. C. retusus (Chinese Fringe Tree) is a little less hardy. Tolerant of dirty air. U.S. native.

Cornus kousa (KOUSA DOGWOOD), USDA zones 5–8, 20–30 feet high—Flowers are similar to C. florida (Flowering Dogwood) though they appear later, after the leaves. Attractive bark, red fall color, decorative edible fruit. Sun or part shade; likes acid, well-drained soil. Tolerates drought better than C. florida; disease- and pest-resistant.

Cornus mas (CORNELIAN CHERRY), USDA zones 5–8, 10–20 feet high—Small yellow flowers in early spring before Forsythia, soft red fall color. Tolerates some shade and many kinds of soil. The Japanese Cornelian Cherry, C. officinalis, has showier exfoliating bark.

Halesia carolina (SILVERBELL), USDA zones 5–9, 10–25 feet high—White bell-like flowers in spring; soft gold fall color. H. monticola 'Rosea' is taller and produces pink bells. Bark is attractive and fruit persists into winter. Enjoys some shelter, tolerates a little shade and city conditions. U.S. native.

Magnolia stellata (STAR MAGNOLIA), USDA zones 4–8, 15–20 feet high—Fragrant white flowers appear before leaves in early spring. Gray bark; attractive fuzzy buds; elegant foliage. Cultivars include 'Rosea' (pink) and 'Royal Star,' a late bloomer and therefore good for colder sections. Fragrant wood once used medicinally.

Malus 'Donald Wyman' (D. WYMAN CRAB APPLE), USDA zones 5–8, 15–20 feet high—Pink buds, white flowers, yellow fall color and resistance to apple diseases make this variety one of the best crab apples to grow.*

Oxydendrum arboreum (SORREL TREE), USDA zones 5–8, 30–40 feet high—Also called Sourwood or Tree Anromeda. The latter name describes its nodding terminal clusters of fragrant summer flowers. Beige-colored fruiting capsules are attractive in winter and against the outstanding red (but variable) fall color. Needs well-drained but moist, acid soil. A little tardy in leafing out in spring when compared to trees like Maple. U.S. native.

---

*Other varieties of ornamental crab apples recommended as disease-resistant include Adams Crab Apple, Professor Sprenger, M. sargentii 'Tina' and 'Sentinel.' Newer cultivars include Autumn Glory and Molten Lava. A complete list of resistant crab apples may be obtained by sending a self-addressed, stamped, business-size envelope to Assistants to the Editor, American Horticultural Society, PO Box 0105, Mt. Vernon, VA 22121.

Stewartia koreana (KOREAN STEWARTIA), USDA zones 6–8, to 50 feet—Small tree that produces large white flowers with many gold anthers in midsummer. Fall color is attractive orange/red; bark of older trees, in shades of rose, gold and gray, appears to be painted by Impressionist artists. This is the hardiest Stewartia and is hardy in southern New England; the beautiful U.S. native, S. ovata (Mt. Camellia) is best from Long Island south.

Zelkova serrata (JAPANESE ZELKOVA), USDA Zones 5–8, to 100 feet—In the Elm family but resistant to Dutch Elm Disease, this tree is a favorite bonsai subject in Japan. Trees are fast-growing when young, have graceful upright habit and red fall color. Cultivar 'Green Vase' recently won the Styer Award. Once established, this tree is said to be tolerant of air pollution, heavy clay soils and drought.

CORNELIAN CHERRY (CORNUS MAS)

I first saw Cornelian Cherries, native to central Europe and western Asia, in Ithaca, New York. Their early yellow flowers, blooming on the Cornell campus after the snows had barely melted, were more than welcome after a winter only a skier could love. I never noticed fruit on the small trees that grew next to the Plant Science Building; perhaps it was eaten before I could. A number of years passed, at any rate, before I learned that not only is the red fruit of some varieties edible, it is highly prized in some parts of the world. Alexander Eppler,* an authority on this small tree, writes that the best varieties have a more complex taste and flavor than cherry: "It can be said to be a wild, refreshing, clean taste, with moderate to low astringency in a fully ripe state. Reminiscent of a mix of conventional cherries, plums and even berries, but not directly related to any of them . . . Wine from this fruit has the body and color of a medium red wine, very aromatic, and if pulp-fermented on the stones, with a noticeable 'almondy' aftertaste." According to Mr. Eppler, flavor is best if fruit is allowed to ripen on the tree. This can be a problem, because birds and squirrels may harvest it first.

This hardy tree is prized for its wood as well as its fruit. The Latin name, Cornus, comes from *cornu,* a horn, in allusion to the hardness of

---

*A. Eppler, a specialist and grower of European Black Currants, Gooseberries and Cornus mas (Cornelian Cherry) can be contacted by writing PO Box 16513, Seattle, WA 98116-0513. His article on C. mas appeared in *Pomona,* a publication of the North American Fruit Explorers, Route 1, Box 94, Chapin, IL 62628 (Dues: $8/year).

the wood. Mr. Eppler, a musician, has used the wood of C. mas to make flutes. Long considered one of Europe's finest hardwoods, Mr. Eppler compares it to some ebonies and other tropical woods. The bark is subtly colored and attractive, especially in winter. There are a number of cultivars; some have white or blue fruit and several have variegated leaves.

Mr. Eppler claims this species is extremely long-lived, perhaps one thousand years or more and capable of regenerating when cut or burned. It is not as susceptible to disease as some of the other great ornamental Dogwoods, and it grows quickly. In addition to its very early show of golden flowers it has fine red fall color. Cornus mas, attractive in all seasons, would be a fine addition to almost any garden.

SOURCES FOR TREES

Theo Grootendorst
Southmeadow Fruit Gardens
15310 Red Arrow Highway
Lakeside, MI 49116

Lucile Whitman
Whitman Farms
1420 Beaumont N.W.
Salem, OR 97304

Michael McConkey
Edible Landscaping
Rt 2, Box 485, AA
Afton, VA 22920

Desirable Rapid Growers

Many desirable trees are slow growers, tempting homeowners to plant faster-growing temporary trees such as Silver Maple, Tree of Heaven and various Poplars and Willows. Removing a half-grown tree, however, can be a nuisance. The following desirable trees are all fairly rapid growers:

Abies concolor (SILVER FIR)
Acer spp. (MAPLE)
Betula spp. (BIRCH)
Cladrastis lutea (YELLOW-WOOD)
Fraxinus quadrangulata (BLUE ASH)
Halesia (SILVERBELL)
Magnolia spp. (MAGNOLIA)
Phellodendron amurense (CORKTREE)
Sorbus (MT. ASH)—Most species of Mt. Ash are attacked by

borers, which eventually kill the tree. S. alnifolia (Korean Mt. Ash) is said to be resistant.

Styrax obassia (FRAGRANT SNOWBELL)

Tilia species (LINDEN, BASSWOOD)—Fine tree with fragrant flowers, but aphids may be troublesome and honeydew is a magnet for sooty mold.

Zelkova serrata (JAPANESE ZELKOVA)

National Champion Big Trees

Touring the country by car? Why not plan a visit to a famous old American tree. The following are only ten of the hundreds of Champion Trees listed by the National Register of Big Trees, American Forestry Association, PO Box 2000, Washington, DC 20013. More than forty of our states contain Champions, with Florida, Michigan, California, Texas and Oregon among the leaders.

Birch, paper (BETULA PAPYRIFERA)—girth 217 inches, 93 feet high. Hartford, Maine (Wilbur Libby, 1971).

Dogwood, flowering (CORNUS FLORIDA)—girth 110 inches, 33 feet high. Glenwood Park, Norfolk, Virginia (B. Carmean, G. Wiliamson and D. Leibman, 1989).

Elm, American (ULMUS AMERICANA)—girth 310 inches, 95 feet high. This giant, known as the Louis Vieux Elm, was about 17 years old when George Washington was born in 1732. It grows near the old Oregon Trail in Louisville, Kansas (Gary Naughton, 1978).

Hemlock, Eastern (TSUGA CANADENSIS)—girth 224 inches, 123 feet high. Aurora, West Virginia (Richard Salzer, 1979).

Holly, American (ILEX OPACA)—girth 119 inches, 74 feet high. Chambers County, Alabama (Jeff Abney, 1987).

Maple, sugar (ACER SACCHARUM)—girth 269 inches, 91 feet high. The two former cochampions grow in Kitzmiller, Maryland; in 1984 New England saved face by locating the present Champion in a commuter parking lot in Norwich, Connecticut (William Linke and Glenn Dreyer, 1984).

Oak, white (QUERCUS ALBA)—girth 414 inches, 107 feet high. This 440 year old, which sprouted when Henry VIII was king of England, recently lost a 35-ton limb. However, it is still putting forth new growth in Wye Mills, Maryland (F. W. Beasley, 1945).

Sequoia (SEQUOIADENDRON GIGANTEUM)—girth 998 inches, 275 feet high. This ancient tree, known as the "General Sherman Tree," is the most massive living thing on earth and was alive 2,000 years prior to Columbus's voyage. It weighs more than 6,000 tons and is located in Sequoia National Park, California (Isabelle Story, 1975).

Spruce, Colorado blue (PICEA PUNGENS)—girth 191 inches, 126 feet high. Gunnison National Forest, Colorado (James A. Lees, 1964).

Willow, weeping (SALIX BABYLONICA), Cochampions—girth 284 inches, 117 feet high. Detroit, Michigan (Mr. and Mrs. Joseph Kropp, 1966)—girth 291 inches, 114 feet high, Asheville, North Carolina (K. Knox and C. Osborne, 1982).

If you know of a big tree and would like to see your name listed after a Champion, write to the American Forestry Association for directions on how to measure a tree. Champions are decided on the basis of circumference (at a height of 4½ feet from the ground), height and crown spread. There are still many types of trees without recognized Champions.

Foundation Plantings

Too many homes are half-hidden by overgrown foundation plantings. In addition to planting varieties destined to become tall forest trees, homeowners are often guilty of planting too closely in order to achieve an immediate effect. A jungle in need of continual pruning is the inevitable result. When planting near buildings it is especially important to consider the ultimate size a plant will attain. Choose low-growing plants when shopping for foundation plantings. Words such as nana, pumila and compacta are sometimes used to designate smallness. Plant ground cover and perennials to fill in between new plantings. Here are twelve low-growing evergreens (see "Flowering Shrubs for Limited Space," pages 256–258, for more low growers):

Berberis verruculosa (WARTY BARBERRY)*
Buxus sempervirens 'Suffruticosa' (EDGING BOX)*
Ilex crenata 'Helleri' (DWARF JAPANESE HOLLY)
Kalmia latifolia 'Myrtifolia' (DWARF MOUNTAIN LAUREL)

*Best where winters are mild.

Leucothoe axillaris (COAST LEUCOTHOE) and L. fontanesiana
   'Nana' (Dwarf Drooping Leucothoe)
Pieris japonica 'Compacta' (DWARF JAPANESE ANDROMEDA)
Pinus mugo 'Compacta' (MUGO PINE)
Rhododendron (HYBRID EVERGREEN AZALEA)
Skimmia japonica (JAPANESE SKIMMIA)*
Taxus baccata repandens (SPREADING ENGLISH YEW)*
Thuja occidentalis 'Pumila' (LITTLE GEM ARBORVITAE)
Viburnum davidii (BLUE-FRUITED VIBURNUM)*

*Best where winters are mild.

R. J. SCANNELL'S FAVORITE FOUNDATION PLANTS FOR THE SOUTH

Professor of Landscape Design at Penn State and Cornell for many years, R. J. Scannell has also been Director of Landscape and Design for the Parks Department in St. Petersburg, Florida. While in the latter post he developed the Boyd Hill Nature Trail, which received the top National Annual Award from the American Nurseryman's Association. The following plants are hardy in all of central Florida; taller plants may be planted at corners and lower-growing species under windows:

Liriope sp. (LILYTURF)—Grows about 12 inches tall, in shade or
   sun, and produces white or lilac summer flowers. Lilyturf
   likes well-drained soil; hardy north to parts of zone 6.
Wedelia trilobata (WEDELIA)—An excellent ground cover like
   Lilyturf, Wedelia grows about a foot tall in average soil
   and has yellow flowers in the spring; zone 10 (only).
Cuphea hyssopifolia (FALSE HEATHER)—Native to Mexico and
   Guatemala, Cuphea grows 2 feet tall and blooms (purple,
   pink or white flowers) all year.
Gardenia jasminoides 'Prostrata' (DWARF CAPE JASMINE)—This
   shrub produces fragrant cream-colored flowers and grows 2
   feet tall.
Ilex vomitoria (DWARF YAUPON)—This Holly, which grows 3
   feet tall, thrives in wet or dry soils. Hardy north to zone
   7; fruit (toxic) may be red or yellow.
Rhapidophyllum hystrix (NEEDLE PALM)—Moisture-loving
   Needle Palm withstands temperatures of zero degrees F and
   is probably hardy to zone 7. It will form clumps and grow
   4 feet tall.
Rhododendron obtusum (KURUME AZALEA)—Produces
   blossoms in many shades of rose and purple; this
   acid-loving plant is hardy to zone 7 and grows 3 feet tall.

Zamia integrifolia (COONTIE)—A "living fossil," Coontie is
similar to Cycad and grows about 2½ feet tall in wet or
dry soils.

Ilex cornuta 'Burfordii' (BURFORD HOLLY)—This Holly has
glossy leaves, red berries and can grow 10 feet tall. Prefers
well-drained soil; hardy to zone 7.

Phoenix roebelenii (PYGMY DATE PALM)—Small dioecious
Palm, native to Laos, which grows about 7 feet tall.

Rhaphiolepis sp. (INDIA HAWTHORN; YEDDA HAWTHORN)—
Native to China and Japan, these evergreen members of the
Rose family have white or pink flowers and grow 5 feet
tall.

Rhododendron indicum (INDICA AZALEA)—Showy spring
flowers in various colors; prefers acid soil. This Japanese
native grows 6 to 8 feet tall and is hardy to zone 6.

Trees to Avoid for Backyard Plantings

Few trees have no faults and most of the trees listed below are
beautiful and fast growing. Tree of Heaven provides shade along polluted
city streets; Box Elder will prosper where choicer maples will not and
its variegated form, not quite as weedy, is highly regarded in the Northwest. The leaves of Cottonwood catch the slightest breeze; Sycamores
have interesting bark and beautiful form. Weeping Willows, with their
graceful golden branches, and elegant Lombardy Poplars are loved by all.
Despite their assets, however, the following trees have serious drawbacks.
Homeowners should consider well before planting—especially when
space is limited.

Acer negundo (BOX ELDER)—Weak and weedy; suckers badly.

Acer platanoides (NORWAY MAPLE)—Heavy feeder that
produces dense shade, lifts sidewalks, invades underground
pipes.

Acer saccharinum (SILVER MAPLE)—A fast grower with brittle
wood; limbs often break in storms causing damage to
nearby buildings, and roots may be troublesome.

Ailanthus altissima (TREE OF HEAVEN)—Fast-growing native of
China, this is a coarse, short-lived weedy tree that suckers
profusely; staminate flowers smell bad.

Morus nigra and alba (MULBERRY)—Weedy trees with edible
but messy fruit. (M. nigra, Black Mulberry, has the largest
and juiciest fruit.) Will attract the birds.

Platanus occidentalis (SYCAMORE)—Beautiful tree though peeling bark and fruits are messy. Releases chemicals that can damage certain kinds of neighboring plants. Platanus is also subject to anthracnose, a fungus disease.

Populus species (POPLAR, COTTONWOOD)—Weak wood; invasive roots. Cottony seeds of female trees a nuisance; much branch and twig drop. P. tremuloides (Quaking Aspen) is the most desirable Poplar; it has fine yellow fall color.

Populus nigra (LOMBARDY POPLAR)—Short-lived and usually succumbs to a fungus infection before maturity.

Salix babylonica (WEEPING WILLOW)—Good near water when there is plenty of room. Poor choice for small yards as roots invade pipes and septic systems; tree is brittle with much branch and twig drop. Attracts aphids.

Ulmus pumilia (SIBERIAN ELM)—Brittle, short-lived and variable.

Some Troubled Trees

Two of the New World's most beautiful trees, American Elm and American Chestnut, were devastated in the early part of the century by fungus diseases from abroad. Recently, other fine trees have come under attack from various quarters (some say pollution is making them vulnerable to pests they once could withstand). Some of the following seem doomed; how others will fare is anyone's guess. Tree lovers should be aware that there is risk involved in planting the following in some locales:

Abies fraseri (SOUTHERN FIR)—Southeastern Firs are plagued with an aphid epidemic and show (together with Red Spruce) general decline in mountain regions of the South.

Acer saccharum (SUGAR MAPLE)—Less tolerant of difficult conditions than other Maples. Trees in the Northeast have been under stress lately, perhaps due to pollution. More recently pear thrips are a problem.

Cocos nucifera (COCONUT PALM)—One of the world's most economically important trees (and aesthetically important in southern Florida), this Palm is suffering from "Lethal Yellowing" caused by microbes.

Cornus florida (FLOWERING DOGWOOD)—Dogwoods have always had a few troubles, but trees in the Northeast (and southern mountains) are recently under attack by anthracnose fungi.

Eucalyptus spp. (EUCALYPTUS)—Japanese researchers have recently discovered that the Chestnut Blight fungus can infect some Eucalyptus species. This finding could have serious implications for California, where the blight has not yet arrived.

Fraxinus americana (WHITE ASH)—Suffering lately from a dieback that Cornell researchers have named "Ash Yellows," an ailment linked to mycoplasmal infection. Ash also appear to be under stress from other unknown causes.

Juglans cinerea (AMERICAN BUTTERNUT)—While not important as an ornamental tree, it is still discouraging to note that Butternut is in serious decline in the United States. A fungal disease (discovered in 1967) threatens the tree with extinction.

Pinus resinosa (RED PINE)—Falling victim to an insect from Japan in the East; decline in the Midwest associated with drought.

Quercus spp. (OAK)—Oak Wilt, caused by a fungus, threatens trees, especially in the Great Lakes region and Texas. The Red Oak group is most susceptible.

Tsuga spp. (HEMLOCK)—Hemlock adelgids have recently arrived in New England from Long Island. This insect (as well as the Red Pine scale) is spreading.

Trees That Tolerate Flooding and Poor Drainage

Acer rubrum* (RED MAPLE)
Asimina triloba (PAWPAW)
Betula nigra (RIVER BIRCH)
Carpinus caroliniana (AMERICAN HORNBEAM, MUSCLEWOOD)
Liquidambar styraciflua (SWEET GUM)
Magnolia virginiana (SWEETBAY)
Nyssa sylvatica (SOUR GUM, PEPPERIDGE, TUPELO)
Quercus bicolor (SWAMP WHITE OAK)
Quercus palustris (PIN OAK)
Salix spp. (WILLOW)
Taxodium distichum (BALD CYPRESS)
Thuja occidentalis (AMERICAN ARBORVITAE)

*Also tolerates quite dry sites.

Other trees of moist ground include Alder, Larch, Franklin Tree, Pagoda Dogwood, Poplar, American Sycamore and Yellow Buckeye.

Trees That Tolerate Drought

Most young trees need adequate water for a year or two until they become established.

Abies concolor (SILVER FIR)
Acer campestre (HEDGE MAPLE)—Tolerates clipping and
  alkaline soil. A. ginnala (Amur Maple) is drought-tolerant
  and very cold hardy.
Cladrastis lutea (YELLOW-WOOD)
Corylus colurna (TURKISH HAZEL)
Fraxinus spp. (WHITE ASH, GREEN ASH, BLUE ASH)—F.
  quadrangulata (Blue Ash) is tolerant of wind and city
  conditions and is hardy into southern Canada.
Ginkgo biloba (GINKGO)
Gymnocladus dioicus (KENTUCKY COFFEE TREE)—Adapts to a
  wide range of pH; hardy from zones 4 to 8.
Koelreuteria paniculata (GOLDEN-RAIN TREE)
Phellodendron amurense (AMUR CORK TREE)—Very cold
  tolerant.
Pinus spp. (SCOTCH PINE, JAPANESE BLACK PINE, MUGO PINE)
Sophora japonica (CHINESE SCHOLAR TREE, JAPANESE PAGODA
  TREE)
Zelkova serrata (JAPANESE ZELKOVA)—'Green Vase' won a 1988
  Styer Award.

Many Hollies (Ilex) also withstand some drought as well as air pollution and coastal conditions; I. pedunculosa (Long-Stalk Holly) is hardy and drought-resistant. The American natives Sassafras albidum, Amelanchier canadensis (Shadbush), Betula populifolia (Gray Birch) and Celtis occidentalis (Hackberry) are also drought-tolerant.

Disease-Resistant Trees

Gone are the beautiful Chestnut trees that flourished during the early part of the century as well as many of the graceful Elms of more recent times. Both were victims of disease and are sorely missed in the landscape although work continues on developing resistant varieties. Many other trees are prone to various diseases that, even if not fatal, can seriously weaken them and produce unattractive symptoms. The following trees are all relatively disease-free. Check with your local extension agent to see if any are subject to insect pests in your area.

Abies concolor (WHITE FIR)—Sun
Acer* ginnala (AMUR MAPLE)—Sun or some light shade
Acer griseum (PAPERBARK MAPLE)—Sun or shade
Asimina triloba (PAWPAW)—Sun or shade
Carpinus caroliniana (AMERICAN HORNBEAM)—Sun or shade
Cercidiphyllum japonicum (KATSURA TREE)—Sun or shade
Chionanthus virginicus (FRINGE TREE)—Sun
Cladrastis lutea (YELLOW-WOOD)—Sun
Cornus kousa (KOUSA DOGWOOD)—Sun or partial shade
Corylus colurna (TURKISH HAZEL)—Sun
Davidia involucrata (DOVE TREE)—Light shade
Diospyros virginiana (PERSIMMON)—Sun or shade
Eucommia ulmoides (HARDY RUBBER TREE)—Sun
Fagus grandifolia (AMERICAN BEECH)—Sun or partial shade
Ginkgo biloba (GINKGO)—Sun
Gymnocladus dioica (KENTUCKY COFFEE TREE)—Sun
Halesia spp. (SILVER BELL)—Sun or shade
Liquidambar styraciflua (SWEET GUM)—Sun or partial shade
Magnolia spp. (MAGNOLIA)—Sun or partial shade
Nyssa sylvatica (SOUR GUM, PEPPERIDGE TREE)—Sun or shade
Ostrya virginiana (HOPHORNBEAM, IRONWOOD)—Sun or partial shade
Oxydendrum arboreum (SOURWOOD, SORREL TREE)—Sun
Parrotia persica (PERSIAN PARROTIA)—Sun
Phellodendron amurense (CORKTREE)—Sun
Pinus cembra (SWISS STONE PINE)—Sun
Pinus parviflora 'Glauca' (JAPANESE WHITE PINE)—Sun
Sassafras albidum (SASSAFRAS)—Sun or partial shade
Stewartia spp. (STEWARTIA)—Sun
Styrax spp. (JAPANESE SNOWBELL, FRAGRANT SNOWBELL)—Sun
Zelkova serrata (JAPANESE ZELKOVA)—Sun or partial shade

*Other disease-resistant Maples include A. campestre and davidii.

DISEASE-RESISTANT ELMS

Lethal and hard-to-control, Dutch Elm Disease hit U.S. shores in the late 1920s and has almost destroyed the beautiful, vase-shaped tree that once was America's most widely planted street tree. Ever since this disaster, researchers have been working with surviving trees in an effort to identify resistant Elms. American Elm (Ulmus americana), because of a different chromosome number, does not hybridize with other species so resistance cannot be introduced via resistant Asian Elms.* Working on selecting disease-free American Elms are:

Elm Research Institute, Harrisville, NH 03450, (800) FOR-ELMS. John Hansel has developed a new strain of American Elm that is said to resist infection. Rootstock of the new 'American Liberty' Elm is available. Fungicide and information on how to protect existing nonresistant trees is also available.**

USDA Research Laboratory, 359 Main Rd., Delaware, OH 43015. This important program has contributed to the development of disease-resistant Asian and European hybrids, including 'Homestead,' 'Pioneer' and 'Urban' Elms. Several American Elms that show tolerance to Dutch Elm Disease have also been developed; 'Delaware II' is one. Researchers are hopeful that newly developed leaf cell techniques will enable them to insert Asian Elm genes for disease resistance into American Elm.

A number of people are working on Asian hybrids that they say closely resemble American Elm:

National Park Service. Horace Wester has developed the 'Washington' Elm (Asian parentage), which was at first

---

*Asian Elms include several species recommended by Garden Club of America: Ulmus japonica (Japanese Elm) and U. parvifolia (Chinese or Lace-Bark Elm). Neither should be confused with the less attractive and brittle-wooded U. pumila. Also in the Elm family, and being billed as a substitute for the graceful American Elm, is Zelkova (see "The Styer Award of Garden Merit," pages 295–297).

**There are several fungicides available for the protection of susceptible Elms which may be inoculated either before or after they show symptoms. Recent tests at SUNY Syracuse showed that Arbotect-20S was the best.

thought to be an American Elm because of the close resemblance.

Morton Arboretum, Lisle, IL 60532. George Ware's Asian hybrids are also said to closely resemble American Elms; some may be hardier and more tolerant of road salt and urban conditions. Three seedlings are obtainable for a $25 contribution to the Arboretum.

SOURCES FOR RESISTANT ELMS

Gurney Seed & Nursery Co.
Yankton, SD 57079

Lake County Nursery Exchange
Box 122, Rt. 84
Perry, OH 44081

Maxalea Nurseries, Inc.
Oak Hill Rd.
Baltimore, MD 21239

Princeton Nurseries
Box 191
Princeton, NJ 08540
(609) 259-7671
Wholesale only

Weston Nurseries
Box 186
Hopkinton, MA 01748

Lake County and Princeton have Elms developed at the National Park Service and the USDA.

DISEASE-RESISTANT CHESTNUTS

The beautiful, dense but easily worked wood of American Chestnut (Castanea dentata) was freely used both in home building and the construction of railroad lines (tannins made Chestnut ties as rot-resistant as Redwood) back when Chestnuts comprised about one-quarter of all trees in the Northeast. This rapidly growing tree also produced an especially flavorful nut. Around the turn of the century a blight fungus from the Far East struck, all but wiping out Chestnuts from our forests. Happily, the species does hybridize with other species, such as blight-resistant C. mollissima (Chinese Chestnut). Working to bring back the American Chestnut are:

American Chestnut Foundation, West Virginia University, College of Agriculture, 401 Brooks Hall, Morgantown, WV 26506-6057. Backcrossing hybrids to American trees is still in progress; hopes are high that a resistant American Chestnut will be available soon. (Asian species are blight-resistant but lack many desirable traits, such as hardiness and form, possessed by American Chestnuts.)

Chestnut Hill Nursery, Inc., Route 1, Box 341, Alachua, FL 32615, (904) 462-2820. The original Dunstan hybrid, developed by Dr. Robert Dunstan, resulted from an American/Chinese Chestnut cross. (The American parent was a blight survivor from Ohio.) Several new Chestnuts, 'Heritage' and 'Carolina,' have just been patented.

Stronghold, Inc., Sugar Loaf Mountain, Route 85, Dickerson, MD 20842, (301) 874-2024. American Chestnuts are inoculated in efforts to produce blight-free trees. Seedlings not available as yet.

Wexford Soil and Water Conservation District, Room 2A, 3060 W. 13th Street, Cadillac, MI 49601, (616) 775-5458. American Chestnut seedlings. For information, send a SASE; add $1.00 for a booklet on growing American Chestnuts. Seedlings offered are not blight-resistant but may be successful in some parts of the country where blight has not arrived, such as parts of the Midwest.

FAVORITE FOLIAGE OF THE GYPSY MOTH

Gypsy moths are on the move south and west and may soon plague other regions of the United States in addition to the Northeast. Many predicted that the drought of 1988 would result in heavy infestations of the moths in 1989.* Fortunately, a wet spring in the Northeast helped a fungus infect caterpillars and the result was little moth damage in New England. Parts of Virginia and Maryland were not as lucky. Although Gypsy Moths are attacked by parasitic wasps, bacteria and viruses as well as fungi, they can cause great devastation in peak years. If you garden in an area where Gypsy Moth infestation could be serious, you may not want to plant one of their favorite food trees:

FAVORITE TREES OF THE GYPSY MOTH:

Acer negundo (BOX ELDER)
Alnus spp. (ALDER)
Betula papyrifera (PAPER BIRCH)

---

*Drought stresses trees and stressed trees are a magnet to pests and diseases. Researchers also speculate that some trees respond to drought by increasing nutrients in their cells; unfortunately, this may be favorable to insect growth and egg laying. The good news is that some trees, when attacked by insects, also appear able to increase the production of toxins to discourage them.

Betula populifolia (GRAY BIRCH)
Crataegus spp. (HAWTHORN)
Larix laricina (AMERICAN LARCH, TAMARACK)
Liquidambar styraciflua) (SWEET GUM)
Malus spp. (APPLE)
Populus grandidentata (LARGE-TOOTHED ASPEN)
Populus tremuloides (QUAKING ASPEN)
Quercus spp. (OAK)—Among the species preferred are Black,
    Bur, Chestnut, Pin, Red, Scarlet, Swamp White and White
Salix spp. (WILLOW)
Tilia americana (AMERICAN LINDEN, BASSWOOD)

FOLIAGE LEAST PREFERRED BY GYPSY MOTHS:

Abies fraseri (FRASER FIR)
Fraxinus spp. (ASH)
Juniperus virginiana (RED CEDAR)
Ilex opaca (AMERICAN HOLLY)
Morus rubra (RED MULBERRY)
Picea rubens (RED SPRUCE)
Platanus occidentalis (AMERICAN SYCAMORE)
Rhus spp. (SUMAC)
Robinia pseudoacacia (BLACK LOCUST)

Street Trees for Northern Urban Environments

The following trees are recommended for street planting in southern New England by Gary L. Koller of the Arnold Arboretum of Harvard University. They were selected as the trees most tolerant of difficult urban conditions such as compacted soil, reflected heat, air pollution and salt spray. Other recommendations (for less inhospitable sites) appear in the booklet "Street Trees" published by the Division of Forest Environment, Rhode Island Department of Environmental Management and Cooperative Extension, University of Rhode Island, Kingston, RI 02881.

Acer platanoides (NORWAY MAPLE)
Acer rubrum (RED MAPLE)
Ailanthus altissima* (TREE OF HEAVEN)
Celtis occidentalis (HACKBERRY)

*Only for the most adverse conditions and locations or as a temporary solution.

Cornus mas (CORNELIAN CHERRY DOGWOOD)
Corylus colurna (TURKISH FILBERT)
Crataegus x lavallei (LAVALLE HAWTHORN)
Crataegus monogyna 'Stricta' (COLUMNAR ENGLISH
    HAWTHORN)
Crataegus laevigata 'Superba' (CRIMSON CLOUD HAWTHORN)
Crataegus phaenopyrum (WASHINGTON THORN)
Crataegus 'Winter King' (WINTER KING HAWTHORN)
Elaeagnus angustifolia (RUSSIAN OLIVE)
Eucommia ulmoides (HARDY RUBBER TREE)
Fraxinus americana 'Autumn Purple' (AUTUMN PURPLE WHITE
    ASH)
Fraxinus americana 'Rosehill' (ROSEHILL WHITE ASH)
Fraxinus pennsylvanica var. lanceolata 'Marshall's Seedless'
Fraxinus pennsylvanica 'Summit' (SUMMIT GREEN ASH)
Ginkgo biloba (GINKGO)
Gleditsia triacanthos var. inermis (THORNLESS HONEY LOCUST)
Ilex decidua (POSSUMHAW-HOLLY)
Maclura pomifera (OSAGE ORANGE—SELECTED THORNLESS MALE
    CLONES)
Malus cultivars (FLOWERING CRABAPPLES)
Platanus x acerifolia (LONDON PLANE TREE)
Pyrus calleryana 'Bradford' (BRADFORD PEAR)
Quercus palustris (PIN OAK—UPRIGHT BRANCHING CULTIVARS)
Quercus rubra (RED OAK)
Sophora japonica (JAPANESE SCHOLARTREE)
Tilia cordata (LITTLELEAF LINDEN)
Tilia x euchlora 'Redmond' (REDMOND LINDEN)
Tilia tomentosa (SILVER LINDEN)
Ulmus carpinifolia 'Christine Buisman' (SMOOTH-LEAF ELM)
Ulmus 'Urban Elm' (URBAN ELM)
Zelkova serrata (JAPANESE ZELKOVA)

TOLERANCE OF PLANTS TO HIGHWAY DE-ICING SALT

Many plants are damaged by de-icing salt using on roads in winter. Symptoms of salt injury are yellowing of leaves and twig dieback; excessive use of salt (in severe winters) for a few consecutive years could be lethal to plantings. To minimize this risk, avoid plants with low tolerance. George Hudler of Cornell University has compiled lists of the relative tolerance of trees and shrubs to highway de-icing salt:

LOW TOLERANCE:

Abies balsamea (BALSAM FIR)
Acer spp. (RED MAPLE AND SUGAR MAPLE)
Carpinus caroliniana (AMERICAN HORNBEAM)
Carya ovata (SHAGBARK HICKORY)
Cornus stolonifera (RED OSIER DOGWOOD)
Euonymus alatus (WINGED EUONYMUS)
Juglans nigra (BLACK WALNUT)
Ligustrum vulgare (COMMON PRIVET)
Malus 'Hopa' (HOPA CRABAPPLE)
Picea abies (NORWAY SPRUCE)
Pinus spp. (RED PINE AND WHITE PINE)
Pseudotsuga menziesii (DOUGLAS FIR)
Tilia americana (AMERICAN LINDEN)
Tsuga canadensis (EASTERN HEMLOCK)
Viburnum trilobum (AMERICAN CRANBERRYBUSH)

MODERATE TOLERANCE:

Acer spp. (AMUR MAPLE, BOX ELDER AND SILVER MAPLE)
Aesculus hippocastanum (HORSE CHESTNUT)
Juniperus virginiana (RED CEDAR)
Pinus sylvestris (SCOTCH PINE)
Syringa vulgaris (COMMON LILAC)
Thuja occidentalis (AMERICAN ARBORVITAE)
Ulmus americana (AMERICAN ELM)

When questioned about Taxus cuspidata (Yew), Professor Hudler writes that it is sensitive to salt in Ithaca, New York. A roadside hedge of Yew seems to be thriving on my property in Storrs, Connecticut. The difference is very likely due to the amount of salt used in the two areas. With a salt mine near Ithaca, road crews use salt profusely. On the other hand, very little salt is mixed with the sand in Storrs.

HIGH TOLERANCE:

Acer platanoides (NORWAY MAPLE)
Betula spp. (YELLOW, CHERRY, PAPER AND GRAY BIRCH)
Elaeagnus angustifolia (RUSSIAN OLIVE)
Fraxinus americana (WHITE ASH)—But not recommended for
    planting
Gleditsia triacanthos (HONEY LOCUST)

Larix spp. (EUROPEAN LARCH AND JAPANESE LARCH)
Lonicera spp. (ZABEL'S HONEYSUCKLE AND EUROPEAN FLY
    HONEYSUCKLE)
Parthenocissus quinquefolia (VIRGINIA CREEPER)
Picea spp. (WHITE AND COLORADO BLUE SPRUCE)
Pinus spp. (MUGO, AUSTRIAN AND PONDEROSA PINE)
Populus spp. (LOMBARDY POPLAR,* COTTONWOOD AND QUAKING
    ASPEN)
Potentilla fruticosa 'Jackmanii' (JACKMAN'S POTENTILLA)
Quercus spp. (WHITE OAK AND RED OAK)
Robinia pseudoacacia (BLACK LOCUST)
Rosa rugosa (RUGOSA ROSE)
Spirea vanhouttei (BRIDAL-WREATH)
Symphoricarpus albus (SNOWBERRY)
Tamarix pentandra (TAMARISK)

*Generally short-lived and not recommended.

AIR POLLUTION DAMAGE TO TREES

EPA warns that forests in many parts of America are suffering a "pronounced decline" in tree growth, possibly caused by air pollution. Donald D. Davis of Penn State University's Center for Air Environment Studies and Raymond G. Wilhour of EPA have compiled lists of woody plants susceptible to sulfur dioxide and photochemical oxidants. Their book *Diagnosing Injury to Eastern Forest Trees* may be ordered for $9.00 from Publications Distribution Center, 112 Agricultural Administration Building, University Park, PA 16802. The following list indicates relative sensitivity of selected woody plants to sulfur dioxide.

SENSITIVE:

Betula spp. (EUROPEAN BIRCH, GRAY BIRCH, YELLOW BIRCH AND
    WHITE OR PAPER BIRCH)
Corylus spp. (BEAKED HAZEL AND CALIFORNIA HAZEL)
Fraxinus pennsylvanica (RED OR GREEN ASH)
Larix occidentalis (WESTERN LARCH)
Pinus spp. (EASTERN WHITE PINE, RED PINE AND JACK PINE)
Populus spp. (LARGE-TOOTHED ASPEN, QUAKING ASPEN AND
    LOMBARDY POPLAR)
Rhus typhina (STAGHORN SUMAC)
Salix nigra (BLACK WILLOW)
Ulmus parvifolia (CHINESE ELM)
Vaccinium angustifolium (LOWBUSH BLUEBERRY)

INTERMEDIATE:

Abies balsamea (BALSAM FIR)
Acer spp. (RED MAPLE AND BOX ELDER)
Cornus stolonifera (RED–OSIER DOGWOOD)
Hamamelis virginiana (WITCH HAZEL)
Hydrangea paniculata (HYDRANGEA)
Philadelphus coronarius (MOCK ORANGE)
Picea spp. (WHITE SPRUCE AND ENGLEMAN SPRUCE)
Pinus spp. (AUSTRIAN PINE, PONDEROSA PINE AND WESTERN
   WHITE PINE)
Populus deltoides (EASTERN COTTONWOOD)
Pseudotsuga menziesii (DOUGLAS FIR)
Quercus alba (WHITE OAK)
Sorbus aucuparia (EUROPEAN MOUNTAIN-ASH)
Spiraea x vanhouttei (BRIDAL WREATH)
Syringa vulgaris (LILAC)
Tilia americana (BASSWOOD)
Ulmus americana (AMERICAN ELM)

RELATIVELY TOLERANT:

Abies concolor (WHITE FIR)
Acer spp. (NORWAY, SILVER AND SUGAR MAPLE)
Arctostaphylos uva-ursi (BEARBERRY)
Ceanothus sanguineus (WILD LILAC, REDSTEM)
Crataegus douglasii (BLACK HAWTHORN)
Forsythia viridissima (FORSYTHIA)
Ginkgo biloba (GINKGO)
Juniperus spp. (COMMON JUNIPER AND WESTERN JUNIPER)
Picea pungens (BLUE SPRUCE)
Pinus spp. (LIMBER PINE AND PINYON PINE)
Platanus acerifolia (LONDON PLANE)
Quercus spp. (PIN OAK AND RED OAK)
Rhus glabra (SMOOTH SUMAC)
Taxus brevifolia (PACIFIC YEW)
Thuja spp. (ARBORVITAE OR WHITE CEDAR AND WESTERN RED
   CEDAR)
Tilia cordata (LITTLELEAF LINDEN)

WOODY PLANTS SENSITIVE OR RESISTANT TO OZONE

Smog is a special problem in some urban areas. It consists of a number of pollutants, such as sulfur dioxide, hydrocarbons and fluorides. The two pollutants that cause growing plants the most difficulty are produced by the chemical action of sunlight on smog; these are ozone and peroxyacetyl nitrate, better known as PAN. Ozone and PAN are known as photochemical pollutants; they cause spotted, streaked and bleached foliage, retarded growth and early leaf drop.

SENSITIVE:

Cotoneaster spp. (ROCK COTONEASTER AND SPREADING COTONEASTER)
Fraxinus spp. (WHITE ASH AND GREEN ASH)
Gleditsia triacanthos (HONEY LOCUST)
Juglans regia (ENGLISH WALNUT)
Larix decidua (EUROPEAN LARCH)
Ligustrum vulgare 'Lodense' (PRIVET)
Liriodendron tulipifera (TULIP TREE)
Pinus spp. (AUSTRIAN PINE, JACK PINE, MONTEREY PINE AND VIRGINIA PINE)
Platanus occidentalis (AMERICAN SYCAMORE)
Populus tremuloides (QUAKING ASPEN)
Prunus spp. (BING, BLACK, HIGAN AND SARGENT CHERRY)
Quercus alba (WHITE OAK)
Rhododendron spp. (TORCH AZALEA, KOREAN AZALEA, KURUME AZALEA)
Rhus aromatica (FRAGRANT SUMAC)
Sorbus aucuparia (EUROPEAN MOUNTAIN-ASH)
Spiraea x vanhoutii (BRIDAL WREATH)
Symphoricarpos alba (SNOWBERRY)
Syringa chinensis (CHINESE LILAC)
Vitis vinifera (WINE GRAPE)

INTERMEDIATE:

Acer negundo (BOX ELDER)
Cercis canadensis (REDBUD)
Forsythia x intermedia (FORSYTHIA 'LYNWOOD GOLD')
Ligustrum vulgare (COMMON PRIVET)
Liquidambar styraciflua (SWEET GUM)*

*Others label Sweet Gum very sensitive.

Philadelphus coronarius (MOCK ORANGE)
Pinus spp. (EASTERN WHITE PINE, PITCH PINE AND SCOTCH PINE)
Quercus spp. (BLACK OAK, PIN OAK AND SCARLET OAK)
Rhododendron spp. (CATAWBA RHODODENDRON AND R. 'ROSEUM
    ELEGANS')
Syringa vulgaris (COMMON LILAC)
Ulmus parvifolia (CHINESE ELM)
Viburnum dilatatum (LINDEN VIBURNUM)

RESISTANT:

Abies spp. (WHITE FIR, DOUGLAS FIR AND BALSAM FIR)
Acer spp. (RED MAPLE, SUGAR MAPLE AND NORWAY MAPLE)
Betula pendula (EUROPEAN WHITE BIRCH)
Buxus sempervirens (COMMON BOX)
Cornus spp. (FLOWERING DOGWOOD AND GRAY DOGWOOD)
Euonymus alata 'Compacta' (DWARF WINGED EUONYMUS)
Fagus sylvatica (EUROPEAN BEECH)
Ilex spp. (AMERICAN HOLLY, ENGLISH HOLLY AND JAPANESE
    HOLLY)
Juglans nigra (BLACK WALNUT)
Juniperus occidentalis (CALIFORNIA JUNIPER)
Kalmia latifolia (MT. LAUREL)
Ligustrum amurense (AMUR PRIVET)
Nyssa sylvatica (BLACK GUM, TUPELO, PEPPERIDGE TREE)
Persea americana (AVOCADO)
Picea spp. (COLORADO BLUE SPRUCE, NORWAY SPRUCE AND WHITE
    SPRUCE)
Pieris japonica (JAPANESE ANDROMEDA)
Pinus resinosa (RED PINE)
Prunus aremeniaca (APRICOT)
Pyracantha coccinea 'Lalandei' (FIRETHORN)
Pyrus communis (BARTLETT PEAR)
Quercus spp. (NORTHERN RED OAK AND ENGLISH OAK)
Rhododendron carolinianum (CAROLINA RHODODENDRON)
Rhododendron molle (CHINESE AZALEA)
Robinia pseudoacacia (BLACK LOCUST)
Rosa woodsii (WOODS ROSE)
Sequoia spp. (REDWOOD AND GIANT SEQUOIA)
Sophora japonica (JAPANESE PAGODA TREE)
Taxus spp. (HATFIELD YEW AND JAPANESE YEW)

Thuja occidentalis (ARBORVITAE)
Tilia spp. (AMERICAN LINDEN AND LITTLE-LEAF LINDEN)
Tsuga canadensis (EASTERN HEMLOCK)
Viburnum spp. (KOREAN SPICE VIBURNUM AND BURKWOOD
VIBURNUM)

Trees for the Northeast Seashore

It may seem strange that a tree from Japan is the most rugged tree available for planting next to saltwater in northeastern America, but this is the case. Pinus thunbergiana (P. thunbergii), Japanese Black Pine, withstands seashore conditions better than other trees although, unsurprisingly, it grows taller in more sheltered spots. Other trees that perform well if they receive protection from direct wind and salt spray:

Acer pseudoplatanus (SYCAMORE MAPLE)
Amelanchier canadensis* (SHADBUSH)
Betula populifolia* (GRAY BIRCH)
Gleditsia triacanthos* (HONEY LOCUST)
Ilex opaca* (HOLLY)
Juniperus virginiana* (RED CEDAR)
Populus alba (WHITE POPLAR)
Salix caprea (GOAT WILLOW) and S. alba var. tristis
Sassafras albidum*

*U.S. native.

Windbreaks and Hedges

EVERGREENS FOR WINDBREAKS

When planted as screens against the wind, trees can help reduce winter fuel bills by perhaps as much as 20 percent. Locating trees correctly is essential. The general rule states that deciduous trees planted on the west, southwest and southeast will reduce air conditioning costs while evergreen windbreaks on the north lower heating bills. Deciduous trees can also act as windbreaks, but evergreens are more effective, and a double row will provide more protection than a single row. Arrange your planting so that trees face the direction of prevailing wind in your area. A windbreak will protect a leeward area that is five to ten times the windbreak's height; your home—and perhaps a garden—should be in this area.

Here are evergreens for windbreaks (space windbreak trees one-third to one-half the height of the mature tree):

Abies concolor (COLORADO OR WHITE FIR)—50 to 100 feet
Abies koreana (KOREAN FIR)—50 to 60 feet
Juniperus virginiana (RED CEDAR)—20 to 90 feet
Picea abies (NORWAY SPRUCE)—100 or more feet
Picea engelmannii (ENGELMANN SPRUCE)—100 or more feet
Picea pungens (COLORADO SPRUCE)—100 feet
Pinus cembra (SWISS STONE PINE)—50 to 100 feet
Pinus flexilis (LIMBER PINE)—50 to 80 feet
Pinus thunbergiana (JAPANESE BLACK PINE)—100 or more feet
Thuja occidentalis (AMERICAN ARBORVITAE)—60 feet

An excellent booklet, "Landscaping to Conserve Energy" by landscape architect Rudy J. Favretti, is available for $1.00 from Publications Office, Cooperative Extension Service, University of Connecticut, Storrs, CT 06268.

PLANTS FOR HEDGES

Walls are some defence, where they are tall and the Garden little; but otherwise they occasion great Reverberations, Whirles and Currents of wind, so they often do more harm than good. I should therefore choose to have the Flower-garden encompassed with Hedges.
  JOHN LAWRENCE, A NEW SYSTEM OF AGRICULTURE, 1776

Hedges have been popular throughout history for defining garden space, hiding unattractive views and providing privacy. They also stop the wind and create comfortable garden "rooms" within the landscape. Today's New Romantics emphasize hedges for privacy. Many plants can be used as hedging and gardeners must first consider their site and the purpose of the hedge. How tall should it be? Will it be clipped and formal, or informal with a minimum need of shearing? Will the hedge be evergreen or composed of deciduous shrubs? Deciduous plants and many broad-leaved evergreens may be cut back severely when you wish to renew an old hedge; this is not possible with most needle-leaved evergreens except for yew. Thorny plants deter animals and other intruders. Is your site sunny, shady or windy? Is the ground moist or dry? Is it near a road where salt may be a problem in winter? Hedges, like trees, are major landscape features and require careful selection.

Hedge material, deciduous or evergreen, should have a dense habit of growth. If the hedge is to be clipped and formal, the plants selected should be able to withstand shearing well. If a low-care hedge is wanted, select slow-growing plants that will attain a desired height and grow slowly thereafter. Remember to trim your hedge so that the bottom is wider than the top. This will allow sun to reach lower branches and keep them from thinning.

EVERGREENS FOR HEDGES

Buxus spp. (BOX)—Too tender for most of the North, B. microphylla (Japanese Box and Korean Box) are apparently the hardiest. The larger Common Box (B. sempervirens) is best in the Southeast and along the Pacific coast. Box will withstand shade; soil should be well drained. There are many forms of Common Box, including slow-growing Dwarf Box. Leaf miner may be troublesome.

Chamaecyparis pisifera filifera (THREAD RETINOSPORA)— Perhaps the hardiest variety, this Chamaecyparis is a medium green evergreen with threadlike twigs. Untrimmed it will grow into a small conical tree; a little yearly pruning will keep it a medium-size hedge.

x Cupressocyparis leylandii (LEYLAND CYPRESS)—This needled evergreen is very fast growing when young and tolerates heavy pruning; also tolerant of a wide range of growing conditions. Narrow form; good tall hedge or screen.

Juniperus chinensis vars. (CHINESE JUNIPER)—There are numerous cultivars of this medium-size columnar tree and some make good hedge plants. 'Pfitzerana' or Pfitzers Juniper is fast growing, broad spreading and grows 6 feet tall. Female plants have attractive fruit.

Pinus mugo 'Mugo' (MUGO PINE, SWISS MT. PINE)—This hardy, low-growing variety (to 5 feet) makes a good hedge that needs little trimming. Mugo Pine likes full sun and tolerates dry, rocky soils and windy conditions; slow growing.

Pseudotsuga menziesii* (DOUGLAS FIR)—Tall, needled tree native to Canada and the United States West; Douglas Fir has a graceful habit of growth. Adapted to a wide range of conditions including drought; probably best in areas of low water tables. Will require regular shearing if grown as a hedge.

*The tallest hedges.

Pyracantha coccinea 'Lalandei' (FIRETHORN)—Suffers from occasional pests and winter foliage burn in the North, but has very good foliage and fruit; tolerant of city conditions. The new disease-resistant variety 'Pueblo' has a broad-spreading growth habit; excellent for large-scale barriers.

Taxus cuspidata (JAPANESE YEW)—Yew is probably the best needle-leaved evergreen hedge shrub for the North. It is a relatively slow grower but tolerates extreme shearing and is available in many forms and sizes, including low-growing 'Nana,' which many call the best substitute for Boxwood in the North. T. baccata (English Yew) is generally not hardy north of Washington, D.C. Taxus will grow in full sun or partial shade; good drainage a must.

Thuja occidentalis* (AMERICAN ARBORVITAE)—Columnar upright tree that tolerates some shade and fairly wet conditions; needs more moisture than Juniper. Average growth rate to about 50 feet. Lateral growth may not be as bushy as desired; makes a good unclipped screen. May also be clipped.

Tsuga canadensis* (HEMLOCK)—Grows in sun or shade; dislikes wind. Hemlock grows rapidly and may be kept clipped to almost any height; it must be trimmed at least once a year if grown as hedging. Soft, graceful foliage. Hemlock adelgids are a new menace.

*The tallest hedges.

DECIDUOUS PLANTS FOR HEDGES

Forsythia, although overplanted, makes a fine hedge plant. It is dense and twiggy and easy to shear. Others to consider are:

Abelia grandiflora (GLOSSY ABELIA)—Handsome semievergreen leaves and fragrant white flowers in summer. Good choice for a low (4 to 5 feet) hedge; not dependably hardy north of New York City.

Acanthopanax sieboldianus (FIVELEAF ARALIA)—Tolerates shade, dry soil and shearing. Makes a hedge of medium height; short prickles.

Berberis thunbergii (JAPANESE BARBERRY)—Makes a dense and thorny low hedge with good red fall color and fruit. Tolerant of shade, shearing and dry soil. B. thunbergii 'Minor' (Box Barberry) is finer textured and lower growing.

Euonymus alatus (WINGED EUONYMOUS)—May be clipped or left unclipped; dense with early foliage; bright red in fall if planted in sun. Medium tall. This shrub and Japanese Barberry may be invasive.

Ligustrum amurense (AMUR PRIVET)—There are many species of Privet; some are semievergreen in the warmer parts of the country. Fast-growing Amur Privet is hardiest for the North; it makes a dense, rather stiff medium-to-tall hedge and will need clipping to keep it in bounds. Smaller Regal Privet (L. obtusifolium Regelianum) has a more horizontal habit than most other Privets, its blue-black fruits (which are toxic and last all winter) are showier and leaves, which become tinged with purple, remain late into fall. All Privets withstand some shade; some claim Regal is the most tolerant. California Privet (L. ovalifolium) is excellent in warmer regions; it has several variegated varieties.

Physocarpus opulifolius 'Nanus' (DWARF NINEBARK)—Smaller and more attractive than the Common Ninebark (P. opulifolius), Dwarf Ninebark makes a low, dense hedge that will tolerate shade and dry soil. Very hardy north; needs little clipping.

Potentilla fruticosa (SHRUBBY CINQUEFOIL)—Low-growing, fine-textured shrub with showy yellow summer flowers. There is a white-flowered variety. Prefers sun but will withstand some shade.

Rhamnus frangula (ALDER BUCKTHORN)—With colorful fruit and yellow fall color, this tall hedge plant can withstand some shade and dry soil. Grows slowly; needs less shearing than Privet. Very hardy north.

Ribes alpinum (MOUNTAIN CURRANT)—Very hardy, dense, medium-size shrub (there is a dwarf form) that grows well in shade and dry soil. Sometimes planted in a Privet hedge where hedge must pass through an area of fairly heavy shade. Currants carry White Pine Blister Rust although this species is very resistant.

Viburnum prunifolium (BLACKHAW)—Dense and twiggy with bright red fall color, this Viburnum makes a beautiful, tall hedge. V. opulus 'Nanum' (Dwarf Cranberrybush) is dense, slow-growing and makes an excellent low hedge. It has no flowers or fruit, but like Blackhaw it has showy red fall color. Several other Viburnums make good hedges.

The low growers usually require little or no clipping: Abelia, Berberis thunbergii, Physocarpus opulifolius 'Nanus,' Potentilla, Ribes alpinum 'Pumilum' and Viburnum opulus 'Nanum.' See also "Herbs for Low Edges and Hedging," page 115.

MIXED HEDGES AND TREE GROUPS

It is not mandatory that a hedge be made up of plants of a single species. The informal hedge rows of England are a happy jumble of a number of different plants. (Even formal hedges can be comprised of more than one species: If part of the hedge is shaded, a shade-loving plant can be planted that will blend in with a sun lover used in another section of the hedge.) Small trees, such as Eleganus, Crataegus and Cornus, can be mixed together with shrubs, evergreen and deciduous, to form interesting and varied low-maintenance screens.

It is also not mandatory that only one specimen tree be planted in a spot slated for a tree. Unless space is extremely limited, why not, as Gary Koller of Harvard's Arnold Arboretum suggests, plant several trees together? They can be planted fairly closely in a small grove, perhaps with a shrub or two. Such plantings not only look more natural, they also provide insurance against an empty yard should one specimen meet with misfortune. Trees planted together in small groves in cities tend to do better than trees planted alone. Plant an odd number, and generally stick to just one or (if the grove is larger) two species. An assortment of different species planted on a property is insurance against pests or disease-decimating plantings, but too much variety, especially if space is limited, leads to confusion and is not thought to be good landscape design.

The late British garden designer Russell Page created gardens all over Europe and the Middle East for many decades. (He also designed many American landscapes; one of the last was the PepsiCo garden in Purchase, New York.) In his book *The Education of a Gardener,* he wrote of one he developed on the shores of Lake Geneva in Switzerland:

> I know of few things in the garden that can be as meaningless and unattractive as a planting of mixed shrubs. Each time I have to devise such a planting I oblige myself to find a simple theme and stick to it. In this case I decided to use hollies and cotoneasters, C. frigida, C. salicfolia and C. cornubia as well as Viburnum rhytidophyllum for my main planting, calculating on a simple play of green foliage and red berries.*

---

*From Russell Page, *The Education of a Gardener* (New York: Random House, 1962).

Narrow-Growing Trees

Sometimes, especially when space is limited, wide-spreading trees are not desired. Trees such as Shadbush (Amelanchier laevis), Hickory (Carya), Pear (Pyrus) and most conifers are all naturally narrow-growing but many other trees have columnar or fastigiate* cultivars that home-owners may wish to consider. Keep in mind that sometimes, as these trees age, some of the narrow form is lost. This may be more likely to happen with Maple than with trees such as Ginkgo or Tulip Tree that are not naturally wide-spreading to begin with. (The same is true with weeping varieties, which can revert or stop "weeping" as they age.)

Acer platanoides 'Columnare' (NORWAY MAPLE)
Acer saccharum 'Monumentale' (SUGAR MAPLE)
Betula spp. (BIRCH)—Several species have upright forms.
Carpinus betulus 'Columnaris' and 'Fastigiata' (EUROPEAN
　　HORNBEAM)—The former is more slender.
Crataegus spp. (HAWTHORN, THORN APPLE)—Several species
　　have fastigiate varieties.
Fagus sylvatica 'Fastigiata' (EUROPEAN BEECH)
Ginkgo biloba 'Fastigiata' (MAIDENHAIR TREE; GINKGO)
Liriodendron tulipifera 'Fastigiatum' (TULIP TREE)
Quercus robur 'Fastigiata' (ENGLISH OAK)
Tilia spp. (LINDEN, BASSWOOD)—Several species have upright
　　forms.

There is also a fastigiate European Mountain Ash (much troubled by borers), a fastigiate Sargent Cherry (Prunus sargentii, a fine and hardy flowering cherry, though intolerant of smog) and even an upright Crabapple, Malus baccata 'Columnaris.'

Weeping Trees

Planted to excess in Victorian times and shunned by landscapers who came later, weeping trees have recently staged a comeback, perhaps due to more individualistic styles of architecture and today's popularity of Japanese-style gardening. Weeping Willows, although beloved, are too large and bad-mannered for the average yard. Most beautiful of all, perhaps, is a mature Fagus sylvatica 'Pendula' or Weeping Beech, but this tree remains an ugly duckling for many years and, like Weeping Willow,

---

*Branches are narrow and upright, similar to Lombardy Poplar.

eventually will need considerable space. Fortunately, there are other weeping trees that are smaller or generally more suitable for limited space; some can be graceful additions to the landscape. Consider your site and choose carefully. Weeping trees do stand out; when weeping habit is combined with unusual color, as in Weeping Blue Atlas Cedar and Weeping Blue Spruce, the results can be less than satisfactory in many settings. Ten deciduous weeping trees are:

Acer palmatum (JAPANESE MAPLE)—Several weeping cultivars with dissected leaves are available.

Betula pendula 'Youngii' (YOUNG'S WEEPING BEECH)—Small weeping tree with white trunk and branches. Borers can be troublesome.

Carpinus betulus 'Pendula' (WEEPING EUROPEAN HORNBEAM)—Small, hardy, neat and tough-wooded. Thrives in moist soil.

Cercidiphyllum magnificum 'Pendulum' (WEEPING KATSURA TREE)—Asian native; can grow to 100 feet in rich, moist soil.

Laburnum anagyroides 'Pendulum' (WEEPING GOLDEN-CHAIN TREE)—Small tree with showy yellow flowers; seeds are toxic.

Malus 'Red Jade' (WEEPING CRABAPPLE)—Pink buds, white flowers and decorative red fruit. Will need some pruning.

Prunus subhirtella 'Pendula' (HIGAN OR WEEPING JAPANESE CHERRY)—Commonly planted with pale pink flowers in early spring; intolerant of smog.

Sophora japonica 'Pendula' (WEEPING PAGODA TREE)—Small tree (smaller than the parent species) with creamy white flowers (sparse) and attractive dark green leaves.

Tilia petiolaris (WEEPING SILVER LINDEN)—Fast growing (to 75 feet) with small fragrant flowers and woolly white undersurfaces of leaves that are attractive in wind. Fairly tolerant of city conditions though white leaf backs may pick up soot and dust. Ginkgo biloba 'Pendula' may be better for city life.

Ulmus glabra 'Camperdownii' (WEEPING SCOTCH ELM)—An old favorite, much planted in Victorian times. Less troubled with Dutch Elm Disease than larger Elms.

Among the weeping conifers (in general, weeping conifers are considerably smaller than the parent species):

Abies alba 'Pendula' (WEEPING WHITE FIR)
Juniperus virginiana 'Pendula' (WEEPING RED CEDAR)
Picea abies 'Pendula' (WEEPING NORWAY SPRUCE)
Pinus strobus 'Pendula' (WEEPING WHITE PINE)
Tsuga canadensis 'Pendula' (WEEPING HEMLOCK)

Woody Plants with Handsome Winter Silhouettes

Many deciduous trees possess distinctive branching and are particularly attractive against an open sky (or, in the case of smaller trees and shrubs, against an evergreen background) in winter. Here are a few of the many attractive species:

Acer palmatum (JAPANESE MAPLE)
Acer griseum (PAPERBARK MAPLE)
Betula papyrifera* (PAPER BIRCH)
Carya ovata (SHAGBARK HICKORY)
Cornus florida (FLOWERING DOGWOOD)
Cornus kousa (KOUSA DOGWOOD)
Diospyros virginiana (PERSIMMON)
Fagus spp. (BEECH)
Ginkgo biloba (MAIDENHAIR TREE)
Gymnocladus dioica (KENTUCKY COFFEE TREE)
Lagerstroemia indica (CRAPE MYRTLE)
Liquidambar styraciflua** (SWEET GUM)
Liriodendron tulipifera (TULIP TREE)
Magnolia spp. (MAGNOLIA)
Nyssa sylvatica (TUPELO, PEPPERIDGE, SOUR GUM)
Oxydendrum arboreum (SOURWOOD, SORREL TREE)
Phellodendron amurense (CORKTREE)
Quercus spp. (OAK)
Rhus typhina (SUMAC)
Sassafras albidium (SASSAFRAS)
Ulmus americana (AMERICAN ELM)***
Vaccinium corymbosum (HIGHBUSH BLUEBERRY)

---

*Especially attractive when open-grown in the North country; maroon twigs produce a reddish haze over trees in winter.
**Attractive round, spiny fruits persist into winter; branches with corky wings.
***American Elms are subject to Dutch Elm Disease; the type with the most attractive weeping form is thought to be the least susceptible.

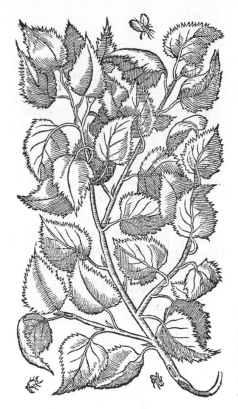

Betula sp. (Birch). Although plagued by serious pests, graceful birches are popular landscape trees. B. nigra 'Heritage' is a pest-resistant, heat-tolerant cultivar with cream-colored bark.

Trees with Interesting Bark

Acer* griseum (PAPERBARK MAPLE)—Showy red-brown bark similar to River Birch. Bark sheds to reveal lighter-colored patches. Autumn leaf color is brilliant red.

Betula nigra (RIVER BIRCH)—Bark very loose and shaggy; red-brown (another name for tree is Red Birch) with patches of tan, orange and gray. Catches blowing snow. B. nigra 'Heritage' with cream/pink peeling bark, is a 1990 Styer Award winner. Not commonly troubled by birch borers.

---

*Other Maples have beautiful bark, including our eastern native, A. pensylvanicum (Striped Maple), which has green and white stripes as its common name implies. If conditions are right in winter the trunk of Striped Maple becomes a rather startling blue, which is quite striking in combination with its red twigs and buds. Like many woodland plants this small tree requires partial shade and moist but well-drained soils. Several Maples from Asia have attractive striped bark; they include A. capillipes, A. davidii and A. tegmentosum.

Betula papyrifera (PAPER OR CANOE BIRCH)—Chalky white peeling bark and beautiful maroon twigs. Bark of young trees is maroon and then pink before turning white. Hybridizes freely with B. populifolia (White or Gray Birch), which also has white bark. These trees are seldom troubled by borers that attack European White Birch, but leaf miners may need control.

Carpinus caroliniana (AMERICAN HORNBEAM)—Smooth gray bark full of irregular, vertical musclelike ridges (another name for tree is Musclewood). Wood is hard and durable and is used to make handles and sporting goods.

Carya ovata (SHAGBARK HICKORY)—Distinctive gray, shaggy bark and picturesque branching. Peeling bark used by trailblazers as kindling, hence another common name, "Pancake Wood." Difficult to transplant. Edible fruit.

Diospyros virginiana (PERSIMMON; POSSUMWOOD)— Slow-growing U.S. native reaching about 50 feet with fragrant flowers and edible golden fruit. Bark deeply cut into small, regular blocks revealing reddish inner bark.

Eucalyptus niphophila (SNOW GUM)—A small, hardy Eucalyptus with smooth, white, peeling bark. Many Eucalyptus species have decorative bark. The trunk of E. citriodora (Lemon Scented Gum) may be tinged pink.

Fagus grandifolia (AMERICAN BEECH)—Large tree, dense and oval in form with smooth, light gray bark. Do not plan to grow much underneath it as branches sweep to ground, shade is dense and roots feed at surface. Stands clipping; fine specimen tree. Long, pointed, brown winter buds.

Parrotia persica (PERSIAN PARROTIA)—A small tree from Iran that grows fairly rapidly and can reach 20 to 40 feet. Flowers in spring before the leaves appear; excellent yellow to red fall color. Exfoliating bark in patches of gray/green/white. Hardy in zones 5 to 8.

Pinus bungeana (LACEBARK PINE)—Native to northwest China; can grow to 100 feet, but often remains shrubby in cultivation. Bark is scaly, revealing patches of gray, green, tan and chalky white.

Platanus occidentalis (SYCAMORE; AMERICAN PLANETREE)—Beautiful, colorful exfoliating bark and majestic form; the upper branches of Sycamore can appear nearly as white as White Birch. This tree needs plenty of room to be at its best; untidy in smaller situations.

Prunus spp. (CHERRY)—Many Cherries produce handsome, shiny reddish-brown bark with interesting horizontal lenticels.

Stewartia spp. (STEWARTIA)—Disease-resistant small trees with large white summer flowers, fine fall color and multicolored, peeling bark. Hardy S. koreana has bark in shades of pale pink, deep rose, gold and gray. Six species are native to eastern Asia and eastern North America.

Ulmus parvifolia (LACEBARK ELM)—Some forms of this small tree, introduced from China and Japan, can resemble American Elm in habit. Reddish brown bark is arrestingly patterned, especially on older trees.

Carya ovata (Shagbark Hickory). Handsome slow-growing native American tree with shaggy bark and rich-flavored nuts.

Trees with Fragrant Flowers

Acer ginnala (AMUR MAPLE)—Yellow, spring
Chionanthus virginicus (FRINGE TREE)—White, spring
Cladrastis lutea (YELLOWWOOD)—White, spring
Elaeagnus angustifolia (RUSSIAN OLIVE)—Yellow, early
    summer
Koelreuteria paniculata (GOLDEN RAIN TREE)—Yellow, summer
Magnolia stellata (STAR MAGNOLIA)—White, spring
Malus spp.* (CRABAPPLE)—White, pink, spring
Prunus serrulata var. Lannesiana (JAPANESE FLOWERING
    CHERRY)—Pink, spring
Robinia pseudoacacia (BLACK LOCUST)—White, late spring
Styrax obassia (FRAGRANT SNOWBELL)—White, spring
Symplocos paniculata (ASIATIC SWEETLEAF,
    SAPPHIREBERRY)—White, late spring
Tilia cordata (LITTLELEAF LINDEN)—Creamy white, summer

*Not all Crabapples are fragrant.

Pittosporum tobira (Japanese Pittosporum, Mock Orange) and Sophora secundiflora (Mescal Bean) both have fragrant flowers but are not hardy north of zone 8. The bright red seeds of the latter are toxic.

SOME ALTERNATIVES TO FLOWERING DOGWOOD

American native Cornus florida is a beautiful tree in all seasons. Tiny flowers are set off by showy pink or white bracts in spring and shiny red fruit (enjoyed by birds) and red leaves are notable in the fall. Those that try to improve perfection have brought us yellow-fruited forms, double-flowered Dogwoods, variegated Dogwoods and even a weeping Flowering Dogwood. Gardeners have always regarded some of Dogwood's troubles—crown rot, canker, borers—as a small price to pay for such an indispensable garden subject. Now, however, a still-mysterious blight is causing concern in many areas, especially the Northeast and mountain regions of the South. So far, not all Dogwoods are being attacked and not all attacked trees succumb. Still, as we wait for further information on the blight's prognosis (and for the resistant hybrids that some are already working on to come to market), gardeners may wish to consider less-troubled alternatives:

Amelanchier spp. (SHADBUSH)—American native that produces
    delicate white flowers in early spring before Flowering
    Dogwood blooms. Fruit is edible and enjoyed by birds; fall

color is red. There are new varieties available with pink
buds and pink-tinged blossoms.

Chionanthus virginicus (FRINGE TREE)—Small native tree that
produces fragrant white flowers about two weeks after C.
florida blooms. Good yellow fall color. Female plants will
produce blue-black fruit.

Cornus alternifolia* (PAGODA DOGWOOD)—Small native tree
with uniquely beautiful horizontal branching. It grows in
sun or shade, has red fall color and striking blue fruit on
red pedicels. White flowers, which are different and not as
showy as those of Flowering Dogwood, appear several
weeks after C. florida has bloomed. In some areas Pagoda
Dogwood is subject to twig blight; C. controversa (its
Asian counterpart) may be substituted in these regions.

*Most Dogwoods have opposite leaves and branching; Cornus alternifolia is an
exception, as the name implies.

Cornus alternifolia (Pagoda
Dogwood). Attractive in all
seasons, Pagoda Dogwood is
a fairly fast-growing small
native tree. There is a variegated cultivar.

Cornus kousa (KOUSA DOGWOOD)—Blooms later than C. florida, and though flowers are similar (C. kousa has pointed bracts instead of the notched bracts of C. florida) they are not quite as striking since they appear after leaves have unfolded. Fall color is a softer red and hanging red fruit is not as bright. C. kousa does have interesting exfoliating bark and is more tolerant of drought than C. florida; most importantly, it appears to be relatively disease-free. Asian native.

Halesia carolina (SILVERBELL)—Blooms about the same time as Flowering Dogwood; blossoms are white and bell-like and fall color is yellow. U.S. native. H. monticola is larger; said to withstand city conditions.

Styrax obassia (FRAGRANT SNOWBELL)—Fast-growing small tree with fragrant white, bell-like flowers. An Asian native, Styrax blooms after Flowering Dogwood; it also has interesting bark and branching. S. japonica is said to be hardier, but flowers are less fragrant.

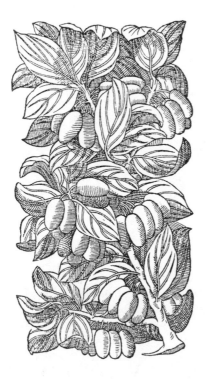

Cornus mas (Cornelian Cherry). A hardy small tree with early yellow flowers that bloom before leaves appear and edible fruit. There are many cultivars.

Symplocos paniculata (ASIATIC SWEETLEAF, SAPPHIREBERRY)—
Another small Asian native with fragrant white flowers, Symplocos has showy bright blue fruit that is quickly eaten by birds. Two different clones should be planted for the best fruit set. Flowers a week or two after C. florida.

Viburnum plicatum tomentosum (DOUBLEFILE VIBURNUM)—
Blooms after C. florida (but before C. kousa) with showy white flowers. Red fruit (eaten by many birds) is also showy, as is red fall color. Asian native with a broad horizontal habit.

Viburnum prunifolium (BLACK HAW)—This dense, fine-textured native can be trained into a small tree. Flowers (late spring) and fruit not as showy as Doublefile, but fall color a more brilliant red. Similar to Hawthorn (Crataegus), but without the Hawthorn troubles.

Trees for Red Fall Color

The brilliant red and orange fall color that North Americans enjoy each year does not occur in most parts of the world, where leaves only yellow before falling. Many associate red color with Maples (especially Red Maple), which can be the brightest of reds, particularly when growing in low, wet spots. However, do not count on red color from Maples; they can also turn yellow. (Norway Maple is always a good, clear yellow.) As I write, my Red Maple "twins," growing so close together that their upper branches mingle, are turning color; for the ten years that I have observed them one always turns red, the other gold. Other Maples will turn combinations of red and yellow.

LARGE TREES (50 TO 100 FEET):

White Ash (FRAXINUS AMERICANA)—Reddish purple
Sweet Gum (LIQUIDAMBAR STYRACIFLUA)—Red
Tupelo or Sourgum (NYSSA SYLVATICA)—Brilliant red
White Oak (QUERCUS ALBA)—Soft purple-red
Scarlet Oak (Q. COCCINEA)—Scarlet
Pin Oak (Q. PALUSTRIS)—Scarlet

THE MAPLES:

Red Maple (ACER RUBRUM)—Red and/or yellow
Sugar Maple (A. SACCHARUM)—Red and/or yellow

Silver Maple (A. saccharinum) also turns red or yellow, but color is duller and the tree is generally inferior to Red Maple for use in the landscape. Norway Maple always turns a beautiful clear yellow in the fall.

BEST SMALL TREES FOR RED FALL COLOR:

Amur Maple (ACER GINNALA)
Blackhaw (VIBURNUM PRUNIFOLIUM)
Callery Pear (PYRUS CALLERYANA)
Dogwood (CORNUS FLORIDA, KOUSA, ALTERNIFOLIA)
Hawthorn (CRATAEGUS VIRIDIS, PHAENOPYRUM)
Sargent Cherry (PRUNUS SARGENTII)
Sourwood, Sorrel Tree (OXYDENDRUM ARBOREUM)

Sassafras (Sassafras albidum), a native American, turns bright orange-red in the fall.

SOME TOLL-FREE HOTLINES FOR NEW ENGLAND
FALL COLOR UPDATES:

Maine: (800) 533-9595
Massachusetts: (800) 343-9072
Rhode Island: (800) 556-2484
Vermont: (800) 634-8984

Variegated and Colorful Evergreens

Evergreens with silvery blue, golden or variegated foliage come in many sizes, shapes and shades of color. The name 'Glauca' describes plants with gray/white foliage; 'Aurea,' 'Aureus' or 'Lutea' all allude to golden color. Although these plants can brighten a dull spot, they do stand out in the landscape; the bluest or most golden specimen obtainable is not necessarily the most effective. Keep in mind that some variegated broad-leaved evergreens are less vigorous than their all-green relatives and generally do better in protected sites.

> **Abies concolor** (SILVER OR WHITE FIR)—Needles are blue
> enough for accent in the landscape, but the tree is more

refined and less stiff than Colorado Blue Spruce. Unlike many other firs, White Fir will tolerate hot, dry summers once established. There are several dwarf cultivars.

Aucuba japonica (JAPANESE AUCUBA)—Shade loving and smog resistant, Aucuba is a large shrub (there is a dwarf form) much grown in the West and South but not hardy north of zone 8. There are varieties with both white and gold variegations. Tolerates drought once established. Plants are dioecious and both sexes must be planted for the attractive red fruit. Ilex aquifolium (English Holly) is another dioecious broad-leaved evergreen with white/gold variegated forms that thrives in the Pacific Northwest.

Cedrus atlantica (ATLAS CEDAR)—Foliage of the species is blue-green; cultivar 'Glauca' (Atlas Blue Cedar) is very blue. This fine tree will tolerate drought (when established) and air pollution but is not hardy north of Long Island.

Chamaecyparis spp. (FALSE CYPRESS)—C. nootkatensis (Nootka Cypress) is probably the hardiest Chamaecyparis for the North; 'Glauca' is very gray. This tree likes a cool, moist environment. C. pisifera 'Squarrosa' (Moss Retinospora) is a conical small tree or large shrub with feathery texture and gray/blue color that may be kept smaller with pruning. C. pisifera 'Aurea' has yellow-tipped foliage. Many other colorful varieties are available, including small variegated plants suitable for rock gardens.

Euonymus fortunei (WINTERCREEPER)—Hardy broad-leaved evergreen vine or shrub from China with a number of variegated forms. 'Emerald Gaiety' is a small shrub with leaves edged in white; 'Emerald 'N Gold' has leaves with gold trim. Both show pink coloration in winter; hardy in zones 5 to 9. E. japonica (Japanese Spindle Tree) is larger but less hardy than E. fortunei; it also has many variegated forms. Both species may be attacked by scale and other insect pests; E. japonica is prone to mildew and needs good air circulation.

Juniperus spp. (JUNIPER)—J. chinensis (Chinese Juniper) is similar to U.S. native J. virginiana in form, but more blue-green in color and not disfigured by cedar rust. There are numerous cultivars in various sizes and colors, including the low-growing J. chinensis 'Procumbens' (blue-green foliage) and J. chinensis 'Sargentii' (Sargent Juniper), gray-green and also low growing. J. horizontalis

(Creeping Juniper) is a native trailing plant with blue-green foliage that turns bronze in the winter sun. J. horizontalis 'Douglasii' (Waukegan Juniper) is very blue, as is dwarf form 'Wiltonii' (Blue Rug). Sargent and Creeping Junipers make good ground covers.

Leucothoe fontanesiana (DROOPING LEUCOTHOE, DOG-HOBBLE)—A graceful broad-leaved evergreen, native to the southeastern U.S., this Leucothoe can grow 6 feet tall and is sometimes wider than tall. Turns a beautiful reddish purple in the winter sun; best in a site shaded in the north to prevent burning. Variety 'Rainbow' is smaller with pink and yellow markings; protect from wind.

Picea spp. (SPRUCE)—P. engelmannii (Engelmann Spruce) is gray-green and similar to Colorado Blue Spruce, but the foliage is softer and the form is less stiff. This beautiful tree is native to the mountains of the West and ranges from Canada to New Mexico. P. pungens (Colorado Spruce) is slightly bluish; there is a P. pungens 'Aurea.' P. pungens 'Glauca' (Colorado Blue Spruce) is rather stiff, with vivid blue needles, making it doubly positive and difficult to place well in the landscape. P. pungens has numerous cultivars which include dwarf, prostrate and weeping forms.

Pieris japonica (JAPANESE ANDROMEDA)—Nodding reddish flower buds makes the species colorful in winter; smaller 'Variegata' has white leaf margins. Several new cultivars have pink or red new growth. Plant Pieris in a shaded spot, sheltered from wind; requires an acid soil.

Pinus spp. (PINE)—Several Pines have a blue-green cast to their foliage, among them the soft-textured P. strobus (White Pine) and P. sylvestris (Scotch Pine); both have numerous named varieties. P. parviflora 'Glauca' (Japanese White Pine) is a variable but beautiful silvery tree with no serious pests or diseases and is tolerant of wind, drought and salt air. P. densiflora (Japanese Red Pine) is a small tree with soft blue-green foliage. Leaf tips of 'Alboterminata' are yellowish white; 'Oculus-draconis' (Dragon's Eye Pine) has needles with two yellow bands.

Thuja occidentalis (AMERICAN ARBORVITAE)—Thuja is one of the two best narrow and slow-growing evergreens for the North (Juniperus is the other); Thuja will stand more shade, but needs more moisture. There are many Thujas with gold and variegated foliage; 'Aurea' has deep yellow leaves and 'Aureo-variegata' has foliage variegated with gold.

Dalechamps, an herbalist, identifies this evergreen as Picea or Spruce. Spruces and Firs (Abies) appear similar but the former have persistent raised leaf bases which make leafless twigs feel rough. Fir twigs are smooth.

BEST EVERGREENS FOR THE CHRISTMAS TREE

The following hold their foliage well after being cut:

Abies (FIR)
Pseudotsuga (DOUGLAS FIR)
Pinus (PINE)
Thuja (ARBORVITAE)
Juniperus (JUNIPER, RED CEDAR)

The following are susceptible to leaf drop:

Picea (SPRUCE)
Tsuga (HEMLOCK)

Leaf drop will be greatly reduced if cut trees are handled properly. Ideally, cut trees shortly before use. Store a cut tree outdoors in a pail of water; keep in a shady spot. Before bringing indoors, make a fresh cut on the trunk about an inch from the bottom. Be sure to keep the tree stand's water reservoir filled. Place the tree in a cool area—or at least away from the fireplace and radiators.

Planting trees and shrubs with an eye to their use as holiday greenery makes good sense; your own grounds can provide plants that are fresher, perhaps more varied—and certainly more economical than the local garden center. The following evergreens are handsome both outdoors in the landscape and indoors as cut greens; as the latter, they are unlikely to be found on the market.

> **Abies concolor** (WHITE FIR)—Blue-green needles; 5-inch cones. Often more attractive outdoors than spruce and better indoors.
>
> **Cedrus atlantica 'Glauca'** (BLUE ATLAS CEDAR)—Silvery blue needles and interesting cones.
>
> **Ilex glabra** (INKBERRY)—A native shrub of medium height, Inkberry has glossy dark green leaves about 1 to 2 inches long. I. crenata (Japanese Holly) has small shiny leaves the size of Boxwood's.
>
> **Juniperus spp.** (JUNIPER, RED CEDAR)—There are bluish junipers, golden junipers and green junipers that bronze in the winter sun. Blue fruit produced by some female junipers is very decorative in summer.
>
> **Kalmia latifolia** (MT. LAUREL)—Beautiful native broad-leaved evergreen; both flowers and foliage are outstanding.
>
> **Leucothoe spp.** (FETTERBUSH)—Another native evergreen with leaves similar to Mt. Laurel. Branches arch gracefully.
>
> **Pieris spp.** (ANDROMEDA)—Both the native P. floribunda and Japanese Andromeda (P. japonica) have evergreen foliage; P. japonica has glossier leaves and reddish winter buds but smaller P. floribunda is hardier. 'Brouwer's Beauty' is a cross between the two species; it is hardy with showy red winter buds.
>
> **Sciadopitys verticillata** (UMBRELLA PINE)—Big, glossy dark green needles. Long lasting when cut. Umbrella Pine, like Ginkgo, is considered an ancient species. It likes protected, moist and shady sites and (unlike Ginkgo) is not tolerant of air pollution.

Trees with Brittle Wood

Not all trees on the list below are undesirable, despite susceptibility of branches to breakage in wind and storms. Plant away from buildings.

Acer negundo (BOX ELDER)

Acer rubrum (RED MAPLE)

Acer saccharinum (SOFT OR SILVER MAPLE)—Choose another Maple.

Amelanchier x grandiflora (SHADBUSH)

Catalpa speciosa (WESTERN CATALPA)

Cladrastis lutea (YELLOWWOOD)—Not weak-wooded like Silver Maple and not prone to breaking limbs, though outer twigs are brittle.

Liriodendron tulipifera (TULIP TREE)

Pinus strobus (WHITE PINE)—As this evergreen ages, it loses its young conical shape as branches grow outward. Susceptible to wind damage, it can become quite picturesque and is a fine tree for the larger landscape though a poor selection for planting near homes.

Populus spp. (POPLAR, COTTONWOOD)

Pyrus calleryana (CALLERY PEAR)

Salix spp. (WILLOW)

Tilia spp. (LINDEN, BASSWOOD)

Best Woods for Indoor Burning

Heating homes with wood has become very popular in some parts of the United States, and it is likely to become even more popular as the costs of other fuels rise. How long your fire lasts and how much heat it generates depends largely on the density and dryness of the wood used. If two logs are dry and equal in size, the heavier one is likely to deliver the most heat. The following lists give relative heat values of various species of trees:

DENSE WOOD WITH HIGH TO HIGHEST HEAT VALUE:

Apple	**Locust, Black**
Beech, American	**Oak, White**
Elm, Rock	**Osage Orange**
Hickory, Shagbark	**Persimmon**
Ironwood	

HIGH HEAT VALUE:

Ash, White
Birch, Yellow
Locust, Honey

Maple, Sugar
Oak, Red

MEDIUM HEAT VALUE:

Ash, Black and Green
Cherry
Elm, American
Juniper (EASTERN RED CEDAR)

Larch
Maple, Red and Silver
Pine, Longleaf and Pitch
Sycamore

LOW HEAT VALUE—FIRES MADE WITH THESE WOODS MAY PRODUCE GOOD FLAMES, BUT PROBABLY WILL NOT LAST AS LONG:

Aspen
Basswood
Fir, Red and Balsam
Hemlock

Pine, White and Red
Spruce, Red and Engelmann
Willow

Among the trees that produce wood of medium or better heat value, the fastest growers are Elms (American and Rock), Green Ash, Silver Maple, Pines, Sycamore and Larch. In addition to the density and dryness of the wood, a long-lasting fire also depends on where you build it. Less dense wood is often not practical for the fireplace, but it is quite satisfactory for an airtight woodstove.

EASE OF STARTING:

Easy	Fair	Poor to Difficult
Aspen	Elm	Apple
Birch	Hickory	Beech
Cedar	Juniper	Cherry
Cottonwood	Willow	Locust
Hemlock		Red Maple
Larch		Sugar Maple
Pine		Red Oak
Poplar		
Spruce		

Ash ranges from fair to difficult in ease of starting.

George Washington's Trees

George Washington, famous general as well as America's first president, was also a farmer and land surveyor. His records reveal a keen interest in horticulture and the newly discovered plants of his new country. We have all heard of the legendary cherry tree he felled as a youth, but few of us have heard of the other trees—some of which may still be seen—with which he was more certainly associated.

The Cambridge Elm—Ulmus americana. Under this tree in Cambridge, Massachusetts, Washington took command of the Continental Army on July 3, 1775. Believed to have been over 200 years old when it fell in October 1923. Although it can no longer be seen, many of its descendants have been planted throughout the U.S.

The Washington Oak—Quercus alba. This ancient tree still stands on Gaylord Road (near the intersection with Newton Road) in New Milford, Connecticut. Washington held a council under its branches while on route to Hartford in 1780.

Washington Sycamore—Platanus occidentalis. It is difficult for us to imagine, in these days of Air Force One and the Secret Service, how "The Father of His Country" got around in the eighteenth century. When General Washington needed to confer with his officers stationed in various parts of the country during the Revolution, he traveled on horseback, sometimes through dangerous country and often with only one or two aides. In July 1782 he was on such a trip in Pennsylvania. After leaving Philadelphia (en route back to his headquarters in Newburgh, New York) he spent the night of July 25 in Bethlehem, Pennsylvania. On July 26 he crossed the Delaware into New Jersey, where he dismounted around noon and rested under a large Sycamore, which still stands near Hope in Warren County.

Timothy Ball Walnut—Juglans nigra. This tree still grows in Maplewood, New Jersey, near the old Ball residence, which was built in 1743. The Balls were Washington's cousins and he visited them on several occasions, hitching his horse, according to tradition, to an iron ring in this tree. The ring is no longer visible but the old Walnut still stands.

Mt. Vernon Trees—Washington planted many trees and shrubs on the grounds of his beloved Mt. Vernon. Mr. Norton, horticulturist of the estate, is quite sure that 12 trees still standing date from this time: Three Fraxinus americana (White Ash), four Ilex opaca (American Holly), two Liriodendron tulipifera (Tuliptree), one Morus alba (White Mulberry), one Quercus muehlenbergii (Yellow Chestnut Oak) and one Tsuga canadensis (Hemlock). Four other trees are believed to date from Washington's time: three more Hollies and one Sweet Buckeye (Aesculus octandra). Tests in process should determine their age.

WASHINGTON'S PLANTS FOR YOUR YARD

A list of plants grown at Mt. Vernon Estate and available for mail order can be obtained by writing Mt. Vernon Ladies' Association, Mt. Vernon, VA 22121. Packages of seed appropriate for eighteenth-century gardens are for sale, as are many other plants. American Holly, Tulip Poplar and English Boxwood, all propagated from original source material planted by George Washington, can be ordered.

A Historic Plant Center is also in operation at Monticello, the restored home of Thomas Jefferson in Charlottesville, Virginia. Seeds of some of the flowers and vegetables grown at Monticello are available by mail. Plants may be purchased on the premises. Write to the Center for Historic Plants, Monticello, Box 316, Charlottesville, VA 22902.

Syrup Trees

Acer barbatum (SOUTHERN SUGAR MAPLE OR SUGAR TREE)
Acer glabrum (ROCKY MOUNTAIN MAPLE)
Acer macrophyllum (BIG-LEAF OR OREGON MAPLE)
Acer rubrum (RED MAPLE)
Acer saccharinum (SILVER MAPLE)
Acer saccharum (SUGAR MAPLE)
Acer saccharum grandidentatum (BIG-TOOTH MAPLE)
Acer saccharum nigrum (BLACK MAPLE)
Betula lenta (BLACK OR SWEET BIRCH)

Sacred Trees

Many species of trees have been (and in some cases still are) venerated by people around the world. Ten of the most famous are:

Cedrus libani (CEDAR OF LEBANON)—Noble trees to ancient Hebrews; mentioned in the Bible many times. Fragrant, slow-to-decay wood used in temple building.

Cleyera japonica (SAKAKI TREE)—Evergreen shrub or small tree with fragrant white flowers; a sacred symbol of Shinto (*sakaki* means "tree of the gods").

Crateva religiosa (SACRED GARLIC PEAR)—Small tree with spots on branches and fruit; sacred to Hindus.

Cycas spp. (SAGO PALM)—A food source and sacred to the Asmattes, a present-day Stone Age tribe of New Guinea.

Ficus religiosa (BO TREE)—Sacred to Hindus and Buddhists; Buddha received enlightenment under this tree. Figs also revered by ancient Romans and others.

Fraxinus spp. (ASH)—This noble tree was venerated by many, including ancient Greeks and Scandinavians.

Ginkgo biloba (MAIDENHAIR TREE)—Probably saved from extinction because of cultivation in Chinese temple gardens.

Phoenix dactylifera (DATE PALM)—Of great importance to biblical peoples; once a symbol of rejoicing. Still distributed by Christians on Palm Sunday.

Quercus spp. (OAK)—Long-lived, majestic Oaks (which are often struck by lightning) were sacred to ancient Greeks and Druids alike.

Thespesia populnea (PORTIA TREE)—Planted near Buddhist temples.* The generic name means "divine" in Greek.

* Edwin Menninger, *Fantastic Trees* (New York: Viking Press, 1967).

SHRUBS

Flowering Shrubs

NATIVE FLOWERING SHRUBS

Dr. Edwin Carpenter, professor of horticulture at the University of Connecticut in Storrs, believes we are coming back to native plants because they are most capable of withstanding today's environmental stresses. On the following pages are lists of his favorite flowering shrubs for use in landscaping:

FOR WET SITES:

Clethra alnifolia (SUMMERSWEET, SWEET PEPPERBUSH)—Fragrant white flowers ('Pink Spire' is available) in summer; attracts bees. Golden fall color.

Cornus amomum (SILKY DOGWOOD, RED WILLOW)—Red branches, white flowers, purple/red fall color. Blue fruit attracts 34 species of birds.

Ilex glabra (INKBERRY, GALLBERRY)—This native evergreen does well in shade. Black fruit (on pistillate plants) once used as ink.

Ilex verticillata (WINTERBERRY, CHRISTMASBERRY, BLACK ALDER)—Will also thrive on drier sites; will tolerate sun but prefers partial shade. Red fruit (on pistillate plants) persists into winter. Dwarf cultivars are available.

Rhododendron periclymenoides (PINXTERBLOOM, HONEYSUCKLE)—Lightly fragrant large pink blooms open before the leaves on this choice deciduous shrub.

Rhododendron periclymenoides (Pinxterbloom). A choice native shrub for moist sites, Pinxterbloom also does well in drier locations.

Rhododendron vaseyi (PINK SHELL AZALEA)—Similar to
Pinxterbloom. Flowers may be brighter colored but are not
fragrant.

Rhododendron viscosum (SWAMP AZALEA, CLAMMY AZALEA,
SWAMP HONEYSUCKLE)—Another deciduous Rhododendron,
this one has glossy leaves and very fragrant white flowers
that bloom in summer after the leaves have unfolded.

Viburnum dentatum (ARROWWOOD)—This Viburnum tolerates
a wide range of conditions, including drought. Small, lacy
white flowers, shiny foliage and brilliant red fall color.

Viburnum trilobum (AMERICAN CRANBERRYBUSH)—Attractive
white flowers, reddish fall color and showy edible red
fruit, which disappears quickly. Tolerates dry soil.

Zenobia pulverulenta (DUSTY ZENOBIA)—Nodding white
flowers and blue-gray foliage. Needs partial shade and
moist, but well-drained, acid soil.

FOR DRY SITES:

Arctostaphylos uva-ursi (BEARBERRY)—Excellent as a ground
cover or container plant in sandy, acid soil. Attractive red
berries. Foliage turns bronze-red in sun.

Fothergilla major (LARGE FOTHERGILLA)—Tolerates fairly dry
soils but not drought; also tolerates light shade. White
flowers and orange/red fall color are both noteworthy.

Juniperus spp. (JUNIPER)—J. communis depressa (Old Field
Juniper) and J. horizontalis (Creeping Juniper) are two fine
evergreens that tolerate hot, dry conditions. Both are low
growing. Female plants produce blue fruit. All junipers are
best in full sun.

Potentilla fruticosa (SHRUBBY CINQUEFOIL)—Early summer
blooming and tolerant of dry sites. There are 30 cultivars;
flowers may be yellow, white or orange. 'Red Ace' won a
1967 All-America Award. Gray-green foliage.

Rhus aromatica (FRAGRANT SUMAC)—Low-growing Sumac
with distinctive fragrance and brilliant red fall color.

Rosa carolina (CAROLINA ROSE, PASTURE ROSE)—A disease- and
maintenance-free rose for dry (or moist) soil and full sun.

FOR SHADE:

Calycanthus floridus (CAROLINA ALLSPICE, SWEET
SHRUB)—Calycanthus has a strawberry scent and exotic
reddish-purple flowers. Golden fall color. Likes moist
shade.

Fothergilla gardenii (DWARF FOTHERGILLA)—Also tolerant of
full sun, this small shrub has attractive white flowers and
outstanding orange or reddish fall color.

Hydrangea quercifolia (OAK-LEAVED HYDRANGEA)—Bold
foliage plant with beautiful red/purple fall color and
peeling bark. Native to the Southeast. Flowers well in
southern New England.

Kalmia latifolia (MOUNTAIN LAUREL)—The best broad-leaved
evergreen for the North; leaves do not curl up when
temperature drops, as do the leaves of many
Rhododendrons. Beautiful white/pink late spring flowers;
many cultivars.

Pieris floribunda (MOUNTAIN PIERIS, MOUNTAIN
ANDROMEDA)—Another broad-leaved evergreen, this native
Pieris has Lily-of-the-Valley-like flowers and green/white
winter flower buds. Pest- and disease-free, unlike Japanese
Pieris. One drawback: Deer relish it.

Viburnum acerifolium (MAPLELEAF VIBURNUM)—Excellent
shrub for woodland plantings. White flowers, black fruit
and soft red/purple (pale rose/pink in shade) fall color.

Viburnum alnifolium (HOBBLEBUSH)—This Viburnum likes
cool, moist conditions; white flowers are showy and fruit
turns from red to purple/black.

FLOWERING SHRUBS FOR LIMITED SPACE

There are a number of books devoted to low-growing woody
plants; one fine one is Donald Wyman's small book *Dwarf Shrubs*. Most
of the following flowering shrubs will not grow over 4 to 5 feet tall;
some, like Deutzia and Dwarf Mountain Laurel, are considerably smaller.

Abelia grandiflora* (GLOSSY ABELIA)—Fragrant white flowers
in summer; semievergreen leaves and fine texture. Hardy to
southern New England.

Daphne mezereum (FEBRUARY DAPHNE)—Fragrant purple or

*Needs or will tolerate some shade.

white flowers appear before the leaves; attractive leaves turn soft red in fall. Drawbacks: All parts of Daphne are poisonous, plants may suffer from twig blight and the genus is famous for being temperamental. D. cneorum (Rose Daphne) is lower growing but harder to grow.

Deutzia gracilis (DEUTZIA)—Showy white flowers in spring; this shrub is dainty, neat and fine textured.

Fothergilla gardenii (DWARF FOTHERGILLA)—Attractive, sweet-smelling white flowers in spring; leaves turn good red or orange color in fall.

Kalmia latifolia* 'Myrtifolia' (DWARF MOUNTAIN LAUREL)—Beautiful white/pink flowers in spring, this is the best broad-leaved evergreen for the North. The species may grow to 6 feet or more; the dwarf form is a tidy 2 feet tall.

Philadelphus coronarius (MOCK ORANGE)—Mock Orange has fragrant white flowers and several dwarf cultivars are available. P. microphyllus is naturally lower growing than P. coronarius.

Pieris floribunda* (MOUNTAIN ANDROMEDA)—Andromedas have showy flower buds and evergreen foliage in winter and Lily-of-the-Valley-like flowers in spring. P. floribunda, an American native, has greenish flower buds in winter; less hardy P. japonica (Japanese Andromeda) has glossy foliage and showier red winter buds. There are several low-growing cultivars of P. japonica; 'Pygmaea' is one.

Potentilla fruticosa* (SHRUBBY CINQUEFOIL)—Fine texture with showy yellow flowers in early summer. There are many cultivars, including a white-flowered variety.

Rhododendron* spp.—There are many dwarf or low-growing species, among them R. fastigiatum, R. kiusianum and R. yakushimanum. The latter has dark evergreen leaves, pink green leaves, pink buds and white flowers and is hardy through zone 6. Many hybrids are available. 'Ramapo' is a hardy dwarf that does well (and stays compact) in full sun. This cultivar has blue-green foliage and lavender flowers.

Spirea x bumalda (ANTHONY WATERER SPIREA)—Showy red flowers in early summer and reddish fall color. There are several dwarf cultivars of Japanese Spirea (S. japonica).

Syringa microphylla (LILAC)—This small, hardy Lilac may

*Needs or will tolerate some shade.

grow as tall as 6 feet, but can be kept in check with pruning. Sweet-scented lilac flowers; cultivar 'Superba' has pink blossoms. S. meyeri is also low growing, but less hardy.

Viburnum farreri 'Nanum'* (DWARF FRAGRANT VIBURNUM)—Fragrant white flowers appear before the leaves; red fall color. Hardy only in protected places in most of New England. V. carlesii (Korean Spice Viburnum), is hardier, showier and taller.

*Needs or will tolerate some shade.

FLOWERING SHRUBS FOR THE NORTH

Here are twelve flowering shrubs for zone 4 and North gardens:

Amelanchier canadensis (SHADBUSH)—Similar to several of the more treelike species, but lower growing. Delicate white flowers in early spring, edible fruit and reddish fall color. Likes moist soils. Zones 3 to 8.

Caragana arborescens (SIBERIAN PEA TREE)—Tall shrubs or small trees with showy yellow flowers; there are several varieties. Useful for windbreaks and hedges. Zones 2 to 7.

Clethra alnifolia (SWEET PEPPERBUSH)—Fragrant white (or pink) flowers in summer and yellow fall color. Not tolerant of dry soils or drought. Zones 3 to 9.

Cornus alba (TARTARIAN DOGWOOD)—White flowers in late spring, showy white fruit and good red fall color. Red stems are attractive in winter. Can grow 10 feet tall. There are many cultivars. Zones 3 to 8.

Lindera benzoin (SPICE BUSH)—Native shrub with small yellow flowers in very early spring and excellent yellow fall color. Female plants have attractive red fruit. Zones 4 to 9.

Lonicera morrowii (MORROW HONEYSUCKLE)—A tall (to 8 feet), wide-growing, dense shrub with white (fading yellow) flowers and red fruit. There is a yellow-fruited cultivar. Zone 4.

Potentilla fruticosa (POTENTILLA, SHRUBBY CINQUEFOIL)—Bright yellow, showy flowers (white-, orange- and red-flowered varieties are available) from late spring until frost. Low growing. Zones 2 to 8.

Prunus tomentosa (NANKING CHERRY)—Early, fragrant, white flowers and edible red fruit; shiny reddish bark. Six to 10 feet tall and hardy in zones 3 to 8.

Rosa rugosa (WRINKLED ROSE)—Lovely flowers, red fruit and yellow fall color. Other hardy roses include R. rubrifolia (Redleaf Rose), Carolina Rose and Virginia Rose. Zones 2 to 10.

Rhododendron spp.—Several native species, such as R. viscosum (very fragrant white flowers) and R. periclymenoides (slightly scented pink or white flowers), are hardy through zone 4. Cold-hardy cultivars include 'Boule de Neige,' 'Duet' and 'Windbeam.'

Syringa vulgaris (COMMON LILAC)—Hardy into zone 3 and cherished for fragrant flowers in spring (see pages 273–274 for list of cultivars). Smaller s. microphylla is hardy through zone 4.

Viburnum trilobum (AMERICAN CRANBERRYBUSH)—Attractive white flowers, edible red fruit and red fall color. There are several cultivars. Hardy through Zone 2.

Vinca minor (Myrtle, Periwinkle). Attractive lilac-blue flowers and dainty leaves make Vinca one of the best evergreen ground covers for shade.

Shrubby Ground Covers for Sun and Shade

Some of the species below are much planted (some would say overplanted), but they are deservedly popular. Evergreen Euonymus, Hedera, Pachysandra and Vinca are all important in defining, unifying and softening landscapes, sometimes on a broad scale, throughout the year. All do well in shade. Others listed are most useful on a smaller scale or for special problem sites. Here are ten useful ground covers (see "Perennial Ground Covers for Sun and Shade," pages 62–63, for more):

Arctostaphylos uva-ursi (BEARBERRY)—Sun and sandy, or stony, acid soil is necessary for Bearberry to be at its best. White spring flowers are followed by showy red berries; leaves turn bronze in autumn sun. This U.S. native will grow in partial shade.

Euonymus spp. (BABY WINTERCREEPER, SHARPLEAF WINTERCREEPER AND RUNNING EUONYMUS)—Partial shade; there are several species and many cultivars to consider. Leaves may be all green or variegated; most are evergreen. E. fortunei (China) is probably the most valuable species for ground cover; native and deciduous E. obovata (Running Strawberry Bush) has red fruit and fall color. Euonymus is generally drought tolerant.

Hedera spp. (IVY)—Sun or shade; Ivy is an excellent evergreen ground cover with dark green leaves. A variegated variety of H. helix, 'Buttercup,' won a 1988 Styer Award.

Juniperus chinensis and J. horizontalis (CREEPING AND HORIZONTAL JUNIPERS)—Sun; many cultivars of these species are available; some quite useful in covering large areas in sun and preventing erosion on slopes.

Lonicera japonica 'Halliana' (HALL'S HONEYSUCKLE)—Sun; invasive and vigorous but useful in difficult areas such as steep banks or in places where it can be kept in bounds. Memorable for long-lasting and very fragrant white (changing to yellow) flowers.

Pachysandra terminalis (PACHYSANDRA, JAPANESE SPURGE)—Shady sites preferred though some sun is tolerated. An indispensable evergreen ground cover that remains useful throughout the winter and can successfully colonize in wooded areas.

Sarcococca hookerana humilis (SWEET BOX)—Shade; low-growing evergreen with glossy, pointed leaves; small, white (bright pink anthers) fragrant flowers and shiny blue-black fruit. This Chinese native is hardy north to zone 8; most useful in the South and Pacific Northwest.

Thymus spp. (THYME)—Low-growing Thymes make good ground covers on sunny, dry sites; T. serpyllum (Wild or Lemon Thyme) and T. praecox (Mother-of-Thyme) will creep over and between paving stones.

Vaccinium angustifolium laevifolium (LOWBUSH BLUEBERRY)—Sun or partial shade; fine but slow-growing native ground cover for naturalistic sites. Acid soil a must; edible fruit, outstanding red fall color.

Vinca minor (MYRTLE, PERIWINKLE)—Another indispensable evergreen ground cover for shade; sun is tolerated if moisture and humus are ample. Daintier than Pachysandra, with smaller leaves that are darker green and glossy, Vinca also has blue or white flowers. The blue cultivar 'Bowlesii' is said to be especially floriferous and white-flowered 'Miss Jekyll's White' tolerant of sun.

Pernicious Woody Immigrants

Plants from many countries now call America home. Some were deliberately imported, others unintentionally introduced; both kinds no doubt arrived on the first European vessels to touch our shores. Many botanical immigrants are choice garden subjects and generally remain where they are planted; indeed, it is often a challenge to keep them thriving. Others are sturdy survivors, standing guard around abandoned homesites as the woods close in. Other immigrants, however, blessed with extraordinary vigor and the absence of predators, are able to invade the native flora, in some instances overwhelming it. In many national parks approximately one-third of the species are now aliens; some of them are the focus of vast eradication programs. Many gardeners also battle aggressive exotic plants; Dandelion comes readily to mind if you are a serious lawn groomer. Even more pernicious, however, are some of the woody invaders, which not only crowd out other flora but change whole ecosystems, harming native plants and animals alike:

Berberis thunbergii (JAPANESE BARBERRY)—Although not without virtues, Japanese Barberry is invading fields and gardens in the Northeast.

Casuarina equisetifolia (AUSTRALIAN PINE, SOUTH SEA

IRONWOOD)—A seashore pioneer tree from the South
Pacific now forming dense groves in the Everglades.

Celastrus orbiculatus (ORIENTAL BITTERSWEET)—A spiny vine
that can grow 40 feet tall, this Bittersweet covers trees and
invades gardens in parts of the East.

Elaeagnus umbellata (AUTUMN OLIVE)—Small tree from Asia
with silvery leaves that is spreading throughout many parts
of the East and Midwest. West Virginia banned its sale
and planting in 1976.

Euonymus alata (WINGED SPINDLE TREE)—This Asian species
has fine red fall color and attractive corky twigs but its
invasive nature is causing concern in the parts of the East
and Midwest.

Lonicera japonica (JAPANESE HONEYSUCKLE)—A serious
woodland pest in the Mid-Atlantic states. Tatarian
Honeysuckle is also an invasive alien.

Pueraria lobata (JAPANESE KUDZU VINE)—Once used for erosion
control, animal fodder and ornament, Kudzu has overrun
millions of acres in the Southeast. It is on its way north,
where many think it can survive.

Rosa multiflora (MULTIFLORA ROSE)—Once touted as a "living
fence," this Asian native has been classified as a noxious
weed in many parts of the country.

Tamarix spp. (TAMARISK OR SALT CEDAR)—Brought to the
United States as an ornamental and windbreak, Tamarisk
now covers many acres in the Southwest, where it hurts
the native flora and fauna by poisoning the soil and
reducing the available water.

Wisteria floribunda (JAPANESE WISTERIA)—On the march in
some South Central states.

There are other invasive woody species. Even dainty Periwinkle can be
a pest; it has invaded two Nature Conservancy preserves in California.
See also "When Does an Herb Become a Weed?" page 148.

Shrubs for Dry Soils

Acanthopanax sieboldianus* (FIVE-LEAF ARALIA)—M
Berberis thunbergii* (JAPANESE BARBERRY)—M

S–Small   M–Medium   L–Large Shrub
*Will tolerate shade.

Cornus racemosa* (GRAY DOGWOOD)—M
Physocarpus spp.* (DWARF NINEBARK AND NINEBARK)—S and
   M
Potentilla fruticosa (SHRUBBY CINQUEFOIL)—S
Pyracantha coccinea 'Lalandei' (FIRETHORN)—L
Rhamnus spp.* (COMMON BUCKTHORN AND ALDER
   BUCKTHORN)—L
Rhodotypos tetrapetala* (JETBEAD)—M
Ribes spp.* (DWARF ALPINE CURRANT AND MOUNTAIN
   CURRANT)—S and M; all Ribes carry White Pine Blister
   Rust, although R. alpinum 'Pumilum' and R. alpinum are
   resistant.
Symphoricarpos orbiculatus* (CORALBERRY)—S
Viburnum lentago* (NANNYBERRY)—L

S - Small   M - Medium   L - Large shrub
*Will tolerate shade.

NATIVE SHRUBS FOR DRY EMBANKMENTS

Ceanothus (NEW JERSEY TEA)
Comptonia (SWEET FERN)
Juniperus (CREEPING SAVIN)
Myrica (BAYBERRY)
Rhus (SUMAC)

DROUGHT-TOLERANT SHRUBS FOR THE MID-ATLANTIC REGION

Rutgers University's Cooperative Extension Service has recently published a booklet, "Landscaping for Water Conservation: A Guide for New Jersey," by Dr. Theodore Shelton and Dr. Bruce Hamilton. The publication advises homeowners to reduce the size of their lawns and lists a number of drought-tolerant trees and shrubs. The bulletin, illustrated with color photographs, may be ordered by writing to New Jersey Dept. of Environmental Protection, Division of Water Resources, Office of Water Conservation CN029, Trenton, NJ 08625. The following shrubs are listed as drought tolerant for New Jersey:

Abelia x grandiflora (GLOSSY ABELIA)
Berberis julianae (WINTERGREEN BARBERRY)
Forsythia spp. (FORSYTHIA)
Hamamelis virginiana (WITCH HAZEL)
Ilex crenata (JAPANESE HOLLY) and I. crenata 'Microphylla'
   (Little-leaf Japanese Holly)

Juniperus spp. (JUNIPER)

Myrica pensylvanica (BAYBERRY)

Pinus mugo mugo (MUGO PINE)

Spirea x bumalda (ANTHONY WATERER SPIREA)—Other Spireas are also drought-tolerant.

Syringa spp. (LILAC)—Japanese Tree Lilac tolerates drought and city conditions.

Taxus cuspidata (JAPANESE YEW)

Viburnum prunifolium (BLACKHAW)*

Vitex agnus-castus (CHASTE TREE)

Weigela spp. (WEIGELA)

Yucca filamentosa (ADAM'S NEEDLE)

*Not all Viburnums are drought tolerant. Doublefile (Viburnum plicatum tomentosum) is an indicator plant for drought for it wilts badly under drought stress.

Cephalanthus occidentalis (Buttonbush). A native American shrub for moist sites, Buttonbush has shiny leaves and fragrant, creamy round flower heads.

Native Shrubs for Wet Sites

There is much interest in native plants today, and homeowners are encouraged to use them in landscaping. Most natives are hardy and resistant to pests and diseases. Some are beautiful anywhere in the landscape; others are particularly suitable to plant at the borders of maintained space, where the garden blends with the native vegetation. In some areas of the country, introduced plants (Barberry, Oriental Bittersweet, Honeysuckle and Multiflora Rose are among those in New England) have escaped gardens to become pests—and threats to the native flora. By planting natives we help preserve them while gaining beautiful plants especially suited to our region. Natives for moist ground include:

Cephalanthus occidentalis (BUTTONBUSH)—Fragrant white flowers shaped like small balls in summer. Fruits enjoyed by ducks. Grows in flooded areas.

Clethra alnifolia (SUMMERSWEET)—Showy, fragrant white flowers in summer. No fall color.

Cornus sericea (RED-OSIER DOGWOOD)—Handsome red twigs and red fall color. There are several cultivars, including a golden-twigged variety.

Ilex glabra (INKBERRY)—A fine-textured dark evergreen with small black fruit on female shrubs. A bee plant.

Ilex verticillata (WINTERBERRY)—Deciduous holly with showy red fruit on female plants.

Kalmia angustifolia (LAMBKILL)—A smaller, less showy relative of Mt. Laurel. There are several cultivars, including a white-flowered form. The leaves of Kalmia are toxic to sheep.

Lindera benzoin (SPICEBUSH)—Handsome large shrub that will tolerate shade. Small, early yellow flowers more effective on male plants; females produce attractive red fruits. Leaves smell spicy when crushed and turn clear yellow in fall.

Rhododendron viscosum (SWAMP AZALEA)—Produces clusters of fragrant white flowers in midsummer.

Vaccinium corymbosum (HIGHBUSH BLUEBERRY)—The commercial Blueberry, this dense shrub produces edible fruit and requires acid soil. Brilliant red fall color.

SOURCES FOR NATIVE SHRUBS

Appalachian Gardens
Box 82
Waynesboro, PA 17268

Bovee's Nursery
1737 S.W. Coronado St.
Portland, OR 97219

Carlson Gardens
Box 305
South Salem, NY 10590

Dutch Mountain Nursery
7984 N. 48th St.
Augusta, MI 49012

Eastern Plant Specialties
Box 226
Georgetown, ME 04548

Forestfarm
990 Tetherwest Rd.
Williams, OR 97544

Wayside Gardens
1 Garden Lane
Hodges, SC 29695

Weston Nurseries
E. Main St.
Hopkinton, MA 01748-0186

Woodlanders, Inc.
1128 Colleton Ave.
Aiken, SC 29801

An excellent bulletin, "Native Shrubs for Landscaping," by Sally Taylor, Glenn Dreyer and William Niering, is available from the Connecticut Arboretum. It contains a number of colored photographs of natives, plant descriptions and other information. Although emphasizing shrubs hardy in the Northeast, plants listed in the bulletin will prosper in other parts of the country. Order Bulletin #30 ($3.50) from the Connecticut Arboretum, Connecticut College, New London, CT 06320. Please include $.70 for postage. Additional Arboretum bulletins are also listed in the publication.

Regional Shrubs

SHRUBS FOR THE NORTHEAST COAST

Aronia arbutifolia* (RED CHOKEBERRY)
Baccharis halimifolia* (SEA-MYRTLE)
Clethra alnifolia* (SUMMER-SWEET, SWEET PEPPERBUSH)
Cotoneaster spp.
Elaeagnus angustifolia (RUSSIAN OLIVE); E. umbellata**
       (Autumn Olive)

*U.S. native.
**Japan native.

Hydrangea macrophylla**—Common blue- or pink-flowered variety
Ilex glabra* (INKBERRY) and I. crenata** (Japanese Holly)
Ligustrum ovalifolium** (CALIFORNIA PRIVET)
Myrica pennsylvanica* (BAYBERRY)
Prunus maritima* (BEACH PLUM)
Rhus copallina* (DWARF OR SHINING SUMAC)
Rosa rugosa** (WRINKLED OR SALTSPRAY ROSE)
Taxus cuspidata** (JAPANESE YEW)
Vaccinum corymbosum* (HIGHBUSH BLUEBERRY)
Viburnum prunifolium* (BLACK HAW, NANNYBERRY); V. opulus

*U.S. native.
**Japan native.

Shadbush, Chokeberry, Summer–Sweet, Viburnums, Inkberry, Bayberry and Japanese Yew are useful for planting in shaded situations.

SHRUBS FOR THE SOUTHERN COAST

Acacia armata (KANGAROO THORN) and A. verticillata (Prickly Moses)
Aucuba japonica (JAPANESE LAUREL)
Baccharis halimifolia* (SEA MYRTLE, GROUNDSEL, SILVERLING, CONSUMPTION WEED)
Buddleja madagascariensis (GRAY BUTTERFLY BUSH)
Carissa grandiflora (NATAL PLUM)
Eugenia foetida* (BOX LEAF EUGENIA, SPANISH STOPPER)
Lavandula stoechas (SPANISH LAVENDER, FRENCH LAVENDER)
Lavatera assurgentiflora* (CALIFORNIA TREE MALLOW, MALVA ROSA)
Myrica cerifera* (WAX MYRTLE, CANDLEBERRY) and M. californica* (California Bayberry)
Pittosporum tobira (JAPANESE PITTOSPORUM, MOCK ORANGE)
Raphiolepis umbellata (YEDDA HAWTHORN)
Rhus integrifolia* (LEMONADE BERRY)
Rosmarinus officinalis (ROSEMARY)
Ruscus aculeatus (BUTCHER'S BROOM, BOX HOLLY)
Tamarix ramosissima (FLOWERING CYPRESS)

*U.S. native.

NATIVE TREES AND SHRUBS OF CALIFORNIA

Most woody plants native to California can tolerate full sun and many are resistant to drought. The following natives, suitable for ornamental use, are all drought-resistant but will also tolerate irrigation—not all drought-resistant species will. This latter feature allows them to do well in gardens that may be watered, as well as in those that are not.

EVERGREEN:

Atriplex hymenelytra (DESERT HOLLY)
Ceanothus arboreus (CATALINA CEANOTHUS)
Ceanothus foliosus (WAVY-LEAF CEANOTHUS)
Ceanothus griseus (CARMEL CEANOTHUS)
Ceanothus impressus (SANTA BARBARA CEANOTHUS)
Ceanothus thyrsiflorus (BLUE BLOSSOM)
Cercocarpus betuloides (MOUNTAIN MAHOGANY)
Comarostaphylis diversifolia (SUMMER HOLLY)
Diplacus sp. (BUSH MONKEY FLOWER)
Encelia californica (BUSH SUNFLOWER)
Encelia farinosa (INCIENSO)
Garrya elliptica (SILK TASSEL BUSH)
Haplopappus canus (HAZARDIA)
Heteromeles arbutifolia (CHRISTMAS BERRY)
Hyptis emoryi (DESERT LAVENDER)
Isomeris arborea (BLADDER POD)
Juniperus californica (CALIFORNIA JUNIPER)
Larrea divaricata (CREOSOTE BUSH)
Lavatera assurgentiflora (TREE MALLOW)
Mahonia nevinii (NEVIN BARBERRY)
Penstemon antirrhinoides (YELLOW BUSH PENSTEMON)
Pinus attenuata (KNOB-CONE PINE)
Pinus monophylla (PINON PINE)
Pinus sabiniana (DIGGER PINE)
Pinus torreyana (TORREY PINE)
Rhamnus spp. (COFFEE BERRY AND RED BERRY)
Rhus ovata (SUGAR BUSH)
Simmondsia chinensis (GOAT-NUT)
Stanleya pinnata (PRINCESS PLUME)
Zauschneria californica (HUMMINGBIRD TRUMPET)

DECIDUOUS (MAY BE PARTLY EVERGREEN IN
SOME CIRCUMSTANCES):

Acacia greggii (CAT'S CLAW)
Cercidium floridum (PALO VERDE)
Chilopsis linearis (DESERT WILLOW)
Fallugia paradoxa (APACHE PLUME)
Fouquieria splendens (OCOTILLO)
Fraxinus velutina (ARIZONA ASH)
Olneya tesota (IRONWOOD)
Prosopis juliflora (MESQUITE) and P. pubescens (Screw Bean)
Styrax officinalis (SNOWDROP BUSH)
Symphoricarpos mollis (DWARF SNOWBERRY)

Adapted from the University of California Extension bulletin, "Native California Plants for Ornamental Use," by Mildred Mathias, Harlan Lewis and Marston Kimball.

Rhododendrons

AWARD-WINNING RHODODENDRONS

Rhododendrons are found on all continents except South America and Africa; they are most abundant in mountainous Southeast Asia. Included in the genus are the broad-leaved evergreens of our gardens as well as Azaleas and the beautiful native shrubs incorrectly called Wild or Swamp "Honeysuckle." There are approximately eight hundred species of Rhododendron and numerous hybrids; many hybrids still in cultivation date back to the nineteenth century. Some of the earliest crosses occurred naturally. Today, horticulturists are busy creating hybrids that exhibit new color combinations, sun tolerance and tolerance to both heat and below-freezing temperatures. The following available hybrids have won the Award of Excellence from the American Rhododendron Society; the section of the country in which the plant was developed is listed. Many of these shrubs are tender.

1960 **Annie Dalton***—5 feet, apricot pink, East
1959 **Atroflo**—6 feet, bright rose, East
1960 **Beechwood Pink***—6 feet, fuchsia, East

*Hardy to minus 15 degrees F or lower.

1961 **Blue River**—5 feet, violet blue, West

1959 **Cadis***—5 feet, light pink, East

1960 **Carolyn Grace**—4 feet, yellow/green, West

1960 **Catalode** (COUNTY OF YORK)*—6 feet, white, East

1962 **Cutie***—3 feet, pink, West, prone to rust

1983 **Cyprus***—3 feet, white (cinnamon blotch), East

1960 **David Gable***—5 feet, pink (red throat), East

1956 **R. degronianum**—3 feet, pink, West

1973 **Gigi**—5 feet, rose-red (deeper spotting), East

1984 **Golden Bee**—2 feet, bright yellow, West

1982 **Hallelujah***—4 feet, rose red, West

1988 **Julia Grothaus**—6 feet, rose/peach, white edge, West

1969 **Ken Janeck***—3 feet, pink, West

1973 **Kim**—1 foot, yellow, West

1969 **Lemon Mist**—3 feet, yellow/green, West

1982 **Lodestar***—5 feet, white or pale lilac (spotted blotch), East

1987 **Luxor***—6 feet, light rose pink, fades yellow, East

1959 **Maricee**—2 feet, creamy white, West

1973 **Mary Fleming***—3 feet, yellow (streaked pink), East

1973 **Meadowbrook***—5 feet, bright pink (white blotch), East

1956 **Mrs. A. F. McEwan**—6 feet, rose (white throat), West

1958 **Mrs. Donald Graham**—6 feet, salmon pink, West

1958 **Opal Fawcett**—5 feet, pink (fading white), West

1973 **Parker's Pink****—5 feet, dark pink (spotted red), East

1973 **Roslyn**—6 feet, violet, East

1973 **Scintillation***—5 feet, pastel pink, East

1983 **Swansdown***—5 feet, white (blotch of yellow spots), East

1988 **Taurus**—6 feet, red, West

1960 **Tyee**—5 feet, yellow (green throat), West

1973 **Wheatley***—6 feet, rose pink, East

1973 **Windbeam****—4 feet, apricot pink (changing to light pink), East

1959 **Wizard**—4 feet, apricot/yellow, West

*Hardy to minus 15 degrees F or lower.
**Hardy to minus 25 degrees F.

The Superior Plant Award of the American Rhododendron Society is the highest award possible for a Rhododendron. It has only been awarded five times in thirty years. The winners:

1971 **Trude Webster**—5 feet, pink, minus 10 degrees F
1971 **Lem's Cameo**—5 feet, apricot/pink, 5 degrees F
1983 **Party Pink**—5 feet, lilac/pink, minus 20 degrees F
1985 **Ginny Gee**—2 feet, pink (with white), minus 10 degrees F
1985 **Patty Bee**—18 inches, yellow, minus 10 degrees F

SUN-TOLERANT RHODODENDRONS

Most northeastern gardeners are familiar with the hybrid 'PJM,' which is not only very cold hardy but tolerant of sun and heat. Although most Rhododendrons like a partly shaded site, a number of others besides 'PJM' are sun tolerant. Greer's guide describes the following as tolerant to sun:

Aunt Martha, 5 feet, red/purple, minus 10 degrees F
Belle Heller, 5 feet, white (gold blotch), minus 10 degrees F
Boule de Neige, 5 feet, white, minus 25 degrees F
Fastuosum Flore Pleno, 6 feet, lavender, minus 15 degrees F, before 1900
Gomer Waterer, 6 feet, white (pink bud), minus 15 degrees F, before 1900
Mrs. Charles E. Pearson, 6 feet, light pink, minus 5 degrees F
Scarlet Wonder, 2 feet, red, minus 15 degrees F
The Honorable Jean Marie de Montague, 5 feet, red, minus 5 degrees F
Trilby, 5 feet, crimson, minus 15 degrees F
Wilsoni, 3 feet, rosy pink, minus 15 degrees F

FRAGRANT RHODODENDRONS

A number of Rhododendron cultivars are listed in catalogs as fragrant; unfortunately, the scent is usually quite mild and cannot compare with the perfume of some of the species Rhododendrons. Many hybrids listed as fragrant in catalogs are also tender. The following plants are all hardy to at least minus 15 degrees F (flower buds may freeze at higher temperatures). Perfume will vary.

Avocet—6 feet, white
Betty Hume—6 feet, pink
Dexter's Spice—6 feet, white, bud hardy to minus 5, plant hardy to minus 20
Great Eastern—5 feet, deep purple/pink (R. FORTUNEI HYBRID)
Helen Everitt—6 feet, white

Marydel—Said to be a natural hybrid of atlanticum x periclymen-lymenoides, flowers white, flushed pink, available from Kalmia Woods

Parker's Pink—5 feet, dark pink

Rhododendron atlanticum—3 to 4 feet, white, blushed pink or purple

R. viscosum—5 feet, white

Wheatley—6 feet, rose pink

RHODODENDRON SOCIETIES

The Rhododendron Species Foundation
PO Box 3798
Federal Way, WA 98063-3798
Members may order plants from a large selection. See hundreds of species of Rhododendron blooming in the Foundation's Sanctuary during the months of March, April and May. A Rhododendron Fall Foliage Festival takes place on Sundays during October. For information call (206) 838-4646.

American Rhododendron Society
PO Box 1380
Gloucester, VA 23061

SOURCES FOR RHODODENDRONS

Briarwood Gardens
14 Gully Lane
E. Sandwich, MA 02537
Catalog $1.00

Cummins Garden
22 Robertsville Rd.
Marlboro, NJ 07746
Catalog $1.00

Eastern Plant Specialties
PO Box 226
Georgetown, ME 04548
Catalog $2.00

Ericaceae
PO Box 293
Deep River, CT 06417
Free list

Greer Gardens
1280 Goodpasture Island Rd.
Eugene, OR 97401
Greer's Guidebook to Available Rhododendrons, Species and Hybrids by Harold Greer is available for $15.95 plus $3.50 shipping; fine overview on the genus, illustrated

Kalmia Woods Nurseries
255 Holden Wood Rd.
Concord, MA 01742

Roslyn Nursery
PO Box 69
Roslyn, NY 11576
Catalog $2.00

Transplant Nursery
Parkertown Rd.
Lavonia, GA 30553
Free catalog

Winterset Nursery
Box 58
Kring St.
Johnstown, PA 15904
Send for price list
Specializes in hardy plants

Lilacs

*Still grows the vivacious lilac a generation after the door and lintel and
the sill are gone, unfolding its sweet-scented flowers each spring . . .
Little did the children think that the puny slip . . . which they
stuck in the ground in the shadow of the house and daily
watered would root itself so, and outlive them.*
                    HENRY DAVID THOREAU, WALDEN

Lilacs, among the oldest and hardiest shrubs in cultivation, were ubiqui-
tous around the dooryards of Colonial America. Many still florish today,
the houses they once graced and those who planted them long gone. They
were brought to America very early by people who had the space only
for a few essentials. Since they were not used in medicine or for food,
we know they performed an even more important function; they her-
alded the coming of spring to a winter-weary and homesick people and
fed the soul. Recently this venerable shrub has fallen from fashion—at
a time when there are more fine varieties to plant than ever before. The
following are some superior Lilac cultivars recommended by Walter
Oakes of the International Lilac Society:

> **Adelaide Dunbar**—Double purple; one of the few nearest to
>   red; tall, leggy; suckers are rare
> **Annabel**—Single, pink, florets cupped; early and fragrant
> **De Miribel**—Single, dark slate-blue, late, fragrant
> **Firmament**—Single, medium blue, large florets; a good grower
> **Katherine Havemeyer**—Double mixture of white, lavender
>   and pink

Krasavitsa Moskvy—Double, pink buds, white flowers; a 1963 Russian introduction; name means Beauty of Moscow
Massena—Single, dark reddish purple; large flowers
Miss Ellen Willmott—Double, white, late
Mrs. WE Marshall—Single, dark reddish purple; may be the darkest colored variety in existence
Paul Thirion—Double, reddish purple, very showy
President Lincoln—Single, bluish; plants become very big
Sensation—Single, purple-red; margin of white around each floret; tall, straggly grower
Vestale—Single, white, perfection in flower and panicle formation

Not all of the listed cultivars are readily available, though most can be tracked down. Three Lilacs reputed to do well in warmer climates are:

Angel White (FRAGRANT)
Blue Skies
Lavender Lady (FRAGRANT)

There are other species of Lilac besides Common Lilac (Syringa vulgaris), the ancestor of most of today's named varieties. The Persian Lilac is a very old hybrid, Cut-Leaf Lilac is native to China, and another Asian native, S. reticulata (Japanese Tree Lilac), grows into a handsome small tree with white flowers and shiny cherrylike bark. S. meyeri, from China, is a dwarf species that produces a profusion of purple lilac flowers late in the season. S. microphylla, from Japan, is hardier and also small; cultivar 'Superba' has fragrant pink flowers. For more information about Lilacs contact the International Lilac Society, Walter W. Oakes, Secretary, Box 315, Rumford, ME 04276.

TO GROW A LILAC

Lilacs (from the Persian word *lilak,* which means "blue") are wonderfully versatile. Originating in Asia and southeastern Europe, they nonetheless thrived in northern Europe and New England when introduced, proving that they can grow in both cold and warm climates. They do need a dormant period in order to bloom; winter assures this in the North; a dry period can fulfill the requirement in warmer areas, such as California. When selecting Lilacs, note whether they have been grafted or not; Lilacs grown on their own roots are best. Plant Lilacs deeply (especially if they have been grafted). They appreciate sunshine and good air circulation. Sprinkle wood ashes around them when you give the grass its first cutting in spring. To keep older plants blooming, remove a few of the largest canes every few years, allowing a sucker or two to mature in their place.

THE FRAGRANCE OF LILACS

Not all Lilacs are equally fragrant; some of the newer cultivars have little scent. The outstanding aroma of the old common Lilac (S. vulgaris purpurea) is the fragrance most people associate with Lilacs. The early-blooming Chinese Lilac (S. oblata) has a lighter but similar fragrance to that of S. vulgaris, and other Asian species have fine, spicy aromas. Other species, however, including the tree Lilacs (S. reticulata, S. pekinensis), have a musky, privetlike scent that some find unappealing. To help select the perfect shrubs for your yard, visit the Lilacs in the following places:

Illinois
(LOMBARD): Lilac Park

Iowa
(DES MOINES): Ewing Park Lilac Collection

Massachusetts
(JAMAICA PLAIN): Arnold Arboretum

New York
(ROCHESTER): Highland Park

Pennsylvania
(SWARTHMORE): Swarthmore College

Washington
(WOODLAND): Hulda Klager Lilac Gardens

Wisconsin
(MADISON): Longenecker Garden, University of Wisconsin-Madison Arboretum

SOURCES FOR LILACS

Heard Gardens, Ltd.
5355 Merle Hay Rd.
Johnston, Iowa 50131

Mellinger's Inc.
2310 W. South Range
North Lima, OH 44452

Spring Hill Nursery
6523 N. Galena Rd.
Peoria, IL 61632

Wayside Gardens
1 Garden Lane
Hodges, SC 29695-0001

Wedge Nursery
Rt. 2, Box 114
Albert Lea, MN 56007

Indispensable Viburnums

White as annunciating angels, and breathing a fragrance of lemons.
MARCEL PROUST

If forced to choose just one group of plants to use in landscaping, it would be difficult to come up with a more useful genus than Viburnum. Cousins to Honeysuckles and Elderberries, Viburnums offer many species to choose from; most are without serious pests and diseases. They are easy to grow and tolerate a wide range of soil pH. There are Viburnums with fragrant flowers and Viburnums that can withstand shade and dry soil. Some species can be trained into small trees; other species make excellent hedge plants; some Viburnums have evergreen foliage. Most Viburnums are attractive throughout the seasons with showy flowers in spring, attractive fruit from summer into winter and fine red autumn color. Birds love the fruit of many species; over thirty kinds devour the fruit of American Cranberrybush (Viburnum trilobum) alone. Plants are not dioecious, so only one of a species is needed for fruit (though fruit set is heavier when several Viburnums of the same species are planted in a group), and fruit is not toxic. In short, these are nearly perfect plants and should be more widely planted.

TALL SHRUB OR TREELIKE VIBURNUMS

Viburnum dentatum (ARROWWOOD)—This dense, clump-forming U.S. native makes a good screen or hedge plant. Flowers are white and berries are blue; the showiest season is fall when leaves turn a brilliant glossy red. Native habitat is often lowlands and stream borders although Arrowwood will grow in moist or dry soils and in sun or shade.

V. lantana (WAYFARING TREE)—Introduced from Europe, this Viburnum, which will tolerate dry conditions, has spread from cultivation in some areas. Attractive, thick, wrinkled and downy leaves turn reddish in autumn. White flowers produce showy fruits that change from red to black; especially fine is the late-summer contrast of bright scarlet fruit against the bold foliage. 'Mohican,' one of the hardiest cultivars, has fruit that turns orange-red and remains attractive for many weeks.

V. lentago (NANNYBERRY)—Tallest of the northern Viburnums, native Nannyberry is a vigorous grower (and thicket former) that can reach 25 feet or more. White flowers, edible blue-black fruit and red fall color are not wildly showy, but shrub is useful in large-scale situations and for its ability to tolerate shade, dry soil (but not drought) and city conditions.

V. opulus (EUROPEAN CRANBERRYBUSH)—This Viburnum has maplelike leaves, flower clusters with a showy outer whorl of sterile flowers and red fall color. Birds usually avoid the fruit, making V. opulus one of the best large deciduous shrubs for red winter fruit; 'Xanthocarpum' has yellow fruit. Proust (see above) may have been referring to the Snowball or Guelder-Rose (V. opulus roseum). This double-flowered variety, which produces no fruit, is much troubled with aphids. The Japanese Snowball, mentioned below, has showier flowers and no aphid trouble. V. opulus has been reported to attract cats.

V. plicatum tomentosum (DOUBLEFILE VIBURNUM)—Doublefile is an outstanding large shrub or small tree. An outer ring of sterile flowers makes showy white flower clusters resemble lace caps. Attractive fruit, which changes from red to black, is held upright above the horizontal branches and is beloved by birds. Fall color is a fine dark red. There are several excellent cultivars (see pages 281–282). Do not confuse with V. plicatum (Japanese Snowball), which has large round clusters of sterile flowers and no fruit.

V. prunifolium (BLACK HAW)—Grows to 15 to 20 feet with dense, twiggy horizontal branching. Small, glossy, oval (prunifolium means plum-leaved) leaves turn brilliant red in fall. Clusters of small white flowers in late spring are followed by blue-black fruit that Colonists used for jams and jellies. Drought tolerant. Another U.S. native, V. rufidulum (Southern Black Haw) is an even better landscape plant for southern areas.

V. sieboldii (SIEBOLD VIBURNUM)—Native to Japan, this large shrub has glossy bright green leaves that turn reddish in fall and remain late on the branches. White flowers produce showy fruits that are pink, then red and finally black (and inconspicuous) all on bright red stalks. V. sieboldii 'Seneca' produces prolific, large fruit clusters that are multicolored orange-red, maturing dark red and persist on the plant up to three months. Older shrubs develop picturesque gnarled trunks.

V. trilobum (AMERICAN CRANBERRYBUSH)—Similar in appearance to the European V. opulus, but hardier than European Cranberrybush for northern gardens. The bright red fruit of V. trilobum is edible and can be used for jams and jellies if the birds don't harvest it first. The scarlet fruits of European Cranberrybush remain decorative on the shrub much longer; they aren't edible and do not attract birds. American Cranberrybush tolerates light shade and urban conditions; best in moist soil. It can grow 12 feet tall; 'Compactum' is a smaller cultivar. Other cultivars include 'Andrews,' 'Wentworth,' 'Hahs' and 'Manito.'

Viburnum acerifolium (Mapleleaf Viburnum). An excellent native shrub for woodlands, Mapleleaf Viburnum features white flowers, purple fruit and rose to pale pink fall color.

MEDIUM AND SMALLER VIBURNUMS

Viburnum acerifolium (MAPLELEAF VIBURNUM)—This small (2 to 4 feet), shade-loving native shrub has an open habit of growth and makes an excellent understory in woodland plantings. White flowers are attractive and blue-black fruit is quickly eaten by birds. Fall color is especially notable and ranges from a soft red-purple to an eye-catching pale pink in shadier sites. Thrives in dry situations.

V. x carlcephalum (FRAGRANT SNOWBALL)—A cross between V. carleesii and V. macrocephalum, this shrub will grow about 9 feet tall and produce large, rounded clusters of fragrant white flowers. Cultivar 'Cayuga' is more compact, free flowering and a better garden plant. Autumn foliage is brilliant. Fragrant Snowball and the following fragrant Viburnum are both hardy in zone 5.

V. carlesii (KOREAN SPICE VIBURNUM)—One of the hardiest fragrant Viburnums (often grafted on to the roots of V. lantana), Korean Spice grows 4 to 5 feet tall, has slightly downy grayish-green leaves and an open habit.* Fall color is a showy, velvety red; fruit is blue-black. Flowers, which appear early with the leaves, are outstanding; pink in bud, they are white when fully open and wonderfully fragrant.

V. cassinoides (WITHEROD)—Also called Wild Raisin, this American native grows 3 to 10 feet high, often favoring low ground and stream borders. It has a rounded, compact form and small laurellike leaves. Scented white flowers are not showy; fall color is a good red. The main attraction is the fruit, which changes color from yellow/green to pink and red to blue and attracts both game birds and songbirds. Decaying leaves have an unpleasant odor.

V. davidii—Much grown in the West, this evergreen Viburnum from China grows 1 to 3 feet tall and is hardy in zone 7. Flowers are white, but shrub is grown mainly for its dark, glossy leaves (to 6 inches long) and its bright turquoise blue fruit. Plant more than one plant for the most abundant fruit production; tidy and attractive in sun or shade.

V. dilatatum (LINDEN VIBURNUM)—Dense and round in form, this Japanese Viburnum can grow as tall as 10 feet. Leaves are nearly round and grayish green; fall color is russet red. Produces a great show of bright red fruits (which birds usually do not disturb); 'Xanthocarpum' produces yellow fruit. Viburnum dilatatum 'Catskill' was selected for compact growth habit and is usually under 5 feet high. 'Erie,' of medium-growth habit, is a heavy fruiting cultivar with bright red fruit that becomes coral after a hard frost. 'Oneida's glossy dark red fruit (abundant in the North;

---

*'Compactum' is of more compact habit.

sparse in the South) persists into late winter, and fine-textured foliage turns pale yellow and orange-red in fall. Flowers may appear off and on throughout the summer. Several cultivars should be planted together for heaviest fruit set.

V. rhytidophyllum (LEATHERLEAF VIBURNUM)—This unusual evergreen, native to China, can grow 10 feet tall in the South and Pacific Northwest. Hardy in the East to southern New York, Leatherleaf has cream-colored flowers (there is a variety roseum) and red fruit that turns black. The main attraction is the large, wrinkled leaves, which can reach more than 7 inches in length. This shrub makes a strong architectural statement in the landscape. The cultivar 'Allegheny' has a rounder, denser growth habit.

Viburnum cassinoides (Witherod, Wild Raisin). This hardy native, also known as Appalachian Tea, favors low ground and stream banks. Its showy fruit attracts many kinds of birds.

Surely Viburnums have a problem or two? As noted above, Guelder Rose, or Common Snowball, often suffers badly from aphid attack but aphids are not a severe problem on other species. Occasionally, spider mites are found on shrubs in hot, dry climates. (Keep sprays containing sulfur off Viburnum leaves.) V. carlesii is susceptible to bacterial leaf spot. Some Viburnums have leaves or bark with unpleasant odors when bruised. V. sieboldii has, perhaps, the most malodorous leaves; V. lentago has odoriferous reddish brown bark. (The dried bark of some species was used medicinally; other common names for American Cranberrybush are "Crampbark" and "Squawbush." V. cassinoides provided the drink known as Appalachian Tea.) In addition, the flower fragrance of several species (notably V. dilatatum) is offensive to some. Fruiting is best when several shrubs of the same species or a compatible cultivar are planted together, but this is true for many plants. A number of Viburnums are sensitive to highway de-icing salt (especially V. carlesii and its hybrids) and some species are fairly intolerant of drought. These few drawbacks are a small price to pay for such a beautiful and dependable group of plants!

U.S. NATIONAL ARBORETUM VIBURNUM CULTIVARS

To the great good luck of gardeners, Donald Egolf, now of the U.S. National Arboretum in Washington, D.C., has been interested in Viburnums since his student days at Cornell. After a long period of neglect, a number of American nurseries are at last beginning to stock some of Dr. Egolf's superior cultivars; they can be recognized by their American Indian names. For more information call the Aboretum at (202) 475-4815. Here are some favorites:

Viburnum x burkwoodii 'Mohawk'—Has inflorescences of dark red buds that open to white petals with red-blotched reverse; strong, spicy clove fragrance and glossy, dark green foliage that turns brilliant orange-red in autumn. Resistant to the leaf spot that affects V. carlesii (a parent), this is a choice medium-size plant for the home landscape.

Viburnum sargentii 'Onondaga'—Distinguished from the species by vividly pubescent dark maroon young foliage that maintains a maroon tinge when mature. In more northern climates, foliage has intense coloration throughout the summer. 'Susquehana,' another V. sargentii cultivar, is a large, heavy-branched and upright shrub with corky trunks, showy white flowers (with large sterile marginal florets) and masses of red fruit. The open-branched structure becomes a distinctive winter feature.

Viburnum plicatum tomentosum 'Shasta'—Has a strongly horizontal growth habit, being twice as wide as high. Flowers are pure white with sterile marginal florets larger than other cultivars. A spectacular garden plant, especially when viewed from above. V. plicatum tomentosum 'Shoshoni' is a compact plant less than 5 feet high and about twice as wide, with abundant flowering and prolific red fruit. ('Mariesii,' selected in the nursery of James Veitch and Sons, is also a superior cultivar.)

V. x 'Chesapeake'—Distinct with leathery, dark green leaves, dense branching and a compact growth habit. Pink buds, white flowers and berries that turn from red/orange to black. Unfortunately, not reliably hardy north of zone 7, but one of the best Viburnums for southern gardens.

V. x 'Chippewa' and 'Huron'—Of different parentage but similar in growth habit, flowering, fruiting and foliage. These cultivars are cross-compatible and by planting both, heavy (red) fruiting is insured. Glossy, semievergreen leaves become plum to bright red for weeks in autumn.

V. x burkwoodii 'Conoy'—The most recent introduction from the U.S. National Arboretum, this Viburnum has compact growth habit, fine-textured evergreen foliage (to Washington, D.C.; semievergreen or deciduous farther north) and persistent, abundant, glossy red fruit. In scale for home landscaping, foundations and low hedges, 'Conoy' appears to be quite cold-hardy.

V. x 'Eskimo'—A compact 4 foot plant with glossy, dark green, semievergreen leaves. In early May it is a mass of pink-tinged cream buds that open to pure-white tubular florets. This is the first three-species hybrid that combines snowball inflorescence and tubular floret characteristics. An outstanding, compact, hardy plant that is much admired and widely available in Europe.

FRUITS

Self-Pollinating Fruit Producers

Some fruiting trees and shrubs self-pollinate with good results; others are self-fruitful but yields are increased if cross-pollination takes place. Still others require that compatible pollinating varieties, blooming at the same time, be planted nearby.

Blackberry
Blueberry (HIGHBUSH)—Bigger and earlier yields with cross-pollination.
Cherry, sour
Citrus (MOST VARIETIES)
Fig
Gooseberry
Grape—Except for some Muscadines.
Nectarine
Peach—With a few exceptions.
Plum—Many European varieties are self-fruitful.
Quince
Raspberry—Usually self-fruitful but crop can improve with cross-pollination.

Two or More Varieties Required for Fruit

Apple—With a few self-fruitful exceptions like Rome and Golden Delicious.
Apricot—Some self-pollinating varieties are available.
Blueberry (RABBITEYE)
Cherry, sweet
Elderberry
Pears—With several self-fruitful exceptions like Flemish Beauty, Dutchess d'Angoulene and sometimes Bartlett.
Persimmon
Plum—Most Japanese varieties need cross-pollination.

Trouble-Free Fruits

Writing in *Pomona,* the journal of the North American Fruit Explorers,* Don Munich listed fruits that can be raised without harmful

*NAFEX is an organization of hobby fruit growers and researchers. For information contact: Jill Vorbeck, Rt. 1, Box 94, Chapin, IL 62628.

sprays. Mr. Munich asked readers to recommend such fruits and though the response was disappointing, a rather large number of different plants were suggested. Here is a partial list:

Actinidia (KIWI)
Amelanchier (SHADBUSH, SERVICEBERRY, JUNEBERRY)
Asimina (PAWPAW)
Diospyros (PERSIMMON)
Ficus (FIG)
Fragaria (STRAWBERRY)
Malus (APPLE VARIETIES: ARKANSAS BLACK, ASHWORTH WORMLESS,
    BRANDISE BLUE, GRIMES GOLDEN, POUND SWEET, REDFIELD,
    WEALTHY AND YELLOW DELICIOUS)
Morus (MULBERRY)
Prunus cerasus (SOUR CHERRY)
Prunus tomentosa (NANKING CHERRY)
Pyrus (PEAR)
Ribes (CURRANT AND GOOSEBERRY)
Rubus (BLACKBERRY AND RASPBERRY)
Sambucus (ELDERBERRY)
Shepherdia (BUFFALOBERRY)
Vaccinium (BLUEBERRY AND CRANBERRY)
Viburnum (BLACKHAW, AMERICAN CRANBERRYBUSH)
Vitis (CONCORD GRAPE, MUSCADINE GRAPE)

American Native: Blueberries

Many fruit-producing trees and shrubs have lovely spring blossoms, but few are handsome in the landscape throughout the year. Many also suffer from a multitude of insect pest and diseases. Blueberries, on the other hand, are almost too good to be true. Long-lived and hardy with few pests, Blueberries have white flowers, bright red fall color, colorful winter twigs and produce a beautiful, delicious fruit rich in iron as well as vitamins A and C.

Enjoyed by Native Americans and Colonists, Blueberries have not been in cultivation long; they were unobtainable in nurseries before the mid-1930s. A New Jersey cranberry grower, Elizabeth White, and F. V. Colville, a plant scientist with USDA, are given credit for first selecting and taming wild Blueberries in the early 1900s. One of their old varieties, now called Rubel, is still available. Other old-timers, high on flavor, include Herbert* and Darrow; the former is said to be hardiest.

*Do not pick too early! Wait a week after the berries turn blue before picking.

Blueberries are easy to grow. Highbush varieties can do well in very sandy soils although some organic matter is preferred. Plenty of moisture is needed but soils should not be soggy. Blueberries also need sun but will produce fruit in partial shade. One requirement: All Blueberries must have acid soil (pH 4 to 5.5). Though many Highbush varieties are self-fertile, two different varieties should be planted for best results. Rabbiteye Blueberries, native to the South, do not need as long a cold period in order to blossom. They are not self-fertile so two or more varieties must be planted. USDA recommends not fertilizing young Rabbiteyes as they are very sensitive to salts; go lightly on fertilizer with older plants as well. The University of Georgia College of Agriculture recommends the following Rabbiteyes for Georgia, the nation's fourth-largest Blueberry-producing state:

RABBITEYE BLUEBERRY VARIETIES

Early Season	Midseason	Late Season
Climax	Bluebelle	Delite
Woodward	Briteblue	Baldwin
Brightwell	Tifblue	
Bonita		

Climax, Bonita and Woodward are not suggested for high mountain areas. Highbush varieties may be grown in cooler and mountain regions of the South.

Most fresh supermarket Blueberries are Highbush varieties; leading producer states are Michigan, New Jersey and Maine. Northland is the hardiest Highbush variety grown. Other hardy and good-tasting varieties include Blueray,* Patriot and Bluecrop.* Spartan and Collins are also superior-tasting but not quite as hardy.

HIGHBUSH BLUEBERRY VARIETIES

Early Season	Midseason	Late Season
Earliblue	Blueray	Darrow
Northland	Patriot	Coville
Spartan	Bluecrop	Elliot*
Collins	Berkeley	
	Herbert	

*An exceptionally high producer.

*Do not pick too early! Wait a week after the berries turn blue before picking.

As mentioned previously, Blueberries are outstanding in the landscape. The branches of Vaccinium ovatum, native to the Pacific Northwest, are the florist's "Huckleberry." Lowbush Blueberries, small, very hardy creeping shrubs, are found on rocky cliffs in the Northeast. They make exceptional ground covers and produce small but sweet and delicious fruit. Minnesota Landscape Arboretum has developed several Lowbush cultivars and Lowbush/Highbush hybrids; among these are Northcountry, Northsky and Northblue. The new hybrids are low growing, productive and extra hardy. Two varieties cultivated for ornamental purposes, Lowbush (18 inches) and Ornablue (4 feet), are said to produce satisfactory crops. Check with your local extension agent for a list of Blueberries recommended for your region.

New Blueberries to watch for: Arlen Draper and Gene Galletta of the Agricultural Research Service, Beltsville, Maryland, describe several newly developed varieties: Cooper, Gulfcoast and Georgiagem (for southern gardens); and Duke, Toro, Sunrise, Sierra, Bluegold and Nelson (for the North). Duke, Toro and Sunrise are all early-fruiting; Nelson is the latest.

SOURCES FOR BLUEBERRIES

A. G. Ammon Nursery
Route 532, PO Box 488
Chatsworth, NJ 08019

Finch Blueberry Nursery
PO Box 699
Bailey, NC 27807

Hartmann's Plantation Inc.,
PO Box E
Grand Junction, MI 49056

New York State Fruit Testing
Cooperative Association, Inc.
PO Box 462
Geneva, NY 14456
Informative catalog
Old and new varieties of many
fruits

Raintree Nursery
391 Butts Rd.
Morton, WA 98356
Also stocks Raspberries

More Native Berries: Raspberries

Members of the great Rose Family (and the genus Rubus), both red and black Raspberries grow wild in many parts of the United States (red Raspberries are also native to Europe and Asia). They are not the beautiful shrubs Blueberries are, but they are attractive, easy to grow and their fruit is incomparable. Put them in a sunny spot; a little shade, especially during the late afternoon, is fine. Avoid planting red Raspberries near black Raspberries; the latter are very sensitive to viral diseases that reds can harbor. If space permits, locate them away from the vegetable garden as well. Water during dry spells.

Although plants will endure neglect, higher crops result if canes are properly tended. There are two types of red Raspberries. Standard Raspberries produce summer fruit on canes that grew the previous summer (floricanes). Everbearing Raspberries will also produce a summer crop on floricanes, as well as a fall crop on the new canes of the current season's growth (called primocanes); everbearing cultivars trace their ancestry back to fall-bearing North American natives. The fall crop is usually the better of the two, and most advise cutting everbearers to the ground when they are dormant to ensure only the fall harvest. This practice keeps pests and disease in check as well. Standard or summer-bearing Raspberries should also be pruned; cut only canes that have borne fruit; primocanes must be left for next season's berries.

As with other fruits and vegetables, few cultivars grow equally well in all regions of the country. Heritage, which does well in many different regions, disappoints some in the Midwest who prefer Amity. A NAFEX member in Maine (zone 3) who had no success with Heritage recommends Canby. Plant virus-free plants and avoid cultivars such as Fall Red and September, which are susceptible to disease-carrying aphids.

GENERALLY GOOD IN THE NORTHEAST:

Heritage (EVER-BEARER)—Excellent flavor; fruit remains in good condition on bush even when overripe. Fine fall crops; disease-resistant. Try this one first.

Redwing (EVER-BEARER)—Developed in Minnesota; fruit said to be sweeter than Heritage though yields may not be as high. Fruits before Heritage.

Taylor (STANDARD)—Large berries; excellent quality. Suggested for a market crop as well as for the home garden. Midseason ripening; introduced in 1935.

Titan (STANDARD)—Largest fruit of all; mild flavor; high yield. Appears to have some resistance to aphids. Good reports from the Midwest.

RECOMMENDED FOR THE SOUTH:

Dormanred—Trailing canes. Fruit must be very ripe to be sweet. Resistant to heat and drought; very large fruit and high yields.

Heritage—Appears to do well in the cooler parts of Georgia.

Indian Summer—Old (1936) pest-resistant cultivar that tolerates hot weather well.

Southland—Large berries of good quality. Resistant to anthracnose, mildew and leaf spot; recommended for upper and mid-South regions. Does well in southern Arkansas.

SOURCES FOR RASPBERRIES

Gurney Seed and Nursery Co.
Yankton, SD 57079

Stark Brothers Nursery
Louisiana, MO 63353

Miller Nurseries
West Lake Rd.
Canandaigua, NY 14424

Waynesboro Nurseries, Inc.
Waynesboro, VA 22980

NY State Fruit Testing
Cooperative Association, Inc.
P.O. Box 462
Geneva, NY 14456
Informative catalog
Old and new varieties of many
fruits

Producers of Edible Pine Nuts

Gardeners in colder regions may not realize that it is possible for them to grow pines that yield edible nuts. Some of the following trees reach heights over 100 feet, but all are slow growers, making them suitable for the small garden. All pines need a sunny site and good drainage. Gardeners wishing to harvest nuts need patience; some trees will not produce for a decade.

Pinus cembra* (SWISS STONE PINE)
P. cembroides (MEXICAN PIÑON OR MEXICAN STONE PINE)
P. edulis (PIÑON)—Hardy in parts of New England.
P. geradiana (NEPAL NUT PINE)—Hardy in parts of the North.
P. koraiensis* (KOREAN PINE)
P. monophyll (SINGLE-LEAF PIÑON)—Can also be grown in some northern areas.
P. pinea (ITALIAN STONE OR UMBRELLA PINE)
P. sabiniana (DIGGER PINE)
P. sibirica* (SIBERIAN PINE)

*Hardy to USDA zone 4.

MORE NUT TREES FOR NORTHERN GARDENS

Carya spp. (SHELLBARK HICKORY AND SHAGBARK HICKORY)
Castanea spp. (CHESTNUT)
Corylus spp. (AMERICAN HAZELNUT AND EUROPEAN HAZELNUT)
Juglans spp. (BLACK WALNUT AND CARPATHIAN WALNUT)

LORE AND MORE

Summer- and Fall-Flowering Trees and Shrubs

In many gardens the woody plants put on dazzling floral displays in April and May but when June arrives the only color seen is supplied by roses, annuals and perennials. This is too bad because there are many summer-blooming woody plants of all sizes to add interest to the garden. Twenty-five summer bloomers are:

Abelia grandiflora (GLOSSY ABELIA)—Small/medium shrub
Albizia julibrissin (MIMOSA; SILK TREE)—Small tree
Buddleja davidii* (BUTTERFLYBUSH)—Small/medium shrub
Calycanthus floridus* (SWEETSHRUB, CAROLINA
    ALLSPICE)—Medium shrub
Caryopteris x clandonensis (BLUEBEARD)—Small shrub
Ceanothus spp. (SUMMER LILAC)—There are many species of
    these tender Pacific coast shrubs represented in the
    Northeast by the low-growing C. americanus (New Jersey
    Tea).
Clethra alnifolia* (SUMMERSWEET)—Medium shrub
Cotinus coggygria** (SMOKEBUSH)—Large shrub/small tree
Franklinia alatamaha (FRANKLIN TREE)—Small tree
Hibiscus syriacus (ROSE OF SHARON)—Medium-large
    shrub/small tree
Hydrangea spp. (HYDRANGEA)—Small and large shrubs; in some
    varieties pinkish flowers and yellow fall color coexist and
    remain decorative until frost.
Hypericum spp. (ST. JOHNSWORT)—Small shrubs
Itea virginica* (VIRGINIA SWEETSPIRE)—Large shrub; the variety
    'Henry's Garnet' won the Pennsylvania Horticultural
    Society's Styer Award of Garden Merit.

*Fragrant.
**The flowers of Smokebush are insignificant, but the large, misty fruiting panicles are showy from the middle of the summer until winter.

Koelreuteria paniculata* (GOLDENRAIN-TREE)—Small tree

Lagerstroemia indica (CRAPE MYRTLE)—Large shrub/small tree

Oxydendrum arboreum* (SOURWOOD, SORREL TREE, TREE ANDROMEDA)—Small/medium tree

Potentilla fruticosa (SHRUBBY CINQUEFOIL)—Small shrub

Rhododendron viscosum* (SWAMP AZALEA)—Medium shrub

Sophora japonica (CHINESE SCHOLAR TREE)—Large tree

Sorbaria spp. (URAL FALSE-SPIREA AND TREE-SPIREA)—Medium and large shrubs, best in large scale situations; aralia is another coarse summer-flowering small tree.

Spirea spp. (SPIREA)—Small/medium shrub. Many Spireas are spring blooming; these are the white-flowered species. Later blooming Spireas are usually pink or red, such as the popular S. x bumalda with its many cultivars. S. tomentosa, our native pink-flowered Hardhack or Steeplebush, is perhaps the latest-blooming Spirea.

Stewartia spp. (STEWARTIA)—Large shrub/small tree

Syringa pekinensis (PEKING LILAC)—Large shrub and S. reticulata (Japanese Tree Lilac) small tree

Tilia spp.* (LINDEN, BASSWOOD)—Large tree

Vitex spp.* (CHASTE-TREE)—Small tree in south; shrubby in north where it may die back to ground in winter.

*Fragrant.

Notes on Plants in Flower*

The Thorns are a very beautiful class of large shrubs, or perhaps we might better call them small trees, as they grow from 12 to 20 feet high. We have seen them the former height when only six or seven years old. They are now in flower and receive, as they well deserve, general admiration. There are few shrubs more beautiful or more worthy of general cultivation. The best varieties are the Single Pink and Single Red, and the Double Red and Double White.

Several varieties of the Spirea are in flower, and among them we notice the S. trilobata and S. crenata, both very neat shrubs of rather dwarfish habit, with trusses of small flowers almost covering the plant. S. ulmifolia is of larger growth, with larger flowers. S. lanceolata is the finest of the class—of the

*From *Moore's Rural New-Yorker,* 20 June 1857.

purest whiteness. Its branches are floral snow-wreaths.
Everybody should plant it.

The Calycanthus is becoming a great favorite, as the
demand for it at the nurseries shows. It is a pretty, sweet-scented
shrub, with large cinnamon-colored flowers.

The Rose-colored Weigela is just coming into bloom. It is
a fine shrub, with flowers of a rosy pink, and is as hardy as a
lilac.

The African Tamarix now shows its delicate pink flowers.
It is delicate and beautiful both in leaf and flower.

The Lilacs are mostly gone, though we gathered a few fine
specimens, and among them the Persian White and a singular
very dark purple variety called Josekea.

That old favorite, the Snowball, is now in perfection.
There is nothing better. Everyone has it, or should have it. It is
a crooked, rambling grower, and the wood is tender; the
consequence is that many plants are broken with the weight of
the flowers, especially in wet weather. Young plants should be
pruned, so as to secure a stiff stem and a compact head.

The Horse Chestnuts are just passing out of bloom. The
common variety and the Red Flowering are fine. The flowers of
the Yellow variety are poor, not differing much from the
Buckeye. The Double White (see illustration) is the finest of
them all. The flowers are white, prettily spotted with red, like

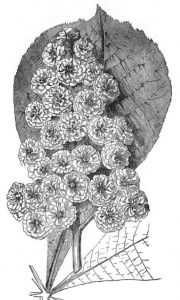

The Double Flowering Horse Chestnut from the June 20, 1857, issue of
Moore's Rural New Yorker.

the common variety, but perfectly double. There is a variegated-leaved variety, with red flowers, but it is not much disseminated.

Last week we noticed the Upright, or Tartarian Honeysuckle. We have now a fine variety in flower, with deep pink flowers, more showy than the common.

American Native: Witch Hazel

Witch Hazels bloom when little else is in flower and their branches were once a favorite tool of water diviners. The shrub's astringent bark was utilized by Native Americans and still is made into a medicinal lotion, manufactured in Connecticut by E. E. Dickinson. Perhaps this combination of factors earned Hamamelis the name of "Witch" Hazel although another common name is "Snapping-Hazel," which refers to the loud snap heard when the shiny black seeds are ejected, sometimes several feet from the bush. These seeds take a year to mature and two years to germinate. Common Witch Hazel (Hamamelis virginiana) is a large, shade-loving native shrub or small tree and is the last of all woody plants to bloom in the fall in the Northland. Sometimes the delicate yellow flowers are accompanied by the golden fall color of the leaves, while other times the shrub blooms after leaves have fallen in early November. The Vernal Witch Hazel, H. vernalis, is smaller, does not range as far north in its native habitats and blooms in winter or very early spring. Its flowers are not as showy as those of Common Witch Hazel but they are more fragrant and make good candidates for early-winter indoor forcing. The temperate regions of eastern Asia also have several native Witch Hazels. H. japonica (Japanese Witch Hazel) and H. mollis (Chinese Witch Hazel) both approximate the size of our Common Witch Hazel and both have showy yellow flowers in spring. H. mollis is not quite as hardy as H. japonica. Many catalogs now feature shrubs that are crosses between the two Asians (H. x intermedia) and some cultivars have red flowers.

Plants at Risk for Fall Planting

In the Northeast and much of the Midwest most bare-root trees and shrubs should be planted in spring. The general rule states that container-grown or balled and burlapped trees and shrubs can be planted anytime the ground is not frozen. However, fall planting requires some care— gardeners should plant early (before November) and water enough to insure good root development. Mulch but do not fertilize until spring. Above all, avoid planting species that are noted for transplanting poorly in the fall. Professor Phil Carpenter of Purdue lists the following woody plants at risk for fall planting (common landscape plants not listed below are good bets for fall planting):

GROUP 1 (PLANTS WITH SIGNIFICANT RISK OF LOSS; PLANT IN SPRING)

Carpinus spp. (HORNBEAM)
Chamaecyparis nootkatensis (NOOTKA CYPRESS)
Koelreuteria paniculata (GOLDENRAIN TREE)
Liriodendron tulipifera (TULIP TREE)
Magnolia spp. (MAGNOLIA)
Nyssa sylvatica (SOUR GUM, TUPELO, PEPPERIDGE)
Populus spp. (POPULAR)
Quercus alba (WHITE OAK)
Quercus coccinea (SCARLET OAK)
Quercus macrocarpa (MOSSYCUP OAK)
Quercus phellos (WILLOW OAK)
Quercus robur (ENGLISH OAK)
Quercus rubra (RED OAK)
Zelkova serrata (JAPANESE ZELKOVA)

GROUP 2 (SOME DEGREE OF RISK; PROVIDE EXTRA CARE)

Acer rubrum (RED MAPLE)
Betula spp. (BIRCH)
Cornus florida (FLOWERING DOGWOOD)
Crataegus spp. (HAWTHORN)
Prunus spp. (PEACH, CHERRY, OTHER STONE FRUITS)
Pyrus calleryana (CALLERY PEAR)
Salix spp. (WILLOW, TREE FORMS)
Tilia tomentosa (SILVER LINDEN)

GROUP 3 (NOT AT GREAT RISK, BUT PLANT EARLY; BEST PLANTED IN LATE AUGUST OR SEPTEMBER)

Berberis julianae (WINTERGREEN BARBERRY)
Cotoneaster salicifolius (WILLOWLEAF COTONEASTER)
Hedera helix (ENGLISH IVY)
Ilex crenata (JAPANESE HOLLY)
Pinus thunbergiana (JAPANESE BLACK PINE)

Rhododendron spp. (RHODODENDRONS AND AZALEAS, EVERGREEN
    TYPES)
Taxus baccata (ENGLISH YEW)
Tsuga canadensis (CANADIAN HEMLOCK)
Viburnum rhytidophyllum (LEATHERLEAF VIBURNUM)

Donald Wyman's Favorites

Dr. Donald Wyman, past president of the American Horticultural
Society and director of Harvard University's Arnold Arboretum for
many years, is also the author of the well-known *Wyman's Gardening
Encyclopedia,* as well as many other books. Several years ago he listed a
dozen of his favorite trees and shrubs in an article that appeared in the
New York Times, November 3, 1976:

Berberis thunbergii 'Aurea' (JAPANESE BARBERRY)—Golden
    yellow and pest-free.
Chamaecyparis obtusa 'Nana' (DWARF HINOKI
    CYPRESS)—Small, dense and neat evergreen.
Cornus kousa (KOUSA DOGWOOD)—Ideal small ornamental tree.
Cornus mas (CORNELIAN CHERRY)—Pest-free dogwood with
    small yellow flowers in early spring.
Fothergilla gardenii (DWARF FOTHERGILLA)—Small white
    flowers, orange autumn color; an unknown native.
Ilex crenata 'Convexa' (JAPANESE HOLLY)—Fine evergreen with
    boxlike leaves; excellent for indoor arrangements.
Leucothoe fontanesiana 'Nana' (DWARF DROOPING
    LEUCOTHOE)—Stays small, as a good foundation plant
    should.
Malus hybrid 'Dorothea' (DOROTHEA CRAB APPLE)—Large,
    double, pink flowers and bright yellow fruit.
Sciadopitys verticillata (JAPANESE UMBRELLA PINE)—Branches
    long-lasting in indoor arrangements.
Stephanandra incisa 'Crispa' (LACE SHRUB)—Low, dense and
    spreading makes this a good bank cover.
Tsuga canadensis (CANADA HEMLOCK)—A graceful evergreen
    that prefer some shade and protection from winter winds.
    There are many cultivars.
Viburnum sargentii (SARGENT VIBURNUM)—Professor Wyman
    liked the yellow-fruited variety of this Asian species.

The Styer Award of Garden Merit

Most nurseries concentrate on just a few varieties of ornamentals and do little to introduce gardeners to the many choice plants that are available but less commonly planted. No wonder many of our gardens look the same! The Pennsylvania Horticultural Society is attempting to remedy the situation by recognizing exceptional garden plants that possess pleasing habit, fine color, ease of culture and pest resistance but are little known to most gardeners—and garden centers. The following plants (all of which survive winter temperatures to minus 10 degrees F) have been honored with the Pennsylvania Horticultural Society's first Styer Award (1988):

Hedera helix 'Buttercup' (ENGLISH IVY)—Accent plant with golden yellow new growth and light-colored veins.

Ilex serrata x I. verticillata (HOLLY 'SPARKLEBERRY')—A deciduous holly that produces bright red berries that last all winter. Grows in a wide range of soils.

Itea virginica (VIRGINIA SWEETSPIRE)—Shrub with fragrant white flowers in summer and purple or maroon fall color. Prefers cool, moist sites.

Magnolia acuminata x M. heptapeta (MAGNOLIA 'ELIZABETH')—The first yellow magnolia. Tree grows to 30 feet and blooms profusely for several weeks.

Prunus incisa x P. campanulata (FLOWERING CHERRY 'OKAME')—One of the earliest blooming cherries. Reaches 25 feet and produces pink flowers.

Zelkova serrata (ZELKOVA 'GREEN VASE'—A tree that withstands air pollution, clay soils and drought. A relative of American elm and recommended as a substitute for it.

Six additional plants were honored by the Pennsylvania Horticultural Society in 1989. All are said to be hardy to zone 5 except for Deutzia, which is hardy to zone 6.

Callicarpa dichotoma (BEAUTYBERRY)—Shrub that produces showy lavender-colored berries in fall when most fall fruits are yellow/orange/red. Three to 5 feet tall; graceful arching branches. Few pests or diseases; prefers full sun or partial shade.

Deutzia gracilis 'Nikko' (DEUTZIA)—Compact and fine textured; perfect for the small garden. Covered with white flowers in spring; reddish fall color. Plants enjoy light afternoon shade in areas of high summer temperatures.

Hamamelis mollis 'Pallida' (CHINESE WITCH HAZEL)—Fragrant flowers with long yellow petals bloom in late winter. Slow growing to 15 feet. Witch Hazels like moist (not wet) soil and tolerate some shade.

Hydrangea quercifolia 'Snow Queen' (OAKLEAF HYDRANGEA)—This Hydrangea, with its handsome bold leaves that turn burgundy in fall, is best in the Mid-Atlantic states and south. 'Snow Queen' has showy, upright white flower clusters in midsummer that last several weeks before turning an attractive russet. Grows 5 to 6 feet tall; will grow in sun or shade.

Malus 'Donald Wyman' (DONALD WYMAN CRABAPPLE)— Named for the well-known horticulturist, this fast-growing tree is an excellent choice for the homeowner who wants a relatively trouble-free Crabapple. 'Donald Wyman' is medium sized, with pink buds and single white flowers. Shiny, bright red fruit persists into late winter. Grafting not necessary; roots readily from summer cuttings.

Malus 'Jewelberry' (JEWELBERRY CRABAPPLE)—A dwarf Crabapple for those with limited space. Dark pink buds open into pink and white flowers (the cooler the spring, the darker pink the flowers) and shiny red fruits are plentiful. Much more disease-resistant than the commonly planted dwarf 'Red Jade.'

Finally, in 1990, the following plants received the Styer award:

Betula nigra 'Heritage' (HERITAGE RIVER BIRCH)—Everyone admires the white birches of New England; unfortunately the native B. papyrifera as well as B. pendula (European White Birch) are subject to serious borer infestations when grown in warmer regions. 'Heritage' has creamy, exfoliating bark rather than the chalk white bark of Paper Birch, but most important, 'Heritage' is heat-tolerant and resistant to borers and leaf spot. Trees grow 40 to 60 feet in moist or drier acid soil. Zones 4 to 8.

Cornus sericea 'Silver and Gold'—Lovers of variegated shrubs can rejoice in this new dogwood with yellow stems and variegated foliage. Said to withstand heat and humidity better than variegated forms of the red-stemmed Cornus alba (Tartarian Dogwood). Pruning keeps shrub in bounds and bark colorful.

Fothergilla gardenii 'Blue Mist' (DWARF FOTHERGILLA)— Relatives of Witch Hazel, Fothergillas are native to the U.S. Southeast but hardy north to zone 5. This small cultivar has early (before the leaves) scented white flowers and brilliant orange/red fall color. The cultivar name comes from the blue-green summer foliage. Tolerates light shade and likes moist, well-drained soil.

Hydrangea macrophylla 'Blue Billow'—Most gardeners know H. macrophylla as the common Hydrangea with large, rounded flower heads which may be pink or blue depending on soil pH. This cultivar from Korea has flat-topped flower heads composed of both fertile and sterile flowers which gives them the lacecap look of many Viburnums. Reliably hardy in the mid-Atlantic states but blue flowers turn redder if soil pH gets above 6.5.

Daphne caucasica—An elegant small shrub with leathery leaves and fragrant, white flowers from spring until frost. Not as hardy as D. cneorum and D. mezereum, but thought to be longer-lived. Needs good drainage. Zone 7.

Stewartia pseudocamellia var. koreana (KOREAN STEWARTIA)—Listed by *Hortus Third* as Stewartia koreana, this hardy tree, beautiful in all seasons, is described in the list "Fine Trees for Your Garden," pages 206–208.

WHERE TO BUY STYER AWARD WINNERS

Ask for these plants at your local garden center. If they cannot help, a source list can be obtained by sending a stamped, self-addressed business-size envelope to Styer Award, Pennsylvania Horticultural Society, 325 Walnut Street, Philadelphia, PA 19106.

Trees and Shrubs for Indoor Forcing

Gardeners do have some winter pleasures: thumbing through seed catalogs, enjoying snow on colorful twigs and branches and bringing in branches of spring-blooming shrubs and trees for forcing. A number of plants can be forced to bloom during the winter months. Bring the earliest bloomers in first. Forsythia, Cornelian Cherry, Red Maple and Witch Hazel can be cut in early January; wait several weeks to bring in later-flowering shrubs and fruit trees. Be sure to select branches that have some fat flower buds; smaller buds will be the leaf buds. For best results soak the branches in a tall container (or bathtub) overnight so as much water as possible will be absorbed. Place the branches in jars of water and keep them in a cool place; as buds begin to swell make sure light is adequate—but do not put them in direct sunlight. Be patient; some branches take a week or longer to show signs of life. Remember that not all shrubs and trees make good candidates for forcing. Some to try:

Abeliophyllum distichum (WHITE FORSYTHIA)—Flowers are pale pink upon opening but soon turn white.

Acer rubrum (RED MAPLE) and A. platanoides (Norway Maple)—Rubrum produces red flowers; platanoides yellow-green.

Aesculus (HORSE CHESTNUT)—Attractive leaves and spikes of flowers.

Alnus (ALDER)—Alders produce interesting catkins. Some birches may also be forced for catkins.

Amelanchier (SHADBUSH)—White flowers; forces quickly.

Cercis (REDBUD)—Hot pink or white flowers. Be patient.

Chaenomeles (FLOWERING QUINCE)—Long-lasting red or orange flowers.

Cornus mas (CORNELIAN CHERRY)—Small yellow flowers; easy to force.

Cornus florida (FLOWERING DOGWOOD)—Slow and difficult sometimes but worth a try. Flowers will not expand fully.

Daphne mezereum (FEBRUARY DAPHNE)—Red-purple flowers; there is a white variety.

Forsythia (FORSYTHIA)—Yellow flowers; easy to force.

Hamamelis vernalis (WITCH HAZEL)—Good fragrance; easy to force.

Larix (LARCH)—Branching and delicate green needles are especially suitable in Oriental-style arrangements.

Lonicera (HONEYSUCKLE)—Some varieties are very fragrant.

Magnolia (MAGNOLIA)—Flowers large; forces easily.

Prunus armeniaca (APRICOT)—Many white flowers; somewhat short-lived.

Prunus spp. (CHERRY)—White or pink flowers.

Prunus triloba (FLOWERING ALMOND)—Easy to force pink flowers.

Malus spp. (APPLES AND CRABAPPLES)—White, pink or red flowers; double-flowered species take longer to force but last longer. Pear (Pyrus communis) also forces well.

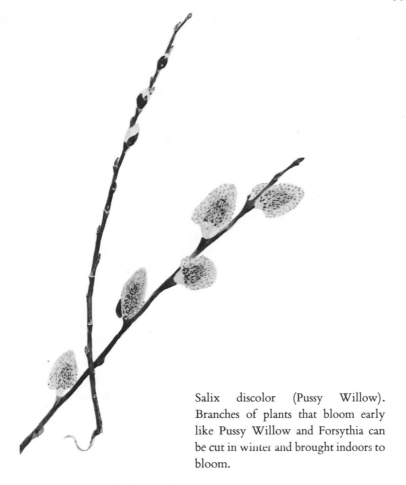

Salix discolor (Pussy Willow). Branches of plants that bloom early like Pussy Willow and Forsythia can be cut in winter and brought indoors to bloom.

Quercus spp. (OAK)—Oaks produce lovely pinkish leaves that turn pale green.
Salix caprea, S. discolor (PUSSYWILLOW)

Water Needs of Container-Grown Ornamental Plants

Recent research results from California confirm what gardeners have always known: some plants are heavy water users while others get by with less.* In general, container-grown plants, like the average lawn,

* David Burger, Janet Hartin, Donald Hodel, Tim Lukaszewski, Steven Tjosvold and Sally Wagner, "Water Use in California's Ornamental Nurseries," *California Agriculture* (September-October 1987), 7.

are water gluttons, but a few plants were found to be fairly light water users. It may be desirable to keep these frugal ones in mind when selecting plants for containers in regions where water is scarce and expensive. Plants are listed in order of descending water use.

HEAVY WATER USERS:

Pyracantha angustifolia 'Gnome' (FIRETHORN)
Buddleia davidii 'Dubonnet' (BUTTERFLY BUSH)

MODERATE WATER USERS:

Chaenomeles x clarkiana 'Minerva' (FLOWERING QUINCE)
Nerium oleander (OLEANDER)
Spiraea vanhouttei (BRIDAL WREATH)
Juniperus horizontalis 'Youngstown Compacta' (CREEPING JUNIPER)
Forsythia intermedia 'Spring Glory'
Platycladus orientalis 'Aureus Nana' (ORIENTAL ARBORVITAE)
Berberis thunbergii 'Atropurpurea' (PURPLE JAPANESE BARBERRY)
Juniperus chinensis 'Spearmint' (CHINESE JUNIPER)
Juniperus sabina 'Buffalo' (SAVIN JUNIPER)
Ligustrum japonicum (JAPANESE PRIVET)
Callistemon citrinus (BOTTLEBRUSH)—Zone 9
Cotoneaster congestus 'Likiang'
Juniperus horizontalis 'Prince of Wales'
Juniperus chinensis procumbens 'Green Mound'
Pittosporum tobira (AUSTRALIAN LAUREL, MOCK ORANGE)—Zone 8

LIGHT WATER USERS:

Arctostaphylos uva-ursi (BEARBERRY, CREEPING MANZANITA)
Euonymus kiautschovica 'Manhattan'
Photinia x fraseri (EVERGREEN PHOTINIA)—Zone 8
Cytisus scoparius 'Moonlight' (SCOTCH BROOM)
Mahonia repens (OREGON GRAPE, HOLLY GRAPE)

Woody Plants for Bonsai

It is not surprising that Japan, a crowded country where open land is at a premium, gave "tray planting" or bonsai to the world. This technique involves restricting roots in a small container and pruning branches. Many plants are suitable bonsai subjects, and the adventurous should experiment with likely candidates among their garden favorites and native flora. The following Asian natives are traditional bonsai subjects:

Acer buergerianum (TRIDENT MAPLE)
Acer palmatum (JAPANESE MAPLE)
Cercidphyllum japonicum (KATSURA TREE)
Chaenomeles japonica (DWARF FLOWERING QUINCE)
Chamaecyparis obtusa (HINOKI CYPRESS)
Ginkgo biloba (GINKGO, MAIDENHAIR TREE)
Juniperus chinensis var. sargentii (SARGENT JUNIPER)
Picea jezoensis (YEDDO SPRUCE)
Pinus densiflora (JAPANESE RED PINE)
Pinus parviflora (JAPANESE WHITE PINE)
Pinus thunbergiana (JAPANESE BLACK PINE)
Prunus mume (JAPANESE FLOWERING APRICOT)
Rhododendron kaempferi x R. kiusianum (KURUME HYBRID
  AZALEAS)
Taxus cuspidata (JAPANESE YEW)
Zelkova serrata (JAPANESE ZELKOVA)

Five American natives to experiment with:

Acer rubrum (RED MAPLE)
Corylus americana (AMERICAN HAZELNUT)
Pinus rigida (PITCH PINE)
Taxodium distichum (BALD CYPRESS)
Tsuga canadensis (HEMLOCK)

Poisonous and Irritating Woody Plants

POISONOUS

Most of the following pose little threat except to small children, who are sometimes attracted to colorful berries and interesting seeds. Children should be taught never to sample an unknown seed—even Apple seeds and the kernels of Apricot, Peach, Loquat and Cherry are poisonous, and commonly collected seeds like Acorns and Horse Chestnuts can cause distress if eaten by small children. Some of the plants listed on the following page are more dangerous than others but all should be avoided:

Aucuba japonica (JAPANESE AUCUBA)—The whole plant contains toxins but the red berry has been the culprit in reported cases of poisoning. Symptoms are not always produced but nausea and fever may occur.

Calycanthus spp. (CAROLINA ALLSPICE)—The big, shiny brown seeds of this handsome native plant should not be eaten. AMA reports that human poisonings have not been reported but seeds cause convulsions in animals.

Celastrus scandens (BITTERSWEET)—Not believed to be extremely toxic, the fruit (and leaves) are still reputed to be poisonous and should be avoided.

Cestrum spp. (JESSAMINE)—Nightshade family member planted in warmer regions of the country for its attractive, fragrant flowers. The variously colored fruits (and sap) cause digestive distress if consumed.

Clematis spp. (CLEMATIS)—All parts of this Buttercup family member are toxic and can cause serious symptoms; fortunately, the pain produced by nibbling on the plant limits ingestion.

Daphne spp. (DAPHNE)—These attractive shrubs produce red or gold fruit; the whole plant, including the flowers, is toxic and can produce life-threatening symptoms.

Euonymus europaea (EUROPEAN SPINDLE TREE)—The fruit (red-pink capsule, orange aril) is poisonous; symptoms can be serious. All members of the genus should be avoided and no parts of the plants used.

Gelsemium sempervirens (YELLOW OR CAROLINA JESSAMINE)—Attractive for its fragrant yellow flowers, this Jessamine is a toxic plant. Children have been poisoned by sucking on the flowers.

Hedera spp. (IVY)—Leaves and berries should not be chewed; stomach discomfort could result, which may be especially worrisome in small children.

Hydrangea macrophylla (HYDRANGEA)—The flower buds contain cyanide and poisoning can occur if enough are consumed.

Ilex spp. (HOLLY, YAUPON)—Holly berries are toxic and should not be eaten; nausea and vomiting are the chief symptoms.

Kalmia spp. (MT. LAUREL)—Leaves are poisonous, as is honey made from the flowers. Symptoms may be frightening and include convulsions and coma.

Laburnum spp. (GOLDEN CHAIN TREE)—The whole plant, but

especially the seeds (produced in showy pods), is toxic. The poison's action is similar to that of nicotine.

Leucothoe spp. (LEUCOTHOE, FETTER BUSH)—As in Kalmia, leaves and nectar are poisonous.

Ligustrum spp. (PRIVET)—The whole plant, including the blue or black berries, is toxic. Consumption of many berries causes severe stomach distress and can be serious in young children.

Melia azedarach (CHINABERRY)—Yellow fruit and bark are toxic, and symptoms are variable but can be serious. Fatalities have been reported, although fruit is eaten in some areas with no ill effects.

Menispermum canadense (MOODSEED, YELLOW PARILLA)—Dark-colored fruit resembles grapes and is poisonous. Convulsions can occur from consumption.

Nerium oleander (OLEANDER)—All parts of the plant are very toxic; so is the water in which the flowers are placed. Poison is similar to digitalis and capable of causing heartbeat irregularities.

Phoradendron spp. (MISTLETOE)—Leaves and stems are poisonous; berries can also be toxic (and even fatal) if enough are eaten.

Pieris spp. (LILY-OF-THE-VALLEY BUSH, FETTERBUSH)—Leaves and nectar are poisonous, as in Kalmia and Leucothoe, and children have been fatally poisoned from eating leaves.

Rhododendron spp. (RHODODENDRON)—Another Heath family member (like Mt. Laurel, Fetterbush and Pieris) with toxic leaves and honey. Symptoms can be serious.

Rhodotypos scandens (JETBEAD)—Glossy black berries are toxic.

Robinia pseudoacacia (BLACK LOCUST)—Leaves, bark and seeds are poisonous. The latter are found in large pods that may attract the young.

Sophora spp. (BURN BEAN, MESCAL BEAN, CHINESE SCHOLAR TREE)—Handsome trees and shrubs with toxic seeds. Attractive U.S. native S. secundiflora has bright-red seeds (in woody pods); S. tomentosa has yellow seeds. These plants belong to the Leguminosae (Bean family)—the seeds of all unknown Legumes should be shunned.

Taxus spp. (YEW)—Much of the plant is toxic, including the seeds. The red aril that surrounds the seed (and attracts children) is not toxic. Yew fatalities are not rare.

Wisteria spp. (WISTERIA)—All parts of the plant are poisonous, including the flowers and seeds. Children are often attracted to the showy seed pods; severe nausea and vomiting can result from eating Wisteria.

There are other suspect plants in our flora (such as Honeysuckle) and some whose fruit causes symptoms only after considerable amounts are consumed (Snowberry). In addition, some plants that are eaten by many people (Elderberry, Pokeweed) without causing ill effects have caused others to become ill—perhaps because they ate unripe or uncooked fruit or other parts of the shrub in the case of Elderberry (the AMA believes that Elderberry flowers are "probably" nontoxic). The good news is that not every berry that woody ornamentals produce is a danger to the young; the fruits of Mt. Ash, Firethorn, Bayberry and Barberry are not considered particularly harmful. Nevertheless, these and all other wild plants should be avoided unless you are very sure they are safe to eat.

IRRITATING

"Leaflets three, let it be!" The familiar couplet warns against Rhus radicans (Poison Ivy), which is responsible for most of the plant-caused rash in the country. A variable plant, Poison Ivy (also known as Poison Oak), may be a trailing or climbing vine or a shrub six feet tall. Leaves may be lobed, resembling oak leaves, or unlobed, but always consist of three leaflets. Berries are white. Rhus vernix (Poison Sumac) is usually (but not always!) confined to wet areas and is sometimes confused with the handsome red-berried Sumac that is not poisonous. Like Poison Ivy, Poison Sumac's fruit is white (another useful couplet for these two: "Berries white, take flight!") While the Rhus cousins are by far the worst offenders, other shrubby plants can cause dermatitis in sensitive persons. A dozen others:

Abies balsamea (BALSAM FIR)
Asimina triloba (PAWPAW)
Campsis radicans (TRUMPET CREEPER)
Cotinus coggygria (SMOKE TREE)
Gingko biloba (GINGKO)
Hedera spp. (ENGLISH IVY AND ALGERIAN IVY)
Hydrangea spp. (HYDRANGEA)
Juglans nigra (BLACK WALNUT)
Juniperus spp. (JUNIPER)
Magnolia grandiflora (MAGNOLIA)
Nerium oleander (OLEANDER)
Schinus spp. (PEPPER TREE, FLORIDA HOLLY)

MORE ABOUT POISON IVY

Most people know that they can get poison ivy by stroking the fur of an animal that has recently walked through an ivy patch. Not so obvious, perhaps, is that clothing, tools, camping gear and smoke (from a fire containing some of the plant) can also be a source of exposure. Suspect articles should be washed well. The allergen can persist on clothing for a year or more and there have been reports of ivy-contaminated clothing causing a rash even after the clothes had been washed. Sometimes we hear of people successfully desensitizing themselves in various ways (such as eating new leaflets in the spring), but this is risky business. Severe reactions, with possible convulsions and even death, can result; if desensitization is achieved it is usually of very short duration. Work is being done on an ointment to protect against the allergen; Oregon's medical school has developed an effective product and Stockhausen, Inc. (Greenville, North Carolina) is working to make this sticky substance cosmetically acceptable. Until then, if you walk unaware through Poison Ivy, you will probably know it in 12 to 72 hours. The rash is usually limited to where you made contact, although previous reaction sites can flare up. Take

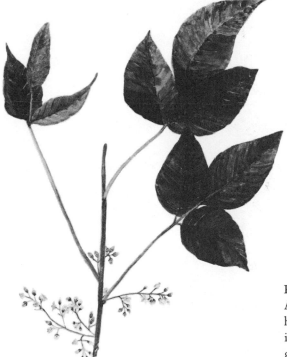

Rhus radicans (Poison Ivy). A plant to avoid, Poison Ivy has compound leaves consisting of three leaflets, small greenish white flowers and waxy, white fruit.

comfort in the fact that, according to the AMA, fluid from blisters cannot spread the rash.

The Language of Trees and Shrubs

Apple—*Temptation*
Arborvitae—*Everlasting friendship*
Ash—*Grandeur*
Aspen—*Lamentation*
Azalea—*Temperance*
Barberry—*Sour temper*
Beech—*Prosperity*
Birch—*Meekness*
Cedar—*Strength*
Cherry—*Good education*
Chestnut—*Luxury*
Cypress—*Death, mourning; despair*
Dogwood—*Durability*
Elm—*Dignity*
Fir—*Time*
Hawthorn—*Hope*
Hazel—*Reconciliation*
Hemlock—*You will be my death*
Holly—*Foresight*
Honeysuckle—*Devotion*
Hydrangea—*Braggart*
Juniper—*Succour; protection*
Larch—*Audacity; boldness*
Lilac (PURPLE)—*First love*
Lilac (WHITE)—*Youthful innocence*
Linden (OR LIME)—*Conjugal love; matrimony*
Locust tree—*Elegance*
Magnolia—*Love of nature*
Maple—*Reserve*
Mockorange—*Counterfeit*
Mt. Ash—*Prudence*
Mt. Laurel—*Ambition*
Oak leaves—*Bravery*
Oak tree—*Hospitality*
White Oak—*Independence*
Olive—*Peace*
Orange tree—*Generosity*

Palm—*Victory*
Pear tree—*Comfort*
Plum—*Fidelity*
Pine—*Pity*
Privet—*Prohibition*
Rhododendron—*Beware; danger*
Spindle tree—*Your charms are engraved on my heart*
Sycamore—*Curiosity*
Weeping Willow—*Mourning*
Witch Hazel—*A spell*
Yew—*Sorrow*

Arbor Day

Newspaper editor J. Sterling Morton surveyed Nebraska's treeless plains in the early 1870s and was inspired to start a tree-planting campaign. The idea spread and by 1894 every state had an official Arbor Day. Today, in an age of heightened concern for the environment (and vast destruction of tropical forests), Arbor Day has taken on new significance. National Arbor Day is the last Friday in April. Below are the current Arbor Day dates for our fifty states and a planting guide for your personal use:

Alabama—Last full week in February
Alaska—Third Monday in May
Arizona—Friday following April 1 for Apache, Navajo, Coconino, Mohave and Yavapai counties; Friday following February 1 for all other counties
Arkansas—Third Monday in March
California—March 7 to 14
Colorado—Third Friday in April
Connecticut—April 30
Delaware—Last Friday in April
District of Columbia—Last Friday in April
Florida—Third Friday in January
Georgia—Third Friday in February
Hawaii—First Friday in November
Idaho—Last Friday in April
Illinois—Last Friday in April
Indiana—Second Friday in April
Iowa—Last Friday in April
Kansas—Last Friday in March

Kentucky—First Friday in April
Louisiana—Third Friday in January
Maine—Third week in May
Maryland—First Wednesday in April
Massachusetts—April 28 to May 5
Michigan—Third week in April
Minnesota—Last Friday in April
Mississippi—Second Friday in February
Missouri—First Friday after the first Tuesday in April
Montana—Last Friday in April
Nebraska—Last Friday in April
Nevada—Southern—February 28; Northern—April 23
New Hampshire—Last Friday in April
New Jersey—Last Friday in April
New Mexico—Second Friday in March
New York—Last Friday in April
North Carolina—First Friday following March 15
North Dakota—First Friday in May
Ohio—Last Friday in April
Oklahoma—Last full week in March
Oregon—First full week in April
Pennsylvania—Last Friday in April
Rhode Island—Last Friday in April
South Carolina—First Friday in December
South Dakota—Last Friday in April
Tennessee—First Friday in March
Texas—Third Friday in January
Utah—Last Friday in April
Vermont—First Friday in May
Virginia—Second Friday in March
Washington—Second Wednesday in April
West Virginia—Second Friday in April
Wisconsin—Last Friday in April
Wyoming—Last Monday in April

You can also visit Arbor Lodge State Historical Park and Tree Trail, Nebraska City, Nebraska. Arbor Day founder J. Sterling Morton's mansion and grounds are open to the public. The 65 acres are planted with more than 250 varieties of trees and shrubs.

Where to Visit the Trees

Some well-known arboreta and botanical gardens where trees can be seen:

California
(San Francisco): Strybing Arboretum

Connecticut
(New London): Connecticut College Arboretum

District of Columbia
National Arboretum

Florida
(Miami): Fairchild Tropical Garden

Georgia
(Pine Mt.): Callaway Gardens

Illinois
(Lisle): Morton Arboretum

Massachusetts
(Jamaica Plain): Arnold Arboretum

Minnesota
(Chanhassen): Minnesota Landscape Arboretum

Mississippi
(Picayune): The Crosby Arboretum

New Jersey
(Gladstone): Rutgers University Willowwood Arboretum

New York
(Oakdale): Bayard Cutting
(Millbrook): Cary Arboretum
(Oyster Bay): Planting Fields Arboretum

Ohio
(Newark): Dawes Arboretum
(Mentor): Holden Arboretum
(Cincinnati): Spring Grove Arboretum

Oregon
(Portland): Hoyt Arboretum

Pennsylvania
> (Philadelphia): Morris Arboretum
> (Media): John J. Tyler Arboretum

Texas
> (Houston): Houston Arboretum

Washington
> (Seattle): Washington Park Arboretum

West Virginia
> (Morgantown): Core Arboretum, W. Virginia University

WOODY PLANT SOCIETIES

In addition to the American Rose Society, American Rhododendron Society and International Lilac Society (listed on pages 2, 272, and 274 respectively), gardeners may seek specialized information from the following organizations (some woody-plant societies are also listed under "Houseplant Societies," pages 192–193). Addresses change frequently, so be patient.

American Bonsai Society, Inc.
Box 358
Keene, NH 03431

American Boxwood Society
Box 85
Boyce, VA 22620

American Magnolia Society
907 S. Chestnut
Hammond, LA 70403

American Willow Growers
Network
Box 124A
South New Berlin, NY 13843
Especially interested in basketry
Willows

Holly Society of America, Inc.
304 North Wind Rd.
Baltimore, MD 21204

International Camellia Society
Box 750
Brookhaven, MS 39601

International Golden Fossil Tree
(Ginkgo) Society, Inc.
201 West Graham
Lombard, IL 60148

International Oleander Society,
Inc.
PO Box 3431
Galveston, TX 77552-0431

North American Fruit Explorers
Rt. 1, Box 94
Chapin, IL 62628

Northern Nut Growers
Association
9870 S. Palmer Rd.
New Carlisle, OH 45344

SOURCES FOR WOODY PLANTS

Berthold Nursery
434 Devon Ave.
Elk Grove Village, IL 60007

Bill Bounds Nursery
2815 Campbell Rd.
Houston, TX 77080

Blue Oak Nursery
2731 Mt. Oak Lane
Rescue, CA 95672

Bovees Nursery
1737 S.W. Coronado
Portland, OR 97219

Brooks Rare Plant Nursery
235 Cherry Lane
Doylestown, PA 18901

Carroll Gardens
PO Box 310
44 E. Main St.
Westminster, MD 21157

Forestfarm
990 Tetherow Rd.
Williams, OR 97544

Four Fives Nursery
5555 Summer Ave.
Memphis, TN 38134

Gossler Farms Nursery
1200 Weaver Rd.
Springfield, OR 97477

Gurney Seed & Nursery
Company
Yankton, SD 57079

Hooks Nursery, Inc.
PO Box 455
Lake Zurich, IL 60047

Kelly Nurseries
19 Maple St.
Dansville, NY 14437

Louisiana Nurseries
Rt. 7, Box 43
Opelousas, LA 70570

Maxalea Nurseries, Inc.
Oak Hill Rd.
Baltimore, MD 21239

Miller Nurseries
West Lake Rd.
Canandaigua, NY 14424

N.Y. State Fruit Testing
Cooperative Association, Inc.
Geneva, NY 14456

Oliver Nurseries
1159 Bronson Rd.
Fairfield, CT 06430

Salter Tree Farm
Box 1332, Rt. 2
Madison, FL 32340

Smithfield Gardens
Rt. 17
Crittenden, VA 23433

Martin Viette Nurseries
Northern Blvd.
East Norwich, NY 11732

Wayside Gardens
1 Garden Lane
Hodges, SC 29695

Weston Nurseries
E. Main St.
Rt. 135, Box 186
Hopkinton, MA 01748

Woodlanders, Inc.
1128 Colleton Ave.
Aiken, SC 29801

6

Special Gardens

$\mathcal{F}$ ASHIONS COME AND GO IN GARDEN DESIGNS AS in many other things. Trendy today are wildflower meadows and "New Romantic" landscapes; scorned are lawns and foundation plantings. The very mention of a "carpet bed" elicits looks of disdain from current cognoscenti. Still appreciated is water—pools and fountains seem to have been welcomed in gardens all over the world since ancient times.

The lawn is a Western invention; it is not found in the gardens of the East. Some say that lawns first appeared around Roman villas; others claim they are outgrowths of open space and pastures that surrounded medieval castles. In America the concept of the New England village green was extended to public green areas in front of every home, which became open and unfenced from neighbors and street. Garden writers of the nineteenth century saw this as democratic and therefore suitable for a new democracy. Lawns became dominant features of American gardens though many today view them as boring, labor intensive and water demanding.

As maligned as modern lawns have become, the fact remains that many people like them. Some find them beautiful; others enjoy lawn games, as the Victorians did when mowers came into use and made them possible. Lawns create open areas around homes, permitting abundant sunshine and good air circulation. Keeping the grass cut is one of the few meaningful chores that is left for many young people. Similarly, carpet beds are pleasing and appropriate around Victorian homes and certain public buildings. Those who must garden in leftover bits of spaces (like gardeners in the Middle Ages) do not have room for the types of plantings now in vogue. As exciting as a wildflower meadow or "New American" garden can be, they are not for everyone. As always, site and architecture must be considered when planning a garden. Foremost to consider, however, is the raison d'être for gardens: human comfort and enjoyment. Gardens, just as indoor rooms, should reflect the interests and needs of their owners. They need not be dictated by fashion or the tastes of others.

PLANTS FOR A BIBLICAL GARDEN

Biblical lands are extremely varied, ranging from mountain peaks over 10,000 feet high to tropical valleys and other areas below sea level, such as the Dead Sea. These varied environments naturally produce a varied flora, although the land today, thanks to centuries of exploitation and warfare, is drier and poorer than it was in biblical times. Scholars and nonscholars alike have long argued over the identification of the many plants mentioned in the Bible. This is not surprising when one considers the age of the texts, the many translations and the fact that those who wrote the originals were not botanists—nor were they particularly interested in natural history. The plants listed, therefore, represent good guesses and are not positive identifications.

Anemone coronaria (ANEMONE, WINDFLOWER)—Thought by many to be the biblical "lilies of the field."

Artemisia (WORMWOOD)—Absinthium may be the closest approximation of the biblical plant that is readily available.

Brassica nigra (BLACK MUSTARD)—Probably the mustard plant of the New Testament parables.

Crocus sativus (SAFFRON CROCUS)—Saffron is mentioned in the Song of Solomon, and other species of crocus are believed to be alluded to in the same book.

Hyacinthus orientalis (GARDEN HYACINTH)—Probably native to the biblical region and thought by some to be the plant called "lilies" in several verses from the Song of Solomon.

Iris pseudacorus (YELLOW WATER FLAG)—Believed to be "the lilies by the rivers of waters" in Ecclesiasticus.

Lilium candidum (MADONNA LILY)—Cultivated for thousands of years, Madonna Lily may have grown in Solomon's garden.

Narcissus tazetta (POLYANTHUS)—Thought to be the "rose" in the passage from Isa. 35:1 "and the desert shall rejoice, and blossom as the rose."

Ornithogalum (STAR OF BETHLEHEM)—Very common in much of the region; thought to be the "dove's dung" of Kings 6:25.

Rosa phoenicia—There is much argument regarding biblical "roses," but it is generally agreed that some passages really do refer to the genus Rosa; R. phoenicia is the native.*

Tulipa montana (TULIP)—Possibly the biblical "Rose of Sharon."

*Rosa phoenicia, according to Peter Beales, is not easy to grow but is worth the effort. It is a slender-growing climber with few thorns, gray-green leaves and white flowers. It likes dry, sandy soil. According to Beverly Dobson's 1988 Combined Rose List (see page 37), it does not appear to be available in the United States at this time.

Iris pseudacorus (Yellow Water Flag). Perhaps the "lilies by the rivers of waters" mentioned in Ecclesiasticus, this Iris is still a handsome plant for the water's edge.

Trees and Shrubs for a Biblical Garden

Acacia (ACACIA)—Used in the construction of the tabernacle.
Buxus (BOX)—Branches used at Jewish thanksgiving Feast of
the Tabernacles.
Ceris—(Judas Tree; Redbud)—According to legend, the tree on
which Judas hanged himself.
Ficus (FIG)—Another legend says Judas used the fig.
Elaeagnus (RUSSIAN OLIVE)—Common to the region; may be
the biblical "oil tree."
Morus (MULBERRY)—Cultivated for the raising of silkworms.
Myrtus communis (MYRTLE)—Ancient symbol of peace and
justice.
Pinus (PINE)—The "green fir tree" that produced fruit
mentioned in Hos. 14:8.
Populus (POPULAR)—Another tree on which Judas may have
hanged himself; also thought by some to be the wood of
the cross—thus the leaves tremble with shame and horror.
Prunus armeniaca (APRICOT)—The "apple" of the Old
Testament?

The Bible also mentions Walnut, Cedar, Olive, Sycamore and Oak,
among others.

The Biblical Garden at the Cathedral of St. John the Divine, New York City

The garden, situated on a quarter acre, was dedicated in 1973. Some
of the ornamental plants are:

Aloe
Anemone
Ceris (REDBUD)
Crocus
Cydonia (QUINCE)
Hyacinthus
Lilium
Linum (ANNUAL FLAX)
Ornithogalum (STAR OF BETHLEHEM)
Prunus (APRICOT)
Tamarix (TAMARISK)

Among the vegetable and herb plants grown are:

Allium (ONION, LEEK)
Anethum (DILL)
Brassica (MUSTARD)
Cichorium (CHICORY, ENDIVE)
Coriandrum (CORIANDER)
Cucumis (CUCUMBER)
Hordeum (BARLEY)
Lens (LENTIL)
Ruta (RUE)
Salvia (SAGE)

Biblical Gardens to Visit

Florida
    (Bristol): Torreya State Park
    (Daytona Beach): Bellevue Biblical Garden

New York
    (Manhattan): Cathedral of St. John the Divine Biblical Garden

North Carolina
    (Salisbury): Poets' and Dreamers' Garden, Livingston College
      Campus

Rhode Island
    (Providence): Temple Beth El Biblical Garden

MARY'S PLANTS

Mystic Rose! that precious name
Mary from the Church doth claim;
In the Lily's silver bells
The purity of Mary dwells.
In the Myrtle's fadeless green,
Mary's constancy is seen.
ATTRIBUTED TO WALAFRID STRABO, A NINTH-CENTURY MONK

Many garden plants (as well as a number of wildflowers) are associated with the Virgin Mary. Long before Christianity, of course, some of these same beloved plants were connected with the gods and goddesses of the old religions. At first, Christianity spurned the pagan flora (roses, for example, were not allowed in the early church), but eventually the plants

Calendula officinalis (Pot Marigold). A hardy annual with large yellow or orange flowers, Pot Marigold was once an important culinary and medicinal herb associated with the Virgin Mary.

won and became symbols of the church's teachings, holidays, saints and Mary. Ten of the most familiar plants associated with Mary are:

Alchemilla (LADY'S MANTLE)—A. vulgaris is an interesting shade-tolerant plant with gray leaves and yellow-green flowers. Legend says Mary wore the plant.

Calendula (POT MARIGOLD)—Important old culinary and medicinal plant with beautiful, large orange flowers. Believed to have been worn by Mary, blossoms were once placed around statues of the Virgin; hence, perhaps, the name "Mary's gold."

Clematis (VIRGINS-BOWER)—Legend says the wild clematis gave shelter to Mary and Jesus on their flight into Egypt.

Chrysanthemum balsamita (COSTMARY)—Another old medicinal with aromatic leaves. According to one legend Mary used this plant to prepare a healing salve. Another legend associates Costmary with Mary Magdalene.

Convallaria majalis (LILY-OF-THE-VALLEY)—Sometimes called "Our Lady's Tears," this fragrant white shade lover blooms in May, Mary's special month.

Lavandula (LAVENDER)—One of Mary's favorite plants according to legend; she used its branches to dry the clothes of baby Jesus. After this, lavender (the genus comes from the Latin "to wash") has been associated with distinctive, clean fragrance.

Lilium candidum (MADONNA LILY)—Since ancient times a symbol of immortality, Madonna Lily also symbolizes purity. Often placed next to Mary in paintings of the Annunciation. Roman legend says Madonna Lily was created by Juno.

Primula veris (PRIMROSE)—Also known as Cowslip and "Our Lady's Keys" (to heaven), this yellow-flowered spring bloomer likes partial shade and rich, moist (not wet) soil.

Rosa (ROSE)—Fable says the rose sprang from the blood of Adonis; eventually it became an emblem of Mary and rosary beads were made of a paste of dried petals.

Rosmarinus (ROSEMARY)—Another plant that legend claims sheltered Mary and Jesus on their flight into Egypt. Afterwards, the formerly white flowers are said to have changed into the blue of Mary's robe. Rosemary is a tall shrub in southern climates.

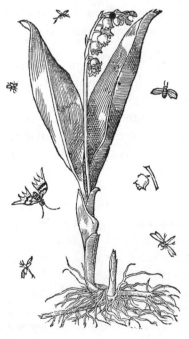

Convallaria majalis (Lily-of-the-Valley). A favorite perennial with fragrant white flowers, Lily-of-the-Valley makes a fine ground cover in shade. All parts of the plant are poisonous.

GARDENS OF THE MIDDLE AGES

Medieval gardens generally lacked two things: space and variety in plant material. Castles and towns were often built on hilltops and walled for defense, which left little ground for gardens. Monasteries were usually more secure and often had the advantage of being located on level and fertile land. With the triumph of Christianity, western Europe entered the great Age of Faith during which sensual pleasures—including the growing of flowers for pleasure—were condemned. Plants were raised for food and medicinal purposes only, but luckily many of them also were very beautiful and no doubt cheered their tenders even during those austere times.

A Monk's Garden

Monks and nuns were the real gardeners of the Middle Ages. Most monasteries were self-supporting and gardens were necessities. Monks often were the only physicians so they also grew medicinal herbs for the entire area in their physic gardens. They sometimes traveled to other religious centers where plants were exchanged. The simple cruciform design of the cloister garden is suitable for small walled or fenced spaces today: Two intersecting paths divide an area into four sections with a tree or fountain at the crossing. Perennials for a Monk's garden include:

Artemisia (WORMWOOD AND SOUTHERNWOOD)
Chrysanthemum (FEVERFEW)
Iris (GERMAN)
Lilium (MADONNA LILY)
Nepeta (CATMINT)
Paeonia* (PEONY)
Papaver (POPPY)
Rosa spp. (GALLICA, ALBA)
Sempervivum* (HOUSELEEK)
Verbascum* (MULLEIN)
Viola (VIOLET)

*Verbascum thapsus (Mullein) was an important medicinal that also was thought to protect against demons. It was believed that Houseleek repelled lightning. Peony, named for Paeon, Greek physician to the gods, also protected against evil.

The monks grew many herbs, including Sage, Rue (used in exorcism), Costmary, Rosemary, Chives, Savory, Mint and Dill.

Mentha sp. (Mint). Easily propagated by cuttings, mints have been used medicinally and for flavoring for thousands of years. Use sprigs to scent bath-water as the ancient Romans did.

A Castle Orchard

The gardens behind castle walls were small and usually allotted to leftover bits of space. They were planted with culinary herbs and other useful plants similar to those grown by monks and nuns. Orchards were outdoor rooms, large or small, sometimes found between the inner and outer moats. Here people gathered in summer for rest and recreation. Trees, especially fruit trees (monks planted theirs in the cemetery) were planted here and grassy areas were strewn with wildflowers, forming "flowery meads." Among the shrubs and trees found in castle orchards:

Apple	Pear
Box	Plum
Chestnut	Privet
Hawthorn	Quince
Honeysuckle	Rose
Medlar	Walnut
Mulberry	Yew

Knot gardens originated in the Middle Ages and arbors and galleries of intertwined trees were common, especially in the later years. Labyrinths and mazes, which were popular in the ancient world, reappeared, and topiary work, using box and yew, was practiced extensively. Some of this helped to make up for the lack of variety in plant material; what existed was cut and trimmed in many different ways. The waning years of the Middle Ages witnessed the introduction of some new plants into Europe (possibly tulips and lilacs) as a result of travel, often connected with the Crusades.

Cloister Gardens to Visit

California
> (Santa Barbara): Santa Barbara Mission

District of Columbia:
> Washington National Cathedral, Bishop's Garden

Florida
> (North Miami Beach): Monastery of St. Bernard

Minnesota
> (Chanhassen): The Minnesota Landscape Arboretum, Mary Cushman Wells Staples Cloistered Garden

New York
> (Manhattan): The Cloisters

Ohio
> (Cleveland): Western Reserve Herb Society Garden

Wisconsin
> (Fond du Lac): St. Paul's Cathedral Cloister

Medieval gardens featured fountains, arbors and galleries but had little variety in plant material.

THE SHAKESPEARE GARDEN

When daisies pied and violets blue
And lady-smocks all silver white
And cuckoo-buds of yellow hue
Do paint the meadows with delight.
Love's Labour's Lost, Act V, Scene II

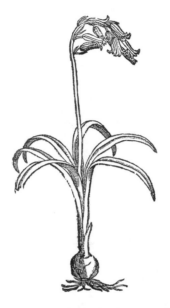

Endymion non-scriptus (English Bluebell, Harebell). The Endymions, sometimes called Wood Hyacinths, have graceful bell-shaped flowers which may be blue, pink or white.

Sixteenth-century Elizabethan England was a rural society. People lived in close contact with plants; they knew which ones would help their ailments and which ones to avoid. From his many references to useful plants we know that Shakespeare was no stranger to this knowledge, but Elizabethans also enjoyed plants for their beauty and fragrance. Strewing herbs were still employed indoors (Meadowsweet was said to be the favorite of Queen Elizabeth) and various rushes and grasses were brought in to decorate the scent walls. Shakespeare mentions close to two hundred flowers in his plays and sonnets; this has prompted the construction of many "Shakespeare Gardens" by his admirers. Not every plant Shakespeare mentions thrives on this side of the Atlantic; here are some to try:

Aquilegia (COLUMBINE)
Artemisia (WORMWOOD)
Calendula—Shakespeare's marigold, or "marybuds"
Endymion non-scriptus (ENGLISH BLUEBELL)—Shakespeare's
   harebell

Fritillaria (CROWN IMPERIAL)

Lavendula (LAVENDER)

Lunaria annua (HONESTY, MONEY PLANT)—Shakespeare's white satin flower

Lythrum (PURPLE LOOSESTRIFE)—Shakespeare's Long Purples

Narcissus (DAFFODIL)

Primula (PRIMROSE)—Shakespeare's cowslips

Ranunculus acris (COMMON BUTTERCUP)—Shakespeare's Cuckoo buds

Rosa (ROSE)—R. eglanteria is specifically noted. Shakespeare mentions roses more than any other plant. He was surely familiar with Gallica, Damask and Alba roses.

Thymus (THYME)

Viola odorata (SWEET OR ENGLISH VIOLET)—Shakespeare mentions violets close to twenty times

Viola tricolor (HEARTSEASE, WILD PANSY)—Shakespeare's Love-in-Idleness

In *The Winter's Tale* Perdita says: "Here's flowers for you; hot lavender, mints, savory, marjoram; the marigold, that goes to bed with the sun, and with him rises weeping: these are flowers of middle summer, and I think they are given to men of middle age." The amused audience would have recognized these herbal remedies for indigestion and flagging energy.

Lunaria annua (Honesty). Shakespeare's "White Satin Flower," Lunaria is a pink or white flowered biennial with decorative fruiting stems much used in dried bouquets.

Vassar College's Shakespeare Garden

Mr. David Stoller, horticulturist at Vassar, has kindly provided a list of plants that grow in Vassar's Shakespeare Garden in Poughkeepsie, New York. Mr. Stoller is aware that not every plant is absolutely authentic for inclusion in a Shakespeare Garden, but notes that when he visited the Shakespeare Garden in Stratford, similar liberties had been taken with regard to the choice of flower species and cultivars. Some plants in Vassar's garden (not a complete list):

Aconitum sp. (MONKSHOOD)
Anemone nemorosa (EUROPEAN WOOD ANEMONE)
Anemone pulsatilla (PASQUE-FLOWER)
Aquilegia sp. (COLUMBINE)
Bellis perennis (ENGLISH DAISY)
Calendula officinalis (POT MARIGOLD)
Crocus sativus (SAFFRON CROCUS)
Dianthus barbatus (SWEET WILLIAM)
Endymion non-scriptus (SCILLA NUTANS)—English Bluebell
Eryngium maritimum (SEA-HOLLY)
Fragaria vesca (WOODLAND STRAWBERRY)
Fritillaria sp. (FRITILLARY)
Iris germanica (GERMAN IRIS)
Lilium candidum (MADONNA LILY)
Linum perenne (PERENNIAL FLAX)
Malva sylvestris (MALLOW)
Mandragora officinarum (MANDRAKE)
Mertensia virginica (VIRGINIA BLUEBELLS)—A U.S. native
Paeonia sp. (PEONY)
Papaver orientale (ORIENTAL POPPY)
Pulmonaria officinalis (BLUE LUNGWORT)
Viola odorata (SWEET VIOLET)

Among the herbs and vegetables grown in Shakespeare Garden are:

Allium spp. (MOLY, SENESCENS, TUBEROSUM)—Onion species
Carum carvi (CARAWAY)
Chamaemelum nobile (CHAMOMILE)
Daucus carota (CARROT AND WILD CARROT OR QUEEN ANNE'S LACE)
Foeniculum vulgare (FENNEL)
Hyssopus officinalis (HYSSOP)

Lavandula angustifolia (LAVENDER)
Melissa officinalis (LEMON BALM)
Mentha sp. (MINT)
Pastinaca sativa (PARSNIP)
Petroselinum crispum (PARSLEY)
Rosmarinus sp. (ROSEMARY)
Ruta sp. (RUE)
Salvia sp. (SAGE)
Satureja hortensis and S. montana (SUMMER AND WINTER
     SAVORY)
Thymus sp. (THYME)

Among the woody plants in Shakespeare Garden are:

Buxus sempervirens (BOX)
Calluna vulgaris (HEATHER)
Cydonia oblonga (COMMON QUINCE)
Cytisus scoparius (BROOM)
Erica sp. (HEATH)
Hedera helix (ENGLISH IVY)
Ilex x meserveae—English Holly, which is not hardy, is one
     of the parents of this hybrid.
Ligustrum vulgare (PRIVET)
Lonicera periclymenum (WOODBINE)
Ribes rubrum (RED CURRANT)
Ribes uva-crispa (ENGLISH GOOSEBERRY)
Rubus arcticus (CRIMSON OR ARCTIC BRAMBLE)
Taxus sp. (YEW)
Ulex europaeus (GORSE)
Vaccinium myrtillus (WHORTLEBERRY, BILBERRY)
Vitis vinifera (WINE OR EUROPEAN GRAPE)

The roses in Shakespeare Garden include:

Rosa x alba 'Maiden's Blush'
R. alba 'White Rose of York'
Rosa centifolia (CABBAGE ROSE)
Rosa damascena 'Versicolor' (YORK AND LANCASTER ROSE)
Rosa eglanteria (EGLANTINE OR SWEETBRIAR ROSE)
Rosa gallica (APOTHECARY'S ROSE)
Rosa moschata (MUSK ROSE)

Shakespeare Gardens to Visit

California
   (San Francisco): Golden Gate Park
   (San Marino): Huntington Botanical Gardens

Illinois
   (Evanston): Northwestern University

Iowa
   (Cedar Rapids): Ellis Park

New York
   (Poughkeepsie): Vassar College

South Dakota
   (Wessington Springs): 508 Alene Avenue North

There is an Elizabethan Garden on Roanoke Island, North Carolina, planted in memory of the "Lost Colony" of 1585.

THIRTEEN PLANTS FOR A WITCH'S GARDEN

Some of the plants listed below have powerful effects on the human body. Monkshood and Belladonna were ingredients of "flying ointments" that witches rubbed into their skin. They are capable of causing the delirium and irregular heartbeat that may have produced the sensation of flying. Foxglove and Yew, also poisonous plants, produce dangerous and unpleasant symptoms, including heartbeat disturbances. Other plants on the list derived their power from magic and were used by ordinary mortals to defend themselves from evil, as well as by sorcerers for evil purposes. Not all are toxic; Elder produces edible berries and the young roots and basal leaves of Rampion are still used in salads.

> **Achillea** (YARROW)—This magical plant could conjure up the Devil or drive him away.
> **Aconitum** (MONKSHOOD, WOLFSBANE)—Beautiful summer- and fall-flowering perennials, which contain some of the most powerful poisons in existence.
> **Artemisia** (MUGWORT AND WORMWOOD)—Witches used the former to raise spirits from the dead; Mugwort was also used medicinally (to treat epilepsy) and magically (to protect from evil).
> **Atropa** (BELLADONNA, DEADLY NIGHTSHADE)—Not a beautiful garden subject and very poisonous but perhaps the plant

most associated with witchcraft. Named for Atropos, the Fate who severs the thread of life, Belladonna is also called Devil's Cherries because of the good tasting but potentially fatal shiny black berries it produces.

Campanula rapunculus (RAMPION)—Supposedly grown as a salad plant by the witch in the fairy tale "Rapunzel."

Digitalis (FOXGLOVE)—Other names include Witches' Gloves and Dead Men's Bells.

Sambucus (EUROPEAN ELDER)—A magic bush, powerful for or against evil depending upon how it was invoked.

Sempervivum (HOUSELEEK)—Also called Devil's Beard, this plant was believed to protect homes from lightning.

Taxus (YEW)—A symbol of sorrow, Yew could be an ingredient of witch's brew, as Shakespeare's witch in *Macbeth* reveals when she throws in the cauldron "slips of yew / Sliver'd in the moon's eclipse."

Valeriana (VALERIAN, GARDEN HELIOTROPE)—A witch's aphrodisiac.

Verbascum (MULLEIN)—Important medicinal planted by monks to ward off evil though some said witches used the dried stalks, dipped in tallow, to light their infamous "Sabbaths."

Verbena (VERVAIN)—A Druid's plant and used by witches, Vervain is also called Herb of Grace and was believed to guard against snakes and bring good luck.

Vinca (PERIWINKLE, MYRTLE)—Another old medicinal that also deters evil though it was used in magic, hence another of its common names, "Sorcerer's Violet."

Verbascum thapsus (Common Mullein). An important old Eurasian medicinal and magic plant, Common Mullein is found naturalized along American roadsides today.

There are many other plants associated with the Devil and witchcraft—among the trees are Walnut, Hawthorne and Savin Juniper. Henbane, Thornapple (Datura) and Poison Hemlock have been excluded in favor of more attractive garden subjects. Even the sunny Dandelion has its devilish associations (Devil's Milk Pail is another of its names), an association many of today's lawn tenders would no doubt agree with.

FLOWERS FOR COLONIAL GARDENS

Although they surely delighted in lovely blossoms, most of the plants that our early settlers cultivated were used for medicines, food or flavorings, cosmetics or to combat pests. Early gardens were often enclosed with hedges or fencing and were a hodgepodge of herbs, flowers and vegetables planted all together. Wealthier people had more elaborate gardens and planted more flowers exclusively for enjoyment, though it must be remembered that many plants we consider purely ornamental have a long history of medicinal use. (Madonna Lily, for example, has been valued as a treatment for wounds and burns since ancient times.) Here are some perennials grown in colonial gardens:

Aconitum (MONKSHOOD)
Artemisia (MUGWORT; WORMWOOD)
Campanula (BELLFLOWER)
Cheiranthus (WALLFLOWER)—Needs winter protection in the North.
Chrysanthemum (FEVERFEW)
Convallaria (LILY-OF-THE-VALLEY)
Dianthus* (D. CARYOPHYLLUS OR CLOVE GILLYFLOWER; D. BARBATUS OR SWEET WILLIAM, WHICH IS USUALLY GROWN AS A BIENNIAL)
Hesperis (DAMES-ROCKET)—Sometimes behaves as a biennial.
Lavandula (LAVENDER)
Paeonia (PEONY)
Primula* (PRIMROSE)
Pulmonaria (LUNGWORT)
Santolina (LAVENDER COTTON)
Sempervivum (HOUSELEEK)
Tanacetum (TANSY)
Valeriana (GARDEN HELIOTROPE)

*Sometimes short-lived.

Vinca (PERIWINKLE)
Viola (VIOLET AND JOHNNY-JUMP-UP*)

*Sometimes short-lived.

AMERICAN NATIVES:

Bloodroot
Columbine
Trout Lily
Canada Lily

Sunflower
Black-eyed Susan
Bayberry
Dogwood

BIENNIALS:

Foxglove
Honesty

Hollyhock

BULBS:

Crocus
Squill

Star of Bethlehem
Madonna Lily

SHRUBS FOR COLONIAL GARDENS:

Privet
Lilac
Mock Orange

Box
Elderberry
Rose (ALBA, DAMASK, GALLICA)

Colonists also grew a large assortment of herbs in addition to a number of useful plants that have become naturalized in our country and are considered "weeds" (see pages 148–149).

Annuals for Colonial Gardens

Balsam
Calendula (POT MARIGOLD OR "MARYGOLDS")
Cornflower (BACHELOR'S BUTTON)
Four O'Clock
Globe Amaranth
Larkspur
Morning glory
Snapdragon
Sweet Pea

Colonial Gardens to Visit

Connecticut
   (Haddam): Wilhelmina Ann Arnold Barnhart Memorial Gardens
   (Greenwich): Putnam Cottage

Maryland
   (Annapolis): William Pace House and Garden

Massachusetts
   (Sturbridge): Old Sturbridge Village

New Hampshire
   (Portsmouth): Strawberry Banke, Moffatt-Ladd Garden

New Jersey
   (Morristown): Schuyler-Hamilton House, Tempe Wick House

New York
   (Croton-on-Hudson): Van Cortland Manor

North Carolina
   (Winston-Salem): Old Salem

Pennsylvania
   (Philadelphia): John Bartram Gardens*
   (Havertown): The Grange**

Rhode Island
   (Westerly): Babcock-Smith House

Virginia
   (Williamsburg): Colonial Williamsburg
   (Surry): Bacon's Castle

*America's first botanic garden.
**Gardens laid out in 1760 have been continuously maintained. George Washington and his cabinet met in these gardens.

AN 1830 GARDEN

Old Sturbridge Village, a historic village in south-central Massachusetts that recreates the period 1790 to 1830, has several gardens in which one can see plants used in the early nineteenth century. Both the Salem Towne

House and Fitch House gardens are planted with annuals and perennials in general use at this time:

Amaranthus caudatus* (LOVE LIES BLEEDING)
Baptisia australis (FALSE INDIGO)
Chrysanthemum leucanthemum (OX-EYE DAISY)
Coreopsis tinctoria* (CALLIOPSIS)—Important old dye plant.
Dianthus spp. (CLOVE PINK, COTTAGE PINK, MAIDEN PINK)
Dictamnus albus (GAS PLANT)
Geranium maculatum (WILD GERANIUM, CRANESBILL)
Gomphrena globosa* (GLOBE AMARANTH)
Iberis sempervirens (CANDYTUFT)
Ipomoea purpurea* (MORNING GLORY)
Lathyrus odoratus* (SWEET PEA)
Lobularia maritima* (SWEET AYLSSUM)
Mirabilis jalapa* (FOUR O'CLOCK, MARVEL-OF-PERU, BEAUTY-OF-THE-NIGHT)
Narcissus (DAFFODIL)
Phaseolus coccineus* (SCARLET RUNNER BEAN)
Reseda odorata* (MIGNONETTE)
Santolina chamaecyparissus (LAVENDER COTTON)
Tagetes erecta and T. patula* (AFRICAN MARIGOLD; FRENCH MARIGOLD)
Tulipa (TULIP)
Tussilago farfara (COLTSFOOT)—Remedy for coughs and colds.
Viola odorata (SWEET VIOLET)

*An annual in Massachusetts.

NINETEENTH-CENTURY GARDENS

As the Colonial period waned, the picket fence of that era disappeared and homes moved back farther from the street. Broad expanses of lawn became important with grass extending right up to the house, which had no foundation plantings in the early part of the century. Mowers did not appear until the mid-1870s so grass was kept rather high and was often full of wildflowers. Formal carpet beds were very popular in early and mid-nineteenth century gardens but later years brought a strong movement away from the formal toward a more natural style of landscaping that included the use of native American plants and herbaceous borders inspired by English cottage gardens. Lawns during these years were well clipped and there were fewer carpet beds—who had time to tend them with all that grass to cut and lawn games to play on the manicured turf? Gardens of this period were crowded with many things in addition to plants, as were the Victorian gardens of England. Cast-iron fencing, statues, urns and vases,* fountains, arbors, trellises, benches and gazebos were all important parts of the home grounds. Above all, gardeners loved their plants—both indoors and out. Bold and exotic specimens with large leaves and showy flowers were much admired, as were vines of all kinds and anything weeping.

Nigella damascena (Love-in-a-Mist). A popular annual in nineteenth-century gardens, Nigella seed heads are attractive in dried arrangements.

Annuals for Carpet Beds

Victorian times were exciting times for gardeners. A number of new plants were being introduced, many from South and Central America, and new seed companies were springing up everywhere. Carpet beds were set in lawns and filled with newly available dwarf annuals to resemble carpets; when beds were filled with plants of varying height the taller annuals were arranged in the middle of the bed. There was greater variety in annual plantings than there is now; in addition to today's Geraniums (luxury plants in early times), Marigolds, Petunias, Sweet Alyssum and Zinnias, Victorians also planted the following annuals:

*Urns and vases were originally left unplanted; they were filled with plants in later gardens.

Amaranthus (LOVE LIES BLEEDING)
Begonia
Caladium
Calceolaria (SLIPPERWORT)
Callistephus (CHINA ASTER)
Canna
Celosia (WOOLFLOWER)
Centaurea (CORNFLOWER)
Cleome (SPIDER PLANT)
Coleus
Dahlia
Fuchsia
Gomphrena (GLOBE AMARANTH)

Impatiens (BALSAM)
Lathyrus (SWEET PEA)
Matthiola (STOCK)
Mirabilis (FOUR O'CLOCK)
Nicotiana
Nigella (LOVE-IN-A-MIST)
Portulaca
Reseda (MIGNONETTE)
Salpiglossis
Tropaeolum (NASTURTIUM)
Verbena
Viola (PANSY)

Impatiens balsamina (Garden Balsam). Balsam is rarely grown today though cultivars of another Impatiens, I. wallerana, are commonly planted.

Perennials for Victorian Gardens

Nineteenth-century gardeners in America used many native plants (such as Butterfly Weed, Foam Flower, Coneflower, Bee Balm, Gaillardia and Coreopsis) in addition to spring-flowering bulbs (such as Tulips, Daffodils and Grape Hyacinth). Other popular perennials included those listed on the following page.

Aconitum (MONKSHOOD)
Aquilegia (COLUMBINE)
Aruncus (GOATSBEARD)
Aurinia (BASKET-OF-GOLD)
Campanula (BELLFLOWER)
Chrysanthemum (FEVERFEW)
Convallaria
    (LILY-OF-THE-VALLEY)
Dicentra (BLEEDING HEART)
Digitalis (FOXGLOVE)
Echinops (GLOBE THISTLE)
Helleborus (CHRISTMAS ROSE)

Hosta (KNOWN AS FUNKIA TO
    VICTORIANS)
Iberis (CANDYTUFT)
Iris (ALL KINDS)
Linum (FLAX)
Lythrum (PURPLE LOOSESTRIFE)
Myosotis (FORGET-ME-NOT)
Papaver (POPPY)
Pennisetum (FOUNTAIN GRASS)
Tradescantia (SPIDERWORT)
Vinca (PERIWINKLE)
Yucca

Shrubs and Trees for Victorian Landscapes

Victorians loved weeping and contorted plants. Evergreens were also much admired; pointed turrets on a house should be echoed by a pointed tree in the landscape. Evergreens also made a fine background for flowers. Favorite evergreens (an American native, Giant Redwood, called Wellingtonia in Victorian England, was a favorite on large estates there):

Picea (SPRUCE); P. abies (Norway Spruce)—Was much planted.
Pinus (WHITE, SCOTCH AND AUSTRIAN PINE)
Thuja (ARBORVITAE)
Tsuga (HEMLOCK)—Two plants were sometimes grown together
    and joined at tops to form an arch.

OTHER TREES:

Acer (MAPLE)—All kinds including Japanese Maple.
Aesculus (HORSE CHESTNUT)
Betula (BIRCH)
Catalpa (INDIAN BEAN)
Cercis (REDBUD)
Chionanthus (FRINGE TREE)
Cornus (CORNELIAN CHERRY)
Fagus (WEEPING BEECH)
Ginkgo (GINKGO)
Halesia (GREAT SILVERBELL)
Hydrangea (PEE GEE)
Laburnum (GOLDEN-CHAIN)
Magnolia (STAR AND SAUCER)

Malus (CRABAPPLE)
Morus (MULBERRY)
Oxydendrum (SOURWOOD)
Populus (LOMBARDY POPULAR)
Prunus (WEEPING HIGAN CHERRY)
Robinia (BLACK LOCUST)
Ulmus (CAMPERDOWN AND AMERICAN)

Shrubs were planted in borders and along property lines; toward the end of the century some were planted next to houses but kept small.

Berberis (BARBERRY)
Callicarpa (BEAUTYBERRY)
Calycanthus (CAROLINA ALLSPICE)
Clethra (SWEET PEPPERBUSH)
Cytisus (BROOM)
Daphne
Deutzia
Forsythia
Fothergilla
Hibiscus (ROSE-OF-SHARON)
Hydrangea

Lonicera (TATARIAN (HONEYSUCKLE)
Paeonia (TREE PEONY)
Philadelphus (MOCK ORANGE)
Rosa (ROSE)
Spiraea
Symphoricarpos (SNOWBERRY)
Syringa (LILAC)
Taxus (YEW)
Viburnum
Weigela

Vines

Vines were necessary in every garden and were planted to provide privacy for porches and garden houses, to cover arbors and trellises—they even climbed among trees in a Victorian landscape. So much were vines admired that one Victorian garden writer extolled the beauty of Poison Ivy but did warn of its irritating properties. Grapes were commonly planted, as were these:

Akebia (FIVELEAF AKEBIA)
Aristolochia (DUTCHMAN'S PIPE)
Campsis (TRUMPET CREEPER)
Celastrus (BITTERSWEET)
Clematis
Hedera (IVY)—A favorite.
Hydrangea (CLIMBING HYDRANGEA)

Ipomoea (MORNING GLORY)
Lonicera (HONEYSUCKLE)
Parthenocissus (VIRGINIA CREEPER)
Thunbergia (BLACK-EYED SUSAN VINE)
Wisteria

Victorian Gardens to Visit

California
(San Francisco): Octagon House

Connecticut
(Hartford): Harriet Beecher Stowe and Mark Twain houses

Delaware
(New Castle): Read House and Garden

Georgia
(Savannah): Green-Meldrim House

Massachusetts
(Stockbridge): Naumkeag Gardens

Missouri
(St. Louis): Tower Grove Park

New Jersey
(Morristown): Acorn Hall Victorian Garden

New York
(Tarrytown): Lyndhurst

Pennsylvania
(Philadelphia): Ebenezer Maxwell House and Garden

Vermont
(North Bennington): Park-McCullough House and Gardens

Virginia
(Staunton): Woodrow Wilson Birthplace and Garden

Wisconsin
(Green Bay): Hazelwood Garden

A SCENTED GARDEN

The New York Botanical Garden claims that its Fragrance Garden, constructed in 1955, is the oldest garden of its kind in the country. The garden was designed to bring visitors into close contact with fragrant plants and touching is allowed. Braille markers are located near plants for the visually impaired. Among the annuals grown there are Sweet Alyssum, Petunia, Nicotiana, Nasturtium, Verbena and Basil. Hardy bulbs such as Hyacinth, Narcissus and Tulip bloom in the spring. The following perennials were planted in the original Fragrance Garden; some of them may still be seen there today:

Achillea ageratum (SWEET YARROW); A. millefolium (Common Yarrow)

Chrysanthemum balsamita (COSTMARY)

Convallaria majalis (LILY–OF–THE–VALLEY)

Dryopteris nevadensis (FRAGRANT FERN)

Dianthus deltoides (MAIDEN PINK); D. gratianopolitanus (Cheddar Pink); D. plumarius (Cottage Pink)

Dictamnus albus (GAS PLANT)

Erysimum allionii (WALLFLOWER)—Probably Cheiranthus

Glechoma hederacea (GILL–OVER–THE–GROUND, RUNAWAY ROBIN)

Hemerocallis citrina (LONG YELLOW DAYLILY); H. flava (Tall Yellow Daylily); H. minor (Dwarf Yellow Daylily)

Hosta plantaginea (FRAGRANT PLANTAIN LILY)

Lavandula officinalis (LAVENDER)

Melissa officinalis (LEMON BALM)

Mentha piperita (PEPPERMINT); M. spicata (Spearmint)

Nepeta mussinii (PERSIAN NEPETA)

Paeonia (PEONY)—Especially fragrant are the double red Mary Brand and Prince of Darkness.

Lavandula sp. (Lavender). A must for the scented garden, deer-proof Lavender needs a sunny, well-drained site.

Papaver alpinum (ALPINE POPPY); P. nudicaule (Iceland Poppy)
Petasites fragrans (WINTER HELIOTROPE); P. hybridus (Purple
    Butterbur)
Salvia officinalis (SAGE)
Santolina chamaecyparissus (LAVENDER COTTON)
Saponaria officinalis (BOUNCING BET)
Satureja montana (WINTER SAVORY)
Sedum spectabile (SHOWY STONECROP)
Tanacetum vulgare (TANSY)
Thymus citriodorus (LEMON-SCENTED THYME); T. vulgaris
    (Common Thyme)
Trifolium repens (WHITE CLOVER)
Viola odorata (SWEET VIOLET)

Perennials not hardy in the North include:

Heliotropium arborescens (HELIOTROPE)
Pelargonium graveolens (ROSE GERANIUM); P. quercifolium
    (Oak-leaved Geranium); P. tomentosum (Peppermint
    Geranium)
Salvia rutilans (PINEAPPLE SAGE)

Some shrubs found in the original Garden of Fragrance:

Chimonanthus praecox (WINTERSWEET)
Citrus* spp. (ORANGE, LEMON, GRAPEFRUIT, ETC.)
Clethra alnifolia (SWEET PEPPERBUSH)
Daphne cneorum and D. mezerium (DAPHNE)
Jasminum nudiflorum (WINTER JASMINE)
Laurus nobilis* (LAUREL)
Myrtus communis* (MYRTLE)
Osmanthus fragrans* (SWEET OLIVE)
Philadelphus coronarius (MOCK ORANGE)
Rhododendron luteum (SWEET AZALEA)
Rosa—Including Alba roses, Damasks and the Hybrid Perpetual
    Mrs. John Laing.
Rosmarinus officinalis* (ROSEMARY)
Syringa villosa (LATE LILAC); S. vulgaris (Common Lilac)
Viburnum carlesii (KOREAN SPICE VIBURNUM)

*Not hardy in the North.

The following is from a letter from Sir Henry Wotton addressed to Thomas Johnson (who revised *Gerard's Herbal*):

> "where might I have for my monye, all kinde of colored Pynkes to sett in a Quarter of my Garden, or any such flowers as perfume the Ayre?"
>
> GERARD'S HERBAL, AMENDED BY THOMAS JOHNSON, 1636

Fragrance Gardens to Visit

Alabama
(Talladega): Helen Keller Fragrance Garden

California
(San Francisco): Golden Gate Park

Idaho
(Gooding): Gooding School for the Blind

Illinois
(Chicago): Garfield Park Conservatory

Missouri
(St. Louis): Missouri Botanical Garden

New Jersey
(Iselin): Garden for the Blind

New York
(Brooklyn): Brooklyn Botanic Garden

Oregon
(Sandy): Gardens of Enchantment, Oral Hull Park

Rhode Island
(Providence): Garden for the Blind

Texas
(Fort Worth): Fort Worth Botanic Gardens

Utah
(Salt Lake City): Perception Garden

Washington
(Mount Vernon): Fragrance Garden for the Blind

THE WHITE GARDEN

Despite differences among the various plants with gray foliage, a garden comprised exclusively of silvery plants would be quite dull. The famous "White Garden" at Sissinghurst, England, is really a green and gray garden, and it is crammed full of a huge variety of white-flowering green-leaved plants, gray-leaved plants and a few variegated plants. Because of good design and the "white" theme, the end result is not confusion. Gardeners do not need to limit themselves to flowers of one color; many prefer to garden using "drifts" of different colors (advocated by another Britisher), but all too often the drifts are comprised of only one or two types of plants. Harold Nicolson and Vita Sackville-West, who designed the White Garden in 1939 (it was not planted until 1949–1950), proved that there is excitement in diversity and that it need not result in chaos. In addition to gray plants such as Artemisia, Lavender-Cotton, Lamb's Ears and Silver Sage, Sissinghurst's White Garden contains white-flowered varieties of the following: Tulips, Pansies, Columbines, Irises, Campanulas, hardy Geraniums, Lupines, Clematis, Wallflowers, Potentillas and Thyme. Here are more:

Dianthus 'Mrs. Sinkins'
Dictamnus albus (GAS PLANT)
Cardiocrinum giganteum (HIMALAYAN LILY)
Cleome 'Helen Campbell'
Crambe cordifolia*
Galega (GOAT'S RUE)
Galium (SWEET WOODRUFF)
Galtonia candicans (SUMMER HYACINTH)
Gypsophila 'Bristol Fairy'
Hosta plantaginea
Hydrangea arborescens grandiflora
Iris florentina
Libertia (IRIDACEAE)
Lilium regale (REGAL LILY)
Nicotiana sylvestris (FLOWERING TOBACCO)
Paeonia suffruticosa (TREE PEONY)

*Crambe is a great favorite with British gardeners. C. cordifolia (Colewort) is a stout perennial with large basal leaves that produces a very tall panicle of airy, white and fragrant flowers. C. maritima (Sea Kale) is a lower-growing perennial grown for tasty new shoots as well as attractive blue-green leaves and white flowers.

Pulmonaria 'Sissinghurst White'
Rosa (MME. ALFRED CARRIERE,** ICEBERG, WHITE WINGS, R.
    LONGICUSPIS)
Thalictrum aquilegifolium 'Album'
Ruta (RUE)

**Graham Stuart Thomas says this rose (a Noisette rated 6.5 by ARS), "raised 100
years ago, flowers more profusely every year than any other rose in the country."
(*Great Gardens of Britain,* New York: Mayflower Books, 1979).

Vita Sackville-West on White Gardens

Vita Sackville-West originally intended to allow a few plants with
pale pink flowers into Sissinghurst's White Garden, but changed her
mind. In *A Joy of Gardening* she writes:

> Obviously the pure candor of whiteness looks best against the
> dark background of a yew hedge, or any dark shrubs if yew is
> not available. There comes a moment at twilight when white
> plants gleam with a peculiar pallor of ghostliness. I dare say of
> white, that neutral tint usually regarded as the absence of color,
> that it is every bit as receptive of changing light as the blues
> and reds and purples. It may perhaps demand a patiently
> observing eye, attuned to a subtlety less crude than the strong
> range of reds and purples we get in, say, the herbaceous phloxes
> which miraculously alter their hue as the evening light sinks
> across them. I love color, and rejoice in it, but white is lovely
> to me forever. The ice-green shades that it can take on in
> certain lights, by twilight or by moonlight, perhaps by
> moonlight especially, make a dream of the garden, an unreal
> vision.*

A VARIEGATED GARDEN

Victorian gardeners had a penchant for the unusual—weeping trees, large,
exotic flowers and plants with variegated foliage. Today's garden designers look askance at such excess, preferring plants that blend into the
landscape instead of standing out. Plants with variegated leaves have
many detractors: Looks aside, many of them are not as vigorous as

*Vita Sackville-West, *A Joy of Gardening* (New York: Harper & Row, 1958).

all-green plants of the same species. Gardens made up exclusively of variegated plants would be decidedly nerve wracking. However, many of them like shade and can brighten dimly lit areas. Here are fifteen to try (the last seven are woody):

Aegopodium (GOUTWEED, BISHOPS-WEED)—Can be weedy as
the name implies.

Athyrium goeringianum 'Pictum' (JAPANESE PAINTED FERN)

Ajuga reptans (BUGLEWEED)—Variegated form not as vigorous
or invasive.

Hosta (PLANTAIN LILY)—Several species have variegated foliage.

Lamium maculatum ('BEACON SILVER')—Has pink flowers;
('WHITE NANCY,')—White flowers.

Liriope muscari 'Variegata' (LILYTURF)—Only young leaves
are yellow-striped.

Molinia caerulea 'Variegata' (VARIEGATED MOOR GRASS)

Pulmonaria saccharata (LUNGWORT)—Pink buds, blue flowers
and silver-spotted leaves.

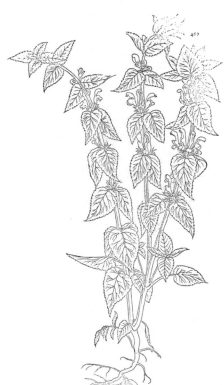

Lamium sp. (Dead Nettle). The low-growing variegated Dead Nettles prefer moist soil but will make a ground cover in dry shade.

Acer negundo 'Variegatum' (VARIEGATED BOX
ELDER)—Smaller and not as weedy as the species.
Cornus alba (TATARIAN DOGWOOD)—There are several
variegated varieties.
Elaeagnus pungens 'Variegata' (THORNY ELAEAGNUS)
Euonymus fortunei (WINTERCREEPER) and E. japonica (Japanese
Spindle Tree)
Hedera helix (ENGLISH IVY)—There are many variegated forms,
including the 1988 Styer Award winner, 'Buttercup.'
Pachysandra terminalis 'Variegata' (JAPANESE
PACHYSANDRA)—Not as vigorous as the more commonly
planted all-green plant.
Pittosporum tobira 'Variegata' (JAPANESE PITTOSPORUM)—Not
hardy beyond zone 8.

Don't forget variegated annuals such as Impatiens, Coleus and Caladium.
See also "Variegated and Colorful Evergreens," pages 244–247.

A MOONLIGHT GARDEN

Plants with Gray Leaves

Silvery foliage is an attractive foil for bright colors in a perennial
border. It appears cool on hot summer days, stands out at dusk and is
lovely by moonlight. The leaves of some gray-green perennials, such as
Iris, Sedum and Dianthus, are smooth, while other plants appear gray
because they are covered with tiny hairs. Hairy foliage helps cut water
loss and deter pests; such plants are often native to sunny, dry regions and
need sun and good drainage to prosper. There are many silvery plants to
choose from; ten of the most useful for the perennial border are:

Achillea (YARROW)—There are several varieties with gray
leaves; 'Moonshine' has pale yellow flowers in summer and
fall.
Alyssum (BASKET OF GOLD)—Bright-yellow flowers in spring.
Artemisia (MUGWORT, WORMWOOD)—Perhaps the most useful
of the gray plants (named for the Greek goddess of the
moon, Artemis); grown mainly for leaves. The many
varieties include 'Silver King' and 'Silver Mound.'

Cerastium (SNOW-IN-SUMMER)—A white-flowered rock-garden favorite.

Lavendula (LAVENDER)—There are many kinds; some have grayer foliage than others and some have white flowers. Not all lavenders are hardy north.

Perovskia (RUSSIAN SAGE)—Shrubby plant with aromatic gray leaves and lavender/blue flowers.

Salvia (SAGE)—The herb Sage has silver leaves, as does S. argentea (Silver Sage), a showier garden subject.

Santolina (LAVENDER COTTON)—Another plant grown mainly for gray leaves although it has attractive yellow flowers that many gardeners remove.

Stachys (LAMB'S EARS)—Grown for beautiful, fuzzy silver leaves; remove flowers for best results or use 'Silver Carpet,' a nonflowering form.

Veronica (SPEEDWELL)—Several Veronicas have gray foliage; incana (Woolly Speedwell) is a low-growing species for edging or the rock garden.

Twelve more plants with gray or blue/green leaves are: Arabis, Baptisia, Dianthus, Festuca ovina var. glauca (Dwarf Blue Fescue, a grass), Gazania,* Helichrysum angustifolium (White Leaf or Curry Plant), Iris, Lychnis, Onopordum, Sanguinaria, Sedum and Senecio.

Shrubs/trees with gray foliage include: Buddleja, Caryopteris, Elaeagnus, Hippophae, Populus alba,* Potentilla, Salix and Tilia* (Silver Linden and Pendant Silver Linden). Plants with light and airy foliage add depth to the landscape and can make small grounds appear larger. See also "Variegated and Colorful Evergreens," pages 244-247.

Moonlight Flowers

Flowers do not scent the air for the pleasure of gardeners; in fact, many smell best after gardeners have retired for the night. Some evening-scented blossoms, such as Yucca, Bouncing Bet and certain Honeysuckles and Orchids, have little daytime fragrance; others, like Evening Primrose and Four O'Clocks, remain closed during daylight hours. Even some Roses, Jasmines and Linden flowers that have sweet daytime fragrance, are thought by some to be richer scented in the evening. Those that save their perfume for sundown do so to lure their pollinators—those noctur-

*Appears silvery due to white down on undersides of leaves.

nal beetles, moths and even bats that are busy at twilight. Many of these "moonlight flowers" are light colored for good nighttime visibility. Listed here are fifteen that are said to smell sweetest at sundown:

Clethra alnifolia* (SWEET PEPPERBUSH, SUMMERSWEET)
Daphne pontica* (TWIN-FLOWERED DAPHNE)—Not hardy
    beyond zone 7.
Hesperis matronalis (DAME ROCKET)—B or P
Hosta plantaginea (PLAINTAIN-LILY)—P
Lilium spp. (MADONNA, GOLDBAND, REGAL)—P
Linnaea** borealis (TWIN-FLOWER)—P
Lonicera* spp. (HONEYSUCKLE)
Matthiola longipetala (EVENING STOCK, PERFUME PLANT)—A
Mirabilis jalapa (FOUR O' CLOCK, BEAUTY OF THE NIGHT)—A, P
    in some southern regions.
Nicotiana alata (EVENING-SCENTED TOBACCO)—A
Oenothera spp. (EVENING PRIMROSE)—B or P
Phlox sp. (SUMMER PHLOX)—P
Saponaria officinalis (BOUNCING BET, SOAPWORT)—P
Silene spp. (CAMPION)—A, B or P
Yucca filamentosa (YUCCA)—P

A—Annual   B—Biennial   P—Perennial
*Woody plants. Clethra, a moisture-loving shrub, produces white flowers in late July; Daphne pontica, an evergreen, has yellowish flowers in the spring; Lonicera, a climbing plant or small shrub, has flowers that may be yellow/white and/or purple.
**Evergreen trailing subshrub admired by and named for Linnaeus, the "Father of Taxonomy." Suitable rock-garden subject.

ROCK GARDENS

Plants for Beginners

Rock gardens traditionally contain those dwarf plants that thrive in alpine environments where summers are cool, soil is thin, drainage is excellent and sunshine is plentiful. Unfortunately for lowland gardeners, most alpine plants are fine-tuned to life at high altitudes and are therefore quite difficult to grow elsewhere, even if given a light, well-drained soil and plenty of sun. Happily, there are a number of attractive, low-growing and dwarf plants available (some are actually alpines; most are not) that are easy to grow and suitable for rockeries; they are listed on the following page. Soil should be well drained, not too rich and the site sunny.

Achillea (YARROW)—There are several small Yarrows for the rock garden; A. tomentosa 'Nana' has woolly, silver leaves, yellow flowers and grows 4 inches tall.

Alyssum (MADWORT)—A. montanum is another gray-leaved plant with yellow flowers that grows 4 inches tall. Fragrant.

Arabis (ROCK CRESS)—There are many small Rock Cresses; A. caucasica is 8 inches tall with fragrant white flowers. There are several lower-growing cultivars.

Armeria (SEA PINK)—A complex group; there are many Armerias with white or rose flowers; some alpine, some from coastal regions.

Aurinia (BASKET OF GOLD)—A. saxatilis has evergreen gray leaves and bright yellow flowers in spring. Cultivars include 'Compacta,' 'Nana' and 'Flore Plena' with double flowers.

Campanula (BELLFLOWER)—C. carpatica is said to be the least fussy of the small Campanulas but needs good drainage. Most small cultivars have blue flowers, but several are white flowered.

Chrysogonum virginianum (GOLDEN-STAR, GREEN-AND-GOLD)—U.S. native with yellow flowers and a long-blooming period. There are several cultivars. Tolerates full sun but prefers light shade.

Iberis (CANDYTUFT)—Noted for handsome evergreen leaves and chalk-white flowers; there are a number of named varieties that are lower growing than I. sempervirens, the common species.

Phlox (MOSS PINK)—There are many small Phlox species; P. subulata is overplanted but reliable and comes in many shades of pink, white and blue.

Sedum (STONECROP)—Succulent leaves, low habit and a preference for light, well-drained soils make Sedums fine rock-garden subjects. The many species have red, pink, yellow or white flowers. Sempervivum (Houseleek, Hens and Chicks) is another low-growing group of succulents that make good rock-garden subjects.

Thymus (THYME)—Several Thymes have a creeping habit and blue, pink or white flowers.

Veronica (SPEEDWELL)—V. spicata 'Nana' is tiny but tough. Speedwells have blue, white or pink flowers and green or gray foliage.

Small plants for the shadier part of the rock garden (most of these perennials would be useful in any small, partially shaded garden):

Ajuga (BUGLEWEED)—Ajugas have blue/purple or pink flowers and green, bronze or variegated foliage.

Aruncus (GOATSBEARD)—A. aethusifolius has feathery white flowers, small fernlike leaves and grows one foot tall.

Asarum (WILD GINGER)—Evergreen or deciduous; some species have mottled foliage. A. wagneri has lemon-scented leaves. Brownish flowers appear near the ground and are hidden by foliage.

Dicentra (WILD BLEEDING HEART)—U.S. natives with finely cut gray-green leaves and heart-shaped flowers. D. eximia produces pink flowers over a long period.

Dodecatheon (SHOOTING STAR)—Not the easiest plant to grow; needs moist, well-drained soil and goes dormant after flowering. This U.S. native has beautiful nodding flowers (white, pink or purple) with reflexed petals and is the symbol of the American Rock Garden Society.

Galium odoratum (SWEET WOODRUFF)—Starlike apple-green leaves and small white flowers. Dried foliage is sweetly fragrant.

Hosta (HOSTA)—H. venusta has small oval leaves and lilac flowers; H. tardiflora has lilac/pink flowers in fall and shiny, narrow leaves. Both grow one foot tall.

Primula (PRIMROSE)—Primulas need richer soil and more moisture than most rock-garden plants; flowers come in many colors. Some Primulas require more sun than others.

Smilacina (SOLOMON'S PLUMES)—S. stellata grows about a foot tall, produces white flowers (red berries in autumn) and tolerates dry soil.

Thalictrum (MEADOW RUE)—T. clavatum has white flowers; T. coreanum has pink flowers. Both of these dainty, one-foot tall species require moist soil.

A Rocky Mountain Rock Garden

Located in Boulder, Colorado, the late Dr. Paul Maslin's rock garden has an advantage over many hotter and more humid areas of the country—altitude. Boulder, well below the natural habitat of most alpine plants, is high enough to permit their growth, although some of them do die out after several years. Ten of the plants in this rock garden are listed on the following page.

Anemone patens (PASQUE FLOWER)
Aquilegia jonesii and A. saximontana
Chionophila jamesii (SNOW-LOVER)
Geum rossii (ALPINE AVENS)
Mertensia alpina (BLUEBELLS)
Sedum rhodanthum
Silene acaulis (CUSHION PINK)
Telesonix jamesii
Thalictrum alpinum (ALPINE MEADOW RUE)
Viola adunca (WESTERN DOG VIOLET)

Herb K's Rock Garden

Herb Kaufman is a professor of psychology at the University of Connecticut, a member of American Rock Garden Society and an avid rock gardener. Groups of people come from miles around to see his rock garden located in northeastern Connecticut (Storrs, elevation 630 feet). Below he lists his favorites, chosen in part because they thrive in his garden:

Aquilegia caerulea,* A. flabellata and A. saximontana*
(COLUMBINE)
Campanula pulla and C. portenschlagiana
(BELLFLOWER)—The latter, once called C. muralis, is a wonderful scree or wall plant.
Chrysogonum virginianum* (GOLDENSTAR,
GREEN-AND-GOLD)—Flowers over a very long season, easy and beautiful.
Erodium manescavii (HERON'S BILL)—This long-season bloomer is supposed to be somewhat tender, but has been perfectly hardy in my garden for the last five years.
Euphorbia epithymoides (FORMERLY E. POLYCHROMA)—Very attractive foliage and the showiest of the spring bloomers in my garden.
Gentiana verna (GENTIAN)—The spring-blooming Gentian with the most beautiful blue flower in the Plant Kingdom. G. scabra and G. septemfida (Crested Gentian) are equally beautiful fall-blooming species.

*U.S. natives.

**Geranium dalmaticum and G. sanguineum var.
prostratum**—The former has rose flowers and red and
yellow fall foliage; the latter pink flowers (with red
veining) for much of the summer.

Lewisia cotyledon* and L. rediviva* (BITTER ROOT)—Both
are spectacular flowering alpines that do well in my
garden.

Saxifraga spp. (SAXIFRAGE, ROCK-FOIL)—Both the foliage
(especially the encrusted sorts**) and the flowers are
appealing.

Tiarella wherryi* (FALSE MITERWORT, FOAM FLOWER)—This
species has pink flowers and semievergreen, red-veined
leaves.

*U.S. native.
**These plants have encrustations of lime along leaf margins and need an alkaline soil
(or limestone chips); they tolerate more sun than other Saxifrages.

Where to Visit Alpine Plants

Colorado
(Mt. Goliath): Walter Pesman Trail (50 miles from Denver)—
Here you can see native alpines at 12,000 feet; managed by
the Denver Botanical Gardens).

New Hampshire
(Mt. Washington): Mt. Washington Arctic Gardens

New Mexico
(Albuquerque): Sandia Peak Botanical Gardens

New York
(Bronx): Thomas H. Everett Alpine House, Wave Hill, 675
W. 252nd Street

Washington
(Longmire): Mt. Rainier National Park

Where to Visit Rock Gardens

Illinois
(Chicago): Lincoln Park, 2400 N. Stockton Drive

Michigan
(Detroit): Meadow Brook Hall and Gardens

New York
(Bronx): New York Botanical Garden

Pennsylvania
(Kennett Square): Longwood Garden's Hillside Garden

American Rock Garden Society
Buffy Parker, Secretary
15 Fairmead Road
Darien, CT 06820

SOURCES FOR ROCK GARDENS

More information about rock gardening can be obtained from inexpensive guides published by Cornell University (Booklet IB 159— send $3.00 to Distribution Center C, 7 Research Park, Cornell University, Ithaca, NY 14850) and the Brooklyn Botanic Garden (1000 Washington Avenue, Brooklyn, NY 11225). Check with your local extension service for additional information.

SOURCES FOR ALPINE PLANTS

Remember that true alpines are fussier than most of the plants listed for beginners on page 346. Most of them prefer neutral soils, snow cover in winter, cool summers, perfect drainage and the presence of rocks and grit. Limestone grit can provide alkalinity; crushed granite will make the environment more acid.

Alpine Gardens
15920 S.W. Oberst Lane
Sherwood, OR 97140
Sedum and Sempervivum

Alpine Plants
Box 245
Tahoe Vista, CA 95732

Chehalis Rare Plant Nursery
2568 Jackson Highway
Chehalis, WA 98532

Colorado Alpines, Inc.
PO Box 2708
Avon, CO 81620

Lamb Nurseries
E. 101 Sharp Ave.
Spokane, WA 99202

John D. Lyon Company
143 Alewife Brook Parkway
Cambridge, MA 02140
Species bulbs

McClure & Zimmerman
108 W. Winnebago St.
PO Box 368
Friesland, WI 53935-0368
Unusual bulbs

Roslyn Nursery
211 Burrs Lane
Dix Hills, NY 11746
For dwarf Rhododendrons,
azaleas and evergreens

Rocknoll Nursery
9210 U.S. 50
Hillsboro, OH 45133-8546

Siskiyou Rare Plant Nursery
2825 Cummings Rd.
Medford, OR 97501

Cold-Hardy Cacti

Many gardeners are unaware that a surprising number of Cacti are quite cold-hardy and can be grown successfully outdoors in zone 6 and even zone 5 gardens. Cacti need five or six hours of sun daily during the growing season and a high percentage of sand and gravel in their soil. Wet, poorly drained sites must be avoided; gardeners in some areas construct roofing over plants to keep them dry. Ten hardy Cacti for the Northeast are:

Coryphantha missouriensis (NIPPLE CACTUS)—Flowers yellow-green and fragrant. Native from the Dakotas and Montana to northern Texas.

Coryphantha vivipara—Small, roundish or cylindrical Cactus with variously colored spines and purple or pink flowers. Native from southern Canada to northern Texas.

Echinocereus chloranthus—A small barrel-type Cactus with greenish yellow flowers and purple-red fruit. Hardy through zone 6 according to the American Horticultural Society.

Echinocereus triglochidiatus (HEDGEHOG)—Red flowers appear in spring and red fruit follows. White spines on a plant about one foot tall. Hardy in parts of New England.

Echinocereus viridiflorus—Very small Cactus, about 6 inches tall, with yellow-green flowers and purple spines. This native species is found from the Dakotas to Wyoming and south to Texas and New Mexico. Lemon scented.

Opuntia erinacea (GRIZZLY-BEAR CACTUS)—Native Opuntias range throughout North and South America and are generally longer-lived than Echinocereus in cultivation.

This cactus grows 1 to 2 feet tall; flowers may be white, red or yellow.

Opuntia humifusa (PRICKLY PEAR)—The East Coast Prickly Pear, O. humifusa, has large yellow flowers and edible red-purple fruit. It is found in dry, rocky or sandy areas from New England to Florida and west to Montana.

Opuntia imbricata (CHAIN-LINK CACTUS)—A tall species with showy purple flowers and yellow fruit. Very spiny; can grow into a treelike plant in some areas. Found from Colorado to Mexico; very hardy.

Opuntia polyacantha—A small Opuntia with yellow flowers (sometimes yellow-tinged red flowers) native to the Dakotas, west to Washington and south to Texas.

Pediocactus simpsonii (SNOWBALL CACTUS)—Small and round with many spines and pink or yellow flowers. Native to western U.S.

JOHN SPAIN'S HARDY CACTI

You don't need to live in the Southwest to have a Cactus garden. John Spain grows Cacti outdoors in western Connecticut without the aid of evergreen branches to protect them from temperature extremes or plastic sheeting to keep them dry. He does give them excellent drainage and plenty of sun. His plants are striking in all seasons, especially in late spring when flowers in iridescent shades of red, pink, purple, yellow, orange, cream and green appear. He grows most of the Cacti listed above, as well as many others. Below are a dozen of his favorites:

Coryphantha vivipara
Echinocereus reichenbachii var. baileyi (LACE CACTUS)
Echinocereus triglochidiatus var. triglochidiatus
    (CLARET-CUP CACTUS; HEDGEHOG)
Echinocereus viridiflorus var. vividiflorus
Opuntia basilaris var. basilaris (BEAVER-TAIL; ROSE TUNA)
Opuntia fragilis
Opuntia imbricata (CHAIN-LINK)
Opuntia kleiniae
Opuntia macrorhiza var. pottsii
Opuntia phaeacantha var. camanchica
Opuntia polyacantha 'Smithwick'
Pediocactus simpsonii var. simpsonii

SOURCES FOR HARDY CACTI

Cactus Patch
Box 159, RR 2
Radium, KS 67550-9111
(316) 982-4670
Send stamp for catalog

Mesa Garden
PO Box 72
Belen, NM 87002
(505) 864-3131
Send two stamps for catalog

Intermountain Cactus
2344 S. Redwood Ave.
Salt Lake City, UT 84119
(801) 972-5149
Send SASE for catalog

A SEASIDE GARDEN

Mary Turner gardens in front of and in back of an ocean-front house on a barrier beach in southern New Jersey. Sedums and Sempervivums thrive in pots, and her annuals (Zinnia, Marigolds, Cosmos, Geranium, Celosia and Impatiens) seem brighter and more beautiful than the same plants grown farther inland. In addition to Mary's green thumb, some researchers would claim that her plants benefit from nutrient-laden coastal fogs, although it is well known that plants are injured if doused with saltwater or subjected to steady winds off the ocean that are unaccompanied by rain. Pliny, a first-century Roman gardener, noted, "Sea breezes are injurious in some places, while at the same time in most places they encourage growth; some plants like having a distant view of the sea but are not benefited by being moved nearer to its saline exhalations."* Drought- and wind-resistant plants found in Mary's seaside garden include:

Ammophila (AMERICAN DUNE GRASS)
Anthemis (GOLDEN MARGUERITE)
Armeria (SEA PINK)
Artemisia (SILVER KING; WHITE SAGE)
Cerastium (SNOW-IN-SUMMER)
Chrysanthemum (DAISY)
Coreopsis (COREOPSIS, TICKSEED)
Dianthus (PINK)
Euphorbia (CYPRESS SPURGE)

---

*Pliny quoted in H. Rackham, *Natural History* (Cambridge: Harvard University Press, 1950), 17.

Gaillardia (BLANKETFLOWER)
Gypsophila (BABY'S BREATH)
Hemerocallis (DAYLILY)
Hudsonia (BEACH HEATHER)
Lathyrus (SWEET PEA; BEACH PEA)
Lilium (SEVERAL KINDS, INCLUDING EASTER LILIES)
Limonium (SEA-LAVENDER)
Optunia (PRICKLY PEAR)
Rosa (R. RUGOSA AND THE SHRUB ROSE SEA FOAM, RATED 7.6 BY
  THE ARS)
Santolina (LAVENDER COTTON)
Solidago (SEASIDE GOLDENROD)
Tradescantia (SPIDERWORT)
Yucca (SPANISH BAYONET)

A GARDEN FOR AUTUMN COLOR

Many people consider only the flowers a shrub will produce, ignoring completely how the plant will appear in fall and winter. This is too bad because a number of deciduous shrubs produce beautiful fall color that often exceeds floral displays. Some shrubs are worth planting for their fall color alone; others will produce showy flowers and/or fruit in addition to fall color; these are noted. Some shrubs for brilliant fall color follow. (Note that Japanese Barberry and Winged Euonymus have become pests in some areas. Doublefile Viburnum can also escape cultivation.)

Berberis thunbergii** (JAPANESE BARBERRY)—Red
Euonymus alatus** (WINGED EUONYMUS; BURNING BUSH)—Red
Cornus alba** (TATARIAN DOGWOOD)—Red
Rhododendron schlippenbachii* (ROYAL
  AZALEA)—Red-orange or yellow
Rosa rugosa*** (RUGOSA ROSE)—Deep yellow
Viburnum carlesii* (KOREAN SPICE VIBURNUM)—Soft red
Viburnum plicatum tomentosum*** (DOUBLEFILE
  VIBURNUM)—Soft red

*Showy flowers.
**Showy fruit.
***Showy flowers and fruit.

NATIVE AMERICAN SHRUBS FOR SPECTACULAR FALL COLOR:

Aronia arbutifolia** (CHOKEBERRY)—Red
Cornus racemosa** (GRAY DOGWOOD)—Reddish purple
Cornus sericea (RED–OSIER DOGWOOD)—Red; C. sericea and C.
   alba have red stems all winter
Fothergilla spp.* (FOTHERGILLA)—Orange or red
Hamamelis spp.* (WITCH HAZEL)—Yellow
Hydrangea quercifolia* (OAKLEAF HYDRANGEA)—Bronze red
Rhododendron vaseyi* (PINK-SHELL AZALEA)—Red
Rhus glabra** (SMOOTH SUMAC)—Red; R. copallina and R.
   typhina are also outstanding in fall
Rosa virginiana*** (VIRGINIA ROSE)—Red; red stems all
   winter
Vaccinium corymbosum (HIGHBUSH BLUEBERRY)—Red; edible
   berries and colorful winter twigs
Viburnum acerifolium (MAPLELEAF VIBURNUM)—Red-purple;
   in woodlands fall color is often pale pink
Viburnum dentatum (ARROWWOOD)—Red
Viburnum prunifolium (BLACKHAW)—Red

*Showy flowers.
**Showy fruit.
***Showy flowers and fruit.

Colchicum autumnale (Autumn Crocus). Leaves appear in the spring but the rose, purple or white flowers do not bloom until autumn. Roots and seeds are the source of the pain-killer Colchicine.

The following perennials will bloom in the late-summer/early-autumn garden:

Aconitum (MONKSHOOD)
Anemone (JAPANESE ANEMONE)
Aster (ASTER)—There are many species and cultivars.
Boltonia—Needs lots of room
Callirhoe (POPPY MALLOW)
Ceratostigma (LEADWORT)
Chrysanthemum (HARDY CHRYSANTHEMUM)
Cimicifuga spp. (BUGBANE)—Do not select C. racemosa, which
    blooms in summer.
Colchicum (AUTUMN CROCUS)
Eupatorium (HARDY AGERATUM)
Helenium autumnale (SNEEZEWEED)—Don't let the common
    name deter you.
Heliopsis (HELIOPSIS)
Hosta (FRAGRANT PLANTAIN LILY)
Liatris (GAYFEATHER)
Nepeta x faassenii (CATMINT)
Physostegia (FALSE DRAGONHEAD)
Sanguisorba (CANADIAN BURNET)
Sedum sieboldii (OCTOBER PLANT) and S. spectabile
Stokesia (STOKE'S ASTER)

Physostegia virginiana (False Dragonhead, Obedience). Native American Physostegia is a fine fall-blooming perennial with pink or white flowers. There are several cultivars.

A WINTER GARDEN

The Japanese plan their gardens to be beautiful in winter as well as the other three seasons. Many North Americans, in contrast, pay scant attention to the garden after the last leaf has fallen. When they do think of winter plantings, they tend to think exclusively of needle-leaved evergreens such as Yew, Spruce and Hemlock. As important as these plants are, their overuse can be tiresome. There are many plants that will add interest to winter gardens that can be colorful, lovely after a snowfall and even boast a flower or two:

Acer palmatum (JAPANESE MAPLE)—Many varieties of this small tree have interesting lacey twigs.

Berberis thunbergii (JAPANESE BARBERRY)—Dense and twiggy with long-lasting red fruits; a fine snow catcher.

Cornus spp. (TATARIAN DOGWOOD, CORAL DOGWOOD, RED-OSIER AND GOLDENTWIG)—Red or yellow stems and twigs.

Cotoneaster horizontalis (ROCKSPRAY)—Low growing semievergreen with spreading habit and many persistent red berries.

Cytisus scoparius (SCOTCH BROOM)—Mass of thin, attractive green stems all winter; best in sandy soil and mild winters.

Euonymus alatus (WINGED EUONYMUS)—Conspicuous corky twigs collect snow; other species are evergreen.

Ilex verticillata (WINTERBERRY)—Red fruits (on pistillate plants) showy in early winter.

Kalmia (MT. LAUREL)—Leaves stay green all winter and do not roll up like some of the Rhododendrons.

Kerria japonica (KERRIA)—Bright-green stems.

Kolkwitzia amabilis (BEAUTY BUSH)—Older stems have exfoliating bark.

Leucothoe—Small, graceful broad-leaved evergreen with burgundy winter color.

Magnolia stellata (STAR MAGNOLIA)—Small and dense, Star Magnolia has gray bark and large, gray, furry winter buds.

Mahonia aquifolium (OREGON HOLLYGRAPE)—Member of the Barberry family with green or bronze leaves in winter; needs a sheltered spot and some shade; there is a hardier creeping species.

Myrica pennsylvanica (BAYBERRY)—Silver fruits (on pistillate plants) are showy in winter.

Pieris (ANDROMEDA)—Glossy evergreen leaves and attractive

reddish winter flower buds on P. japonica; P. floribunda
has green/white flower buds in winter.

Prunus tomentosa (NANKING CHERRY)—Very winter hardy with
shiny reddish exfoliating bark and picturesque branching.

Rhododendron (AZALEA)—Persistent bronze leaves.

Rhus typhina (STAGHORN SUMAC)—Good in larger landscapes;
fuzzy twigs and showy fruit clusters (on pistillate plants).

Sassafras albidum (SASSAFRAS)—Green twigs and interesting
branching.

Vaccinium corymbosum (HIGHBUSH BLUEBERRY)—Gray, green
and red twigs; older plants have attractive winter silhouette
Vinca (which often surprises with winter flowers), English
Ivy and Pachysandra make good evergreen ground covers;
Christmas Fern is an evergreen native Fern. Another native,
Hamamelis vernalis (Vernal Witch Hazel), produces
fragrant yellow flowers in late winter. See also "Trees with
Interesting Bark," pages 237–239, and "Variegated and
Colorful Evergreens," pages 244–247.

A QUIET GARDEN

A friend once owned a small, gray, contemporary house on Towd Point,
Long Island, New York. The neighborhood was wooded and traversed
by sandy lanes. My friend felt that flowers would distract from the
architecture and setting and wanted a garden without showy blossoms or
bright fall color. (She did want some berried shrubs for birds.) The
following shrubs are attractive, but neutral and low-key, and will give
privacy without attracting too much attention to themselves. Most are
ideal for informal, "naturalistic" plantings. (See also "Native Flowering
Shrubs," pages 253–256.)

Aronia melanocarpa* (BLACK CHOKEBERRY)—Shade tolerant;
smaller and less showy than A. arbutifolia and can tolerate
drier soil.

Amelanchier stolonifera* (RUNNING SHADBLOW)

Comptonia peregrina* (SWEET FERN)

Cornus rugosa* (ROUNDLEAF DOGWOOD)—Best in shade.

Elaeagnus multiflora (CHERRY ELEAGNUS); E. angustifolia
(Russian Olive)—These plants can spread from cultivation.

Lonicera canadensis* (AMERICAN FLY HONEYSUCKLE)—Prefers
shade.

*U.S. native.

Myrica pennsylvanica* (BAYBERRY)
Rhamnus frangula (ALDER BUCKTHORN)—May spread from
    cultivation.
Rhodotypos tetrapetala (JETBEAD)—Tolerates shade.
Viburnum trilobum* (AMERICAN CRANBERRYBUSH)

*U.S. native.

The shrubs listed above do well on fairly dry to normal sites; the following five natives like somewhat moister conditions (all are shade tolerant):

Calycanthus florida (CAROLINA ALLSPICE)
Hamamelis spp. (WITCH HAZEL)
Ilex verticillata (WINTERBERRY)
Lindera benzoin (SPICE BUSH)
Viburnum cassinoides (WITHEROD; WILD RAISIN)

The following ten perennials are for the green garden; most do best in
semishade (see also "Wildflowers for Woodland Gardens," pages 365–
368):

Alchemilla (LADY'S MANTLE)—Chartreuse flowers; gray-green
    leaves.
Arisaema (JACK-IN-THE-PULPIT AND GREEN DRAGON)
Asarum (WILD GINGER)—Low-growing plants for deep shade.
Astilbe—'Bridal Veil' and 'Deutschland' are among those with
    white flowers.
Convallaria (LILY-OF-THE-VALLEY)
Epimedium x youngianum 'Niveum'—A white-flowered
    Epimedium.
Galium odoratum (SWEET WOODRUFF)—Starlike leaves; tiny
    white flowers.
Hosta—There are many to choose from, some with white
    flowers.
Polystichum (CHRISTMAS FERN)—This fern likes moisture and
    acid soil. (See also "Ferns for the Shady Garden," pages
    80–81.)
Thalictrum spp. (MEADOW RUE)—Most species need moist soil.

PLANTS FOR A JAPANESE GARDEN

There are some who believe that Japanese gardens cannot be properly
exported; stylized, symbolic, sophisticated and often labor intensive, they

are the culmination of very long traditions in philosophy and garden art. However, there are ideas in these gardens that travel well. Rock, sand and gravel (which in Japan are used to suggest mountain, seacoast or water) need not be precisely placed or carefully raked. Winding paths, much loved in Oriental gardens generally, are delightful anywhere. Restrained use of plant material creates tranquility, and the fact that Japanese gardens are often quite small makes them, like a Monk's garden, suitable for enclosed city spaces or a quiet corner of a larger landscape.

The following shrubs and trees usually are left untrimmed, although sometimes they are clipped to suggest wooded hillsides, clouds or ocean waves:

Abelia grandiflora (GLOSSY ABELIA)
Acer palmatum (JAPANESE MAPLE)
Buxus microphylla japonica (JAPANESE BOX)—The hardiest box; there is a dwarf variety.
Euonymus spp. (SPINDLE TREE)—There are many species, some from Japan. E. fortunei is an excellent ground cover (avoid the variegated form).
Ilex crenata (JAPANESE HOLLY)—There are many varieties.
Juniperus chinensis (JUNIPER)—There are many low-growing cultivars.
Kerria japonica—Green twigs give this shrub winter color.
Pinus spp. (JAPANESE BLACK PINE) and P. mugo (Swiss Mt. Pine)—Pines are often planted in Japanese gardens to evoke the sea.
Pieris japonica (JAPANESE ANDROMEDA)
Prunus serrulata (JAPANESE FLOWERING CHERRY)—Has pink or white flowers and excellent red fall color; 'Takasago' (Naden Cherry), a smaller tree, has pink flowers, as does P. subhirtella (Higan Cherry), which is a profuse bloomer with a weeping form. There are many cultivars of these trees.
Rhododendron spp. (AZALEA)—There are many excellent Asian species.
Taxus cuspidata (JAPANESE YEW)—There are many cultivars.
Viburnum plicatum tomentosum (DOUBLEFILE VIBURNUM)

Here are some perennials. A Japanese garden is not a flower garden—use plants with showy flowers sparingly.

Astilbe

Chrysanthemum

Hemerocallis (DAYLILY)

Hosta* (PLANTAIN LILY)

Iris kaempferi (JAPANESE IRIS)—I. sibirica is also effective.

Liriope (LILYTURF)

Miscanthus sinensis (EULALIA)—Tall Asian grass; there are
several cultivars.

Pachysandra (JAPANESE SPURGE)

Paeonia (PEONY)—The Japanese types have flowers with five or
more petals surrounding a center of decorative stamens.

Tradescantia virginiana (SPIDERWORT)—An American native
with Asian relatives.

*Hosta is greatly admired in Japan, where it is native. The various varieties are used as edging, ground covers and in rock gardens—several kinds are even eaten. These long-lived plants offer gardeners a huge range of sizes, form and color. Hostas are noted for their shade tolerance. Blue-leaved hostas are best for shadiest sites while those with glossy leaves, variegated leaves or yellow in the leaf prefer at least some sun. Slugs and deer can cause damage; otherwise Hostas are relatively pest-free. The Japanese often use them as specimen plants, especially in a small garden where they may be planted alone or in a group of three. Sometimes a plant will be raised to be nearer the viewer. Hostas do well in much of the country, except in parts of the deep South and Southwest.

Ferns are also suitable for use in Japanese-style gardens, as are many native American plants. Gardeners in warmer parts of the country can experiment with Bamboo. Remember—a Japanese garden is a four-season garden (there are stone lanterns specially designed to show off a snowfall and shrubs are often pruned to do likewise) and should never be overcrowded.

Western garden design relied heavily on the straight line until the gardens of the East, with their curves and surprises, impacted British landscape architecture in the eighteenth century. In his book *Siftings,* Jens Jensen (1860–1951), an advocate of naturalistic design, wrote: "Parks and gardens of curves are always new, always revealing new thoughts and new interests in life. Straight lines are copied from the architect and do not belong to the landscaper . . . Landscaping must follow the lines of the free-growing tree with its thousands of curves."

Mr. Jensen, who came to America in his twenties, practiced garden design in the Midwest. His work can be seen at Fair Lane, the estate of Henry Ford, in Dearborn, Michigan, and Lincoln Memorial Garden in Springfield, Illinois.

A Japanese Floral Calendar

January—Pine
February—Plum
March—Peach and Pear
April—Cherry
May—Azalea, Peony and Wisteria
June—Iris
July—Morning Glory
August—Lotus
September—The Seven Grasses of Autumn
October—Chrysanthemum
November—Maple
December—Camellia

Japanese Gardens to Visit

California
(San Mateo): Japanese Garden in Central Park

Hawaii
(Hawaii Island): Liliuokalani Garden Park

Illinois
(Geneva): Japanese Garden, Fabyan's Forest Preserve

Maine
(Northeast Harbor): Asticou Gardens

Massachusetts
(Edgartown): Mytoi Japanese Garden

Missouri
(St. Louis): Missouri Botanical Gardens*

New York
(Brooklyn): Brooklyn Botanic Garden

Oregon
(Portland): Washington Park

Texas
(Austin): Zilker Park

*The Japanese Garden, Seiwa-En, is the largest in the country.

Washington
(Seattle): University of Washington Arboretum

WILDFLOWER GARDENS

Wildflowers for the Border

There is new interest today in using native American plants, both in shady wildflower gardens and in open wildflower meadows. If you do not choose to replace the lawn with a meadow or create a garden in the woods, you can still grow native plants—a number of them, hardy, beautiful and pest free, make excellent border subjects. Several, such as Asclepias, Baptisa and Liatris, grow naturally in sunny, open areas and are also good plants for meadows. Some of the following are already commonly grown and readily available from nurseries; others deserve more recognition.

Amsonia tabernaemontana (BLUESTAR)—Grows about 3 feet tall with steel-blue flowers and willowlike leaves that turn gold in the fall. A lower-growing species (montana, 15 inches) is recognized by some.

Asclepias tuberosa (BUTTERFLY WEED)—This orange-flowered beauty (there are yellow and reddish forms as well) needs sun and well-drained soil. Attracts butterflies.

Baptisa australis (BLUE FALSE INDIGO)—Beautiful blue-green compound foliage and periwinkle blue flowers, this species grows 3 to 4 feet tall and produces decorative seed pods. There are white and yellow-flowered species. B. tinctoria is a dye plant.

Boltonia asteroides (BOLTONIA)—Valuable for its white, aster-like fall flowers, Boltonia can grow 6 feet tall; the cultivar 'Snow Bank' is more compact and several feet shorter. 'Pink Beauty' is listed.

Chelone glabra (TURTLEHEAD)—This moisture-loving member of the Snapdragon family grows 3 to 6 feet tall and has white flowers (sometimes with pink blush) in late summer. C. lyonii is shorter (to 3 feet) and has rose flowers. These plants like sun or light shade and moist to wet soil.

Cimicifuga racemosa (BUGBANE, BLACK SNAKEROOT)—Tall, imposing plants (5 or more feet) with long spires of small white flowers in summer. There are several bronze-leaved forms. C. americana is shorter and produces fragrant flowers later in the season.

Gillenia trifoliata (INDIAN PHYSIC, BOWMAN'S ROOT)—A little-known member of the Rose family, Gillenia has narrow-petaled white or pale rose flowers and leaves divided into 3 leaflets. It grows about 3 feet tall. In spite of its delicate, airy appearance, William Brumback of Garden in the Woods calls Gillenia "as tough a perennial as there is" and says it thrives in a dry area of the Garden's parking lot as well as in shadier and damper native haunts. Sanguisorba (Canadian Burnet), which needs more moisture, is another border possibility belonging to the Rose family.

Heuchera spp. (ALUM ROOT; CORAL BELLS)—There are a number of species and cultivars of these dainty plants. Flower color may be red, pink, white or even greenish; foliage is often attractively colored. H. americana (Alum Root) is suitable for a woodland wildflower garden; it is also a useful ground cover.

Liatris spp. (BLAZING STAR, GAYFEATHER)—These choice plants range in height from 18 inches to 5 feet; most are prairie natives and like sun and well-drained soil. (L. spicata will grow in fairly moist spots.) Gayfeathers have narrow leaves and spikes of long-lasting thistlelike purple (may also be white or pink) flowers in late summer. Striking vertical accent plants.

Polemonium reptans (JACOB'S LADDER)—A small plant, with dainty, compound leaves (resembling ladders), this species produces blue flowers with white centers from midspring to midsummer. P. caeruleum, taller and more upright, is a European native. Both prefer moist soil and tolerate light shade. There are cultivars with white flowers.

Silene caroliniana (CATCHFLY, WILD PINK)—A foot or less tall, with sticky blue-green leaves, Catchfly produces masses of pink flowers in spring. Short-lived but self-sows; likes sun and good drainage. Subspecies wherryi is only 4 inches tall and has bright pink flowers.

Vernonia noveboracensis (IRONWEED)—Not for small gardens, Ironweed can reach 8 feet, but abundant, purple thistlelike flowers in late summer make this plant a standout. Should be considered (along with Joe-Pye Weed and Blue Vervain) as an alternative to Lythrum.

There are many other natives that are suitable for the perennial border, including species of Iris, Lily and Phlox. Ten others are: Anemone virginiana (Thimbleweed), Aster spp., Chrysogonum (Goldenstar), Dicentra (Fringed Bleeding Heart), Lobelia (Cardinal Flower), Lupinus (Lupine), Mertensia (Virginia Bluebells), Monarda (Bee Balm), Rudbeckia (Coneflower) and Stokesia (Stokes Aster). Do not overlook the charms of Solidago (Goldenrod); this plant does not cause hay fever.

Wildflowers for Woodland Gardens

Most of the wildflowers below prefer dappled shade, not the very dark shade found under mature stands of conifers. Species that like (or tolerate) denser shade of this kind are noted. Soils should be moist but well drained. When establishing a colony, plant two or three plants of the same species together to insure cross-fertilization and good seed production. Twelve easy-to-grow wildflowers for moist woodland conditions are listed on the following page.

Polygonatum sp. (Solomon's Seal). Native Polygonatums are found in America, Europe and Asia. P. odoratum, a Eurasian species, has fragrant white flowers with greenish tips.

Arisaema triphyllum (JACK-IN-THE-PULPIT)—Interesting brown/green/white striped flowers. Plant can change sex, and if satisfied with growing conditions will produce bright red berries in fall.* Acid soil.

Asarum canadense (WILD GINGER)—Pretty, heart-shaped leaves; makes a good ground cover. Brownish flowers are often overlooked. Acid to nearly neutral soil. Needs shade and will tolerate a considerable amount.

Erythronium americanum (TROUT LILY, DOG-TOOTH VIOLET)—Small bulb that produces beautifully mottled leaves and yellow flowers with brown freckles. Like many spring-blooming bulbs, these go dormant in summer. Acid to neutral soils. White Fawn Lily (E. albidum) is said to flower more readily.

Geranium maculatum (WILD GERANIUM)—Showy pink flowers, a long-blooming period and attractive leaves make unfussy Wild Geranium an asset in the wildflower garden. Acid soil; prefers a moist soil but will grow on drier sites. Goes dormant in late summer. There are several cultivars with white flowers.

Jeffersonia diphylla (TWIN LEAF)—Named in honor of Thomas Jefferson, this handsome native has white flowers and decorative foliage and seed capsules. Acid to neutral soils. There is a blue-flowered species from China.

Medeola virginiana (INDIAN CUCUMBER)—Attractive whorled leaves and small greenish flowers with red styles. Fall brings dark purple berries and golden leaves; top whorl with red leaf bases. Medeola is low-key but charming; needs moist, acid soil and will tolerate quite wet conditions and considerable hade.

Podophyllum peltatum (MAY APPLE)—Large, umbrellalike leaves and white flowers (handsome but often hidden by foliage) in spring. Makes a spreading ground cover if conditions are right; not for the small wildflower garden. Plant is toxic though yellow fruit is edible. Acid to neutral soils.

Polygonatum biflorum (SOLOMON'S SEAL)—Grows about 3 feet tall; produces greenish yellow bell-like flowers in

---

*Red berries of Jack-in-the-Pulpit will cause a burning sensation of mouth and throat if eaten, but are not deadly poisonous.

spring, blue berries and yellow fall color. Classic plant for wildflower gardens. Acid to neutral soils. Tolerant of sun or fairly deep shade and moist or dry soils.

Sanguinaria canadensis (BLOODROOT)—Showy early white flowers, lobed, gray-green leaves and ease of culture make Bloodroot a good choice for woodsy sites. Slightly acid to neutral soils. 'Flora Plena' (or 'Multiplex') has double flowers.

Smilacina racemosa (SOLOMON'S PLUME; FALSE SOLOMON'S SEAL)—Grows 1 to 3 feet tall, with feathery white flowers in late spring and attractive fall berries. Acid soil. Will tolerate dry woods.

Trillium grandiflorum (WHITE TRILLIUM)—Large white flowers, fading pink. Slightly acid to neutral soil. T. erectum (Purple Trillium) favors more acid soils.

Uvularia grandiflora (MERRYBELLS)—Produces pale yellow bells in late spring; this species can grow 2 feet tall. Slightly acid to neutral soil. There are several other species and a variegated variety.

Medeola virginica (Indian Cucumber). A plant for shade and damp soil, Indian Cucumber has attractive foliage and showy purple fruit on red stems in autumn. Edible roots have a cucumber flavor.

Try the following twelve in drier woodlands. Some of them prefer dry conditions while others prefer more moisture, but all will grow in average to somewhat dry woodland soils:

Aster divaricatus (WHITE WOOD ASTER)—Acid to neutral soils
Chimaphila maculata (PIPSISSEWA, STRIPED
    WINTERGREEN)—Acid soil
Gaultheria procumbens (WINTERGREEN)—Acid soil
Geranium maculatum (WILD GERANIUM)—Acid soil
Goodyera pubescens (RATTLESNAKE PLANTAIN,
    LATTICE-LEAF)—Acid soil
Maianthemum canadense (CANADA MAYFLOWER)—Acid soil
Mitchella repens (PARTRIDGE BERRY)—Acid soil
Polygonatum biflorum (SOLOMON'S SEAL)—Acid to neutral
    soil
Pyrola elliptica (SHINLEAF)—Acid to neutral soil
Smilacina racemosa (SOLOMON'S PLUME)—Acid soil
Tiarella cordifolia (FOAM FLOWER)—Slightly acid to neutral
    soil
Trientalis borealis (STARFLOWER)—Acid soil

Wildflowers for Meadows

American prairies and sunny open spaces are full of beautiful native grasses and meadow flowers, and there is new interest today among highway departments as well as homeowners in duplicating them. Obviously, climate and soil will determine what kind of plants will do best in your meadow; the following natives generally perform well in several regions of the country. Check with your county extension agent or the National Wildflower Research Center for lists of plants best suited to your area. Twelve native wildflowers for meadow gardens are:

Aster novae-angliae (NEW ENGLAND ASTER)—This
    fall-blooming beauty produces showy purple flowers; there
    are many named cultivars with pink, red or white flowers.
    Prefers moist soils; not for the Southwest. There are many
    other species of beautiful native asters.
Coreopsis lanceolata (COREOPSIS)—Golden-flowered Coreopsis
    thrives in dry soils and will grow in most regions of the
    country. Cultivars grown in borders include those with
    double flowers.
Cosmos spp. (COSMOS)—Several species are native to the

American Southwest; the annual C. bipinnatus is popular in the flower garden. Most flower rather late in the season and are best on light, sandy soils in regions with long growing seasons.

Echinacea purpurea (PURPLE CONEFLOWER)—The pink flowers (orange/brown centers) of Purple Coneflower attract butterflies. Echinaceas, especially some of the tidier cultivars, are also suitable in borders. All like moist soil.

Erigeron pulchellus (ROBIN'S PLANTAIN)—Erigerons or Fleabanes are valuable for their hardy aster or daisylike flowers in early summer. Robin's Plantain, a short-lived perennial, has fairly large lilac (or pink or white) flowers and spreads by runners. There are other species to consider.

Eupatorium purpureum (JOE-PYE WEED)—Joe-Pye Weed has delicately scented, fluffy rose-pink flowers in late summer. It can grow 6 or more feet tall and requires plenty of moisture. Good companion for New England Aster. There are several other Eupatoriums suitable for meadow plantings.

Gaillardia aristata (BLANKETFLOWER)—Gaily colored yellow and red summer flowers; another native that thrives on dry, sandy sites. The hybrid, G. x grandiflora, is the most commonly cultivated Gaillardia; it has many named varieties.

Linum perenne lewisii (PRAIRIE FLAX)—Native to western North America and more vigorous than the European species (L. perenne), Prairie Flax has large blue flowers and will grow in most sections of the country.

Monarda fistulosa (WILD BERGAMOT)—Not as showy as scarlet-flowered M. didyma (Bee Balm), Wild Bergamot, with lavender flowers, can succeed on drier sites. M. pectinata (Plains Bee Balm), an annual, also likes dry soils and has pink (or nearly white) flowers.

Rudbeckia hirta (BLACK-EYED SUSAN)—One of our most beautiful natives (and ancestor of 'Gloriosa Daisy'), Black-eyed Susan has golden petals and brown centers. Often behaving as a biennial, R. hirta was once used medicinally by native Americans. Other native Rudbeckias (Coneflowers) also make good meadow plants.

Sisyrinchium spp. (BLUE-EYED GRASS)—There is a native Sisyrinchium for most regions of the country, though not all of them have blue flowers and none of them are grasses.

Members of the Iris family, Sisyrinchiums have blue, white or yellow flowers and thrive in wet meadows or dry waste places.

Solidago spp. (GOLDENROD)—There are many beautiful species that will thrive in the meadow. S. canadensis is tall-growing with graceful, golden flower heads; S. odora (Anise-scented Goldenrod) is daintier and thrives on drier sites. Acquaint yourself with the Goldenrods.

There are many other meadow natives to consider. Autumn-blooming Gentians may be possible to establish in moist meadows, along with summer-blooming Lilies such as L. canadense (Meadow Lily) or L. superbum (Turk's Cap). Prairie-Smoke or Pasque Flower (Anemone nuttalliana) ranges from Alaska south to Washington, Utah and Nebraska; it is the state flower of South Dakota. Filipendula rubra, known as Queen of the Prairie, is a showy plant with fragrant pink flowers. Grasses, too, are important plants to include in wildflower meadows. Select clump-forming species such as Little Bluestem, Spangle Grass and Blue Grama (Bouteloua gracilis); turf-forming types will hinder reseeding of short-lived perennials such as Blanketflower and Black-eyed Susan.

Also a hindrance to native meadow flowers are the alien species found throughout our flora and in many meadow mixes. Admittedly, many of them are beautiful in a meadow but their extraordinary vigor often enables them to choke out all but the most robust native species. A list of immigrant plants is given on pages 148–149. Other aliens include Queen Anne's Lace, Celadine, White Campion, Cornflower and that menace to low spots, Purple Loosestrife.

Meadows in a Can

Mixtures of wildflower seed planted in some areas of the country can be quite successful—especially in the West, where competition from tree seedlings is not a problem. In other areas, however, "instant" wildflower meadows are doomed to failure; most will take patience and hard work to establish. Read labels on cans carefully. Often the labels are decorated with unusual species while the seeds inside are predominantly those of common plants such as Goldenrod or aliens such as Queen Anne's Lace. Goldenrod is a desirable plant, but you may not want a whole field of it. Germination rates vary: some wildflowers take several years to sprout; meanwhile, hardier, faster-germinating species will choke out late arrivals. Most mixes contain large numbers of alien species that you may or may not want. (David Longland and Susan Storer rate a number of available meadow mixes in the New England Wild Flower Society's 1985 fall/winter "Wild Flower Notes." Send requests to the New England Wild Flower Society, Inc., Garden in the Woods, Hemenway Road, Framingham, MA 01701.*) The best way to establish a meadow is to decide what plants, of the species that will do well in your region, you wish to grow. You may have some volunteers to encourage. Purchase additional plants or seed of desired individuals (wildflower seed is becoming increasingly obtainable) from reliable growers.

Wildflowers for the City

Recently, the city of Charleston, South Carolina, planted wildflowers on a number of sites within the city limits. Parks and highway departments are looking at such plantings as a way not only of beautifying the landscape but of cutting maintenance costs. Both of these positive goals were attained in Charleston where most of the sites remained unmowed and colorful from March through September, with some plants blooming into December. Following is a list of species that have proven most successful in field trials conducted by Charleston's Parks Department:

Rudbeckia hirta (BLACK-EYED SUSAN)—P
Coreopsis lanceolata (COREOPSIS)—P
Ratibida columnaris (MEXICAN HAT)—P
Achillea millefolium* (WHITE YARROW)—P
Gaillardia pulchella (INDIAN BLANKET)—A
Phlox drummondii (DRUMMOND'S PHLOX)—A
Castilleja indivisa (INDIAN PAINTBRUSH)—A
Coreopsis tinctoria (TICKSEED COREOPSIS)—A; also known as
  Calliopsis
Monarda citriodora (LEMON MINT)—A
Lobularia maritima* (SWEET ALYSSUM)—A

*Not a U.S. native.
A—Annual; P—Perennial

An article on Charleston's wildflowers by Steve and Sara Livingston appeared in the *Journal of the National Wildflower Research Center,* spring 1989.

---

*The New England Wild Flower Society also publishes excellent booklets on the cultivation and propagation of wildflowers.

Where to Visit the Wildflowers

Arizona
(Flagstaff): The Arboretum at Flagstaff
(Douglas): Chiricahua National Monument

California
(Santa Barbara): Santa Barbara Botanic Garden, Mission Canyon Road
(Lancaster): Antelope Valley California Poppy Reserve

Connecticut
(New London): Connecticut College Arboretum

Florida*
(Winter Park): Mead Botanical Garden, S. Denning Drive
(Homestead): Everglades National Park

Louisiana
(Opelousas): Louisiana State Arboretum

Maine
(Woolwich): Robert Tristram Coffin Wild Flower Reservation

Massachusetts
(Framingham): Garden in the Woods, Hemenway Road

New York
(Ithaca): Mundy Wildflower Garden, Cornell University

North Carolina
(Chapel Hill): North Carolina Botanical Garden, University of North Carolina

Pennsylvania
(Washington Crossing): Bowman's Hill Wildflower Preserve, Washington Crossing Park

Texas
(Austin): National Wildflower Research Center
(McKinney): Heard Natural Science Museum and Wildlife Sanctuary, Inc.

*The National Wildflower Research Center recommends Highway 20 from Valparaiso to Tallahassee as excellent for viewing Pitcher Plants.

NATIVE PLANT SOCIETIES

There are many organizations throughout the country in addition to National Wildflower Research Center that champion the cause of America's native flora. Native plant societies (some addresses courtesy of *Flower and Garden* magazine):

Alabama Wildflower Society
Box 115
Northport, AL 35476

Alaska Native Plant Society
PO Box 141613
Anchorage, AK 99514

American Penstemon Society
1569 S. Holland Ct.
Lakewood, CO 80226

Arizona Native Plant Society
PO Box 41206 Sun Station
Tucson, AZ 85717

California Native Plant Society
909 12th St., Suite 116
Sacramento, CA 95814

Colorado Native Plant Society
PO Box 200
Fort Collins, CO 80522

Connecticut Botanical Society
1 Livermore Trail
Killingworth, CT 06417

Florida Native Plant Society
1203 Orange Ave.
Winter Park, FL 32789

Georgia Botanical Society
1676 Andover Ct.
Doraville, GA 30360

Idaho Native Plant Society
Box 9451
Boise, ID 83706

Illinois Native Plant Society
Dept. of Botany
Southern Illinois University
Carbondale, IL 62901

Kansas Wildflower Society
Mulvane Art Center
Washburn University
17th and Jewell St.
Topeka, KS 66621

Louisiana Native Plant Society
PO Box 151
Saline, LA 71070

Minnesota Native Plant Society
University of Minnesota
1445 Gortner Ave.
St. Paul, MN 55108

Mississippi Native Plant Society
202 N. Andrews Ave.
Cleveland, MS 38732

Missouri Native Plant Society
Box 6612
Jefferson City, MO 65102

Montana Native Plant Society
Biology Dept.
University of Montana
Missoula, MT 59812

Nevada (Northern) Native Plant Society
Box 8965
Reno, NV 89507

New England Wildflower
Society
Hemenway Rd.
Framingham, MA 01701

New Jersey Native Plant Society
Box 1295R
Morristown, NJ 07960

Native Plant Society of New
Mexico
PO Box 5917
Santa Fe, NM 87502

New York Torrey Botanical
Club
New York Botanical Garden
Bronx, NY 10458

North Carolina Wildflower
Preservation Society
UNC–CH Totten Center 457A
Chapel Hill, NC 27514

Ohio Native Plant Society
6 Louise Dr.
Chagrin Falls, OH 44022

Native Plant Society of Oregon
Dept. of Biology
S. Oregon State College
Ashland, OR 97520

Pennsylvania Native Plant
Society
1806 Commonwealth Bldg.
316 4th Ave.
Pittsburgh, PA 15222

Philadelphia Botany Club
Academy of Natural Sciences
19th and Benjamin Franklin
Pkwy.
Philadelphia, PA 19103

Tennessee Native Plant Society
Dept. of Botany
University of Tennessee
Knoxville, TN 37916

Native Plant Society of Texas
PO Box 23836–TWU Station
Denton, TX 76204

Utah Native Plant Society
University of Utah
Bldg. 436
Salt Lake City, UT 84112

Virginia Native Plant Society
PO Box 844
Annandale, VA 22003

Washington Native Plant Society
Dept. of Botany
University of Washington
Seattle, WA 98195

West Virginia Native Plant
Society
Brooks Hall
W. Virginia University
Morgantown, WV 26506

Wyoming Native Plant Society
PO Box 1471
Cheyenne, WY 82003

SOURCES FOR WILDFLOWERS

Appalachian Wildflower Nursery
Honey Creek Road
Rt. 1, Box 275A
Reedsville, PA 17084
(717) 667-6998

Bluemount Nurseries
2103 Blue Mount Rd.
Monkton, MD 21111
(301) 329-6226

Canyon Creek Nurseries
3527 Dry Creek Rd.
Oroville, CA 95965
(916) 533-2166

Carroll Gardens
Box 310
Westminster, MD 21157
(800) 638-6334

Gardens of the Blue Ridge
Box 10
Pineola, NC 28662
(704) 733-2417

Montrose Nursery
Box 957
Hillsborough, NC 27278
(919) 732-7787

Prairie Nursery
Box 365
Westfield, WI 53964
(608) 296-3679

Prairie Seed Source
PO Box 83
North Lake, WI 53064
Seed only

Sharp Plants, Inc.
Rt. 2, Box 265C
Asheville, NC 28805
(704) 298-4751

Siskiyou Rare Plant Nursery
2825 Cummings Rd.
Medford, OR 97501
(503) 772-6846

We-Du Nurseries
Route 5, Box 724
Marion, NC 28752
(704) 738-8300

Wildseed, Inc.
1101 Campo Rosa Rd.
Box 308
Eagle Lake, TX 77434
(800) 848-0078; (409) 234-7353
in Texas
Seed only; natives and exotics

National Wildflower Research Center
2600 FM 973 North
Austin, TX 78725

A WEDDING GARDEN

Here are ten plants associated with love and used at weddings:

Achillea (YARROW)—If a couple carries this magical plant at
their wedding they can expect at least seven years of
married bliss.

Convallaria majalis (LILY-OF-THE-VALLEY)—Also known as Lily
Constancy, this plant was believed to encourage virtue and
faithfulness.

Hedera (IVY)—One of the earliest symbols of fidelity, ivy wreaths were given to brides and grooms in ancient Greece.

Lonicera (HONEYSUCKLE)—Has long been the symbol of faithful love.

Lilium (LILY)—A symbol of purity and associated with Juno, goddess of marriage, lilies were used to crown the heads of Roman brides and grooms.

Myrtus communis (MYRTLE)—Some German brides still wear myrtle wreaths, which symbolize love and constancy.

Origanum (MARJORAM)—An herb of happiness to the Greeks and Romans; couples wore betrothal crowns of wild marjoram.

Rosa (ROSE)—A symbol of love.

Rosmarinus (ROSEMARY)—An emblem of fidelity, rosemary was much used at weddings in the past; brides and bridesmaids wore it, gilded sprigs were given as favors and a few leaves were even mixed into the wedding cake.

Ruta (RUE)—Sometimes woven (together with rosemary, rowan berries and flowers) into a wedding wreath by the bride on her wedding eve; the Polish expression *siac rue* (sow rue) meant to be marriageable.

Wedding Seeds and Trees

Owners of Lemon trees or Linden trees may like to know that Linden blossoms are a symbol of conjugal love according to the "Language of Flowers" and Lemon flowers stand for fidelity in love. Orange blossoms (which send the message "Your purity equals your beauty") became popular in medieval bridal bouquets because the newly introduced Orange fruit was strongly associated with the union of the sexes.* In ancient Rome, Apples were symbols of love and were used in the marriage ceremony. Various seeds have also been connected with weddings; the custom of throwing Walnuts, reputed to promote love, dates back to ancient Greece. Wedding cakes in Mediterranean regions are still sometimes sprinkled with Sesame seeds to confer blessings. And then there is Rice! Pelting newlyweds with Rice probably originated in China or

---

*John Williamson, *The Oak King, The Holly King and the Unicorn* (New York: Harper & Row, 1986).

India as a fertility rite to grant couples many children and abundant harvests. In Connecticut bird lovers recently introduced a bill to ban this ancient custom, fearing that Rice thrown at weddings would swell in birds' stomachs and cause them to explode. It was suggested that birdseed be substituted. Ornithology experts at Cornell, however, have assured us that the time-honored custom is harmless and Rice is enjoyed by birds if not by brides.

A CITY GARDEN

City gardens suffer many drawbacks. Space is usually very limited and light deficient. While the garden is in shade much of the time, sunlight can suddenly become intense and, if reflected off pavement, cause damage in summer as well as winter. Often, there is below normal air circulation. Rooftop gardens, at the other extreme, suffer from too much sun and wind. The air itself may be high in pollutants. Most important, nearby buildings and overhangs can prevent adequate rainfall from reaching plants, making them quite dependent on water supplied by gardeners. For all of this gardeners need tough plants, but also, since space is limited, plants that look attractive throughout the season.

*Perennials for the Shady City Garden**

Aquilegia (COLUMBINE)
Astilbe (ASTILBE)—Needs moisture.
Bergenia (BERGENIA)—Prefers damp shade but grows anywhere.
Brunnera (SIBERIAN BUGLOSS)—Produces true blue flowers.
Convallaria (LILY OF THE VALLEY)—Tolerates dry soil.
Epimedium (EPIMEDIUM, BARRENWORT)—Likes shade and
    moisture-retentive soil but will tolerate dry soils in shade.
Galium (SWEET WOODRUFF)—Sun or shade.
Hemerocallis (DAYLILY)
Hosta (HOSTA, PLANTAIN LILY)
Polemonium (JACOB'S LADDER)
Pulmonaria (LUNGWORT)
Tradescantia (SPIDERWORT)—Also tolerates sun and poor
    conditions.

*Most have outstanding foliage.

Perennials for a Rooftop Garden

Achillea (YARROW)
Cerastium (SNOW-IN-SUMMER)
Chrysogonum (GOLDENSTAR)
Coreopsis (COREOPSIS, TICKSEED)
Gaillardia (BLANKETFLOWER)
Geranium (HARDY GERANIUM)*
Iberis (CANDYTUFT)
Lavandula (LAVENDER)
Liatris (BLAZING STAR)
Rudbeckia (BLACK-EYED SUSAN)
Stokesia (STOKES ASTER)
Yucca (YUCCA)

*Some species tolerate shade and drought. Sedums and fuzzy gray-leaved plants also do well in this type of garden. Pachysandra, Hedera (English Ivy), Vinca, Ajuga and some varieties of Euonymus are ground covers that will tolerate city conditions.

Shrubs for City Gardens

Abelia grandiflora (GLOSSY ABELIA)—Fragrant white flowers in summer. Not completely hardy north of New York City.
Berberis thunbergii (JAPANESE BARBERRY)—Red fall color and fruit.
Forsythia suspensa—This forsythia has good yellow fall color.
Ilex crenata (JAPANESE HOLLY)—Small evergreen leaves.
Kerria japonica (KERRIA)—Yellow flowers. Green twigs in winter.
Philadelphus coronarius (MOCK ORANGE)—Dense and tough with fragrant white flowers and yellow fall color.
Potentilla (SHRUBBY CINQUEFOIL)—Bright yellow flowers and fine texture; will withstand some shade in normal soil.
Pyracantha coccinea 'Lalandei' (FIRETHORN)—Evergreen with showy orange fruit; tolerates drought and air pollution. The U.S. National Arboretum's new variety, 'Pueblo,' is resistant to fire blight and scab and has a wide-spreading habit.
Rhodotypos tetrapetala (JETBEAD)—Black fruit remains all winter.
Taxus cuspidata (JAPANESE YEW)—One of the best evergreens for the city garden.
Viburnum opulus (EUROPEAN CRANBERRYBUSH)—White

flowers, red fall color and red fruit all winter. There is a dwarf form without flowers.

See also "A Moonlight Garden," pages 343–345, "Street Trees for Northern Urban Environments," pages 221–228, and "Water Needs of Container-Grown Ornamental Plants," pages 299–300.

DROUGHT-TOLERANT GARDENS

Recent studies have shown that water use in the United States has been declining, largely due to a drop in supply. If the future holds scarcer and more expensive water, and summers continue hot and dry as some predict, gardeners may want to consider plants that favor light, dry soils and can survive periods of low rainfall. Here are twenty-six drought-resistant perennials for sunny, well-drained sites (see also "Plants with Gray Leaves," pages 343–344, and "Herbs for Sunny, Dry Sites," pages 113–114).

Achillea (YARROW)
Amsonia (BLUE STAR)—Sun or partial shade; moist or dry soils.
Anthemis (CHAMOMILE; GOLDEN MARGUERITE)—May bloom in partial shade.
Armeria (SEA-PINK; THRIFT)
Artemisia—If grown just for foliage, some kinds will stand some shade.
Asclepias (BUTTERFLY WEED)
Callirhoe (POPPY MALLOW)
Centaurea (CORNFLOWER, HARDY BACHELOR'S BUTTON)
Coreopsis (COREOPSIS)
Echinops (GLOBE THISTLE)
Eryngium (SEA HOLLY)
Euphorbia (FLOWERING SPURGE AND CUSHION SPURGE)
Gaillardia (BLANKET FLOWER)
Gillenia (INDIAN PHYSIC)
Gypsophila (BABY'S BREATH)—Add lime if your soil is acid.
Heliopsis (HELIOPSIS)—Double-flowered forms are less drought tolerant.
Iberis (CANDYTUFT)—Moderately drought tolerant.
Lewisia (LEWISIA)—Likes moist springs and dry summers.
Liatris (BLAZING STAR)—L. spicata not as drought resistant as L. scariosa.
Limonium (SEA LAVENDER)

Opuntia (PRICKLY PEAR)
Sedum (STONECROP)
Sempervivum (HEN-AND-CHICKENS)
Stokesia (STOKE'S ASTER)—Protect where freezing and thawing
    alternate in winter.
Tradescantia (SPIDERWORT)
Yucca (YUCCA)

Grasses Tolerant of Dry Soil

Andropogon scoparius (LITTLE BLUESTEM)
Bouteloua gracilis (BLUE GRASS)
Festuca ovina (BLUE FESCUE)
Hordeum jubatum (SQUIRREL'S TAIL GRASS)
Panicum virgatum (SWITCH GRASS)
Stipa pennata (FEATHER GRASS)

FIRE-RESISTANT GARDENS

California is a fire-prone state; much of its native vegetation is easily ignited and even nonoily plants become increasingly flammable during the long summer dry season. Extension services and gardening magazines alike encourage gardeners to plant "fire-retardant" plants around their homes to help control damage from brush fires. The use of "gasoline" natives is discouraged, as is the planting of resinous trees such as pines and junipers. Plants should be kept well trimmed and cut back. The following appear on lists of plants suggested for fire protection, although it is well to remember that all plants will burn if conditions are right and most plants listed will need some irrigation during dry seasons if they are expected to slow fires.

Carpobrotus edulis (HOTTENTOT FIG)
Crassula spp. (FLOWERING CRASSULA; MINIATURE PINE TREE)
Delosperma spp. (ICEPLANT)
Drosanthemum spp. (ROSEA ICE PLANT)
Gazania rigens (TREASURE FLOWER)
Malephora crocea (CROCEUM ICEPLANT)
Osteospermum fruticosum (AFRICAN CREEPING DAISY)
Phyla nodiflora (FROGFRUIT)
Sedum spp. (SEDUM)
Yucca (YUCCA)

Some Shrubby Plants for Fire Protection

Arctostaphylos uva-ursi (BEARBERRY)
Baccharis pilularis (DWARF BACCHARIS, COYOTE BRUSH)
Ceanothus griseus var. horizontalis (CARMEL CREEPER)
Cistus spp. (ROCKROSE)
Hedera canariensis (ALGERIAN IVY)
Helianthemum nummularium (SUNROSE)
Heteromeles arbutifolia (TOYON)
Rosmarinus officinalis 'Prostratus' (CREEPING ROSEMARY)
Santolina spp. (LAVENDER COTTON)
Vinca spp. (PERIWINKLE)

AN ALLERGY-FREE GARDEN FOR THE SOUTHWEST

The Tucson Medical Center has published a list of plants recommended for planting in gardens of southwestern desert areas that will not contribute to the already high allergenic pollen counts of the region. Besides being "allergy-free," the plants on the following list have low water requirements.

Acacia farnesiana (SWEET ACACIA)—Flowers are visited by hummingbirds.
Agave spp.
Caesalpinia pulcherrima (DWARF POINCIANA)
Carnegiea gigantea (SAGUARO)—This cactus, which can grow 60 feet tall, has nocturnal white flowers and is Arizona's state flower.
Cassia artemisioides (FEATHER CASSIA)
Chilopsis linearis (DESERT WILLOW)—This small tree, which is not a willow, has trumpet-shaped flowers that attract hummingbirds.
Dasylirion wheeleri (DESERT SPOON)
Echinocactus (BARREL CACTUS)
Echinocereus (HEDGE HOG)
Fouquieria splendens (OCOTILLO)—Has red tubular flowers.
Hesperaloe parviflora (RED YUCCA)—Has showy nodding red flowers; this plant and Ocotillo probably attract hummingbirds.

Larrea tridentata (CREOSOTE BUSH)—The flower buds are pickled and eaten like capers.

Leucophyllum frutescens (TEXAS RANGER; BAROMETER BUSH)

Melampodium leucanthum (BLACK FOOT DAISY)

Oenothera spp. (DRUMMOND EVENING PRIMROSE AND MEXICAN EVENING PRIMROSE)—O. drummondii and O. speciosa var. childsii.

Opuntia violacea (SANTA RITA PRICKLY PEAR)—The pads or joints have a purplish color; flowers are yellow.

Salvia greggii (AUTUMN SALVIA; TEXAS SALVIA)—Another hummingbird plant with showy red flowers.

Simmondsia chinensis (JOJOBA)—Female shrubs produce an edible fruit with a high oil content.

Verbena sp. (DESERT VERBENA)

Yucca aloifolia (SPANISH BAYONET)

Yucca elata (SOAPTREE YUCCA)

Yucca rigida

The Tucson Medical Center warns that people who move to Arizona hoping to find relief from allergies in a desert environment will no doubt develop symptoms in response to new allergens in that area. The following plants are common offenders in southern Arizona:

Arizona Ash	Palo Verde*
Bermuda Grass	Pecan
Cottonwood	Rabbit Bush
Johnson Grass	Saltbush
Mesquite	Ragweed
Mulberry	Tumbleweed
Olive	

*This interesting native desert tree has heavy pollen that is not airborne but is allergenic. Gardeners are advised not to plant it next to windows and to avoid close contact with flowering trees.

Plants That Cause Hay Fever

Some plants depend upon insects for pollination while others, more self-sufficient, produce light, windborne pollen. It is this latter group that causes the seasonal suffering among those allergic to various pollens. Plants that are pollinated by insects, such as the much-maligned Goldenrod* generally do not cause hay fever. (Goldenrod is mistakenly blamed because it blooms in such profusion during the height of the fall hay-fever season, when the real villain, unspectacular Ragweed, often goes unnoticed.) Doctors call it pollinosis, but the common term "hay fever" is apt; pollen from grasses causes much of the summer discomfort in the East and Midwest. Below are the main plants responsible for hay fever during spring, summer and autumn:

SPRING:

Acer (MAPLE)
Betula (BIRCH)
Fraxinus (ASH)
Populus (COTTONWOOD)
Quercus (OAK)
Salix (WILLOW)
Ulmus (ELM)

Other trees, such as Alder, Cedar, Mulberry, Walnut and Pecan, may cause problems.

SUMMER:*

Agrostis (REDTOP)
Anthoxanthum (SWEET VERNAL GRASS)
Dactylis (ORCHARD GRASS)
Phleum (TIMOTHY)
Poa (JUNEGRASS, BLUEGRASS)

*Once mistakenly referred to as "Rose Fever" season.

AUTUMN:

Ambrosia (RAGWEED)—There are hundreds of varieties of Ragweed and it is the major cause of hay fever in the country; unfortunately, its pollen travels better than the spring pollen of most trees. The season depends on where you live. The East and Midwest experience the worst in late summer and early autumn; the season starts earlier and

*Very close contact with certain Composites, such as Zinnia, Cosmos and Goldenrod, may occasionally cause symptoms in Ragweed-sensitive people. The pollen of these plants, though heavy and insect borne, does resemble that of windborne Ragweed.

lasts longer in the South. There is a spring hay-fever season in the Southwest. Due to development, the plant has invaded many parts of the country once touted as Ragweed free—the desert regions of the Southwest, the forest regions of the North, many beach communities and the southern tip of Florida.

Other plants that can cause problems in parts of the country include Bermudagrass, Johnsongrass, Corn, the Artemisias (Sagebrush), Amaranth, Pigweed, Marsh Elder, Firebush, Russian Thistle, Sorrel, Cocklebur, Lamb's Quarters, English Plantain and Cannabis (Hemp).

THE "NEW AMERICAN" GARDEN

Recently, much has been written about the "New Romantic" or "New American" garden. Essentially this garden downplays lawns and is noted for lavish use of ornamental grasses and masses of perennials (some native or naturalized) that provide seasonal interest all year long. Foundation plantings are abolished, homes and gardens are screened from the street and the use of water is featured. There is no peak season in the New American garden, which is full of surprises and strives to be low care. Many of these New American ideas actually originated in the gardens of the Orient and have recently been championed by European garden designers. They go hand in hand with the new interest in meadow gardening that is sweeping the country. Given the right site and the right architecture, plantings of this kind can be very effective. Some plants favored by New Romantic designers follow.

PERENNIALS:

Achillea (YARROW)
Astilbe (ASTILBE)
Ceratostigma plumbaginoides (LEADWORT)
Coreopsis (COREOPSIS, TICKSEED)
Hibiscus moscheutos (ROSE MALLOW)
Hosta species (HOSTA)
Lythrum salicaria (PURPLE LOOSESTRIFE)*

*See "The Purple Tide," pages 150–151.

Rudbeckia (CONEFLOWER)
Sedum spectabile
Yucca (YUCCA)

MEDIUM- TO TALL-GROWING GRASSES:

Arundo donax (GIANT REED)—Coarse two-ranked blue-green leaves and height (which may reach more than 15 feet) make Giant Reed a stand out. A fine specimen near water but not hardy beyond zone 7. Flowers from midfall into winter in the South. There is a shorter but less hardy variegated form.

Calamagrostis x acutiflora 'Stricta' (FEATHER REED GRASS)—Clump-forming and upright to 5 feet; interesting from spring well into fall. Will tolerate some shade. C. arundinacea is similar but more arching.

Cortaderia selloana (PAMPAS GRASS)—South American native that can grow 10 feet tall; not reliably hardy north of zone 8. White or pale pink fall flowers are showiest on female plants.

Erianthus ravennae (PLUME GRASS, RAVENNA GRASS)—Another fall-blooming grass, hardy to zone 5, with upright but open and graceful form. Brown fall color is tinged with orange or purple.

Miscanthus sinensis (EULALIA GRASS)—This grass, which can reach 10 feet, has fluffy pinkish plumes in September. Fall color is beige/orange/brown. Sun or partial shade (clumps may need staking if grown in too shady a spot). There are several cultivars including a variegated form.

See pages 99–109 for more grass lists.

There are many other species of decorative grasses, including some beautiful American natives (see "Decorative Perennial Grasses and Sedges," pages 99–101). Beardgrass or Little Bluestem (Andropogon scoparius) is 1 to 2 feet tall, turns rosy-pink in the fall when it produces graceful tufts of fluff. Even Common Reed, Phragmites, the invasive halophyte that has choked out Cattails in low spots along highways, can be beautiful. This plant, which now ranges worldwide and covers large areas of former salt marsh in the Northeast, has blue-green leaves and purplish brown plumes in summer. Foliage may briefly turn gold in autumn when flower plumes change to shades of taupe, gray and brown.

7

Flowers That Attract Birds, Bees and Butterflies

FLOWERS FOR SONGBIRDS

Some birds, like House Wrens and Eastern Pewees, consume insects almost exclusively; most birds, however, eat a combination of animal (insects, worms) and plant material. Cardinals, Chickadees and Robins all consume insects during the summer and increase their intake of seeds during the fall and winter. The diet of a few birds (like Mourning Doves) consists solely of plant material such as weed seeds. Growers of Blueberries, Cherries and Grapes may not wish to attract birds to their grounds, but many gardeners do. Birds are allies in the war against insect pests and they brighten the landscape throughout the year.

Many garden flowers, especially members of the great Composite or Sunflower family, produce seeds that songbirds enjoy. The National Audubon Society recommends the following twenty bird-attracting flowers for your garden:

Amaranthus caudatus (LOVE-LIES-BLEEDING)
Aster spp. (ASTER)
Calendula (POT MARIGOLD)

Callistephus chinensis (CHINA ASTER)
Campanula spp. (BELLFLOWERS)
Celosia spp. (PRINCE'S FEATHER AND PRINCE'S PLUMES)
Centaurea spp. (BACHELOR'S BUTTON, BASKET FLOWER AND
    CORNFLOWER)
Chrysanthemum spp. (CHRYSANTHEMUM)
Commelina spp. (DAYFLOWERS)
Coreopsis spp. (COREOPSIS)
Cosmos spp. (COSMOS)
Helianthus annuus* (SUNFLOWER)
Phlox spp.—especially P. drummondii
Portulaca spp.—especially P. grandiflora (Moss Rose)
Rudbeckia spp. (BLACK-EYED SUSAN)
Scabiosa atropurpurea (SWEET SCABIOUS)
Silene spp. (CAMPION)
Tagetes spp. (MARIGOLDS)
Verbena hybrida (GARDEN VERBENA)
Zinnia elegans (ZINNIA)

*Seeds eaten by at least 42 bird species.

"WEEDS" FOR THE BIRDS

Many so-called weeds produce seeds and berries that are important food sources for birds. It may please gardeners to know that the seeds of two of their least-loved plants, Ragweed and Crabgrass, are beloved by many birds. Ten important weeds are:

Ambrosia (RAGWEED)—Seeds eaten by 60 species of birds.
Capsella (SHEPHERD'S PURSE)
Digitaria (CRABGRASS)—Over 20 bird species enjoy crabgrass
    seeds.
Chenopodium (LAMB'S QUARTERS)
Phytolacca (POKEWEED)—Loved by birds but may intoxicate
    some.
Plantago (PLANTAIN)
Polygonum (KNOTWEED)
Rumex (SORREL)
Setaria (BRISTLE GRASS)
Stellaria (CHICKWEED)

TREES AND SHRUBS THAT ATTRACT BIRDS

Evergreens such as Hemlock, Spruce, Pine, Juniper and Arborvitae provide refuge for birds in summer as well as winter and are important nesting sites. They are also important food trees. Here are twenty-five deciduous trees and shrubs that are favored by birds:

Amelanchier (SHADBUSH)
Carya (HICKORY)
Celtis (HACKBERRY)
Cornus (DOGWOOD)
Crataegus (HAWTHORN)
Elaeagnus (RUSSIAN OLIVE AND AUTUMN OLIVE)
Fagus (BEECH)
Gaylussacia (HUCKLEBERRY)
Ilex (WINTERBERRY AND AMERICAN HOLLY)
Lindera (SPICEBUSH)
Lonicera (HONEYSUCKLE)*
Malus (APPLE; CRABAPPLE)
Morus (MULBERRY)
Myrica (BAYBERRY)
Nyssa (SOURGUM, TUPELO)
Prunus (CHOKECHERRY)
Pyracantha (FIRETHORN)
Quercus (OAK)
Rosa (ROSE)
Rhus (SUMAC)
Sambucus (ELDERBERRY)
Sassafras (SASSAFRAS)
Sorbus (MOUNTAIN ASH)
Vaccinium (BLUEBERRY)
Viburnum (AMERICAN CRANBERRYBUSH, DOUBLEFILE, NANNYBERRY AND OTHERS)

*Some imported Honeysuckles (such as Tatarian) have become pests in the woods, choking out more desirable native species. Ecology-minded gardeners may wish to refrain from planting invasive nonnatives (see also "Pernicious Woody Immigrants," pages 261–262).

Birds are also very fond of the various species of Rubus (Blackberries, Raspberries), which provide food, cover and safe nesting sites. Viticulturists are well aware of birds' fondness for grapes.

How to Discourage Birds

If you like birds but want to raise Blueberries or Grapes on a scale that rules out netting, a new product from Japan may be of interest. Inflatable bird-scare balloons decorated with giant "eyes" and reflective stickers that hang above crops seem to be very effective at scaring off all types of birds except robins.

FLOWERS THAT ATTRACT HUMMINGBIRDS

Hummingbirds are New World natives, so it's not surprising that many of the plants that attract them are native to the Americas. Hummingbirds can't smell, so flowers need not be fragrant, but the tiny birds do seem to have a preference for red. When planting for hummingbirds, therefore, "think red" (and pink and orange) and look for big solitary blossoms or loose, drooping clusters.

GARDEN FLOWERS:

Althea (HOLLYHOCK)
Fuchsia (FUCHSIA)
Lilium (TIGER LILY)
Mirabilis (FOUR O'CLOCK)
Petunia (PETUNIA)
Phlox (PHLOX)
Salvia (SCARLET SAGE)
Tropaeolum (NASTURTIUM)

WILDFLOWERS:

Aesclepias (BUTTERFLY WEED)
Aquilegia (COLUMBINE)
Castilleja (PAINTED CUPS)
Gilia (SCARLET GILIA)
Impatiens (JEWELWEED)
Lobelia (CARDINAL FLOWER)
Monarda (BEE BALM)
Oenothera (EVENING PRIMROSE)

SHRUBS AND VINES FOR HUMMINGBIRDS

Ten shrubs and vines that attract hummingbirds are:

Arctostaphylos (MANZANITA)
Buddleia* (BUTTERFLY BUSH)
Campsis* (TRUMPET VINE)
Hibiscus (ROSE OF SHARON, SHRUB-ALTHEA)
Ipomoea (MORNING GLORY)
Kolkwitzia (BEAUTYBUSH)
Lonicera (HONEYSUCKLE)
Rhododendron (AZALEA)
Symphoricarpos (CORALBERRY)
Weigela (WEIGELA)

*Also attracts butterflies.

The following trees also attract hummingbirds, although they may not be easy to spot among the treetops: Horse Chestnut, Red Buckeye, Mimosa, Siberian Peatree, Crabapple, Quince, Black Locust, Pacific Madrone and Citrus.

FLOWERS FOR BUTTERFLIES

Like hummingbirds, butterflies also respond to color. Purple seems to attract them most, followed by yellow, pink and white. Butterflies flock to certain nectar-producing flowers and also to plants that are food sources for their young. For example, Monarch larvae feed on Milkweed* leaves and adult Monarchs feed on (and pollinate) Milkweed flowers as well as flowers of other plants, such as Joe-Pye Weed and Seaside Goldenrod (the latter is a food source during the long migration south in late summer). Entice "floating flowers" to your landscape by planting some of the following:

Ageratum (FLOSSFLOWER)
Arabis (ROCK CRESS)
Aristolochia (DUTCHMAN'S PIPE VINE)
Asclepias (BUTTERFLY WEED)

*Birds do not molest Monarchs; the toxins they ingest from Milkweed (but are immune to) protect both larvae and adults.

Buddleia (BUTTERFLY BUSH)
Cornus (DOGWOOD)—Attracts the Common Blue or Spring
    Azure.
Cosmos (COSMOS)
Echinacea (PURPLE CONEFLOWER)
Echinops (GLOBE THISTLE)
Impatiens (IMPATIENS)
Lantana (LANTANA)
Lavandula (LAVENDER)
Monarda (BEEBALM)
Paeonia (PEONY)
Phlox (PHLOX)
Primula (PRIMROSE)
Rudbeckia (CONEFLOWER, BLACK-EYED SUSAN)
Salix caprea (PUSSY WILLOW)—Attracts hibernators such as
    Mourning Cloak and Tortoiseshell.
Salvia (SAGE)
Sedum spectabile (STONECROP)—Sedum is a foodplant for
    Buckeye larvae.
Syringa (LILAC)
Tagetes (MARIGOLD)
Zinnia (ZINNIA)

Wild Plants That Attract Butterflies

The following are plants that larvae feed upon (some caterpillars, such as Monarchs, feed on only one type of plant; others, like Painted Ladies, eat a wider variety):

Asters (FIELD CRESCENTS)
Clover (CLOUDED SULPHURS, SKIPPERS)
Gerardia (BUCKEYES)
Hackberry (MOURNING CLOAK)
Milkweed (MONARCHS)
Nettles (RED ADMIRALS, PAINTED LADIES, QUESTION MARKS)
Painted Cups (CHECKERSPOTS)
Queen Anne's Lace (BLACK SWALLOWTAIL*)
Sassafras (SPICEBUSH SWALLOWTAIL)
Thistle (PAINTED LADIES)

---

*Beautiful Swallowtail caterpillars also feed on parsley, parsnip, carrot, dill, fennel and citrus.

Turtlehead (BALTIMORES)
Violets (FRITILLARIES)

Where to Visit the Butterflies

California

(Vallejo): Live butterfly exhibit at Marine World/Africa USA.

Florida

(Coconut Creek): Butterfly World. See 3,000 live butterflies from around the world.

Georgia

(Pine Mountain): Callaway Gardens. Recently opened Day Butterfly Center is the largest glass-enclosed butterfly conservatory in North America. The Center also houses hummingbirds.

OF BUTTERFLIES AND HUMMINGBIRDS

Milkweeds fend off many insect predators with their toxic milky sap, but not Monarch Butterfly caterpillars, which prefer Milkweed exclusively. Monarchs are not affected by the poison and even use it to discourage their own predators. Relationships between plants and their insect predators and pollinators are ancient ones; scientists at the University of Arizona have recently reported an aphid/Rhus association believed to be 48 million years old. It is an ongoing race. Plants develop protective toxins; predators then develop the ability to ingest them without harm. Some even acquire a special taste for the once-avoided substance! Other insects appear to "disarm" plants with toxic sap by simply cutting a vein and letting juices drain. With this chore completed, a safe meal is enjoyed.

Plants are not without some tricks of their own. Quite a few seem able to increase their production of poisons when predators appear. They are expert at luring pollinators, often promising a drink of sweet nectar but not delivering. Still others lure insects into fatal traps. According to recent reports,* Scarlet Gilia, a native of the western United States, is especially versatile when it comes to attracting pollinators. Instead of

*Ken Paige and Thomas Whitham, "Individual and Population Shifts in Flower Color by Scarlet Gilia: A Mechanism for Pollinator Tracking," *Science,* vol. 227, 18 January 1985, p. 315.

relying on just one, it can attract two, changing flower color to suit the color preference of the pollinator at hand. During the early part of the flowering season, Scarlet Gilia's flowers are red to attract hummingbirds. Sometimes, however, hummingbirds leave the area before the flowering season is over; Scarlet Gilia then changes the color of its blossoms to white or pink to suit the Hawk Moth, which takes over for the absent hummingbirds. Scarlet Gilia, true to its name, prefers red. In areas where hummingbirds remain, blossoms stay red throughout the growing season.

PLANTS FOR HONEYBEES

Honeybees, pollinators par excellence, should be welcome by all gardeners. They are not the only bees that are important pollinators in home orchards, but they are the only species of bee out of several thousand other species in the United States that makes honey. Honeybees have excellent color vision (although they do not see red well) and can detect patterns and nectar guides in flowers that appear solid white to us. They collect both pollen and nectar; pollen is the protein source used to feed their larvae. Below are some valuable food sources for honeybees:

Arabis
Aster
Bergamot
Borage*
Buckwheat
Clover—Especially white.
Crocus
Dandelion
Goldenrod
Lavender
Lythrum
Marjoram
Melissa—Name means "bee" in Greek.
Raspberry*
Rosemary
Sage
Sweet Cicely**

*Special favorite that provides superior honey; frequented by bees even in wet weather.
**Leaves of this plant were once rubbed over the interior of hives to induce new swarms to enter.

Canada Thistle
Thyme

Trees that honey bees favor are Fruit trees (especially Apple), Linden, Locust, Hawthorn, Sugar Maple, Sycamore, Tulip Tree and Willow.

If a Honeybee Stings

Only a female bee can sting, although males may go through the motions. Most bees and wasps sting only as a last resort. Honeybees are especially reluctant to sting: They fly off leaving their stinger behind in the victim (the only bee in the U.S. to do so) and always die shortly after. If you (and the bee) are unfortunate enough to make contact, never squeeze the stinger in an effort to remove it. You will succeed only in giving yourself another injection of venom. Rather, brush the stinger off with a sideways movement. There are many effective products on the market to relieve the pain of bee sting. Before they appeared, people relied on herbal remedies such as the crushed leaves of Plantain and Savory or the juice from ripe Honeysuckle berries, still thought by many to give excellent results.

8

Vegetables

SOME RECENT ALL-AMERICA SELECTIONS
VEGETABLE WINNERS

1988 Cucumber 'Salad Bush'—Said to be high yielding and to require only two square feet of growing space.

1988 Okra 'Burgundy'—Unique fruit color; ornamental and edible.

1988 Pepper 'Mexi Bell'—Bell Pepper with a pungent flavor.

1988 Pepper 'Super Chili'—Said to be hotter than a Jalapeno.

1988 Sweet Corn 'Honey 'N Pearl'—Bicolor corn that supposedly "retains excellent eating quality several days after harvest."

1987 Pumpkin 'Autumn Gold'—Vigorous hybrid yielding 10-pound fruits and turning gold at the immature stage.

1986 Sweet Corn 'How Sweet It Is'—This white corn is extra sweet with good holding quality.

1986 Okra 'Blondy'—Early, dwarf Okra with tender pods; performs even in short-season areas.

1985 Lettuce 'Red Sails'—Decorative red Lettuce handsome for the flower garden.

1985 Scalloped Squash 'Sunburst'—First hybrid scalloped yellow squash with a rich, buttery flavor. Fifty days from sowing to harvest.

1984 **Tomato 'Celebrity'**—Flavorful, high yielding and disease resistant.

1984 **Snap Pea 'Sugar Ann'**—Early and dwarf; can be grown in garden or container.

The following All-America Gold Medal Vegetable Winners are still in commerce:

Bean 'Topcrop'—1950
Bush Lima Bean 'Fordhook 242'—1945
Broccoli 'Green Comet'—1969
Cabbage 'Ruby Ball'—1972
Cabbage 'Savoy Ace'—1977
Cantaloupe 'Honey Rock'—1933
Corn 'Iochief'—1951
Cucumber 'Straight Eight'—1935
Lettuce 'Salad Bowl'—1952
Pea Edible Podded 'Sugar Snap'—1979
Squash 'Caserta'—1949
Watermelon 'New Hampshire Midget'—1951

PLANT SOURCES OF IRON AND CALCIUM

Although iron and calcium are more readily absorbed from the animal products we consume, plants should not be overlooked as sources for these minerals. Many wild-food enthusiasts, such as the late Euell Gibbons, extolled the virtues of plants such as Marsh Marigold, Purslane, Chickweed and Stinging Nettle as rich sources of iron. Here are some less exotic plant sources of iron. Be sure to eat iron-rich foods together with foods high in Vitamin C to insure the best absorption.

Beta (BEET GREENS AND SWISS CHARD)
Brassica (MUSTARD GREENS, TURNIP GREENS, COLLARDS, KALE, BROCCOLI, BRUSSEL SPROUTS)
Cicer (CHICK PEA*)
Glycine (SOY BEAN*)
Ipomoea (SWEET POTATO)
Lens (LENTIL*)
Lycopersicon (TOMATO)

*Extra-rich source.

Nasturtium (WATERCRESS)
Petroselinum (PARSLEY)
Phaseolus (GREEN BEAN,* KIDNEY BEAN,* PINTO BEAN*)
Solanum (EGGPLANT, POTATO)
Spinacia (SPINACH*)
Taraxacum (DANDELION GREENS)
Vigna (MUNG BEAN,* BLACK-EYED PEA)

*Extra-rich source.

Raisins, dried Apricots, dried Prunes and Prune juice are also rich in iron. Persimmons, Elderberries, Dates, Strawberries, Raspberries, Watermelon, Blueberries, Blackberries, dried Apples and Peaches, Bananas, Figs, Apple juice, Peanuts, Pecans, Walnuts and seeds such as Sesame, Sunflower and Pumpkin also contain the mineral. Process foods as little as possible and don't forget to use an iron pot!

Some calcium-rich foods:

Brassica (MUSTARD GREENS,* TURNIP GREENS,* COLLARDS,* KALE,*
      BROCCOLI,* CABBAGE)
Cicer (CHICK PEA*)
Citrus (ORANGE)
Glycine (SOYBEAN*)
Pastinaca (PARSNIP)
Phaseolus (LIMA BEAN, RED KIDNEY, SNAP BEANS)
Phoenix (DATES)
Rheum (RHUBARB*)
Spinacia (SPINACH*)
Taraxacum (DANDELION GREENS*)

*Extra-rich source.

Dried Peaches and Apricots, Prunes, Blackberries, roasted Peanuts, Almonds, Filberts and Sesame seeds are also good sources of calcium. Canned Sauerkraut also contains a fair amount of this mineral.

HEIRLOOM VEGETABLES

Home owners who want to plant flowers in keeping with their colonial houses may wish to try a few heirloom vegetables in the vegetable garden. Horticulturists at Cornell University claim that old varieties of celery, cucumber and muskmelon are disease prone and difficult to grow. All listed below were grown in the nineteenth century; some were in cultivation long before. Ten to try:

Bean—Lazy Wife
Beet—Early Blood Turnip
Carrot—Early Scarlet Horn*
Cabbage—Late Flat Dutch*
Corn—Stowell's Evergreen (New World native)
Lettuce—Paris White Cos*
Onion—White Portugal*
Peas—Dwarf Sugar
Radish—Black Spanish*
Squash—White Patty-Pan* (New World native)

*Probably grown in America before 1800.

Most of these varieties (and many others) can be seen in the Ronald U. Pounder Heritage Garden, Cornell Plantations, Ithaca, New York. An information bulletin, "The Heirloom Vegetable Garden," may be obtained by writing to: Distribution Center, 7 Research Park, Cornell University, Ithaca, NY 14850. Contact your local extension service for suggested heirloom varieties for your area.

SOURCES FOR HEIRLOOM VEGETABLE AND FLOWER SEEDS

It is a good idea to order from a supplier near you.

Abundant Life Seed Foundation
PO Box 772
Port Townsend, WA 98368

W. Atlee Burpee Company
Warminster, PA 18991

Gurney Seed & Nursery
Company
Gurney Building
Yankton, SD 57079

Heirloom Garden Seeds
PO Box 138
Guerneville, CA 95446

Johnny's Selected Seeds
Albion, ME 04910

Park Seed Company
Greenwood, SC 29647

Plants of the Southwest
1812 Second St.
Santa Fe, NM 87501

Shepherd's Garden Seeds
7389 W. Zayante Rd.
Felton, CA 95018

Thompson & Morgan, Inc. Vermont Bean Seed Company
PO Box 1308 Garden Lane
Jackson, NJ 08527-0308 Fair Haven, VT 05743

Garden Seed Inventory, which lists all seed catalogs that have nonhybrid vegetable seeds available in the U.S. and Canada, may be ordered from Seed Saver Publications, RR 3, Box 239, Decorah, IA 52101.

ORNAMENTAL VEGETABLES

No space for a vegetable garden? Take heart! Not all vegetable plants usually confined to plots in back of the house are ugly ducklings that deserve to remain there. Some, because of decorative foliage, flowers or even fruit are attractive enough for flower borders, planters or accents in the landscape. A dozen ornamental edibles:

Allium (ONION)—Common Chives (A. schoenoprasum) and Garlic Chives (A. tuberosum) are both beauties in flower; the former with small rose pompons, later-blooming Garlic Chives with white, sweet-smelling clusters. Both are perennials and both have attractive, grasslike foliage in clumps 1 to 2 feet tall.

Beta (BEET, SWISS CHARD)—These plants have handsome leaves, many with red-violet stems and veining and most will tolerate a little shade. Some crimson-leaved cultivars are grown for ornament alone.

Brassica (KALE)—Small culinary Kales such as 'Vates' and 'Blue Surf' have frilly blue-green leaves. Ornamental Kale, which turns colorfully pink/purple in the fall, is also edible though not as succulent. Sea Kale (Crambe) has decorative large blue leaves as well as masses of attractive white flowers. It does best in full sun and limy, sandy soil; spring leaves are tasty blanched.

Capsicum (PEPPER)—Most Peppers are tidy plants with glossy, dark green leaves, small white flowers and shiny golden, red or purple fruit.

Cichorium (RADICCHIO)—A variety of Chicory (and a relative of Endive), Radicchio turns maroon in the fall and can be grown in many parts of the United States. Try 'Giulio' or 'Rosso di Verona' in New England.

Cynara (ARTICHOKE, CARDOON)—Spectacular plants that need plenty of room and moisture. Artichoke has beautiful gray (but spiny) foliage; try 'Violetto,' one of the smaller cultivars with dark purple heads. Cardoons, also with silvery leaves, are grown for wide, edible stems.

Lactuca (LETTUCE)—The leaf Lettuces, several with puckered, red-tinted leaves, are especially decorative. Try 'Red Sails,' 'Ruby' or 'Lollo Rossa.'

Lycopersicon (TOMATO)—Most Tomato plants would not win a beauty contest, but some of the new compact varieties are attractive. 'Red Robin' produces good-tasting fruit (above the leaves so it can be seen); 'Pixie II' is a little taller and disease-resistant.

Phaseolus (SCARLET RUNNER BEAN)—Pink, white or red-flowered vines are available and flowers, pods and seeds all make good eating. 'Common Scarlet' (red) and 'Desiree' (white) are excellent.

Rheum (RHUBARB)—Large, round leaves with wavy margins are showy; several cultivars (such as 'Cherry') have bright red leaf stalks. Some garden cultivars do not produce flowers while others will blossom on impressive 6-foot stalks.

Solanum (EGGPLANT)—Fuzzy leaves, purple flowers and glossy purple (or white) fruit make Eggplant a decorative addition to the garden. Perennial and shrubby in the South; cultivated as an annual in most of the country. Small 'Ruffled Red' is especially attractive; 'Easter Egg' is a compact plant that produces small white fruits.

Spinacia (SPINACH)—Attractive, deep green leaves; a cool-weather crop that will take a little shade. (Unrelated New Zealand Spinach, Tetragonia, does better in hot weather.) 'Vienna' is an early, disease-resistant variety with glossy, curly leaves.

Don't forget to include Strawberries, Nasturtiums and herbs such as Parsley and 'Opal' or 'Purple Ruffles' Basil in your garden of beautiful edibles.

TOMATOES FOR EVERYONE

Who does not grow tomatoes? They are the most popular vegetable (really a fruit) grown in U.S. gardens today (followed by Peppers,

Onions, Cucumbers, Green Beans and Lettuce)—not bad for a food once shunned and believed poisonous. Native to the Americas, and related to other New World members of the Nightshade family such as Potato and Peppers (Eggplant is an Old World member), there are hundreds of named varieties of the Tomato we cultivate, Lycopersicon lycopersicum.

Which Tomatoes to Plant?

One mistake gardeners make is to select only one variety. If space permits, plant several: one for fruit early in the season, one for midseason and a late producer. Another mistake is to select Tomato varieties on the basis of fruit size alone. Some highly advertised "Big" and "Beefy" Tomatoes are inferior to many others. Be sure to plant disease-resistant varieties. So many fine cultivars are resistant to Verticillium wilt (V) and two races of Fusarium wilt (F) that it makes little sense to plant varieties that are not. Look for the letters VF on labels and seed packages. Plants resistant to Nematodes (N) are also available. Experimenters will be glad to learn that, according to *Hortus Third*, the selection of a cultivar for the home garden is much less crucial than for many other vegetables. Nevertheless, regional lists vary; your local extension agent can recommend varieties for your area.

Tomato Lists from around the Country

Here are suggested Tomato varieties for New England (based on "1988 New England Vegetable Production Recommendations," ed. E. Bouton, and "Suggested Vegetable Varieties for Connecticut," by R. A. Ashley, Connecticut Cooperative Extension Service, University of Connecticut Storrs, Connecticut). Note: Determinate (Det.) plants produce bushy growth, are not as tall and rangy as Indeterminates (Ind.) and generally do not bear fruit for as long a period of time. Indeterminates always need caging or staking.

EARLY:

Springset (VF) Det.
Spring Giant Hybrid* (VFN) Det.
Ultra Girl (VFN) Semi-Det.
Early Girl (v) Ind.
Basket Vee (v) Det.—Of special value in northern New England.

*All-America Selection. Celebrity, selected in 1984, is also resistant to Tobacco Mosaic Virus.

MIDSEASON:

Terrific (VFN) Ind.
Pik-Red (VFFN) Det.
Better Boy (VFN) Ind.
Roadside Red (VF) Ind.
Ole (VFF) Det.

Jet Star (VF) Ind.
Celebrity* (VFFN) Det.
Ultra Boy (VFN) Ind.
Mountain Pride (VFF) Det.
Monte Carlo (VFN) Ind.

LATE:

Supersonic (VF) Det.   **Burpee's Long Keeper**** Ind.

FOR PASTE:

Roma (VF) Det.

CHERRY:

Small Fry (VFN) Det.
Sweet 100** Ind.
Pixie II (VF) Det.—Noted for its very early maturity, small
    size and adaptibility to pot culture.

*All-America Selection. Celebrity, selected in 1984, is also resistant to Tobacco
Mosaic Virus.
**Do not appear to be disease-resistant, but are sufficiently unique to merit planting.

The following wilt-resistant Tomato varieties are suggested for California (based on the recommendations of William Simms, extension vegetable specialist, and Dennis Hall, extension plant pathologist, University of
California, Davis).

EARLY:

Royal Flush   **Pakmor B**
Peto 6718

MID- TO LATE SEASON:

Pearson A1 (NOT RESISTANT   **VF Royal Ace**
    TO FUSARIUM WILT)   **VFN-8***
Castlemart   **Calmart***
Ace 55   **VFN-Bush***

*Nematode resistant.

Dennis R. Pittenger, extension urban horticulturist, University of California, Riverside, recommends the following varieties for the central and north coastal areas and cool valleys (that is, cool to moderate summers with evening temperatures often in the 45 to 55 degree F range) from Santa Maria north to the Oregon border including the San Francisco Bay area (those marked *TMV* are resistant to Tobacco Mosiac Virus.):

Bingo (VFTMV) Det.—Large fruit
Carmelo (VFNTMV) Semi-Det.
Valerie (VFN) Det.—Early medium fruit

Among Mr. Pittenger's suggestions for the warmer sections of California:

Ace Hybrid (VFN) Det.
Better Boy (VFN) Ind.
Celebrity (VFNTMV) Semi-Det.
Champion (VFNTMV) Ind.
Early Girl (V) Ind.
Early Pick (VF) Ind.
Floramerica (VF) Det.—AAS Winner in 1978.
Jet Star (VF) Ind.
Quick Pick (VFNTMV) Ind.
Royal Flush (VFN) Det.
7718VF (VF) Semi-Det.—Widely adapted; also called San Diego Hybrid.
Whopper (VFNTMV) Ind.—Medium-size fruit in spite of the name.

Here are some Tomato varieties for Georgia suggested by J. Barber, P. Colditz and W. McLaurin, Cooperative Extension Service, University of Georgia College of Agriculture, Athens, Georgia:

Bigset (VFN) Det.
Bonnie (VFN) Ind.
Better Boy (VFN) Ind.
Monte Carlo (VFN) Ind.
Walter Villemarie (FF) Det.—Resistant to blossom end rot, cracking, catface and graywall.
Manapal (F) Ind.—Resistant to gray leaf spot.

The American Horticultural Society recommends the varieties on the following page for the South:

Chico (F) Det.　　　　　　　**Roma** (VF) Det.

Note: Floradade (VFF) Det., a University of Florida introduction, is adapted to calcareous soils and resistant to gray leaf spot. Floramerica (VFF) Det., also developed by the University of Florida, was an All-America Winner in 1978. It is disease-resistant and adapted to a wide range of growing conditions.

SOURCES FOR TOMATO SEEDS

Abundant Life Seed Foundation
Box 772
Port Townsend, WA 98368

W. A. Burpee & Co.
300 Park Ave.
Warminster, PA 18991

Harris Seeds
961 Lyell Ave.
Rochester, NY 14606

Johnny's Selected Seeds
310 Foss Hill Rd.
Albion, ME 04910

Park Seed Company
Cokesbury Rd.
Greenwood, SC 29647-0001

Pinetree Garden Seeds
New Gloucester, ME 04260

Shepherd's Garden Seeds
7389 W. Zayante Rd.
Felton, CA 95018

Siberia Seeds
Box 2026
Sweetgrass, MT 59484
Cold-hardy and heirloom
Tomatoes including the Siberia
Tomato

The Tomato Seed Company
PO Box 323
Metuchen, NJ 08840
Modern varieties as well as
heirlooms

Tomato Growers Supply
Company
PO Box 2237
Fort Meyers, FL 33902

Otis S. Twilley Seed Company
PO Box 65
Trevose, PA 19047

The Best Tomatoes, 1877

Writing in the December 1877 *Rural New-Yorker,* Professor W. J. Beal recommends the following "choice" Tomato varieties for planting in the spring of 1878. Professor Beal grew these varieties in a test garden during the previous summer and listed them according to their productivity, with The Conqueror being the best producer and Trophy producing the least number of fruits (though they were of exceptional size).

The Conqueror	Arlington
The Hundred Days	Cheeney
Canada Victor	Hathaway
Golden Trophy	Hathaway (COLLEGE)
Emily	Trophy

Professor Beal writes: "The Conqueror came off conqueror for early use. From previous experience, when the plants are started early, I prefer Trophy for the late pickings. I must confess that Hathaway has fallen behind my expectations, although the form and ripening are almost perfection. Canada Victor and Hundred Days also rank high. It is possible that experiments made with seeds of these varieties, all raised in one place, would give different results from those above."*

Seed Saver's Exchange

Where is The Conqueror today? Apparently lost, along with the other subjects of Professor Beal's experiments and many other old vegetable varieties. Why does it matter, when we have good, disease-resistant modern hybrids? It matters because agricultural crops are placed at risk when genetic diversity is lost. Old varieties, which were often particularly suited to local conditions, also carried genes that might, at some future date, prove valuable should new diseases strike—or growing conditions change dramatically.

Seeds Savers Exchange, founded by Kent Whealy of Decorah, Iowa, is dedicated to preserving what remains of our agricultural heritage. Garden Seed Inventory, first published in 1985, catalogs every available nonhybrid vegetable variety and encourages gardeners to buy and plant them. Seeds from the old varieties may be saved to plant next season, unlike hybrid seed, which must be purchased from the developer each year. Mr. Whealy declares that hybrid corn is vastly superior to nonhybrid corn, but that little difference exists between other hybrid and standard varieties of self-pollinated crops; in other words, the best standard tomatoes and peppers have never been surpassed by the hybrids. For more information write to: Seed Saver Publications, Rural Route 3, Box 239, Decorah, IA 52101.

---

*All seeds used in Professor Beal's study came from New York, although from various locations within the state.

The Cannibal Tomato

The Garden Tomato and its close relatives are a vast and enterprising group of plants. A cold-hardy Siberian Tomato is said to set fruit at 38 degrees F; a Tomato on the Galapagos Islands is tolerant of saltspray and another South American variety is so drought resistant that it survives on the moisture it receives from fog alone.* John Riley, editor of the *Solanaceae Enthusiasts Quarterly* (3370 Princeton Ct., Santa Clara, CA 95051; annual dues $10.00), writes of a Tomato found in Samoa and the Cook Islands known as the Cannibal Tomato (Solanum anthropophagorum): "The fruit may be red or yellow; the skin is tough and thick. The shrub is 2–4 or even 6 feet high. Leaves are dark glossy green, 3–5 inches long. The name (anthropophagorum) has to do with the fact that the leaves were used to wrap human bodies for cooking." Mr. Riley is growing the Cannibal Tomato. He has found the pot liquor pleasant. The leaves have a good texture and a "nice vegetablelike taste." He also describes a "nutlike" flavor. Others who sampled the leaves said they were at least as good as spinach. The small red fruit is "sour but edible" and the plant makes "a good houseplant," according to Mr. Riley.

Tomato Facts and Fancies

- Tomatoes that are refrigerated lose flavor and aroma. When possible, eat tomatoes right after picking; flavor peaks within a few minutes.

- One medium-size Tomato contains about three-fourths of the adult recommendation (RDA) for Vitamin C and about one-third the RDA for Vitamin A. Tomatoes also contain B vitamins and iron.

- Because of their acidity, Tomatoes retain their Vitamin C content exceptionally well during storage and cooking.

- Tomatoes are very low in sodium. They are also low in calories, with about 40 calories per Tomato.

- The fruit of the Tomato plant may be red, orange, yellow, pink or white. White Beauty is a modern white-fruited variety; its fruit matures in 85 to 90 days.

---

*From Rebecca Rupp, *Blue Corn and Square Tomatoes* (Pownal, Vt.: Storey Communications, Inc., 1987). Ms. Rupp claims that the "small yellow egg-shaped fruit" of the Cannibal Tomato was eaten "routinely by Islanders as a stomach-settling chaser after a main meal of their human foes."

- Orange-hued Tomatoes contain more carotene than red ones.
- Researchers in South Carolina report that Tomato plants grown over a red plastic mulch produced higher yields than those grown using ordinary black plastic for mulch.
- Researchers at Penn State concluded that high-density planting may increase Tomato production.
- Cracks on Tomatoes develop when a sudden downpour follows a dry period. To prevent this from happening keep plants mulched and water regularly.
- To help Tomato plants grown in cooler climates set fruit, lightly shake plants or wiggle the tops of stakes. This enhances pollination.
- Tomatoes (from the Aztec word *tomatl*) once were called "love-apples" and were believed to be aphrodisiacs. They were also once thought to be poisonous.
- Thomas Jefferson raised Tomatoes at Monticello long before they were accepted as desirable food by the average American.
- Italians were the first Europeans to recognize the culinary potential of the Tomato.

THRIPS-RESISTANT CABBAGE

After several years of testing, the New York State Agricultural Experiment Station at Geneva, New York, has identified several cabbage varieties as resistant or tolerant to thrips. No variety tested was totally resistant, but the following all remained essentially undamaged by these pests. For updated or additional information (early fresh market varieties have not yet been screened though testing begins soon for worm resistance), contact the Experiment Station, Dept. of Horticultural Sciences, Hedrick Hall, Geneva, NY 14456.

Falcon	**Ocala**
Genesis	**Pennant**
Grand Prize	**Picus**
Grand Slam	**Rio Grande**
King Cole	**Round Up**
Little Rock	**Sunre 4018**

HOT PEPPER CHECKLIST

Both Sweet and Chili Peppers belong to the genus Capsicum, and capsaicin is the magic ingredient that makes Peppers hot. The amount of this firey resin present in Peppers depends on the variety and the weather—dry weather generally produces hotter Peppers. Dr. Ben Villalon of the Texas Agricultural Experiment Station has recently compiled a revised heat scale for Peppers (10 is the hottest rating):

Bahamian, Habanero (10)
Santaka (JAPANESE), **Chiltecpin** (THAI) (9)
Piquin, Cayenne, Tabasco (8)
De Arbol (7)
Yellow Wax, Serrano (6)
Jalapeno, Mirasol (5)
Sandia, Cascabel, Rocotillo (4)
Hot Ancho, Pasilla (3)
Big Jim, Anaheim (2)
R-Naky, El Paso, Cherry (1)
Bells, Pimento, Sweet Banana (0)

Peppers rated 5 and above can burn the skin and eyes. Rinsing the mouth with beer or soda can make a burning mouth worse. John Riley, editor of the *Solanaceae Enthusiasts Quarterly,* advises rinsing the mouth with cool milk for best relief.

Capsicum sp. (Pepper). The source of chili powder and paprika, Peppers are one of tropical America's gifts to the world.

MARY SHERWOOD'S EASY-TO-MANAGE
COMPOSTING

Why pay for soil conditioners when you can make your own with ingredients many pay to have hauled away? It is estimated that nearly a quarter of all household garbage consists of material that can be composted. Mary Sherwood owned and operated a wildflower nursery in Maine for forty years. Below she gives her recipe for easy composting:

Locate a shady area, away from hungry tree roots if possible. Start with a bushel of last year's leaves; spread on the ground where you want the compost pile. On top of the leaves throw spring clean-up sods, plant debris and vegetable scraps from the kitchen. Water this pile and throw a couple of shovels of soil over it and sprinkle with water again. Next, add more plant debris, lawn clippings and so on as the summer progresses, tossing in some soil now and then. If no soil is available (Mary carries a bucket in her car in case she happens upon a chance to fill it), throw in some gravel. Cow or horse manure, if available, is a nice addition. Avoid the seed heads of weeds and acid plant materials such as pine needles and cones, peat and Rhododendron leaves.* Last, but not least, encourage earthworms. To Mary they are the chief workers in the compost pile, breaking it down safely and doing away with the need for chemicals and/or constant turning. Mary rescues them from puddles to add to her pile; you can also buy compost earthworms. In late fall, spread a bit of soil over your pile (add a little manure if you have it), sprinkle with water and cover all with a foot or more of leaves. Mary suggests Maple. Cover the leaves with burlap or an old tablecloth (no plastic; moisture and air must get in) and tie down ends. A few old boards on top will keep things in place. A good snow cover is desirable. In the spring, take some leaves from the top to start a new pile. Your old pile will supply your plants with rich fertilizer all season.

ORIGINS OF COMMON FOOD PLANTS**

Artichoke—Mediterranean area and Canary Islands
Avocado—Central America
Banana—Malay Peninsula

---

*Avoid acid plant materials unless you want acid compost. Rotted hemlock needles, pine needles and cones, and oak and beech leaves will produce acid compost: Use leaves of basswood, birch, hickory, ash and maples for a less acid compost pile.
**From the New York Botanical Garden, Bronx, New York.

Black-eyed pea—West Africa (probably)
Black pepper—India
Cassava—Central and South America
Chick pea—Asia or Caucasia (doubtful)
Chili pepper—South America
Coffee—Southwest Ethiopia
Corn—Mexico
Eggplant—India
Garlic—Central Asia
Lentil—Near East (probably)
Mango—India
Olive—Mountains of Eastern Mediterranean
Onion—Central Asia
Peanut—South America
Pomegranate—Iran
Potato—Highlands of Bolivia and Peru
Rice—Southeast Asia
Scarlet Runner bean—Mexico
Soy bean—Northeast China
String bean—Central and South America
Sugar cane—New Guinea
Sunflower—Central United States
Sweet pepper—Central America
Sweet potato—Peru
Tomato—Mexico or lower Andes of tropical South America
Wheat—Near East to the shores of the Caspian Sea

9

Historical and Miscellaneous Lists

PLANT MATERIAL FOUND IN
TUTANKHAMEN'S TOMB

Three wreaths and bits of Papyrus were found in the caskets, which contained:

Centaurea (CORNFLOWER)
Cyperus (PAPYRUS)
Mandragora (MANDRAKE)
Nymphaea (LOTUS)
Olea (OLIVE)
Salix (WILLOW)
Solanum (NIGHTSHADE)

Several other less easily identified plant remnants were also found. The presence of Cornflowers and Mandrake fruits help establish that the funeral took place in March or April. Death would have occurred seventy days earlier.

PLANT SYMBOLISM IN CHRISTIAN ART

Plants long have served as symbols, and many of the ancient gods and goddesses were associated with special flowers. With the rise of Christianity some plants took on special Christian meanings; saints also became connected with special flowers. The meanings listed below are not necessarily the only ones a particular plant could have: Viola was also a symbol for lust; in Victorian times it became a symbol for modesty. Flowers adorn many fifteenth-century masterpieces: the Ghent Altarpiece, the Unicorn Tapestries and Leonardo da Vinci's *Madonna of the Rocks,* to name only a few. A knowledge of Christian plant symbols is helpful in appreciating these works. Here are the Christian meanings of a dozen commonly depicted flowers:

Aquilegia canadensis (Columbine). Once associated with Aphrodite, Columbine later became a Christian symbol. Painters sometimes added two extra petals so the flower would agree with the seven gifts it represented.

Anagallis (SCARLET PIMPERNEL)—*Salvation*

Aquilegia (COLUMBINE)—*The seven gifts of the Holy Spirit*

Calendula (MARIGOLD)—*Salvation; sacred to Mary*

Chrysanthemum (DAISY)—*Innocence (of the Holy Child)*

Cirsium (THISTLE)—*Sin; symbol of the expulsion from Eden*

Dianthus (CARNATION)—*Divine love; martyrs' blood, the Crucifixion*; also associated with betrothal in medieval and Renaissance times*

Lilium (MADONNA LILY)—*Purity (symbol of immortality to ancient people)*

Iris—*Royalty; their appearance in nativity scenes emphasizes the royalty of the Christ child; yellow flag was one of the emblems of St. John*

Primula (PRIMROSE)—*Common names for P. veris include St. Peter's Keys, Our Lady's Keys and Keys of Heaven*

Rosa (ROSE)—*Lilies and Roses were once condemned as heathenish; roses eventually became associated with Mary and also with the Crucifixion*

Silene (WHITE CAMPION)—*Connected with the devil and death*

Viola (VIOLET, PANSY)—*Connected with the Trinity*

---

*John Williamson, in his book *The Oak King, the Holly King and the Unicorn* (Harper & Row, 1986), points out that Pinks or Carnations have a clove smell and cloves resemble small nails; both cloves and Pinks were therefore connected with the Crucifixion.

PLANTS DESCRIBED BY LEWIS AND CLARK

In 1803 President Thomas Jefferson instructed captains Lewis and Clark to explore the pristine wilderness that stretched from the Missouri River to the Pacific Ocean. Not yet part of the very new nation of the United States, this territory covered 8,000 miles; the journey was to last more than two years. The journals of Lewis and Clark describe close to 200 plants, and, although Lewis (the "botanist" of the trip) had little formal training and did not use Latinate binomials, his descriptions of both flora and fauna were lengthy and precise. Not surprisingly, the edible qualities of some of the specimens were especially noted. Listed are ten of the "new" wonders recorded; many make handsome garden subjects:

Allium cernuum (NODDING ONION)—Lewis describes great stands of this onion growing on an island (which he names Onion Island) and pronounces them delicious.

Camassia quamash (CAMASS)—Bulbs of this beautiful blue-flowered plant were an important food source for native Americans and also were enjoyed by the Expedition. On June 12, 1806, Lewis describes a field of "quawmash" in bloom, "from the color of its bloom, it resembles lakes of fine clear water . . . on first sight I could have sworn it was water."

Ceanothus sanguineus (WILD LILAC)—White-flowered shrub with reddish older stems; there are many blue-flowered ornamentals in this mostly western genus.

Clarkia pulchella (GODETIA)—A "singular" annual with lavender flowers described by Lewis, who regretted that seed would not be ripe to collect during his "residence in this neighborhood." There are 33 species of Clarkias native to western North America and southern South America.

Cornus nuttalii (PACIFIC DOGWOOD)—Clark noted that this Dogwood has smoother bark and grows taller than the eastern Dogwood. Perhaps even more spectacularly beautiful than C. florida, C. nuttalii adapts less readily to cultivation.

Cypripedium montanum (MOUNTAIN LADY SLIPPER)—Clark wrote "Capt. L. showed me a plant in blume which is sometimes called ladies slipper or Mockerson flower . . . it is in shape and appearance like ours only that the corolla is white marked with small veigns of pale red longitudinally on the inner side, and much smaller."

Lewisia rediviva (BITTER ROOT)—A root not enjoyed by Lewis though much eaten by native Americans. Flowers may be rose or white; several Lewisias are useful in rockeries.

Linum perenne subsp. lewisii* (PERENNIAL FLAX)—Decorative plant with sky blue flowers; used today in "xeriscaping" because of its very low water requirements.

Mahonia spp. (OREGON GRAPE OR HOLLY GRAPE)—Lewis carefully described two species of these handsome evergreen native shrubs; Clark sketched the leaves. They did not see the attractive yellow flowers or the blue-black fruit.

Symphoricarpos albus (SNOWBERRY)—Pink-flowered, white-berried native shrub commonly planted in Victorian gardens. S. orbiculatus (Indian Currant or Coralberry) has bright coral-red fruit.

---

*Often found as L. lewisii, *Hortus Third* classifies this Flax as a subspecies of the European native L. perenne.

ERNEST H. WILSON

Ernest H. Wilson was one of the last great plant explorers, and one of the most famous. In 1899 he left his native England for the long journey west to China. A new employee (and just twenty-three years old) of the nursery firm Veitch and Sons, Wilson was instructed to return with the fabled Dove Tree (Davidia involucrata), which had been described by an earlier plant explorer. Wilson found the Dove Tree—and much more, despite his employer's belief that there was little new material left to collect in China. Mr. Veitch must have been surprised indeed when his young worker returned with hundreds of other specimens. Wilson later made other trips to Asia, became director of the Arnold Arboretum and was responsible for introducing hundreds of plants, previously unknown in the West, into our gardens. A few of Wilson's introductions are:

Acer griseum (PAPERBARK MAPLE)
Actinidia chinensis (CHINESE ACTINIDIA)
Berberis julianae (WINTERGREEN BARBERRY)
Buddleia davidii vars. magnifica and **wilsonii** (SUMMER LILAC)
Buxus microphylla koreana (KOREAN BOX)
Clematis montana rubens (ROSY CLEMATIS)
Cornus kousa (KOUSA DOGWOOD)
Davidia involucrata (DOVE TREE)
Kolkwitzia amabilis (BEAUTYBUSH)
Lilium regale (REGAL LILY)*
Meconopsis (YELLOW CHINESE POPPY)
Pyrus calleryana (CALLERY PEAR)
Rheum alexandrae (CUT-LEAF RHUBARB)
Rhododendron (KURUME AZALEA)
Rosa moyesii
Viburnum rhytidophyllum (LEATHERLEAF VIBURNUM)

*"Found" in 1903, when Wilson was twenty-seven, near the China-Tibet border.

ALL-AMERICA SELECTIONS

AAS, founded in the 1930s, is a nonprofit organization that conducts objective trials of new varieties of seed-grown flowers and vegetables from around the world. Tests are conducted in test gardens throughout the country; AAS also maintains a number of display gardens where gardeners may view winners. AAS's purposes are to encourage breeders to develop "new and improved" varieties and to provide home gardeners with superior new flowers and vegetables. Some of the more recent winners have been compact plants for the smaller garden. Before a winner is introduced, AAS requires that enough seed be available to meet anticipated demand. Judges are volunteers from the seed industry, universities and botanical gardens. The three trial categories, Bedding Plant Flower, Flower and Vegetable, are all represented in 1990s winners (descriptions are based on information provided by AAS):

Achillea 'Summer Pastels'—This cultivar grows only 2 feet tall and is easily raised from seed. Flower color ranges from pink, apricot, beige and red to pure white. Perennial, drought tolerant and sun loving.

Bean 'Derby'—A new green bean on a bush-type plant; pods remain tender even when quite large and slip easily from stems during harvesting. Resistant to bean mosaic virus.

Celosia 'Pink Castle'—Semidwarf plant with a pink flower; heat- and drought-tolerant annual.

Pansy 'Jolly Joker'—Unique purple/orange flowers on a compact plant. Said to exhibit above-average heat and weather tolerance.

Pepper F1 'Super Cayenne'—A decorative hot pepper that can be harvested green or left to mature to red. Good yield of long, thin peppers on a 2-foot plant.

Petunia F1 'Polo Burgundy Star'—A Bedding Plant Winner, 'Polo Burgundy Star' is also a multiflora petunia that tolerates heat, drought and bad weather. No pinching necessary for continuous bloom. White star pattern with bright red/violet trim.

Petunia F1 'Polo Salmon'—Another AAS Bedding Plant Winner, 'Polo Salmon' is a multiflora heat- and drought-tolerant petunia that also recovers quickly after storms. While blooms are not as large as grandifloras, they are profuse and the plant does not require cutting back or deadheading to keep flowers coming. Salmon/pink color.

Squash F1 'Cream of the Crop'—An acorn squash with a compact habit and white fruit (interior is a creamy golden color). Stores well after harvest.

Squash F1 'Sun Drops'—Compact bush that produces oval-shaped, yellow summer squash. Matures in 50 to 55 days; can be spaced 20 to 24 inches apart.

Zinnia F1 'Scarlet Splendor'—A scaled-down plant with large red flowers on stems long enough for cutting. New blooms quickly replace cut flowers on this showy annual.

Here are the 1989 All-America Selections Winners; all were flowers, an event that had not occurred for twenty-two years:

Coreopsis 'Early Sunrise'—Also a Gold Medal* winner (the first flower to win a Gold Medal in 15 years), Early Sunrise is a hardy perennial, easily grown from seed and the earliest Coreopsis to flower. Eighteen inches tall; needs no staking or pinching and will flower all summer. Fluffy, double golden flowers. Excellent throughout the country.

Dianthus F1 'Telstar Picotee'—Heat-tolerant Dianthus, 10 inches tall; also thrives in cool summer growing conditions. Red/white bicolor.

Impatiens F1 'Tango'—This is an Impatiens with large, orange flowers; the first F1 hybrid New Guinea Impatiens introduction in the world; 18 to 24 inches tall, 'Tango' thrives in semishade or up to a half day of full sun (if given sufficient moisture).

Marigold 'Golden Gate'—The first Marigold in 9 years to receive an award, 'Golden Gate' is an orange/red bicolor 8 inches tall with very early bloom.

Petunia F1 'Orchid Daddy'—Very floriferous, this cultivar has pink blossoms with plum veination. Combines nicely with violet/blue annuals. Won the Flower Award plus the new Bedding Award; the first AAS dual-award winner.

Torenia F2 'Clown Mixture'—Shade-loving annual with a dwarf habit and flowers that are bi- and tri-colored in shades pink, white and purple. Common name is Wishbone Flower.

Verbena 'Novalis Deep Blue'—Winner of the Bedding Plant Award; dwarf and compact plant with purple flowers with white centers. Keeps blooming even in hot weather.

Verbena 'Sandy White'—Dwarf, compact Verbena with large, pure white flower umbels. Heat and weather tolerant throughout the country.

---

*Gold Medals are reserved for varieties representing a major breakthrough, while regular AAS winners represent the best of their class.

Other recent AAS flower winners include:

1988 Celosia 'New Look'—Bronze foliage and scarlet plumes on dwarf plants.

1988 Shasta Daisy 'Snow Lady'—All-summer-blooming perennial; the first Shasta to combine earliness and dwarf (10 inches) habit.

1987 Basil 'Purple Ruffles'—Ornamental annual herb with glossy purple leaves and strong fragrance.

1987 Petunia 'Purple Pirouette'—Large double blooms with deep purple centers and white edges.

1987 Sanvitalia 'Mandarin Orange'—First orange-flowered Sanvitalia; low-spreading habit. Tolerates full sun and high heat.

1987 Snapdragon 'Princess White with Purple Eye'—Bicolor; 14 to 16 inches.

1986 Cosmos 'Sunny Red'—Bright red single flowers; heat tolerant.

1985 Celosia 'Century Mixed'—Plants are 28 inches tall with a wide color range.

1985 Gazania 'Mini-Star Tangerine'—Bright orange flowers; thrives in poor soils and tolerates high heat and humidity.

1985 Geranium 'Rose Diamond'—Rose-pink blooms; zoned leaves.

1985 Verbena 'Trinidad'—Compact and upright with rose flowers.

1984 Zinnia 'Yellow Marvel'—Early-blooming yellow flowers.

1984 Zinnia 'Border Beauty Rose Hybrid'—Rose-pink; touch of salmon.

1983 Petunia 'Red Picotee'—The first red and white picotee petunia; abundant bloom.

1983 Ornamental Pepper 'Candlelight'—Produces a profusion of thin, light green, edible hot peppers.

The AAS Bedding Plant Flower Award is a new category that tests for improved performance in both greenhouses and gardens. The following Petunia is the first AAS winner in this category:

1988 Petunia 'Ultra Crimson Star'—Large flower with a white star pattern on deep crimson; continuous bloom.

The following Gold Medal Flower Winners are still in commerce:

Cosmos 'Sunset' (1966)
Linaria 'Fairy Bouquet' (1934)
Lobelia 'Rosamund' (1934)
Morning Glory 'Scarlet O'Hara' (1939)
Nasturtium 'Golden Gleam' (1935)
Nasturtium 'Scarlet Gleam' (1935)
Zinnia 'Peter Pan Pink' (1971)
Zinnia 'Peter Pan Plum' (1971)
Zinnia 'Scarlet Ruffles' (1974)
Zinnia 'Thumbelina' (1963)

FLOWER SPIRES

Plants that produce spike- or steeplelike flowers add a vertical line to the garden that contrasts nicely with rounded shapes of other flowers like roses and daisies. (Some of them, such as the spires of Astilbe and Liatris, stand tall throughout the winter, adding interest to the dormant garden.) Many tall plants listed elsewhere have a spikey inflorescence (Aconitum, Aruncus, Cimicifuga, Delphinium, Digitalis, Liatris, Sanguisorba and Thermopsis); ten lower-growing plants with flower spires are:

Antirrhinum majus (SNAPDRAGON)—P or A, depending on climate
Astilbe spp. (ASTILBE)—P
Consolida ambigua (ROCKET LARKSPUR)—A
Dictamnus albus (GAS PLANT)—P
Lobelia spp. (LOBELIA)—P
Lupinus spp. (LUPINE)—P
Lysimachia spp. (LOOSESTRIFE)—P
Physostegia cultivars (FALSE DRAGONHEAD)—P
Salvia farinacea (MEALY-CUP SAGE)—P or A, depending on climate; and S. x superba—P
Veronica spp. (SPEEDWELL)—P

A—Annual   P—Perennial

SEEDPODS FOR WINTER BOUQUETS

Many garden flowers produce fine seedpods for use in dried arrangements. Supplement the following with seedpods found in fields and woods from plants such as Evening Primrose, Mallow, Milkweed and Sensitive Fern (Onoclea). Woody plants such as Sweet Gum, Tulip Tree and Rose also produce attractive seedpods.

> **Baptisia australis** (WILD INDIGO)—P
> **Catananche caerulea** (CUPID'S DART)—P
> **Dictamnus albus** (GAS PLANT)*—P
> **Dipsacus fullonum** (TEASEL)—B
> **Iris spp.** (WILD IRIS, SIBERIAN IRIS)—P
> **Lunaria annua** (HONESTY, SILVER DOLLAR, MONEY PLANT)—B
> **Nigella damascena** (LOVE-IN-A-MIST)—A
> **Papaver orientale** (ORIENTAL POPPY)—P
> **Physalis alkekengi** (CHINESE/JAPANESE LANTERN)—P
> **Yucca spp.** (YUCCA, SPANISH BAYONET)—P

*Seedpods were used as holders for small candles by early settlers.
A—Annual   B—Biennial   P—Perennial

EASILY DRIED GARDEN FLOWERS

The following flowers can all be air dried easily by hanging them in a dry, shaded, warm but well-ventilated place for several weeks (remove excess foliage to minimize the risk of mildew):

> **Achillea spp.** (YARROW)—P
> **Celosia spp.** (COCKSCOMB)—A
> **Echinops spp.** (GLOBE THISTLE)—P
> **Eryngium spp.** (SEA HOLLY)—P
> **Gomphrena globosa** (GLOBE AMARANTH)—A
> **Gypsophila spp.** (BABY'S BREATH)—P
> **Helichrysum bracteatum** (STRAWFLOWER)—P; grown as an annual
> **Lavandula spp.** (LAVENDER)—P
> **Limonium spp.** (SEA-LAVENDER, HARDY STATICE)—P
> **Salvia farinacea** (MEALY-CUP SAGE)—P; annual north of Maryland

A—Annual   P—Perennial

Sedum 'Autumn Joy'—P; dried flower heads are attractive
shades of reddish brown and beige
Tanacetum vulgare (TANSY)—P

A—Annual   P—Perennial

The flowers of some woody plants, such as Heather and Hydrangea, are also easily air dried, and foliage of Artemisias like Silver Mound are useful for wreath making as well as in dried bouquets.

LIME- AND ACID-LOVING PLANTS

Soil acidity is measured on a pH scale of 1 (extremely acid) to 14 (extremely alkaline), with 7 being neutral. It is important because it affects the health of plant roots and the availability of nutrients to them. Many gardeners in the East have highly acid soils to contend with; some areas in the West have soils that are too alkaline. While many plants will tolerate a fairly wide pH range, most prefer soils in the neutral (6.5 to 7) area. However, many members of the Ericaceae (Blueberry, Cranberry, Rhododendron, Azalea, Heath, Mt. Laurel, Trailing Arbutus) need acid soil to thrive, and the addition of acid fertilizer is often necessary to keep them healthy. Many wildflowers, such as Cimicifuga, Indian Cucumber and Cardinal Flower, also prefer acid soils as do Lilies (except Madonna) and Japanese Iris.

A number of garden favorites are native to areas of limy soil and appreciate the addition of a little limestone (mix well into soil; do not let roots touch lime) when grown in the acid soils of many eastern and midwestern gardens. Among the lime lovers:

Aethionema (STONECRESS)
Clematis (CLEMATIS)
Delphinium (DELPHINIUM)
Dianthus (PINKS)
Geum montanum (GEUM)
Gypsophila (BABY'S BREATH)
Helleborus (HELLEBORE, CHRISTMAS ROSE)
Iris (BEARDED IRIS)
Lavendula (LAVENDER)*

*Many herbs appreciate slightly limy soils. A number of woody plants, such as Cornus mas and Syringa, also like a little lime even though they tolerate more acid soils.

Puschkinia (STRIPED SQUILL)
Reseda (MIGNONETTE)
Saxifraga (LIME-SECRETING SPECIES SUCH AS S. PANICULATA)
Scabiosa (PINCUSHION FLOWER)

pH Ranges for Vegetable Plants

Most (but not all) vegetable plants grow best when soil pH is between 6 and 7. Keeping pH in the correct range also helps prevent diseases such as clubroot. Here are some vegetables and their preferred pH:

Asparagus—6.8
Bean—6.5–7.0
Beet—6.5–6.8
Beet (GOLDEN)—6.5–8.0
Broccoli—6.5–7.5
Cabbage—5.8–7.0
Cauliflower—6.5–7.0
Lettuce—6.5–7.0
Onion—6.0–6.5
Potato—5.0–5.5*
Pumpkin—6.5–7.5
Spinach—6.0–6.7
Tomato—6.5

*Although Potatoes will grow in less acid soils, the fungus that causes Potato Scab is discouraged when pH levels are lower than 5.5.

Hydrangea: An Indicator Plant for pH

H. macrophylla produces large, rosy pink or deep sky blue flowers in the middle of summer. When I lived on top of a limestone cliff in southeastern Pennsylvania, the flowers were reliably pink and perfect for centerpieces for a daughter's August 4 birthday party. The same plant produces only blue flowers in its present location in southern New England's acid soils. If your Hydrangea has pink flowers, your soil pH is probably somewhere above 7; if the flowers are blue your soils are probably under 6.5. Hydrangeas grown in soils near 7 may produce blossoms that exhibit many shades of pink and blue.

EDIBLE FLOWERS

People have eaten flowers since time began; ancient Romans were fond of serving them and they were popular in the Middle Ages as well. Today we commonly eat artichokes, broccoli and cauliflower (all immature flowers), but other blossoms are enjoying a revival. Several, like Daylily buds (barely boiled and then sauteed) and spicy Nasturtium flowers are considered gourmet fare. Others, while edible and even nutritious, are mainly used to beautify the main course. Avoid flowers that may have been chemically sprayed such as those found along roadsides or purchased from a florist. Ten to try:

Borago* (BORAGE)
Calendula (POT MARIGOLD)—Flowers once used to color
    cheese.**
Dianthus (CLOVE PINK)
Hemerocallis (DAYLILY)
Hosta (HOSTA)
Rosa (ROSE)
Syringa (LILAC)
Tagetes (MARIGOLD)
Tropaeolum (NASTURTIUM)
Viola (PANSY, VIOLET)

*The true blue flowers of borage have been a favorite through the ages. Pliny said the flowers (served in wine) made men merry and joyful. Gerard said the flowers in salad exhilarate the mind, comfort the heart and drive away sorrow. Sir Francis Bacon claimed borage cures "dusky melancholie." Many other herb blossoms are edible.
**Cheese is still colored botanically by anatto, an orange-red dye made from the pulp surrounding the seeds of Bixa orellana, a Central American plant.

Caution!

Taste only flowers that are known to be edible! Among the attractive but poisonous flowers are Lily-of-the-Valley, Wisteria, Autumn Crocus, Monkshood, Rhododendron, Azalea, Oleander, Clematis, Foxglove and Christmas Rose. There are others. Never sample an unknown plant.

SOURCES FOR EDIBLE FLOWERS

Balducci's
424 Avenue of the Americas
New York, NY 10011
Call the wholesale department at
(718) 361-1300 for information

Fox Hill Farm
Box 9
440-T West Michigan Ave.
Parma, MI 49269-0009
(517) 531-3179
Fox Hill raises several hundred
varieties of herbs and some
culinary flowers and ships
throughout the country

Paradise Farms
PO Box 436
Summerland, CA 93067
(805) 684-9468
Paradise Farms grows herbs and
flowers (organically) and they
ship year round via overnight
mail
They offer baskets of six different
flowers for around $30

Datura sp. (Thorn Apple). An ornamental but very toxic plant, Datura
is a member of the Nightshade or
Tomato Family.

Toxic Garden Plants

While a number of garden flowers make fine additions to the salad bowl, do not be tempted to try them all! The following poisonous plants are all grown in gardens and some of them are capable of causing serious symptoms. Be suspicious of all plants (especially those in the Buttercup, Lily, Poppy, Pea, Parsley and Nightshade families) until proven innocent. (See also "Poisonous and Irritating Woody Plants," pages 301–305.)

Aconitum spp. (MONKSHOOD)—The whole plant, especially leaves and roots, is poisonous. The toxic alkaloids cause dizziness, visual blurring and possible cardiac distress.

Adonis spp. (PHEASANT'S EYE)—All parts of this rock-garden plant are toxic and contain digitalislike substances.

Anemone spp. (PASQUE FLOWER, THIMBLEWEED, WINDFLOWER)—Like Monkshood and Adonis, Anemones belong to the questionable Buttercup* family (as do Delphinium and Larkspur, which are also best avoided.) Toxins cause blisters and acute irritation of skin and mucous membranes.

Atropa (BELLADONNA)—Infamous though not commonly grown, Atropa poisoning can cause fever and delirium. Nightshade family.

Colchicum spp. (AUTUMN CROCUS)—All parts of the plant are toxic and can cause severe colic and diarrhea.

Convallaria (LILY-OF-THE-VALLEY)—The whole plant is poisonous, as is water in which flowers have been placed. The orange-red fruit occasionally produced can be especially attractive to children. Nausea, cramps and heart irregularities are possible after ingestion.

Digitalis purpurea (FOXGLOVE)—All parts of the plant are toxic; abdominal pain and cardiac irregularities are common and can be serious.

Helleborus (CHRISTMAS ROSE)—The whole plant is toxic, causing nausea, cramping, diarrhea and possible rhythm disturbances. Another member of the Buttercup family.

Iris sp. (IRIS AND YELLOW FLAG)—The rootstock of some (perhaps all) Irises is toxic and may cause nausea and vomiting.

*Beggars once elicited sympathy by using Buttercups to blister their skin.

Nicotiana spp. (TOBACCO)—Serious poisoning has resulted when leaves of this genus have been mistaken for salad greens. Symptoms can include convulsions and respiratory failure. Nightshade family.

Physalis spp. (CHINESE OR JAPANESE LANTERN)—The unripe berries of this Nightshade family member are poisonous, especially to children.

Ricinus (CASTOR BEAN)—This large, decorative annual has attractive mottled seeds that taste good but are very toxic. Eating only 2 to 6 seeds may be fatal.

More Poisonous and Irritating Plants

While not usually found in flower borders, some of the following are planted in wildflower gardens; others are common weeds in many regions of the country:

Actaea spp. (BANEBERRY, COHOSH, DOLL'S EYES)—Berries and roots are toxic.

Arisaema spp. (JACK-IN-THE-PULPIT)—Any part of the plant can cause burning irritation of the mouth and throat but no serious systemic symptoms.

Baptisia spp. (WILD INDIGO)—The whole plant is toxic, and "peas" might be especially attractive to children.

Chelidonium majus (CELANDINE)—All parts of the plant are poisonous; the orange sap once was used as a wort remedy.

Cicuta (WATER HEMLOCK)—Tall plants of wet ground; all parts (especially roots) are very toxic and can be quickly fatal.

Conium (POISON HEMLOCK)—The famous Hemlock reputedly given to Socrates, Conium (like Cicuta) is a member of the Parsley family. Both can be mistaken for edible plants like carrot or parsnip and look somewhat like Queen Anne's Lace. Coma or death due to respiratory failure are possible if poisoning is severe.

Datura spp. (THORN APPLE, JIMSON WEED)—All parts of the plant are toxic; belladonna poisons are present in this member of the Nightshade family.

Euphorbia spp. (SPURGE)—The sap of some species is poisonous and can produce sores on skin and (if eaten) stomach distress.

Hyoscyamus niger (HENBANE)—The seed of this weedy Nightshade family plant contains belladonna alkaloids.

Lobelia spp. (CARDINAL FLOWER, INDIAN TOBACCO, GREAT BLUE LOBELIA)—The whole plant is poisonous and symptoms are similar to those produced by nicotine.

Phytolacca americana (POKEWEED)—Roots and uncooked leaves are capable of causing severe nausea and cramps.

Podophyllum peltatum (MAYAPPLE)—The entire plant (except fruit) is toxic. Fatalities have occurred from repeated application of the poisonous resin on the skin or the ingestion of large amounts of the plant.

Solanum spp. (NIGHTSHADE, BITTERSWEET)—The green fruit is toxic, especially to children.

Veratrum spp. (FALSE HELLEBORE)—All parts of this plant can produce nausea, blurred vision and chest pain.

Ricinus communis (Castor Bean). Admired for its decorative foliage, Castor Bean should not be planted in areas where children play.

Toxic Bulbs

The bulbs listed below are poisonous and have been mistaken occasionally for onions. (It would be prudent to refrain from nibbling on the above-ground parts of the following as well; the leaves of several, including Spider Lily and Star of Bethlehem, are also toxic.)

Amaryllis	**Sea Onion** (RED SQUILL)
Autumn Crocus	**Snowdrop**
Hyacinth	**Spider Lily**
Lycoris	**Star of Bethlehem**
Narcissus, Daffodil	**Squill**

Never sample unknown bulbs or roots; the tubers of Glory Lily contain colchicine and the roots of many wild plants, such as Wild Garlic and Wild Calla to name just two, may also be injurious.

Common Garden Plants That Can Irritate the Skin

Poison ivy is the most notorious rash-causing plant, but there are others! Fortunately, not everyone is sensitive to all of the following and some on the list must be handled extensively before trouble is likely (see also "Poisonous and Irritating Woody Plants," pages 301–305).

Achillea (YARROW)*
Apium graveolens (CELERY)*
Artemisa (MUGWORT)
Aster spp. (ASTER)
Chrysanthemum spp. (CHRYSANTHEMUM)
Cypripedium spp. (LADY'S SLIPPER)
Daucus carota (QUEEN ANNE'S LACE)* and D. carota var. sativus
    (Garden Carrot)*
Dicentra spectabilis (BLEEDING HEART)
Dictamnus albus (GAS PLANT)*
Hyacinthus spp. (HYACINTH)
Lactuca spp. (LETTUCE)
Lycopersicon (TOMATO)—Also Potato, in the same family.
Narcissus spp. (DAFFODIL)
Pastinaca sativa (PARSNIP)*
Pelargonium (GERANIUM)

*Ultraviolet light also necessary for dermatitis to develop.

Primula spp. (PRIMROSE)
Rudbeckia (BLACK-EYED SUSAN)
Ruta graveolens (RUE)*
Tagetes spp. (MARIGOLD)
Tanacetum (TANSY)
Tulipa spp. (TULIP)

*Ultraviolet light also necessary for dermatitis to develop.

Some plants have irritating sap, which is released when the plant is injured, or stinging hairs; among these are Anemone, Marsh Marigold, Clematis, Buttercup, Spurge, Prickly Pear and Stinging Nettle.

PLANTS DEER LIKE / PLANTS DEER AVOID

Deer prefer young growth on shrubs to almost anything else (except, maybe, choice items from your garden like young beans, apples and corn) but will lower their standards considerably when hungry. They can also be fickle, avoiding certain plants for a long time and then suddenly developing an appetite for them. (This summer, for the first time, local deer seemed to consider my Tomato plants a gourmet item.) Furthermore, eastern white-tail deer and western black-tails seem to have somewhat different preferences. The following plants are among those favored by eastern white-tail deer:

Lilium (CANADA LILY)
Euonymus (EVERGREEN)
Hosta
Ilex (JAPANESE AND CHINA GIRL HOLLY)
Rhododendron (EVERGREEN AZALEAS)
Taxus (YEW)
Thuja (ARBOVITAE)
Tulipa (TULIP)
Viburnum (CARLESII)

Although there is no such thing as a deer-proof garden, some plants are less appealing to deer than others. In general, deer seem to avoid plants with hairy or aromatic foliage, so herb gardens are relatively safe. The plants listed on the following page show up on lists of plants that both eastern and western deer are reputed to dislike:

Astilbe
Barberry
Buddleja (BUTTERFLY BUSH)
Buxus (BOXWOOD)
Cotinus coggygria (SMOKE BUSH, SMOKE TREE)
Digitalis (FOXGLOVE)
Epimedium (BARRENWORT)
Iris
Narcissus
Pachysandra
Pieris (ANDROMEDA)
Syringa (LILAC)

Options for Gardeners

When deer herds are large and damage severe, a fence may be the only answer to deer in the garden. However, if the problem is not intolerable there are other things home owners can consider. There are a number of repellants on the market; all give some protection—Hinder and BGR reduced damage the most in recent tests in Connecticut. Human hair (unwashed) is said to deter deer and some try tying small bags of hair in their shrubs. An apple grower in Connecticut claims good success with small bars of soap (the more perfume the better) taped to young fruit trees at the point the tree begins to branch.

PLANT PREFERENCES OF JAPANESE BEETLES

These flashy imported beetles may be attractive but their habits are definitely obnoxious. Not only do the beetles seem to savor every plant in sight, the white larvae work underground destroying the roots of grasses, vegetables and nursery plants. It is satisfying to learn that not all plants appeal equally to these pests. Research done by USDA scientist T. L. Ladd* has determined that the following plants are among the top favorites, with Rosa (to the surprise of no one) being number one:

Rosa spp. (HYBRID TEA)—petals
Vitis vinifera (WINE GRAPE)

---

*One wonders if the experimental subjects were given the opportunity to eat Gooseberry leaves, an apparent favorite of beetles in my garden.

Rubus idaeus (RED RASPBERRY)
Ulmus americana (AMERICAN ELM)
Zea mays (CORN)—silks
Acer platanoides (NORWAY MAPLE)
Hibiscus syriacus (ROSE OF SHARON)—petals
Polygonum pensylvanicum (SMARTWEED)
Brassica oleracea (CABBAGE)
Acer palmatum (JAPANESE MAPLE)
Tilia cordata (EUROPEAN LINDEN)
Betula populifolia (GRAY BIRCH)
Malus baccata (SIBERIAN CRAB)
Vitis labrusca (FOX GRAPE)
Parthenocissus quinquefolia (VIRGINIA CREEPER)
Tilia americana (AMERICAN LINDEN)
Quercus palustris (PIN OAK)
Sorbus americana (AMERICAN MT. ASH)
Sassafras albidum (SASSAFRAS)
Platanus x acerifolia (LONDON PLANE)
Prunus domestica (PLUM)
Rosa ssp. (ROSE)—foliage
Ambrosia trifida (GIANT RAGWEED)
Rhus toxicodendron (POISON IVY)

PLANTS NOT FAVORED BY JAPANESE BEETLES

Larix was the least eaten:

Larix decidua (EUROPEAN LARCH)
Ambrosia artemisiifolia (RAGWEED)
Betula pendula (EUROPEAN WHITE BIRCH)
Prunus serotina (BLACK CHERRY)
Prunus persica ('ELBERTA' PEACH)—leaves from old wood
Catalpa bignonioides (CATALPA)
Asparagus officinalis (ASPARAGUS)
Zea mays (CORN)—foliage
Prunus persica ('ELBERTA' PEACH)—leaves from new shoots
Taxodium distichum (BALD CYPRESS)
Trifolium pratense (RED CLOVER)
Medicago sativa (ALFALFA)
Rheum rhabarbarum (RHUBARB)

Prunus cerasifera (CHERRY PLUM)
Cydonia oblonga (QUINCE)
Clethra alnifolia (SWEET PEPPERBUSH)
Malus pumila ('ROME' APPLE)

COMMON LATIN AND GREEK ROOTS

A Swede, Carl von Linne, is known as the "Father of Taxonomy" for he first arranged all plants known to him into a binomial, or two-name system. Latin, the universal language of scholars, was chosen; Linne Latinized his own name to Linnaeus. Relationships between various groups of plants had long been recognized; many of the early herbalists grouped plants together into what later became the great families, such as the Grasses (Gramineae), Lilies (Liliaceae) and Roses (Rosaceae). Linnaeus's two-volume *Species Plantarum* (1753) further gave each plant a genus (the first name of the binomial) and a species (the second and last portion of the binomial). For example, all Roses were placed in the genus Rosa. Today more than one hundred species of these favorite shrubs are recognized, among them Rosa alba (White Rose), R. canina (Dog Rose) and R. foetida—the ill-smelling yellow Austrian Rose, which really came from Asia and was so important to Rose breeders as a source of yellow color. Rosa, of course, was placed in the Rosaceae as were other related genera such as Strawberry (Fragaria), Apple (Malus) and Raspberry (Rubus).

The binomial system of identification was sorely needed. A single plant may have many common names; worse still, the same common name was (and still is) often applied to several plants. Linnaeus's binomials ended the confusion among botanists in various parts of the world and made positive identification possible. Ideally, the Latin (sometimes Greek) used in a plant's name is descriptive of that plant or its habitat. The following words are all used to describe plant genera and species:

Color

alba—white
argentea—silvery
aurea—gold
azurea—sky blue
caerulea—blue

candida—pure white
cardinalis—red
chrysos—gold*
cinereus—ash colored (light gray)
flava—yellow
fuscatus—dark brown
glauca—the gray bloom found on some plants
griseus—gray
lutea—yellow
nigra—black
purpura—purple
rubra—red
sanguinea—blood red
versicolor—variously colored
virens, viridis—green
xanthinus—yellow

*The genera Helichrysum (Strawflower), Chrysopsis (Golden Aster) and Chrysanthemum all imply golden flowers.

Habit

communis—growing in a community; gregarious
crassus—thick
divaricata—spreading
elata—tall
gigantea—giant
liana—climbing
minor—smaller
nana—dwarf
nutans—nodding
patens—spreading
pendula—hanging
procumbens—procumbent
pumila—dwarf
reptans, repens—creeping
robusta—robust
scandens—climbing
suffructicosa—shrubby
tenua—thin

Geography

allegheniensis—native of the Allegheny Mountains
amurensis—of the Amur River region (northeast Asia)
australis—southern
borealis—from the north
canadensis—Canadian
carolinia—North or South Carolina
chinensis—Chinese
damascenus—of Damascus
europaeus—European
gallicus—Gaul (France)
germanicus—German
hesperius—of the West
japonica—Japanese
novae-angliae—of New England
occidentalis—western
olympicus—Mr. Olympus (Greece)
orientalis—from the Orient
pekinensis—of Peking (China)
pennsylvanicus—of Pennsylvania
philadelphicus—Philadelphia region
sibiricus—of Siberia
sinensis—Chinese
virginiensis—of Virginia

Habitat

alpinus—alpine
arenarius—of sandy places
arvensis—of (cultivated) fields
graniticus—granite loving
halophilus—salt loving
maritimus—of the sea
montanus—of mountains
muralis—of walls
nivalis, niveus—pertaining to snow
palustris—of swamps
pratensis—of meadows
saxatilis—of rocks
sylvatica—of woods
uliginosus—wet or marshy places

Other Characteristics

angustifolia—narrow leaved
asper—rough
barbata—barbed, bearded
biennis—biennial
campanula—bell flowered
cristata—crested
elegans—elegant
eximia—excelling, distinguished
foetida—ill-smelling
fragrans—fragrant
maculata—spotted
majalis—of May
mollis—soft, soft-hairy
nobilis—famous, noble
officinalis—of the apothecary
odorata—fragrant
rugosa—wrinkled
sanctus—holy
scaber—rough
sempervirens—ever-living
spectabilis—spectacular
speciosa—showy, good-looking
spicata—spiked
tomentosa—woolly
vernalis—of the spring
vulgaris—common

COMMON GARDEN FLOWERS IN FAMILY GROUPINGS

Families listed in order according to L. H. Bailey's *Manual of Cultivated Plants:*

ARACEAE—ARUM FAMILY

Arisaema triphyllum (JACK-IN-THE-PULPIT)
Caladium bicolor (CALADIUM)

Also in this family are common houseplants such as Philodendron and Dieffenbachia.

COMMELINACEAE—SPIDERWORT FAMILY

Tradescantia virginiana (COMMON SPIDERWORT)

LILIACEAE—LILY FAMILY

Chionodoxa luciliae (GLORY-OF-THE-SNOW)
Colchicum autumnale (AUTUMN CROCUS)
Convallaria majalis (LILY-OF-THE-VALLEY)
Hemerocallis spp./hybrids (DAYLILY)
Hosta spp. (HOSTA)
Hyacinthus orientalis (HYACINTH)
Lilium spp./hybrids (LILY)
Muscari botryoides (GRAPE HYACINTH)
Scilla spp. (SIBERIAN SQUILL AND SPANISH SQUILL)
Trillium spp. (WAKE ROBIN, TRILLIUM)
Tulipa spp./hybrids (TULIP)

AMARYLLIDACEAE—AMARYLLIS FAMILY

Allium spp. (ONION)
Galanthus nivalis (SNOWDROP)
Narcissus spp./hybrids (DAFFODIL)

IRIDACEAE—IRIS FAMILY

Crocus spp. (CROCUS)
Gladiolus spp./hybrids (GLADIOLUS)
Iris spp./hybrids (IRIS)

ORCHIDACEAE—ORCHID FAMILY

Cypripedium spp. (LADY'S SLIPPER)
Goodyera spp. (RATTLESNAKE-PLANTAIN)

CARYOPHYLLACEAE—PINK FAMILY

Cerastium tomentosum (SNOW-IN-SUMMER)
Dianthus spp. (PINK)
Gypsophila spp. (BABY'S BREATH)
Lychnis coronaria (DUSTY MILLER)
Silene spp. (CAMPION, CATCHFLY)

RANUNCULACEAE—BUTTERCUP FAMILY

Aconitum spp. (MONKSHOOD)
Actaea spp. (BANEBERRY OR COHOSH)

Anemone spp. (ANEMONE)
Aquilegia spp./hybrids (COLUMBINE)
Cimicifuga racemosa (SNAKEROOT)
Clematis spp. (CLEMATIS)
Delphinium spp./hybrids (DELPHINIUM AND LARKSPUR)
Helleborus spp. (CHRISTMAS AND LENTEN ROSE)
Nigella damascena (LOVE-IN-A-MIST)
Paeonia spp./hybrids (PEONY)*
Thalictrum spp. (MEADOW RUE)
Trollius spp. (GLOBEFLOWER)

*Today Peonies are placed by most in their own family, the Paeoniaceae.

BERBERIDACEAE—BARBERRY FAMILY

Epimedium spp. (EPIMEDIUM)
Podophyllum peltatum (MAY APPLE)

PAPAVERACEAE—POPPY FAMILY

Eschscholzia californica (CALIFORNIA POPPY)
Papaver spp. (ORIENTAL, ICELAND AND SHIRLEY POPPY)
Sanguinaria canadensis (BLOODROOT)

FUMARIACEAE—BLEEDING HEART FAMILY

Dicentra spp. (BLEEDING HEART, DUTCHMAN'S BREECHES)

CRUCIFERAE—MUSTARD FAMILY

Arabis spp. (ROCK CRESS)
Aurinia saxatilis (BASKET OF GOLD)
Iberis spp. (CANDYTUFT)
Lobularia maritima (SWEET ALYSSUM)
Lunaria annua (HONESTY)
Matthiola spp. (STOCKS)

SAXIFRAGACEAE—SAXIFRAGE FAMILY

Astilbe spp. (ASTILBE)
Bergenia spp. (BERGENIA)
Heuchera spp. (CORALBELLS)
Hydrangea spp. (HYDRANGEA)

Common flowering shrubs in this family include Deutzia and Philadelphus (Mock Orange).

ROSACEAE—ROSE FAMILY

Aruncus dioicus (GOATSBEARD)
Filipendula spp. (MEADOWSWEET)
Rosa spp./hybrids (ROSE)
Sanguisorba spp. (BURNET)

Shrubs in this family include Cotoneaster, Pyracantha (Firethorn), Chaenomeles (Flowering Quince), Kerria, Potentilla and Rubus (Raspberry and Blackberry). Trees in the Rose family include Malus (Apple), Amelanchier (Shadbush), Crataegus (Hawthorn), Pyrus (Pear), Sorbus (Mt. Ash) and Prunus (Plum, Cherry, Apricot, Peach).

LEGUMINOSAE—PEA FAMILY

Baptisia spp. (FALSE OR WILD INDIGO)
Cytisus spp. (BROOM)
Lathyrus odoratus (SWEET-PEA)
Lupinus spp. (LUPINE)
Thermopsis spp. (FALSE LUPINE)

GERANIACEAE—GERANIUM FAMILY

Geranium spp. (CRANESBILL)
Pelargonium (GERANIUM)

RUTACEAE—RUE FAMILY

Dictamnus albus (DITTANY, GAS PLANT)
Ruta graveolens (COMMON RUE)

Citrus trees are also members of the Rue family.

MALVACEAE—MALLOW FAMILY

Alcea rosea (HOLLYHOCK)
Althaea officinalis (MARSH MALLOW)
Callirhoe involucrata (POPPY MALLOW)
Hibiscus spp. (HIBISCUS, MALLOW)

The Cotton plant (Gossypium) is a member of the Mallow family.

ONAGRACEAE—EVENING PRIMROSE FAMILY

Clarkia spp. (CLARKIA)
Fuchsia hybrids (FUCHSIA)
Gaura spp. (GAURA)

PRIMULACEAE—PRIMROSE FAMILY

Androsace spp. (ROCK JASMINE)
Cyclamen spp. (CYCLAMEN)
Dodecatheon spp. (SHOOTING STAR)
Lysimachia nummularia (CREEPING JENNY)
Primula spp./hybrids (PRIMROSE)

PLUMBAGINACEAE—PLUMBAGO OR LEADWORT FAMILY

Armeria spp. (THRIFT, SEA PINK)
Ceratostigma plumbaginoides (LEADWORT)
Limonium spp. (SEA LAVENDER, STATICE)

POLEMONIACEAE—PHLOX FAMILY

Phlox spp. (MOSS PINK, SUMMER PHLOX, WILD BLUE PHLOX)
Polemonium caeruleum (JACOB'S LADDER)

BORAGINACEAE—BORAGE FAMILY

Anchusa azurea (BUGLOSS)
Heliotropium arborescens (HELIOTROPE)
Mertensia spp. (BLUEBELLS)
Myosotis spp. (FORGET-ME-NOT)
Pulmonaria spp. (LUNGWORT)

SOLANACEAE—NIGHTSHADE FAMILY*

Atropa belladonna (BELLADONNA)
Browallia spp. (BROWALLIA)
Hyoscyamus niger (HENBANE)
Mandragora officinarum (MANDRAKE)
Nicotiana alata (FLOWERING TOBACCO)
Petunia hybrids (PETUNIA)
Salpiglossis sinuata (PAINTED TONGUE)

*The family of Potato, Tomato, Eggplant, Pepper and Tobacco.

SCROPHULARIACEAE—FIGWORT FAMILY

Antirrhinum majus (SNAPDRAGON)
Chelone spp. (TURTLEHEAD)
Digitalis spp. (FOXGLOVE)
Linaria spp. (TOADFLAX, BUTTER-AND-EGGS)
Mimulus spp./hybrids (MONKEY-FLOWER)
Penstemon spp. (BEARDTONGUE)
Torenia fournieri (BLUEWINGS, WISHBONE FLOWER)
Verbascum spp. (MULLEIN)
Veronica spp./hybrids (SPEEDWELL)

CAMPANULACEAE—BELLFLOWER FAMILY

Campanula spp. (BELLFLOWER)
Platycodon grandiflorum (BALLOON-FLOWER)

COMPOSITAE—DAISY OR SUNFLOWER FAMILY

Achillea spp./hybrids (YARROW)
Ageratum spp. (AGERATUM)
Artemisia spp./hybrids (WORMWOOD, 'SILVER KING/MOUND')
Aster spp./hybrids (ASTER)
Boltonia asteroides (BOLTONIA)
Calendula officinalis (POT MARIGOLD)
Centaurea spp. (CORNFLOWER)
Chrysanthemum spp. (CHRYSANTHEMUM, SHASTA DAISY)
Chrysogonum virginianum (GOLDENSTAR, GREEN-AND-GOLD)
Coreopsis spp./hybrids (TICKSEED)
Cosmos spp. (COSMOS)
Dahlia hybrids (DAHLIA)
Echinacea spp. (PURPLE CONEFLOWER)
Echinops spp. (GLOBE THISTLE)
Gaillardia spp. (BLANKETFLOWER)
Helianthus spp. (SUNFLOWER)
Liatris spp. (BLAZING STAR, GAYFEATHER)
Rudbeckia spp./hybrids (BLACK-EYED SUSAN)
Santolina chamaecyparissus (LAVENDER COTTON)
Solidago spp. (GOLDENROD)
Stokesia laevis (STOKES ASTER)
Tagetes spp./hybrids (MARIGOLD)
Zinnia hybrids (ZINNIA)

SOME FOLK NAMES FOR GARDEN FLOWERS

A number of once-important plants, today considered weeds, have many common names that attest to many former uses. Bouncing Bet (Saponaria officinalis) was called Soapwort and Bruisewort as well as Sweet Betsy and Wild Sweet William. Common roadside Mullein has a long list of folk names: Candleflower, Hightaper, Torches, Velvet Plant, Flannel Plant and, recalling its use as a remedy for bronchial ailments in cattle, Bullock's Lungwort. Folk names may be confusing to taxonomists, but they are part of a plant's history; many are poetic and imaginative. Listed are some folk names of ten common garden plants:

Aconitum napellus (MONKSHOOD)—Helmet Flower, Friar's Cap, Soldier's Cap, Bear's Foot, Blue Rocket, Garden Wolfsbane, Auld Wife's Huid

Aquilegia spp. (COLUMBINE)—Dove's Foot, Granny's Nightcap, Blue Starry, Rock Bells and Meeting House

Viola Tricolor (Johnny-Jump-Up) A charming annual or short-lived perennial with many common names, Viola Tricolor is one of the parents of our modern garden Pansy.

Campanula spp. (BELLFLOWER)—Lady's Nightcap, Our Lady's
Thimble, Throatwort, Canterbury Bells, Coventry Bells
and Bats-in-the-Belfry

Convallaria majalis (LILY-OF-THE-VALLEY)—Our Lady's Tears
(or Virgin's Tears or Mary's Tears), May Lily, Mayflower,
Glovewort and Muguet (French)

Dianthus spp. (PINK)—Dianthus means "divine flower"; other
names include Carnation, Gillyflower and Sops-in-Wine

Dicentra spectabilis (BLEEDING HEART)—Lady's Locket, Lyre
Flower and Chinamen's Breeches. D. cucullaria
(Dutchman's Breeches) has several other charming names
including White Eardrop, Soldier's Caps, Bachelor's Kittens
and Butterfly Banners

Digitalis spp. (FOXGLOVE)—Fairy Thimbles, Fairy's Petticoats,
Fairy Cap, Fairy Glove, Our Lady's Gloves, Lion's Mouth,
Rabbit Flower, Throatwort, Witches' Thimbles, Bloody
Fingers and Dead Men's Bells

Lunaria annua (HONESTY)—The round, silvery seed pods of
Lunaria have inspired many names: Money Plant, Silver
Penny, Pennyflower, Silver Shilling, Money-in-the-Pocket,
Moonwort and Satin Flower

Primula spp. (PRIMROSE)—Keys of Heaven, Our Lady's Keys,
Saint Peter's Keys, Cowslip and Fairy Basins

Viola tricolor (JOHNNY-JUMP-UP)—Hearts-ease, Monkey Faces,
Peeping Tom, Love-in-Idleness, Meet-Her-in-the-
Entry-Kiss-Her-in-the-Buttery and Herb Trinity

PLANTS NAMED FOR PERSONS

As useful and appropriate as it is to name plants for distinguishing
characteristics, many plants were named for people. Plants new to Europe
streamed into the continent during the exciting Age of Exploration. Since
naming these new wonders was in the hands of Europeans, it is not
surprising that taxonomy books are full of names based on European
surnames. There are some exceptions; Sequoia was named for the Chero-
kee chief who devised an alphabet for his people, and Linnaeus himself
named Quassia in honor of a black slave who used the bark to cure fevers.
There is also a genus of the Malvaceae (Mallow family) named for the

Aztec ruler Montezuma and Camassia, a genus of beautiful American plants too-little planted in gardens, comes from its Indian name, *quamash*. But there are many more named for well-known (and not so well-known) Americans and Europeans, including genera named for Washington, Jefferson and Franklin:

Begonia—Michel Begon (1638–1710), patron of botany
Buddleja—Adam Buddle (1660–1715), English botanist
Camellia—G. J. Camellus (or Kamel), Moravian Jesuit who traveled in seventeenth-century Asia
Claytonia—John Clayton (1686–1773), American botanist
Dahlia—Andreas Dahl (1751–1789), Swedish botanist and pupil of Linnaeus
Deutzia—Johann van der Deutz (1743–1784), patron of Thunberg (see Thunbergia)
Dieffenbachia—J. F. Dieffenbach (1794–1847), German physician and botanist
Forsythia—William Forsyth (1737–1800), English horticulturist
Fuchsia—Leonard Fuchs (1501–1565), German professor of medicine and botanical author

Leonard Fuchs, 1501–1566. Fuchs was a professor of medicine at the University of Tübingen and author of the herbal *De Historia Stirpium* (1542). The genus Fuchsia was named in his honor.

Gardenia—Alexander Garden (1730–1791), physician in South Carolina who corresponded with Linnaeus

Heuchera—Johann Heinrich von Heucher (1677–1747), German botanist

Hosta—N. T. Host (1761–1834), Austrian physician and botanist

Kalmia—Peter Kalm (1717–1779), Swedish botanist who traveled in North America

Kerria—William Kerr (died 1814), Kew gardener and collector

Lewisia—Meriwether Lewis (1774–1809), of the Lewis and Clark Expedition; there is also a genus, Clarkia, named for Captain Clark

Linnaea—Named for Linnaeus by Gronovius; L. borealis (Twin-flower) is a small evergreen, shrubby plant with fragrant white or rose flowers; suitable for rock gardens; said to be a favorite of Linnaeus

Lobelia—Matthias de Lobel (1538–1616), Flemish botanist, author and physician to King James I

Magnolia—Pierre Magnol (1638–1715), French botany professor

Moraea—J. Moraea, Swedish physician, Linnaeus's father-in-law

Nicotiana—Jean Nicot (1530–1600), French diplomat, may have been the first to present Tobacco to the French and Portuguese courts

Saintpaulia—Baron Walter von Saint Paul-Illaire (1860–1910), "discoverer" of the plant (African Violet)

Thunbergia—Carl Thunberg (1743–1822), student and successor of Linnaeus

Weigela—C. E. Weigel (1748–1831), German professor

Wisteria—Caspar Wistar (1761–1818), professor at University of Pennsylvania

Zinnia—J. G. Zinn (died 1759), German botanist

Many others, including J. Poinsett (Poinsettia), J. Linder (Lindera) and M. Gaillard (Gaillardia) have the distinction of a genus named in their honor. The names of women, the traditional gathers and caretakers of plants, are glaringly underrepresented in this roster. It is true that Fittonia was named for the Fitton sisters, who wrote *Conversations in Botany* in 1817, and the giant South American water lily, Victoria, was named in honor of the British queen. For the most part, however, we must rest content with saints (Veronica, Barbara), nymphs (Calypso) and goddesses (Iris, Artemis)—and not very many of these.

Linnaea borealis (Twin-flower). A hardy little evergreen trailing plant with pink or white flowers, Linnaea was named for Linnaeus, "The Father of Taxonomy."

THE LANGUAGE OF GARDEN FLOWERS

Anemone—*Estrangement; forsaken*
Begonia—*Warning; dark thoughts*
Bluebell—*Loyalty*
Cardinal flower—*Distinction*
Carnation (PINK)—*Encouragement*
Carnation (RED)—*Ardor*
Carnation (WHITE)—*Devotion*
Carnation (YELLOW)—*Disdain*
Chrysanthemum (RED)—*I love you, too*
Chrysanthemum (WHITE)—*Trust*
Clematis—*Intelligence*
Columbine—*Folly*
Columbine (PURPLE)—*Resolved to win*
Columbine (RED)—*Worried; trembling*
Coreopsis—*Always cheerful*
Crocus (SPRING)—*Youthful joy*
Daffodil—*Vanity; regard*

Dahlia—*Instability; rebuff*
Dahlia (YELLOW)—*Distaste*
Daisy (WHITE)—*Innocence*
Daylily—*Coquetry*
Forget-Me-Not—*Forget me not; true love*
Foxglove—*Insincerity*
French marigold—*Jealousy*
Geranium (SCARLET)—*Comforting*
Goldenrod—*Precaution*
Heliotrope—*Devotion*
Hollyhock—*Ambition; fecundity*
Honesty—*Honesty; fascination*
Hyacinth—*Sport; dedication*
Iris—*Faith; valor; message*
Iris (YELLOW)—*Sorrow*
Lily (WHITE)—*Purity; modesty*
Lily (YELLOW)—*Falsehood*
Lily-of-the-Valley—*Friendship; happiness*
Lobelia—*Dislike, rebuff*
Marigold—*Despair; grief*
Morning Glory—*Affectation*
Narcissus—*Egotism*
Nasturtium—*Patriotism; affectation*
Pansy—*Thoughts*
Peony—*Bashfulness; contrition*
Phlox—*Friendship*
Pink—*Boldness; fragrance*
Poppy (RED)—*Consolation; moderation*
Poppy (WHITE)—*Sleep; indecision*
Snapdragon—*Refusal*
Sweet Pea—*Tenderness; departure*
Sweet William—*Gallantry*
Tulip (RED)—*I love you*
Tulip (YELLOW)—*Hopeless love*
Violet—*Faithfulness; modesty*
Wake Robin—*Ardor*
Water lily—*Pure of heart*
Zinnia—*Thinking of absent friends*

FLOWERS OF THE MONTH

January—Carnation; Snowdrop
February—Violet; Primrose
March—Daffodil
April—Daisy; Sweet Pea
May—Lily-of-the-Valley; Hawthorne
June—Rose
July—Larkspur
August—Poppy; Gladiolus
September—Aster; Morning Glory
October—Calendula
November—Chrysanthemum
December—Holly; Narcissus

TEN FLOWER DOS AND DON'TS

FTD publishes a booklet of "Floral Faux Pas and How to Avoid Them" which contains the following:

- Do not give red flowers in Mexico for this color is associated with witchcraft and the casting of spells (white lifts spells).
- In Japan red signifies health and healing and red flowers are appropriate for hospital patients.
- Do not send yellow flowers in France; the color stands for infidelity.
- Avoid even-numbered bouquets of cut flowers in France; likewise send odd-numbered bouquets of roses in Italy and Switzerland.
- Avoid the number 13 in France and Latin America.
- Yellow flowers are associated with death and are only appropriate at funerals in Latin America.
- Do not send flowers to men in Italy; send a potted plant instead. However, do not send plants to elderly people in Japan as the superstitious believe it may make sickness "take root."
- Sending a cactus to a Swede signifies the end of a romance.

- Be careful of Chrysanthemums! Best not to send them, especially white ones, in France unless it's for a funeral. Send them only to funerals in Italy and note that white and yellow 'Mums are reserved for funerals in China. The sending of Chrysanthemums is also tricky in Japan; here one must not send the 16-petal type that is used in the Imperial Family Crest.

- Do not send strongly scented flowers to a Swiss Miss—or anyone else in Switzerland.

NATIVE LANDS OF COMMON GARDEN FLOWERS

Hortus Third lists the following native lands:

Alcea (HOLLYHOCK)—Eastern Mediterranean region to central Asia

Astilbe (ASTILBE)—Asia (two species are found in the eastern United States)

Calendula (POT AND FIELD MARIGOLD)—Europe, northern Africa, Iran

Celosia (WOOLFLOWER)—Tropical Africa, America

Convallaria (LILY-OF-THE-VALLEY)—Eurasia

Coreopsis (TICKSEED)—North and South America, Africa

Cosmos—Southwestern United States to tropical regions of America (North, South and Central)

Dahlia—Central and South America, Mexico

Dianthus (PINK)—Eurasia

Digitalis (FOXGLOVE)—Europe, northwest Africa, central Asia

Epimedium (BARRENWORT)—Eurasia

Gaillardia (BLANKETFLOWER)—North and South America

Geranium (CRANESBILL)—Worldwide in Temperate Zone and tropical mountains

Hemerocallis (DAYLILY)—Eurasia, especially Japan

Heuchera (CORAL BELLS)—North America

Hosta (PLANTAIN LILY)—Japan (a few species are found in China and Korea)

Iberis (CANDYTUFT)—Europe, Mediterranean region

Iris—Native rhizomatous Irises in Europe, Asia, Northern Africa and North America (the ancestors of the tall-bearded Irises of our gardens are Old World natives)

Lilium (LILY)—80 to 90 species of Lilies are found throughout the northern Temperate Zone

Lobelia (CARDINAL FLOWER)—North America; there are close to 400 species of Lobelia, most native to warm regions

Lunaria (HONESTY, MONEY PLANT, SATIN FLOWER)—Europe

Narcissus (DAFFODIL)—Europe, northern Africa

Paeonia (PEONY)—Eurasia; there are several species native to western North America; the common garden Peony is native to Asia

Pelargonium (GERANIUM)—southern Africa

Phlox (PHLOX)—North America (one species is native to Siberia)

Tagetes (MARIGOLD)—North and South America

Trillium (TRILLIUM, WAKE ROBIN)—North America, Himalayas, eastern Asia

Tropaeolum (NASTURTIUM)—Cool highlands of Mexico, Central and South America

Tulipa (TULIP)—Eurasia, especially Central Asia

Zinnia—southwestern United States, Mexico, Central and South America

TEN BOTANICAL WONDERS

Bambusa (BAMBOO)—Giant, long-lived evergreen grass that produces a woody trunk. World's largest grass.

Equisetum (HORSETAIL, SCOURING RUSH)—Horsetails, like Clubmosses, were dominant plants of the Coal Age (close to 100 million years before the dinosaurs roamed the planet). Because of silica found in their stems, Horsetails have been used in polishing, hence the name Scouring Rush.

Lodoicea (DOUBLE COCONUT OR COCO-DE-MER)—This Palm produces the largest seeds in the plant kingdom. Fruit can weigh 33 to 44 pounds and take seven years to mature.

Lycopodium (CLUBMOSS, GROUND PINE)—Low-growing evergreen plants of northern woods, Clubmosses, like Horsetails, once grew much larger and dominated the Coal Age flora. Ancestral Clubmosses were important additions to the plant deposits that later became coal.

Musa (BANANA)—Treelike plant, but technically the world's largest perennial (nonwoody) herb. Bananas have ill-smelling flowers that are pollinated by bats.

Pinus—P. aristata or Bristle-Cone Pines are thought to be the Earth's oldest living trees; some are nearly 5,000 years old. A clonal Creosote Bush in California, over 11,000 years old, may be the Earth's oldest living plant.

Rafflesia—This parasitic plant, first discovered on Sumatra, produces the world's largest flowers. (All other parts of the plant are small or missing.) Flowers may reach over a yard in diameter, they are reddish brown and ill-smelling.

Sequoia—A huge western American conifer, possibly the world's largest tree.

Wolffiella (DUCKWEED)—World's smallest flowering plant.

Zamia (COONTIE)—Handsome native of Florida used in landscaping, Coontie's cycad ancestors covered the globe during the Dinosaur Age.

SUMMER'S FRAGRANCE: MAKING POTPOURRI

From *American Agriculturist* (July 1893): "All through the winter you may have the fragrance of woods and fields about you if you will take the trouble to gather it during the summer months. This will be a delightful task for the children. Send them out with little baskets during the month of July to pick clover blooms from the road side and pastures. Dry them on the garret floor, turning them over daily until cured. Rose leaves, especially those of the wild rose that blooms so abundantly in the hedges, and lemon verbena are also excellent as well as bay leaves, sweet fern, wild thyme and the young shoots of sassafras. These when dried should be mixed with common salt to keep out worms; add a few pot pourri spices, pack between layers of wool and into pillows."

ANTIQUARIAN AND OUT-OF-PRINT BOOKSELLERS SPECIALIZING IN GARDENING BOOKS

America's first garden book, Bernard M'Mahon's *The American Gardener's Calendar,* published in 1806, is still available from dealers specializing in antique books. (The genus Mahonia, Oregon Grape-Holly, was named in M'Mahon's honor.) Most of the following issue catalogs and will search for a particular title:

Anchor and Dolphin
30 Franklin St.
Newport, RI 02840
(401) 846-6890

Carol Barnett Books
3562 N.E. Liberty
Portland, OR 97211
(503) 282-7036

Bell's Book Store
536 Emerson St.
Palo Alto, CA 94301
(415) 323-7822

Exeter Rare Books
200 High St.
Exeter, NH 03833
(603) 772-0618 or 772-8356

Hurley Books
RR1, Box 160
Westmoreland, NH 03467
(603) 399-4342

Ian Jackson
PO Box 9075
Berkeley, CA 94709
(415) 548-1431

Landscape Books
PO Box 483
Exeter, NH 03833
(603) 964-9333

Timothy Mawson Books
New Preston, CT 06777
(203) 868-0732

Savoy Books
PO Box 271
Bailey Rd.
Lanesborough, MA 01237

Stubbs Books and Prints
835 Madison Ave.
New York, NY 10021
(212) 772-3120

Wilkerson Books
31 Old Winter St.
Lincoln, MA 01773
(617) 259-1110

Elisabeth Woodburn
Booknoll Farm
Hopewell, NJ 08525
(609) 466-0522

FLOWER SHOWS

Many flower shows are held throughout the country every year. Here are some major exhibitions and their 1991 dates (they are held at approximately the same time each year; check by phone for exact dates):

Atlanta Flower Show
    March 6–10
    Atlanta Apparel Mart
    Atlanta, GA
    (404) 876-5859

Cincinnati Home and Garden Show
February 2–10
Cincinnati Convention Center
Cincinnati, OH
(513) 825-1600

Indiana Flower and Patio Show
March 9–17
Indiana State Fairgrounds
Indianapolis, IN
(317) 255-4151

Metropolitan Louisville Home-Garden and Flower Show
March 7–10
Kentucky Fair and Exposition Center
Louisville, KY
(502) 637-9737

New England Flower Show
March 9–17
Bayside Exposition Center
Boston, MA
(617) 536-9280

New York Flower Show
March 8–17
Pier 92
52nd St. and 12th Ave.
New York, NY
(212) 757-0915

Philadelphia Flower Show
March 10–17
The Philadelphia Civic Center
34th St. and Civic Center Blvd.
Philadelphia, PA
(215) 625-8250

Portland Home and Garden Show
February 16–24
Multnomah County Exposition Center
Portland, OR
(503) 246-8291

San Francisco Garden Landscape Show
April 17–21
Piers Two and Three
Fort Mason, Marina Blvd. and Buchanan St.
San Francisco, CA
(415) 221-1310

Southland Home and Garden Show
August 17–25
Anaheim Convention Center
Anaheim, CA
(714) 978-8888

Washington (D.C.) Flower and Garden Show
February 20–24
Washington Convention Center
New York Ave. & 9th St. NW
Washington, DC
(703) 569-7141

FLOWER FESTIVALS

These are 1990 dates; dates will vary slightly from year to year.

Apple Blossom Festival
May 3–6
Winchester, VA
(703) 662-3863

Azalea Trail
March 1–May 31
Mobile, AL
Azalea Run and Festival
March 31
(205) 476-8828

Bluebonnet Trail and Festival
April 7–8; 14–15
Austin, TX
(512) 478-9085

Camellia Festival
March 2–11
Sacramento, CA
(916) 442-7673

Cherry Blossom Festival
April 1–8
Washington, DC
(202) 737-2599

Daffodil Festival
March 31–April 8
Tacoma, WA
(206) 627-6176

Dogwood Festivals
April 19–22
Piedmont Park, Atlanta, GA
(404) 525-6145.

April 6–22
Knoxville, TN
(615) 637-4561

April 10–22
Charlottesville, VA
(804) 358-5511

Lilac Festival
May 18–27
Highland Park, Rochester, NY
(716) 546-3070

Rose Festival
April 28–29
Shreveport, LA
(318) 938-5402

Tulip Time Festival
May 14–19
Holland, MI
(800) 822-2770

MOTHERS OF INVENTION

An Unfinished List

We know plants have inspired poets, writers, artists and musicians. What about scientists? Of course they have been the source of many modern drugs, but have they been an inspiration to inventors as well? Undoubtedly a log floating in water inspired the first boat; perhaps a seed like Dandelion's, borne aloft on the wind, inspired the first parachute. Listed below is one recent invention suggested by a plant. There must be others. Readers—please send your nominations to Box 123, Mansfield Center, CT 06250.

Plant	Invention
Cocklebur	A Swiss inventor, G. de Mestral, returned from a hike with his trousers covered with burs. Microscopic examination of the burs inspired the hook and loop fastener which he called Velcro, from the French for velvet (velour) and hook (crochet).

Selected Bibliography

FOR THE LATIN NAMES OF PLANTS I HAVE FOL-
lowed *Hortus Third* with only a few exceptions: I have stuck to
the old species name in the case of Aloe vera because of its wide
recognition; I have also kept the old genus, Andropogon, for Little
Bluestem for the same reason. Cultivars have not been enclosed with
single quotation marks except when preceded by their Latin names, such
as in Hosta fortunei 'Albomarginata'. Also, to simplify matters, I have not
capitalized species names.

Bailey, L. H. (Rev. by Staff of L. H. Bailey Hortorium). *Hortus Third: A Concise Dictionary of Plants Cultivated in the United States and Canada.* New York: Macmillan, 1976.

————*Manual of Cultivated Plants.* New York: Macmillan, 1969.

Beales, Peter. *Classic Roses.* New York: Holt, Rinehart and Winston, 1987.

————*Twentieth-Century Roses.* New York: Harper & Row, 1988.

Bergon, Frank. *The Journals of Lewis and Clark.* New York: Penguin Books, 1989.

Cumming, Roderick, and Robert E. Lee. *Contemporary Perennials.* New York: Macmillan, 1960.

Lampe, Dr. Kenneth, and Mary Ann McCann. *AMA Handbook of Poisonous and Injurious Plants.* Chicago: AMA, 1985.

Menninger, Edwin. *Fantastic Trees.* New York: Viking Press, 1967.

Millspaugh, Charles. *American Medicinal Plants.* New York: Dover, 1974.

Moldenke, Harold N., and Alma L. *Plants of the Bible.* New York: Dover, 1986; first published 1952.

Pesch, Barbara, ed. *Perennials: A Nursery Source Manual.* New York: Brooklyn Botanic Garden Handbook #118, 1988/89.

Pickston, Margaret. *The Language of Flowers.* London: Michael Joseph Ltd., 1968.

Poor, Janet M., ed., (Garden Club of America) *Plants that Merit Attention.* Vol. 1: Trees. Portland, Oreg.: Timber Press, 1984.

Randall, Charles E., and Henry Clepper. *Famous and Historic Trees.* Washington, DC: The American Forestry Association, 1977.

Rapaport, Howard, M.D., and Shirley Linde, M.S. *The Complete Allergy Guide.* New York: Simon & Schuster, 1970.

Ray, Mary Helen, and Robert P. Nicholls. *The Traveler's Guide to American Gardens.* Chapel Hill: University of North Carolina Press, 1988.

Scott-James, Anne. *Sissinghurst: The Making of a Garden.* London: Michael Joseph Ltd., 1975.

Sherwood, Mary. *Wild Petals.* 1979, unpublished.

Wyman, Donald. *Dwarf Shrubs.* New York: Macmillan, 1974.

Index